This illustrated book is the first full-length study of Inigo Jones as a stage-designer. Jones's designs for the Stuart court masques (and associated court entertainments) between 1605 and 1640 played a crucial role in transmitting the visual language of the Italian Renaissance tradition into English culture, where, because of geographical and historical factors, it had not yet become acclimatised. John Peacock shows that almost all of Jones's designs were copied and adapted from Italian and continental sources (many identified here for the first time), and argues that this is to be understood in terms of 'imitation', a concept and a practice central to the very tradition of which Jones is a messenger and propagandist. His exploration adds a new dimension to our knowledge and understanding of a figure who is generally considered the most important English artist of the seventeenth century.

Mae'r eitem yma ar gael i chi hyd y dyddiad neu'r amser a nodir isod, oni bai fod darllenydd arall yn ei alw'n ôl ynghynt.

This item is on loan to you until the date or time shown below, unless it is recalled sooner by another borrower.

The Stage Designs of
INIGO JONES

The Stage Designs of
INIGO JONES
The European Context

JOHN PEACOCK
Lecturer in English
University of Southampton

CAMBRIDGE UNIVERSITY PRESS
Cambridge, New York, Melbourne, Madrid, Cape Town, Singapore, São Paulo

Cambridge University Press
The Edinburgh Building, Cambridge CB2 2RU, UK

Published in the United States of America by Cambridge University Press, New York

www.cambridge.org
Information on this title: www.cambridge.org/9780521418126

© Cambridge University Press 1995

This publication is in copyright. Subject to statutory exception
and to the provisions of relevant collective licensing agreements,
no reproduction of any part may take place without
the written permission of Cambridge University Press.

First published 1995
Reprinted 1998
This digitally printed first paperback version 2006

A catalogue record for this publication is available from the British Library

Library of Congress Cataloguing in Publication data
Peacock, John, 1941–
The Stage Designs of Inigo Jones / John Peacock.
p.   cm.
Includes bibliographical references and index.
ISBN 0 521 41812 7 (hardback)
1. Jones, Inigo, 1573–1652 – Criticism and interpretation.
2. Theatres – England – Stage-setting and scenery – History –
17th century. I. Title.
PN2096.J66P43 1995
792'.025–dc20 94-23475 CIP

ISBN-13 978-0-521-41812-6 hardback
ISBN-10 0-521-41812-7 hardback

ISBN-13 978-0-521-03500-2 paperback
ISBN-10 0-521-03500-7 paperback

Main Library
PN2096.J66 P43 1995
30110007604730
The stage designs of Inigo
Jones : the European context

To my parents

Contents

List of plates		page x
Acknowledgements		xvii
List of abbreviations		xxi
	Introduction: the court masque	1
1	*The theory and practice of imitation*	6
2	*The masques as pictures*	35
3	*Architecture*	55
4	*Figures*	113
5	*Landscape*	158
6	*Ornament*	208
7	*Antiquity*	267
	Conclusion	325
	Notes	328
	Bibliography	366
	Index	376

Plates

1	Inigo Jones, Atlas, for *Coelum Britannicum*, Chatsworth	page 16
2	Francesco Albani, Hercules bearing the globe, Chatsworth	17
3	Fragment of a frieze, from the Arundel Marbles, Museum of London	23
4	Jones, A Roman atrium, for *Albion's Triumph*, Chatsworth	25
5	Domenico Fontana, Catafalque for Sixtus V, from B. Catani, *La Pompa Funerale di Papa Sisto il Quinto*, 1591, plate 24, British Library	31
6	Jones, Catafalque for James I, Worcester College, Oxford	31
7	Donato Bramante, Tempietto di S. Pietro in Montorio, from Serlio, *Architettura*, 1619	33
8	Jones, Proscenium, for *Albion's Triumph*, Chatsworth	43
9	Nicholas Hilliard, Young man among roses, Victoria and Albert Museum	45
10	Paul van Somer, James I, Royal Collection	46
11	Andrea Mantegna, Triumph of Julius Caesar, Royal Collection	47
12	Jones, Temple Bar, RIBA	49
13	Jones, Archway, Chatsworth	62
14	Serlio, Perspective construction, from *Architettura*, 1619	63
15	Serlio, City gate, from *Architettura*, 1619	63
16	Jones, Temple of Apollo, Chatsworth	65
17	Bramante, Tempietto, from L. Sirigatti, *Prospettiva*, 1625, British Library	65
18	Jones, A Throne, Chatsworth	66
19	Bramante, Exedra of the Belvedere, from Serlio, *Architettura*, 1619	67
20	Remigio Cantagallina after Giulio Parigi, Palazzo della Fama, from *Il giudizio di Paride*, 1608, Victoria and Albert Museum	72

21	Jones, The House of Fame, for *The Masque of Queens*, Chatsworth	73
22	Jones, Palace within a Cavern, for *Oberon*, Chatsworth	76
23	Jones, Oberon's Palace, for *Oberon*, Chatsworth	77
24	Philibert de l'Orme, Gateway of the château of Anet, from J. A. du Cerceau, *Les plus excellents bastiments de France*, 1609, Bodleian Library	78
25	Fountain of Anet, from G. Simeoni, *Les Illustres Observations Antiques*, 1558, British Library	79
26	Salomon de Caus, Grotto design, from *Les Raisons des forces mouvantes*, 1615, Bodleian Library	80
27	Château of Chenonceau, from J. A. du Cerceau, *Les plus excellents bastiments de France*, 1609	81
28	Jones, A Street in Perspective, for *The Vision of Delight*, Chatsworth	83
29	Serlio, Comic Scene, from *Architettura*, 1560	84
30	Serlio, Tragic Scene, from *Architettura*, 1560	84
31	Bartolomeo Neroni called Riccio, Design for *L'Ortensio*, Victoria and Albert Museum	85
32	Jones, Cupid's Palace, Chatsworth	86
33	Jones, Proscenium and Standing Scene, for *Artenice*, Chatsworth	87
34	Jones, The Vale of Tempe, for *Tempe Restored*, Chatsworth	89
35	Jones, Whitehall Banqueting House, for *Time Vindicated*, Chatsworth	90
36	Jones, English Houses with London and the Thames afar off, for *Britannia Triumphans*, Chatsworth	91
37	Cantagallina after Parigi, Tempio della Pace, from *Il giudizio di Paride*, 1608, Victoria and Albert Museum	93
38	Jones, An Amphitheatre, for *Albion's Triumph*, Chatsworth	94
39	Amphitheatre, from O. Panvinio, *De Ludis Circensibus*, 1600, British Library	95
40	Jones, The Forum or Piazza of Peace, for *The Triumph of Peace*, Chatsworth	96
41	Jacques Callot, Capitano Spagnuolo, British Museum	97
42	Jones, A Palace, Chatsworth	98
43	Jan Vredeman de Vries, Perspective construction, from *Perspective*, 1605	99
44	Agostino Carracci after Federigo Barocci, Aeneas fleeing Troy	100
45	Jones, the Temple of Diana, for *Florimène*, Chatsworth	101
46	Vredeman de Vries, Ionic portico, from *Perspective*, 1605	101
47	Jones (?), The Second Temple of Diana, for *Florimène*, Chatsworth	102

48	Antonio Labacco, Temple of Jupiter Stator, from *Architettura*, 1569, Bodleian Library	103
49	Jones, The Palace of Fame, for *Britannia Triumphans*, Chatsworth	104
50	Vredeman de Vries, Courtyard, from *Perspective*, 1605	105
51	Jones, The Tragic Scene, Chatsworth	106
52	Oliviero Gatti after G. B. Aleotti, Scena Tragica del Teatro di Ferrara	107
53	John Webb after Jones, The Suburbs of a Great City, for *Salmacida Spolia*, Chatsworth	108
54	G. B. Vanni after Paolo Veronese, The Marriage at Cana	109
55	Callot, Christ Presented to the People, from *La Petite passion*	110
56	Jones, Design for Bridge, for *Salmacida Spolia*, Chatsworth	110
57	Willem van Nieulandt, Ponte Quattro Capi	111
58	Van Nieulandt, Isola Tiberina and Ponte Quattro Capi (detail)	111
59	Jones, Naiad, for *Tethys' Festival*, Chatsworth	126
60	Marcantonio Raimondi after Raphael, Temperance	126
61	Jones, Page Bearing a Helmet, Chatsworth	127
62	Marcantonio after Francesco Francia, David with the Head of Goliath	127
63	Jones, A Fiery Spirit, for *The Lords' Masque*, Chatsworth	128
64	Marcantonio, Two Fauns carrying a Child	129
65	A. V., Apollo Belvedere	129
66	Jones, An Indian, for *The Memorable Masque*, Chatsworth	131
67	Adamo Scultori after Mantegna, Allegory of Servitude, British Museum	131
68	Jones, Albanactus: Preliminary Sketch, for *Albion's Triumph*, Chatsworth	132
69	Marcantonio, Trajan between Rome and Victory	133
70	Marcantonio, Lion Hunt	133
71	Adamo Scultori after Michelangelo, Ignudo from the Sistine Ceiling, British Museum	134
72	Jones, The Sons of Peace, for *The Triumph of Peace*, Chatsworth	135
73	Jones, Sketches of heads, from the *Roman Sketchbook*, Chatsworth	136
74	Odoardo Fialetti, Heads in foreshortening, from *Il vero modo et ordine*, 1608, British Library	137
75	Jones, Satyrs, for *Oberon*, Chatsworth	142
76	Marcantonio, Satyrs abducting a Nymph	143
77	Jones, A Watery Spirit, for *The Temple of Love*, Chatsworth	144
78	Daniel Rabel, Entrée des Sorcières et des Monstres, from *Ballet du château de Bicêtre*, 1632, Paris, Bibliothèque Nationale	145

142	Boyvin after Thiry, *Toison d'or*, plate 26, British Library	255
143	Webb after Jones, Reworking of proscenium from *The Triumph of Peace*, Chatsworth	256
144	Jones, Proscenium, *The Temple of Love*, RIBA	257
145–6	Diana Ghisi after Giulio Romano, Fresco from Palazzo del Tè (details)	258
147	Tempesta, Grotesque panel, Victoria and Albert Museum	259
148	Jones, Truth, for the proscenium of The Tragic Scene, Chatsworth	260
149	Theodoor van Thulden after Primaticcio, *Les Travaux d'Ulysse*, plate 50	261
150	Hercules, for the proscenium of The Tragic Scene, Chatsworth	262
151	Van Thulden after Primaticcio, *Les Travaux d'Ulysse*, plate 9	263
152	Master L. D. after Primaticcio, Diana	263
153	Tarquinio Ligustri, Designs for consoles	264
154	Robert Peake after Edward Pearce, Frieze design, British Museum	264
155	Jones, Two half elevations for an overmantel, possibly for Basing House, RIBA	265
156–7	Jones, Panels of frieze, for *Salmacida Spolia*, RIBA	266
158	Title-page of V. Scamozzi, *Discorsi Sopra L'Antichità di Roma*, 1582, British Library	269
159	Title-page of Serlio, *Architettura*, Book III (English version of 1611)	273
160	Frontispiece of Nero, from Serlio, *Architettura*, 1619	274
161	Jones, The Release of the Daughters of the Morn, for *Love Freed from Ignorance and Folly*, Chatsworth	275
162	Jones, A Cave and Mount, Chatsworth	281
163	Trofei di Mario, from A. Donato, *Roma Vetus ac Recens*	283
164	Jones, A Horse Caparison, Chatsworth	284
165	Tempesta, Domitian, from *The Twelve Caesars*, Metropolitan Museum of Art	284
166	Jones, Elephant Pageant, Chatsworth	285
167	Jones, Oberon, for *Oberon*, Chatsworth	286
168	Tempesta, Caligula, from *The Twelve Caesars*	286
169	Jones, The Fallen House of Chivalry, for *Prince Henry's Barriers*, Chatsworth	287
170	Jones, St George's Portico, for *Prince Henry's Barriers*, Chatsworth	287
171	Du Cerceau, Les Tutelles, Bordeaux	288
172	Van Nieulandt, Torre delle Milizie	288
173	Paolo Farinati, Virgin and Child with St John	289

List of plates

174 Etienne du Pérac, Tempio di Jani Quadrifronte, from *I Vestigi Dell'Antichità di Roma*, 1575, British Library — 291
175 Weeping Dacia, from G. Franzini, *Le cose maravigliose dell'alma città di Roma* — 292
176 S. Giovanni in Laterano, from G. F. Bordino, *De Rebus Praeclare Gestis a Sixto V*, 1588, British Library — 292
177 Jones, Headdress for Tethys, *Tethys' Festival*, Chatsworth — 294
178 Aegidius Sadeler, Livia, Courtauld Institute — 295
179 Jones, Emperor's habit in war, from the *Roman Sketchbook* — 300
180 Scene from Trajan's Column, from Chacón, *Historia Utriusque Belli Dacici*, 1576, British Library — 301
181 Sleeping Cupids, from the inventory of the Mantua Collection, Royal Library, Windsor Castle — 304
182 Daniel Mytens, Thomas Howard Earl of Arundel, Arundel Castle — 305
183 Pudicitia, from G. B. Cavalieri, *Antiquarum Statuarum Urbis Romae Primus et Secundus Liber*, 1585 — 306
184 Hercules, from G. B. Cavalieri, *Antiquarum Statuarum Urbis Romae Primus et Secundus Liber*, 1585 — 307
185 Jones, A Captive King, for *Albion's Triumph*, Chatsworth — 312
186 Reges Captivi, from O. Panvinio, *De Triumpho Romanorum Commentarius*, 1600, Bodleian Library — 313
187 Jones, Design for Albanactus's Headdress, *Albion's Triumph*, Chatsworth — 315
188 Jones, Classical Ruins, Chatsworth — 316
189 Van Nieulandt, Flight into Egypt — 317
190 Van Nieulandt, Temples in the Forum, British Museum — 317
191 Jones, Temple of Peace and SS. Cosma e Damiano, Chatsworth — 318
192 Van Nieulandt, Temple of Peace and SS. Cosma e Damiano, British Museum — 319
193 Jones, A City in Ruins, for *Coelum Britannicum*, Chatsworth — 320
194 Van Nieulandt, Temple of Jupiter Stator, British Museum — 320
195 Battista Pittoni, Monte Quirinale, from V. Scamozzi, *Discorsi Sopra L'Antichità Di Roma*, 1582, British Library — 321

Acknowledgements

This study has relied at every turn on the fundamental work of Stephen Orgel and Roy Strong. Their publication of the masque designs in *Inigo Jones: The Theatre of the Stuart Court*, with the accompanying discussion, opened up a whole new field of enquiry. The exhibition which they and John Harris organised in 1973 was equally important. Each of the three organisers had already made substantial individual contributions to the study of Jones, and has continued to do so. I also owe a great debt to the work of John Summerson, Howard Colvin, John Newman and John Orrell. All those distinguished scholars have enabled another generation to cast further light on Jones's manifold achievements; and I have benefited, not only from their research, but from stimulating conversation with Edward Chaney, Jeremy Wood, Christy Anderson, and especially Gordon Higgott, whose new appraisal of Jones's architectural drawings brilliantly informed the exhibition organised by him and John Harris in 1989/90. The continuing work of Anthony Johnson and Richard Peterson on Ben Jonson has also been invaluable.

   I am grateful to Peter Day, Keeper of Collections at Chatsworth, for all his help; to Lesley Le Claire, former Librarian of Worcester College, Oxford, for hospitably enabling my study of Jones's books, and to the present Librarian, Dr Joanna Parker; to the staffs of the British Library, the Bodleian Library, the National Art Library, the Department of Prints and Drawings at the British Museum, the Print Room of the Victoria and Albert Museum, and the Conway Library at the Courtauld Institute. I owe a special debt of gratitude to the staff in the Library and Photographic Collection of the Warburg Institute, for its unique atmosphere of intellectual optimism.

   My research has been funded at different times by the British Academy,

Acknowledgements

the Leverhulme Trust, and the Arts Faculty of Southampton University, and I thank them all.

I am grateful to the following journals for permission to reprint material which they have previously published: *Apollo*, *Architectural History*, *The Art Bulletin*, *The Journal of Medieval and Renaissance Studies*, and *Renaissance Studies*; and to Manchester University Press and Reaktion Books for permission to reprint parts of chapters in *The Court Masque*, ed. David Lindley, and *Renaissance Bodies*, ed. Lucy Gent and Nigel Llewellyn.

Friends and colleagues have given support, help and advice, and I am especially grateful to Liz, Michael and Matthew Pountney for lending me their flat in Bloomsbury; to the past and present members of the Lark household in north London for hospitality and friendship over many years; to John Birtwhistle, Tony Crowley, Barbara Garvin, Edmund Papst, Philip Rylands, Jonathan Sawday, Kevin Sharpe and Frank Stack; to Germaine Greer, for help at a critical moment, and Peter Caldwell, to whom I owe more than I can say. A more general debt can only be expressed sentimentally. The original motive for this book was that infatuation with Italy to which the visitor from northern Europe is so notoriously susceptible. Although this feeling may be scarcely evident in the interstices of a thousand footnotes, it is present everywhere, and the more strongly at this time, prompted by a sympathetic anxiety for the historic future of the Italian people.

I am grateful to the following for permission to reproduce illustrations.

Plates 24, 26, 48, 98, 186	Bodleian Library, Oxford
Plates 12, 140, 144, 155, 156, 157	The Royal Institute of British Architects, The British Architectural Library/RIBA
Plates 5, 17, 25, 39, 74, 82, 93, 112, 133, 134, 135, 139, 141, 142, 158, 174, 176, 180, 195	By permission of the British Library
Plates 41, 67, 71, 85, 109, 121, 125, 138, 154, 190, 192, 194	British Museum, Department of Prints and Drawings
Plates 1, 2, 4, 6, 8, 12, 16, 18, 21, 22, 23, 28, 32, 33, 34, 35, 36, 38, 40, 42, 45, 47, 49, 51, 53, 56, 59, 61, 63, 68, 72, 73, 75, 77, 79, 81, 83, 86, 87, 90, 92, 94, 96, 97, 99, 101, 103, 106,	The Devonshire Collection, Chatsworth. Reproduced by permission of the Chatsworth Settlement Trustees. Photo: Courtauld Institute.

110, 111, 114, 115, 117,
118, 119, 121, 123, 124,
126, 128, 129, 131, 143,
148, 150, 161, 162, 164,
166, 167, 169, 170, 177,
178, 179, 185, 187, 188,
189, 193

Plate 52	*Enciclopedia dello Spettacolo*
Plate 165	All rights reserved, the Metropolitan Museum of Art, New York
Plate 54	Museo Correr, Venice
Plate 3	Museum of London
Plate 182	By courtesy of the National Portrait Gallery, London
Plates 78, 80	Paris, Bibliothèque Nationale
Plates 10, 11	Reproduced from the Royal Collection by gracious permission of Her Majesty the Queen
Plate 181	Royal Library, Windsor Castle. Reproduced by permission of Her Majesty the Queen
Plate 91	From the Collections of the Theatre Museum
Plates 9, 20, 31, 37, 102, 104, 107, 108, 113, 147	By courtesy of the Board of Trustees of the Victoria and Albert Museum
Plates 60, 62, 64, 65, 69, 70, 76, 84, 88, 89, 105, 130, 145, 146, 149, 151, 152, 163, 168, 171, 173, 175, 183, 184	Warburg Institute

Note on the illustrations

A few of the illustrations may be found not as easily legible as the majority; this is because the drawings or prints from which they are photographed themselves present problems of definition.

Abbreviations

Allsopp	Bruce Allsopp, ed., *Inigo Jones on Palladio*, 2 vols., Newcastle upon Tyne, 1970
Barbaro	Daniele Barbaro, *I Dieci Libri Dell' Architettura Di M. Vitruvio*, Venice, 1567
Barocchi, *Scritti*	Paola Barocchi, ed., *Scritti d'arte del Cinquecento*, 3 vols., Milan and Naples, 1971–7
Barocchi, *Trattati*	Paola Barocchi, *Trattati d'arte del Cinquecento*, 3 vols., Bari, 1960
Bartsch	Adam von Bartsch, *Le Peintre graveur*, 21 vols., Vienna, 1802–21
Haydocke, Lomazzo	G. P. Lomazzo, *A Tracte Containing The Artes of curious Paintinge Carvinge Buildinge*, trans. Richard Haydocke, Oxford, 1598
H&H	John Harris and Gordon Higgott, *Inigo Jones: Complete Architectural Drawings*, London and New York, 1989
H&S	*Ben Jonson*, ed. C. H. Herford and Percy and Evelyn Simpson, 11 vols., Oxford, 1926–52
Hollstein	F. W. H. Hollstein, *Dutch and Flemish Etchings, Engravings and Woodcuts ca. 1450–1700*, 41 vols., Amsterdam, 1949–92
King's Arcadia	John Harris, Stephen Orgel and Roy Strong, *The King's Arcadia: Inigo Jones and the Stuart Court*, London, 1973
Lomazzo, *Scritti*	Gian Paolo Lomazzo, *Scritti sulle arti*, ed. Roberto Paolo Ciardi, 2 vols., Florence, 1973–4

O&S	Stephen Orgel and Roy Strong, *Inigo Jones: The Theatre of the Stuart Court*, 2 vols., Berkeley, Los Angeles and London, 1973
Palladio, *Quattro Libri*	Andrea Palladio, *I Quattro Libri Dell'Architettura*, Venice, 1570
Serlio	Sebastiano Serlio, *Tutte L'Opere D'Architettura, Et Prospetiva*, Venice, 1619
Vasari, Milanesi	Giorgio Vasari, *Le opere di Giorgio Vasari*, ed. Gaetano Milanesi, 9 vols., Florence, 1878–85
Vitruvius	Vitruvius, *On Architecture*, trans. Frank Granger, 2 vols., London and Cambridge, Mass., 1931–4

Introduction: the court masque

Most of Inigo Jones's surviving stage designs (there are over 470) were made for the court entertainments known as masques. Although the masque has a history stretching back to the early Tudor period, and a prehistory even lengthier,[1] in its fully developed form it belongs to the reigns of James I and Charles I. The Stuart court masque emerged with its recognisable character in 1605 and flourished until 1640. That character was shaped in collaboration by Jones and the poet Ben Jonson; and although other poets and designers were sometimes employed, and other artists (composers and choreographers) added their indispensable contributions, it was Jonson and Jones who made the masque into a highly sophisticated aesthetic and cultural form. Their partnership, based on common intellectual ground, was also charged with conflict. When it broke down after twenty-five years, Jonson was discarded and Jones left in control of the productions; so his commanding involvement with the Stuart masque, either as co-equal or 'sole Monarch' (a tactless but revealing phrase of his own), lasted from start to finish.

The term 'masque' is difficult to define, and contemporaries never seem to have attempted this, although practitioners were quite prepared to generalise prescriptively about the masque,[2] and spectators to make critical judgments on performances, as if the nature of the form was clear to them. The alternative spelling 'maske' suggests that the salient feature was a concealment or change of identity. Jonson drops a helpful piece of folk-memory into *The Masque of Augurs* (1622) by having one character say 'Disguise was the old English word for a Masque.'[3] This derives the masque from the older 'disguising', and highlights the adoption of roles. That older format, as recorded in the time of Henry VIII, involved the entry of a group of disguised courtiers, often in a movable scenic machine (a 'pageant'), who performed a series of dances, and then retired.[4] But there are parallel records of a new kind of entertainment imported from Italy, the 'maske': here a

I

group of courtiers, similarly disguised but designated 'maskers', would arrive attended by torchbearers; they would take partners from the assembled company and dance with them; and finally make a formal departure.[5] It seems that the masque as Jonson knew it had a more complex ancestry than his character suggested, combining the theatrical representation of the 'disguising' with the social ritual of the Tudor 'maske', the common factor being the masquers' assumption of some symbolic role.

In the Stuart masque the theatrical dimension is much elaborated. The hall where the entertainment takes place is set up as a theatre, and a quasi-dramatic fiction explains the appearance of the masquers in their appointed roles, and envelops the entire action, including the social dancing (known as the 'revels'). A preliminary episode called the 'antimasque' (there might be more than one of these) leads into the masque proper or 'main masque', and serves both as an exposition and a contrast.[6] At its fullest extent the structure comprises an introductory poetic dialogue (perhaps including song), one or more antimasques, the main masque, the revels (sometimes punctuated by song), and an epilogue as the masquers withdraw to the stage, from which they have descended to dance their set pieces and join in the revels.[7]

The word 'masque' could still be applied to the central part alone of the elaborate structure which bore the same name – the part where the masquers appeared in their splendid costumes, performed their rehearsed dances, and then danced with the spectators. So on a design for *The Temple of Love* (1635) Jones has written 'for the Quenes Masque of Indianes',[8] referring to the roles taken by Queen Henrietta Maria and her ladies, who were to appear at the climax of the whole piece. This interchange of name between the whole and a part indicates a persistent sense of where the central emphasis lay in a now complex structure: on a revelation of, and communion with, symbolically transfigured persons.

These quasi-religious terms are appropriate, as masques were not just luxurious recreations. William Davenant, introducing the published text of *Britannia Triumphans* (1638), wrote:

> Princes of sweet and humane natures have ever, both amongst the ancients and moderns in the best times, presented spectacles and personal representations, to recreate their spirits wasted in grave affairs of state, and for the entertainment of their nobility, ladies and courts.[9]

The issue is not pleasure as such, but the 'nature' of the 'Prince', whose generosity bestows such pleasure on his subjects. Jonson called masques 'the donatiues, of great Princes, to their people':[10] their very gratuitousness proves the magnanimity and 'magnificence' of the monarch. They also represent those virtues. In *Britannia Triumphans* Charles I appears as

'Britanocles, the glory of the western world'; and the action concludes with an ingenious scenic tableau of his 'great fleet', financed by ship-money.[11] The pleasures of the masque were a function of politics. Jonson did insist from the start that the masque should strive to transcend its immediate political concerns and 'lay hold on more remou'd *mysteries*',[12] on arcane moral and philosophical truths. But since masques always focussed on the King, and the King (whether James or Charles) was not only head of the Church but sponsor of his very own political metaphysic, the '*mysteries*' were usually those of divine right monarchy.

It is difficult for us, over three and a half centuries later, to imagine what a masque was like. Masques were made for performance; there was little systematic effort to give them an after-life by publishing full records of those performances, as was done with court festivals in Italy. Any publication was usually undertaken by the poet who had written the text; but this, even if he tried to give some account of the whole occasion, still placed undue emphasis on only one constituent. The masque was a combination of different arts: poetry (and sometimes prose), music, dance, and visual spectacle (both costume and scenery). As we have seen, the collaboration that was required could generate conflict, so that the relationship between the constituent arts could be volatile and unsettled. The present study, in emphasising the art of the designer, is necessarily partial.

Since our easiest access to the masque is as readers of the texts which survive, especially the outstanding corpus by Ben Jonson, we may tend to overstress the literariness of the form. It is tempting to see it as an effete version of the drama performed in the public theatres of 'the age of Shakespeare'. To avoid such misconceptions we must take account of the specific social conditions which made it what it was.

The masque was a courtly form. There are instances of courtiers putting on masques in their own houses: *Lovers Made Men* (1617) was offered by Lord Hay to the French ambassador, and *The Gypsies Metamorphosed* (1623) by Buckingham to King James.[13] But most masques took place at court, 'presented' by members of the royal family and nobility to their fellows, an élite community. Fierce efforts to obtain admission were made by those outside this élite. They might range from foreign ambassadors (an invitation conferred diplomatic prestige) to mere citizens or adventurous nobodies, as documented in Jonson's comic antimasque for *Love Restored* (1612). The principal masquers were always courtiers,[14] usually grouped around a royal personage: Anne of Denmark, Prince Henry, Charles I and Henrietta Maria were all keen masquers. King James alone never took part, but as chief spectator he would always be complimented, and drawn into the symbolic action. This action was governed by the decorum of the court. The masquers never impersonated characters as if they were actors on the dramatic stage; they never spoke or sang. They simply appeared in costume, their real identities enhanced by symbolic roles, and danced – dancing being a proper courtly accomplishment. Dialogue and song, and the histrionic dancing seen in the antimasque, were delegated to professional actors and musicians.[15]

Masques were occasional, that is, linked to specific occasions. These were of two kinds. There were the regular seasonal festivities, such as Christmas: it was customary to present a masque on Twelfth Night (as on Shrove Tuesday). There were also special celebrations, such as a royal coming-of-age or wedding: *Tethys' Festival* marked the investiture of Henry as Prince of Wales in the summer of 1610; and three masques were presented (two by the Inns of Court) at the marriage of Princess Elizabeth to the Elector Palatine in February, 1613. Since the action of a masque was related to its occasion (the seasonal productions often had a topical sub-text), masques could only receive a unique performance. In fact some masques were repeated: Queen Anne had missed *Pleasure Reconciled to Virtue* (1618) because of illness, so it was restaged for her benefit; and an exceptionally successful piece, like *The Temple of Love* (1635), might be repeated more than once.[16] But in principle masques could not be revived like plays.

Unlike plays moreover, masques were theatrical without being intrinsically dramatic. They professed to represent higher realities beyond the ordinary world of appearances and natural vicissitudes. The action achieved its climax by transcending drama: the 'discovery' of the masquers was always a moment of triumph or apotheosis, when negative forces released in the antimasque would be confounded with glory. Any elements of drama were confined to the antimasque. Not an original part of the overall structure, this was developed by Jonson in *The Haddington Masque* (1608) and *The Masque of Queens* (1609). It might be an episode of 'antic' dance inserted in the poetic prologue (as in the former), or a semi-dramatic scene with demotic or fantastic characters filling the entire space before the main masque (as in the latter). Jonson gave his talent for comedy generous scope in the antimasque, while the poets who succeeded him allowed it to become more and more demonstratively balletic. Again, like the sometimes uncertain consensus of the contributory arts, the shifting relation between symbolic and dramatic action showed the economy of the masque to be more volatile than was theoretically allowed.

The generic affinities of the masque were European rather than domestic, less with contemporary English drama than with courtly continental forms like the Italian *intermedio* or the French *ballet de cour*. Other kinds of court entertainment also belong in this international context: tilts (chivalric tournaments with a theatrical setting), barriers (tilts on foot), and the pastoral plays favoured by Queen Henrietta Maria. Jones's work as a designer covers the whole spectrum; but it was the masque designs which made the strongest impression, taking the culture of the English court into the mainstream of European art.

I

The theory and practice of imitation

L'artiste sera ou plagiaire ou révolutionnaire
Gauguin

Delight and profit

We think of Inigo Jones as the first classical architect in England, who showed his compatriots a version of what had been going on in Italian architecture over the previous 150 years. But well before he was in a position to do this, becoming Surveyor of the King's Works in 1615, he was introducing the Stuart courtiers to the traditions of Renaissance art, with which they were still largely unfamiliar, on a broader front. He did this through the court masques; and he did it with some deliberation.

It may seem strange to see the masques as vehicles of a didactic programme. Bacon called them 'toys', trivial diversions. But the rulers who commissioned these extravagant spectacles, and the artists who produced them, both took them very seriously.[1] When the Dowager Grand Duchesses of Tuscany granted a *privilegio* to Giulio Parigi in 1626, it included among his works the famous *intermedi* staged in 1608.[2] Ben Jonson, who wrote many of the masques which Jones designed, was fond of stressing the significance of their content: 'though their *voyce* be taught to sound to present occasions, their *sense* . . . should alwayes lay hold on more remou'd *mysteries*'.[3] In his preface to *The Masque of Queens* (1609) he described himself as 'obseruing that rule of the best *Artist*, to suffer no object of delight to passe without his mixture of profit, & example.'[4] Here, in specifically invoking the Horatian principle of delightful teaching, he is speaking for himself as a poet, but – being perfectly aware on Horace's authority that '*Poetry*, and *Picture*, are Arts of a like nature' – he might just as well be speaking for Jones as designer;[5] and the Cockpit-in-Court theatre which Jones built later incorporates a Horatian motto about instruction and delight above the proscenium.[6] In fact Jones's contribution to the masques is doubly didactic: his teaching is aesthetic as well as moral. Not only is he using 'picture', in collaboration with Jonson's poetry, to communicate philosophical, ethical and political ideas; he is inducing his audience to revise radically their ideas about what 'picture' is, to adopt a wholly new concept of visual art.

Rubens described Jones's friend and patron the Earl of Arundel as an evangelist of art.[7] The term could have been even more aptly applied to Jones. As the first English artist to acquire a deep and inward knowledge of the whole Renaissance tradition, he was able to grasp just how marginal to that tradition was the visual culture of his own country: in spite of the impact of Holbein and numerous lesser continental artists, English art was still in outer darkness. It was to this situation that he addressed himself. At the outset of his career, his friend the antiquarian Edmund Bolton identified him as a person of peculiar promise, 'through whom there is hope that . . . all that is praiseworthy in the elegant arts of the ancients, may one day find their way across the Alps into our England'.[8] These words were written in a copy of Gianfrancesco Bordino's *De Rebus Praeclare Gestis a Sixto V*,[9] a book of poems celebrating the energetic pope who had combined ecclesiastical reforms with a sweeping architectural transformation of the city of Rome. Bolton was setting out a programme for Jones, and Jones responded to the challenge. By the end of his career he had realised Bolton's hopes.

The programme

Bolton's inscription is couched in formal, public terms, but it has an irreverent undercurrent which makes it partly private. Since it hovers between public and private, we have to consider what it leaves half-said or unsaid, as well as what it manifestly states.

> Tertio Calendas Januar. MDCVI Styl. Angl. Arrham, tesseramque amicitiae, futurae cum Ignatio Jonesio sempiternac, Edmundus Bolton do libellum hunc. Ignatio Jonesio suo per quem spes est, Statuariam, Plasticen, Architecturam, Picturam, Mimisim, omnemque veterum elegantiarum laudem trans Alpes, in Angliam nostram aliquando irrepturas. MERCURIUS IOVIS FILIUS.

> 30 December 1606. As an earnest and a token of a friendship which is to endure forever with Inigo Jones, I, Edmund Bolton give this little book. To his own Inigo Jones through whom the hope is that sculpture, modelling, architecture, picture, theatrical representation, and all that is praiseworthy in the elegant arts of the ancients, may some day insinuate themselves across the Alps into our England. MERCURY SON OF JOVE.[10]

The final reference to Mercury, messenger of the gods, is appropriate, since Jones is given the role of mediator or go-between. And the formula 'Mercurius Iovis filius' is explained by the British mythographer Alexander Ross: 'They called him the son of *Jupiter*; to shew, that eloquence, sciences, and ingenuous arts are the gift of God.'[11] According to Cartari, quoting a string of classical authors, Mercury was the discoverer and patron of 'tutte le buone arte'; and the characteristic Greek statues of him, called herms, were placed in schools and academies.[12] Now we know that the great project of Bolton's life was to found a national academy under royal patronage, for which he petitioned James I ten years later, and that Jones was to be one of the members.[13] Whether he is alluding at this earlier stage to his vision of an academy, and to Jones as a future academician, we cannot be certain. But clearly in a sense he is already acting as a cultural entrepreneur: he invokes Mercury as the god who teaches humans 'all the good arts', and salutes Jones as the potential messenger to England of those best known to him – what we would call the fine arts, and he knew as the arts of design.[14]

Bolton's words could almost be read as a joint statement. Even if the idea of an academy is far from fully formed, Bolton sees his relationship with Jones like those between the scholars and artists who joined together in the Italian academies, where the artists were absorbed into the humanist tradition, and seen not as craftsmen with manual tasks to discharge but intellectuals with knowledge to impart. One function of the *letterati* in these relationships was to encourage and assist the artists to articulate their ideas, not only in the visual discourses of art but in speech and writing. In this perspective Bolton's inscription can be seen not just as a one-sided demand, imposing a programme on Jones, so much as a collaborative statement recording Jones's aspirations as they have emerged in the intercourse between artist and writer.

Putting this statement in Latin – which offers the artist a voice he could otherwise not have used – adds to its meaning.[15] The Latin language stresses the scope of Jones's project, which crosses national and temporal boundaries, extending in space across Europe and in time back to antiquity. It also allows Bolton to use a conventional form of words which gives that project a specific historical character. His listing of the arts follows a humanist formula from the fifteenth century. The concept of the 'veterum elegantiae' derives from the preface to Lorenzo Valla's *Elegantiae linguae latinae*, produced around 1440, the influential anthology of the arts of language as practised by the best Roman writers. Valla identifies in his own age an artistic 'revival' – what came to be seen by Vasari in the next century as a 'rinascità' and by writers of the nineteenth century as 'the Renaissance':

I do not know why the arts most clearly approaching the liberal arts – painting, sculpture in stone and bronze, and architecture – had been in so long and so deep a decline and almost died out together with literature itself; nor why they have come to be aroused and come to life again (ac reviviscant) in this age; nor why there is now such a rich harvest both of good artists and good writers.[16]

The list of arts in Valla's Latin runs: 'illae artes quae proximae ad liberales accedunt, Pingendi, Scalpendi, Fingendi, Architectandi . . . ' This was followed by Erasmus, about fifty years later, comparing the revival of eloquence and the visual arts, whose products he listed as 'caelaturas, picturas, sculpturas, aedificia, fabricas et omnium denique officiorum monimenta . . . '[17] Others used the same list in the same context;[18] and, more than a century and a half after Valla, Bolton, with his 'Statuariam, Plasticen, Architecturam, Picturam', is still using essentially the same formula, together with Valla's idea of recovering the 'veterum elegantiae', the choicest aesthetic effects of the ancients.

Bolton's use of a conventional structure of words and ideas first fashioned by Valla enables him to make a vital point without spelling it out, and so preserve the elliptical terseness proper to a Latin inscription, which is also a somewhat private communication. The coming of the arts to England will be a journey not only across Europe but across time or history, a revival or rebirth. For Bolton to take up the stance of a literary humanist welcoming an artistic revival, a stance over a century and a half old, may seem anachronistic. But by speaking of 'hope' rather than achievement he suggests that England is still only on the verge of that revival. The passage of the arts across the Alps will produce a rehearsal of that rebirth of antiquity which brought the arts in Italy to their modern fulfilment. By reusing a rhetorical formula from the context of Quattrocento humanism, designed to greet self-consciously the dawn of Italian Renaissance art, Bolton more resonantly acknowledges the backwardness of his native culture and asks Jones to transform it, by initiating the Renaissance in England.

His appeal takes a radical view of English culture, since it sweeps out of account whatever responses to the revival of the arts England had already made in the course of the sixteenth century. The idea of a whole new programme of work to be inaugurated springs from the poetic text he is inscribing to Jones, which is itself a part of what he has to communicate. It celebrates Sixtus V as a protagonist of the counter-Reformation, a figure who revives the energy of the High Renaissance papacy but in a radically reforming spirit, who makes a fresh start, and hopes to win back lost ground. The text includes illustrative prints, showing the powerful feats of architecture and urban planning which gave concrete cultural expression to the

Pope's new plans for the Church. The Sixtine *renovatio Romae* resumed the earlier building campaigns of Renaissance popes like Julius II, but carried them out more thoroughly, as if for a second Renaissance charged with the dynamic of reform. These are the points of reference, Renaissance compounded by reform, which make Bolton's words so resolute. Whatever has been gained or lost in the past, a radical new beginning is to be made.

How is this to be done? The answer lies in the word which Bolton adds to the conventional list of the arts, 'Mimisim'. This is a quasi-Latinised form of the Greek 'mimesis', and is best glossed from its original context. Unlike Valla or Erasmus, who speak of the arts as practices or products, Bolton refers to them in conceptual terms, using abstract nouns; he is not expecting Jones to practise all the arts which figure in his neo-classical conspectus. All his terms come from impeccable ancient authorities: 'Statuaria', 'Plastice' and 'Pictura' are used by Pliny in his account of the arts; 'Architectura' is obviously sanctioned by Vitruvius. And 'Mimesis', as part of the vocabulary of the arts, is given its definitive meaning for the Renaissance in the *Poetics* of Aristotle. There it has a broader and a narrower meaning. In general it denotes the universal human instinct for imitation[19] which Aristotle sees as one of the root causes of poetry, and of representation in all art. More specifically it describes the imitative function of poetry, or rather – since Aristotle's discussion of tragedy does not focus exclusively on poetry as a verbal medium – of poetic drama performed with all the resources of the theatre. Although he wrote occasional verses, Jones was no poet; but up to the time of Bolton's dedication nearly all his work had been in the theatre. If we insert this fact into the context provided by Aristotle, we can define the term 'Mimesis' used by Bolton to Jones as 'theatrical representation' or 'the imitative arts of the theatre as detailed in Aristotle's *Poetics*'.

Jones had already revived the theatre of antiquity in the plays he designed and produced before the King at Oxford in 1605, which included a tragedy, a comedy and a satyr play all in Latin, and used the scenic *periaktoi* (rotating prisms) described by Vitruvius, together with costumes of 'Antique fashions'.[20] But a royal visit to the university was a rare occasion: he did not work again in Oxford for thirty years; and Bolton cannot be looking for that kind of archaeological revival on a regular basis. The crucial point about 'Mimesis', the art of theatrical representation as described by Aristotle and practised anew by Jones, was that in its fullest form it was a composite of various other arts: poetry, music, dance and spectacle.[21] And it was not the university but the court at Whitehall that offered the resources and opportunities for realising a modern idea of the aesthetic complexity of the ancient theatre, in the annual productions of the masques. When Bolton wrote his dedication, Jones's theatre work at Oxford was receding into the past, but the court offered a future. He had already staged *The Masque of*

Blackness and *Hymenaei*, on Twelfth Night 1605 and 1606 respectively; the sequel to *Blackness*, *The Masque of Beauty*, was awaited (eventually to be done in 1608); and in a few days, on Twelfth Night 1607, *Lord Hay's Masque* was to be produced. Whether Jones was responsible for that production is not certain, but likely,[22] and if so, the impending challenge to his powers would have given a special point to Bolton's words. But in any case both men would have understood that Jones's obvious vehicle for reviving the ancient art, or arts, of theatrical representation was the masque, which combined several arts in a single art of 'Mimesis'.

This neo-classical view of the masque is not so odd as it may seem. Obviously the masque was not meant to be a doctrinaire recreation of the theatre of antiquity – as attempted by Jones at Oxford, by the Vicentine Academy in Palladio's Teatro Olimpico, or by the Florentine Camerata – since the format which united its various arts was not that of antique drama. But within this modern format Jones's two masque productions to date had been consciously neo-antique in content. Ben Jonson's already published text of *Hymenaei* (1606) had insisted that the 'inventions' of masques must be 'grounded upon antiquity', and he stressed this with an apparatus of scholarly notes (a practice to be repeated in later texts) giving references to classical sources.[23] *Hymenaei* was constructed around a recreation of a Roman wedding ceremony, all carefully documented by Jonson; and Jones's costume design for the masquers 'had part of it . . . taken from the *antique Greeke* statue'.[24] While not reproducing the representational format of the ancient theatre, the masque was certainly going in the general direction hoped for by Bolton.

It was possible to see much of the court theatre of the late Renaissance through neo-classical eyes. The Italian perspective scenery which Jones introduced into England was far from replicating the kind of illusionistic scenery used by the Greeks and Romans. Nevertheless, the Italians from whom he learnt it were quite accustomed to having their art praised for reviving the achievements of the ancients. Buontalenti's Florentine *intermedi* of 1586 were compared to antiquity; and his work for the opera *Il rapimento di Cefalo* in 1600 was described as a unique revival of the artistic glories of the Romans.[25] This is not just hyperbole, or chauvinism. The idea of regarding advances in knowledge and performance as successful returns to the past is central to the mentality of Renaissance art. Daniele Barbaro, in his theoretical treatise on perspective scenery, uses the Greek-derived term 'scaenographia' to trace the origins of modern scenography back to the Greeks.[26] According to this way of thinking all aspects of the arts of Jones's theatre could be seen as antiquity revived.

But if the master art of 'Mimesis' is Jones's vehicle for reviving various particular arts, how will it convey into England those specifically named by

Bolton: picture, sculpture and architecture? The final answer to the question turns on the double meaning of the word 'Mimesis', revealing an irreverent undercurrent in Bolton's resounding Latin tribute. As producer of the masques, with overall responsibility for staging them, Jones practised 'Mimesis' in one sense; in his more specialised role as designer he practised it in another. In Aristotle's discussion, the basic meaning of the word, before one comes to the notion of representation, is simply 'replication' or 'mimicry'. Jones the designer is mimetic in this sense. All his stage designs are copied. They reproduce existing works of pictorial art, sculpture and architecture. This is why Bolton uses the odd word 'irrepturas', meaning that through Jones's efforts the arts will cross the Alps and come into England surreptitiously.[27] And this covert campaign is appropriately under the aegis of Mercury, who is not only divine patron of the arts but also god of thieves.

Mercury's doubleness here is illustrated by two later paintings associated with the court (the first directly and the second allusively). Honthorst's *Mercury Presenting the Arts to Apollo and Diana* shows the Duke of Buckingham as a kind of divine courier of the arts received by Charles I and Henrietta Maria, in a scene which has been compared to a masque. Robert Walker's *Self-Portrait* admits his plundering of Van Dyck's compositions, as he points to a figure of Mercury.[28] These are the two roles which Bolton compounds into one.

The ambiguity of Bolton's words is in general accord with the ambivalence of their context, the dedication to an English artist of the *res gestae* of a counter-Reformation Pope. Bordino's 'little book', as Bolton calls it with seeming innocence, reads awkwardly in the setting of a Protestant country, and especially a Protestant court, where the monarch is also head of the church. Sixtus V is seen as the hero of a renewed Catholicism, who looks to reverse the losses of the Reformation. One result, Bordino piously hopes, will be the spread of Rome's influence to the heretical hinterlands, including the English,[29] and their reabsorption into the Church. Bolton paraphrases this dangerous topic into his own hope for a benign invasion by the arts, rather than the religion, of Italy. But Bolton was a Catholic, and could appreciate that England was still beyond the full reach of Renaissance art not only geographically (being 'across the Alps') but through stern resistance to the culture of Catholicism. Jones too may have been a Catholic – we cannot be sure. But whether Bolton is addressing a co-religionist or not, his own Catholicism is enough to give his words a dimension of covert suggestiveness, as the link between art and religion is left undeclared.

The sense of covert communication is turned to account by shifting it onto a specific theme, focussing wider ambivalence into particular ambiguities which have a practical point. What English history has failed to deliver – because of the alternation of religious reform and reaction, and the eventual triumph of Protestantism, in the sixteenth century – is now looked for from one promising individual. By laying the burden of history on Jones's shoulders, and requiring him to be the mediator of Renaissance art to England, Bolton is asking a very great deal. The only feasible response can be to maximise the means available, as Bolton's word-play, with its doubling of meanings, suggests – to practise Mimesis in its grandest and its simplest forms,[30] invoking the god of mediations in his highest and lowest roles. In reviving the antique *Gesamtkunstwerk*, the total theatrical representation which can be the vehicle for all the other arts,[31] Jones at the same time is to mimic the artistic achievements of the Renaissance. Bolton's 'hope' can only be achieved through a campaign of grand larceny.

Both modes of Mimesis are necessary, the covert trawl for material to copy and the public production of the results in a manifestly coherent form. Wide range – the stereotypical faculty of the 'Renaissance man', which Jones genuinely exercised – must be complemented by coordination and firm composition; replication is no good without representation. Within the total composition which it constructed from the elements of poetry, spectacle, music and dance, Jones's theatre, in its crucial visual dimension which he designed, also compendiously represented the work of the countless sculptors, architects and pictorial artists from whom he derived his stage designs. The affective power of the masque was to instil a whole unknown history of art. Bolton implies that the arts of the ancients, revived in Italy, will implant themselves in England because they will be tacitly introduced through the theatre; they will infiltrate or insinuate themselves; they will civilise and instruct by stealth.

Copying

Jones pursued his programme through the whole range of his work. His most public intervention was his architecture, and his official title from 1615 was Surveyor of the King's Works. But his key activity was bound to be his designing of the masques, which began earlier (in 1605) and was more intensively focussed, in the restricted but crucially influential circle of the court. He used the masques to represent Renaissance art to the leaders of taste, and his method was simply to copy. Nearly all the surviving masque designs have identifiable sources, which cover an almost encyclopedic range. These are not only Italian, but also French, Netherlandish and German; and they are not only stage designs, but prints of architecture, sculpture and painting, as well as original paintings and drawings. By casting his net so widely Jones was familiarising the Stuart court with the whole repertory of images, styles and visual conventions which had long been established on the continent. Over a period of thirty-five years he staged this repertory before the courtiers' eyes, recapitulating a development of nearly two centuries, in what looks like a project to naturalise Renaissance art in England once for all.

The idea that the Renaissance tradition could be seen as unfolding in a great theatre occurred to Carlo Ridolfi, and he expresses it in a way which coincidentally illuminates Jones's efforts. Looking back from the seventeenth century over the great age of Venetian painting, he appeals to his readers' sense of its unequalled achievements, 'the last century having been a very theatre, and its scenery the choicest wonders of art . . .'[32]

Jones's method of copying has not always been understood by modern scholars. The crux of the matter has been well expressed by John Newman: 'Jones's artistic career was . . . a sustained campaign to educate his compatriots in the appreciation and understanding of the visual arts. Had he been less a copyist he would have been a less sure teacher . . .'[33] Roy Strong on the other hand sees Jones's copying not as self-conscious and systematic but as opportunistic: 'Jones was a relentless plagiarist, a magpie artist who lifted from a multiplicity of sources ideas for scenery and costumes.'[34] Perhaps these explanations are not so far apart. Both have a central motif in common: they see Jones as compulsive, in complementary ways, acting on the compulsion to acquire material and then to impart it. The motives of creative expediency and pedagogic zeal mix well in his case. It matters also that his stage designing had a long history, and its educational possibilities may not have been as clearly formulated in the earlier phases as they were later. But to call him simply a plagiarist seems wrong, especially as in historical terms the concept itself may be rather misleading.

The criticism is reiterated in Orgel and Strong's edition of the masque designs. Noting that many set designs of the 1630s are taken from Florentine sources, they speak of a 'declining originality of vision.'[35] Here are two fundamental misconceptions. One is that Jones's copying varied in degree at different stages of his career, when it was in fact consistent. The other is that 'originality of vision', a favourite (and perhaps mistaken) idea of our post-Romantic culture, could mean much for an artist of the early seventeenth century. The greatest artist of Jones's time, Rubens, was an avid student of ancient and modern art, assimilating a vast range of it into his own work (and he habitually retouched drawings by Cinquecento painters with no apparent sense of trespassing on their 'originality'). In this respect the exceptional figure is typical. Works which Jones copied had sometimes themselves been copied from other works; for example, his drawing of Atlas in *Coelum Britannicum* (1634) (plate 1) is copied from Francesco Albani (plate 2), who had in turn based his image on a well-known antique sculpture, the Atlante Farnese (also copied by Annibale Carracci in the

Camerino Farnese).³⁶ The engravings which he frequently used were used equally by other artists: for example, the prints of Roman ruins by Hieronymus Cock and Battista Pittoni were copied not only by Jones but by Veronese in the frescoes at Maser;³⁷ etchings by Paul Bril and Callot which he copied were reworked as paintings by Pozzoserrato and Teniers.³⁸ Sometimes he knew that a particular motif had been copied by another artist: in the Roman Sketchbook appears a head of the Virgin from Parmigianino's etching of the Annunciation, reused in reverse in another etching of the Entombment, which was itself copied in turn by Schiavone and Guido Reni; next to one of his various versions of this head Jones has written 'Parmigianino il meglio'.³⁹ These instances could be multiplied.

Jones belonged to a culture where the interrelationships of works of art were more obvious than any value placed on 'originality' in the modern sense. Inside this context he evolved his own specialised project, in which copying becomes a method or system. Even here he was not wholly unusual. Jill Finsten has shown that Isaac Oliver, who was associated with Jones in the service successively of the Earl of Rutland, Anne of Denmark and Prince Henry, was engaged on a similar programme of work.⁴⁰ Oliver produced not only the portrait miniatures for which he is famous but a series of much more elaborate compositions – some limnings, the majority finished drawings – in which he adopts the characters of various continental artists, often mingling different styles in the same composition. The result is a corpus of work in which the whole gamut of continental mannerist styles is self-consciously represented. These drawings were apparently done for a small circle of court patrons prepared to appreciate their sophisticated representation of new aesthetic styles.⁴¹ Oliver's activity here is a more refined, circumscribed version of Jones's dissemination to the court in general of the broadest range of continental art.

Both Oliver and Jones must have been aware that they were doing similar things. Each had started from the same point. There was no-one in England to teach them about continental art, so that pastiche and copying became necessary means of self-education. They capitalised by turning the means of self-education into a means of educating their public, creating a context in which their work could be understood.

The idea of copying as an activity which was formative for the artist was sanctioned by the artistic tradition which Jones and Oliver were trying to introduce. The sanction was ambiguous, since the increasing volume of theoretical writing which had appeared in Italy by the turn of the sixteenth century did not produce a consensus on the point. The practices of copying as a means of learning or developing one's métier, and of following the ancients (and moderns) as a way of generating new work, had come to overlap with the imitation of the 'great masters' of the Cinquecento in

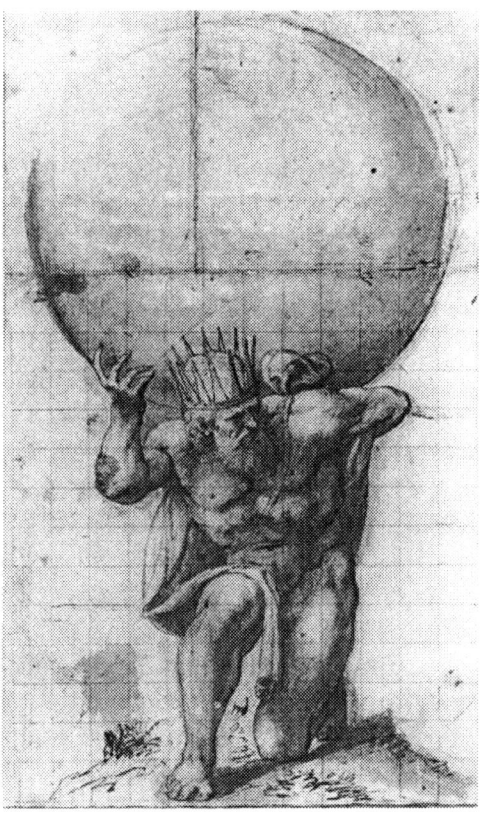

Plate 1. Inigo Jones, Atlas, for
Coelum Britannicum, Chatsworth

pursuit of a beautiful style or *maniera*; as Jones wrote, paraphrasing Vasari, 'gudd / manner coms by Copii/nge ye fayrest thinges'.[42] The resulting problems are most readily displayed in the case of Michelangelo, whose deification turned him for many lesser artists into a monstre sacré. Vasari's life records him as an apprentice copying a complicated engraving by Schongauer, making deceptively perfect copies of 'various old masters', and drawing Masaccio's frescoes in the Brancacci Chapel.[43] A later round-up of anecdotes includes his attacks on derivative artists, especially a sculptor who claimed to have imitated and surpassed antique statues: 'One who follows others never surpasses them, and an artist who cannot do good work of his own is unable to use that of others to advantage.'[44] There is a clear distinction in the narrative between learning from others' work and learning to use others' work. In fact the quotation goes back to Quintilian, and restates a classic topos about practising imitation in order to be oneself. But this issue became confused by the overbearing example of Michelangelo's achievement, reinforced by Vasari's deification, so that in the second edition

Plate 2. Francesco Albani, Hercules bearing the globe, Chatsworth

of the *Lives* Vasari is forced to complain of all the artists who follow Michelangelo in a slavish and inept fashion.[45] The cult of greatness and the Vasarian myth that art had reached its apogee threatened to compromise modern artists' imitative relationship with their predecessors.

The problem is acknowledged in Lomazzo's *Idea del tempio della pittura* (1591), where the painter, advised to learn by drawing on the work of the best artists, is also warned not to go against the grain of his own individual 'genius';[46] as if, while deferring to the overpowering example of the 'governors' of art, he can still exercise a prerogative similar to theirs, resemble their singularity, and exist in a state of independent subjection. The difficulty here is spelt out more obviously in G. B. Armenini's treatise *De' veri precetti della pittura*.[47] Armenini distinguishes between two kinds of artists who borrow from the work of others. There are 'those who because of their poor intellect lack inventiveness', and others, more talented, who use copying as a means to develop 'una bella e dotta maniera'.[48] Armenini's example of the second type is Perino del Vaga, whose copies (after Raphael, Michelangelo, and a range of engravings) 'had been adapted to his pleasing style with such skill that one could say they had been born of, and been created by, Perino . . .'[49] But Armenini also suggests that every artist faces the same situation: 'Since, now, as many believe, it is impossible to create anything which has not already been found and made, it follows that one can and must use another's inventions, provided one takes care to adapt them with some changes and has the ability to make them appear as if born of, and created by, one's own mind.'⁵⁰ This sentence occurs in his advice to the artist of 'poor intellect', but it describes a general crisis for all artists, and recommends a method identical to that ascribed to Perino, the superior artist of an earlier age. Armenini's argument is certainly not consistent, but what he is saying becomes plain enough: that copying, which was once customary for the novice and an option for the master, is now for the modern artist inevitable.

The conclusion to be drawn from his discussion – that copying is not just formative for the artist but inevitably constitutive of his work – could be seen as underwriting Jones's practice as a copyist, including the ambiguity of that practice. Because Armenini's argument is inconsistent it produces a kind of anamorphosis, in which Jones can be seen either as a typical artist of the modern epoch or an opportunist of 'poor intellect' ingeniously compensating for his deficiencies. This suggestive image perhaps shows us Jones in his historical situation. But it cannot take account of his peculiar geographical situation, and it now needs to be compared with Jones's picture of himself.

The motto

Jones's idea of himself as one who learned to be an artist through copying is expressed in his motto, 'Altro diletto che imparar non trovo.' He took this from Daniele Barbaro's commentary on Vitruvius. In Book 1, chapter 2, Vitruvius details the six parts of architecture. The second of these is *dispositione* (Lat. *dispositio*, arrangement) which Jones in his notes translates simply as 'disposition'. It divides into plan, elevation and perspective; and these arise from *pensamento* (Lat, *cogitatio*, reflection; Jones, 'thinkynge') and *inventione*. *Pensamento* combines intellectual labour with pleasure; and Barbaro pauses to explain this relationship. Jones paraphrases a key statement in the margin, 'Arte seekes to repre/sent effectes like / nature', which gives the tendency of Barbaro's comments. He is discussing the strenuous intellectual qualities required for the practice of art in the Aristotelian sense, and the resulting pleasure which the products of art give to the human mind. Jones summarises: 'Pleasure of the inte/llect to aprehend / truth'; Barbaro had written:

> the pleasure of the intellect is to apprehend what is true, for nothing is more fitting to the intellect than truth, hence the saying: Altro diletto ch'imparar non trovo.⁵¹

This is a quotation from Petrarch's *Trionfo dell'Amore*, but Barbaro is offering it as an Aristotelian dictum. He follows contemporary editors of Petrarch such as G. A. Gesualdo, who glossed the statement from Aristotle's

Metaphysics, which begins with the axiom 'All men naturally desire knowledge.'[52] A similar point comes near the conclusion of the *Ethics*: since the intellect is the most characteristic of human faculties, the intellectual life will be the happiest for a human being.[53] But the Aristotelian text which presents this doctrine in a context specifically pertinent to Jones is the *Poetics*. The fourth chapter, introducing the detailed discussion of poetry as mimesis, propounds the fundamental existence of the mimetic instinct and the pleasure of learning through imitation:

> the instinct of imitation is implanted in man from childhood, one difference between him and other animals being that he is the most imitative of living creatures, and through imitation learns his earliest lessons, and no less universal is the pleasure felt in things imitated . . . to learn gives the liveliest pleasure, not only to philosophers but to men in general; whose capacity, however, of learning is more limited.[54]

This passage, like much of the *Poetics*, was endlessly reproduced by sixteenth-century Italian theorists. The last part is paraphrased by Minturno as follows:

> Nè già per altro, se non che pur i Philosophi, ma ciascuno altro maggior diletto, che imparar non prova . . .[55]

Minturno's wording links the Aristotelian association of mimesis and knowledge with Barbaro's Petrarchan aphorism, and shows clearly how Jones's motto acquires its point from the *Poetics*.

Why should Jones have turned to the Aristotelian theory of poetry in order to express a central conviction about himself as a visual artist? His rupture with Ben Jonson about the relative importance of poetry and 'picture' in the masques may make the question look more difficult than it is. Long before that, at the beginning of his employment by Queen Anne, he had to design three plays at Oxford; and he may have read Aristotle, and a modern Aristotelian such as Minturno (whose treatise contains a great deal on 'poesia scenica') for guidance about principles. Vitruvius had said the architect should be familiar with 'lettere', a point reinforced and elaborated by Barbaro.[56] But whatever prompted him to read the *Poetics* or texts based on it, the general situation of the arts in this period meant he would have inevitably become familiar with Aristotelian poetic theory. In a classic study, Rensselaer Lee has shown how the *Poetics*, along with Horace's *Ars poetica*, was appropriated by theorists of visual art in order to supply the absence of any comparable treatise on art surviving from antiquity. Aristotle's theory of mimesis, which he had expounded in any case partly through analogies with painting, became a particularly important doctrine in art theory of the sixteenth and seventeenth centuries.[57] Jones's contemporary Franciscus Junius begins *The Painting of the Ancients* as a matter of course with 'a generall observation of the inbred delight men take in the imitation of the workes of Nature . . . ,'[58] and this approach is typical of Italian writers of previous generations. It is not surprising that Jones should have used the theory of mimesis to express the essential point of his own work.

So the motto 'Altro diletto che imparar non trovo' characterises Jones as an imitator. This may be understood in two senses. Vasari explains:

> I know that our art consists entirely of imitation, first of Nature, and then, as it cannot rise so high of itself, of the things which are produced by those who are acknowledged the greatest masters.[59]

This expresses succinctly the sophistication of Aristotle's concept made by later writers of antiquity: that in order to imitate nature one also has to imitate art. The first kind of imitation (*mimesis*) entails the second (*imitatio*). Vasari's claim that art 'consists entirely' of imitation in this complex sense is borne out later, when he defines the term 'disegno':

> *Il disegno* fu lo Imitare il piu bello della natura in tutte le figure, cosi scolpite, come dipinte, la qual parte viene dallo haver la mano, e l'ingegno, che rapporti tutto quello, che vede l'occhio in sul piano . . .

Jones underlined the first term and paraphrased: 'what desine is / To Imitate yᵉ best of / nature'.[60] Since 'design' is Vasari's most inclusive concept – painting, sculpture and architecture being for him the 'arti del disegno' – to equate imitation with it is to stress the inclusiveness of that concept too. Ben Jonson complained in his *Expostulation* that the idea of 'design' was 'Omnipotent' for Jones;[61] by analogy we may deduce from his motto that imitation is an equally powerful motif in his thinking (Jonson could never have mocked at that because it was at the centre of his own work).[62]

Imitating and 'composing'

In this context of thought, the masque designs, which are 'copied', are much closer to Jones's architecture, which is 'original', than our anachronistic discourse of originality and copying can convey. Both could come under the rubric of imitation. According to Jones's mentor Palladio, architecture, like all the other arts, was 'imitatrice della natura';[63] and Alberti and Barbaro had maintained the same point. The argument was that architecture operated according to 'the laws upon which she [nature] herself acted in the Production of her Works',[64] the Aristotelian view being that art imitated Nature's *modus operandi*. Other writers reinforced this argument by seeing quasi-representational elements in classical buildings. Vitruvius had derived the concept of proportion in architecture from the model of the human body.⁶⁵ Vasari, in describing a well-proportioned building, turned this abstract analogy almost into an allegory, in which a palace was seen to 'represent' the human organism in its plan and function.⁶⁶ Lomazzo saw the architect as imitating the human body like the painter.⁶⁷ Again, Vitruvius derived the proportions of the Doric column from the male body, and of the Ionic from the female; although he then also suggested that the form of the latter in part actually represented a woman.⁶⁸ This gives a cue for Vasari to claim that the form of the Doric column 'resembles that of Hercules'.⁶⁹ Not only did Vitruvius prompt this anthropomorphic view of architecture, but he stresses its likeness to natural forms. He wrote that columns, in thickness, 'ought ... to imitate the natural growth of trees'; this is repeated by Palladio and Sir Henry Wotton.⁷⁰ On a smaller scale, Jones himself writes on an illustration in his Palladio that the ovolo of the Temple of Neptune 'imitates the almond rather the[n] the chestnut'.⁷¹ From the most general and abstract down to the most detailed and naturalistic level, architecture imitated nature.

Appropriately then, one occurrence of Jones's motto is in his copy of Barbaro's Vitruvius.⁷² Quite apart from the fact that he discovered it in Barbaro's text, its implication about learning through imitation chimes with the idea that the architect imitates nature. Barbaro explains how this is:

> Art as far as it can imitates nature; and this comes about because the motive principle of art, which is the human intellect, is very similar to the motive principle of nature, which is also an intelligence. From the similarity of powers and principles springs a similarity in functioning – which for the moment we may call 'imitation'.⁷³

This can be compared with Jonson's description of the first scene in his and Jones's first masque, *The Masque of Blackness* (1605):

> an artificiall sea was seene to shoote forth, as if it flowed to the land, raysed with waues, which seemed to moue, and in some places the billow to breake, as imitating that orderly disorder, which is common in nature.⁷⁴

Jonson credits Jones the artist with an imitation of nature which works on exactly that fundamental level identified by Barbaro. The implications for Jones are obvious: whether as architect or masque designer he is an artist in the full Aristotelian sense, a fundamental imitator of nature.

His own interest in the theory, as well as the practice, of *mimesis* is documented in his copy of Plato's *Republic*. He chooses three sections for continuous comment, all dealing with art as *mimesis*: in Book III, the discussions of narration and dramatisation in poetry, and of music; in

Book X, the famous attack on art because its mimetic method ensures its estrangement from the truth. While following Plato's account of music with sympathetic attention, Jones stands back from his critical argument in the other two passages. In Book III, when Socrates maintains that the dramatic element in poetry must be minimised because its essentially mimetic quality represents both good and evil impartially, Jones simply notes the technical distinctions he makes: 'what poesi / is Imitatio[n] . . . what poesie is not Imita/tion . . . nar/ration in pr/ose no immi/tation';[75] but he refrains from endorsing the conclusion. He Aristotelianises the passage, as it were, reading from it the contrasting analysis of narration and dramatisation that was to be elaborated in the *Poetics*. He follows the condemnation of art in Book X in an even more detached spirit. Homer is challenged to show the practical effect of his representations of the world:

> Be so good as to tell me, what city was ever better governed and ordered through your example, as Sparta was by the methods of Lycurgus, and many cities both great and small have been by the methods of many other men? Of what city do men proclaim you to be an excellent lawgiver?

Jones, less docile than the usual Platonic interlocutor, answers back: 'I think yt homer tau/ght lawgi/uers'.[76] When Socrates declares,

> I said that painting, and every kind of imitation, operates at a great distance from truth; and again, it relates to that part of us which is especially devoid of prudence, and allies itself to that, having no particle of truth or honesty,

Jones notes in the margin: 'Painti[n]g / is Imita/tion'.[77] This and similar comments can only be described as Aristotelian stonewalling. Plato's account of mimesis clearly compelled his attention, but in the end he subscribed to Aristotle's more positive view, as reinterpreted in the Renaissance, that art productively and truly imitates nature.

But in order to imitate nature he was, in both the fields of architecture and stage design, an imitator of art. Jones's ideas as an architect on using the work of others are revealingly documented in his notes on Palladio. In those notes, made over many years,[78] the most frequently recurring phrase is the recommendation, addressed to himself, 'to be imitated'. Occasionally this refers to solving a practical problem, such as the placing of stairs or the extension of columns which are too short.[79] But usually it refers to a formal solution. Sometimes, especially when it occurs in the negative, 'not to be imitated', Jones spells out his criteria of judgment.[80]

The masque designs may seem at first to be in a different universe from Jones's architecture, but these notes on the topic of imitation suggest the

Plate 3. Fragment of a frieze, from the Arundel Marbles, Museum of London

opposite. One of them concerns the fragment of a temple frieze among the Arundel Marbles (plate 3),

> wch I thinke was of the tempell of Minerua at Smirna by reason of ye gorgons heades in the mettopes of [the] freese beetwene ye Cartottzi wch are in the stead of Trigliffios a rare inuention and to bee imitated sheauing how the Ansientes varied and composed ther o(r)ders according to the nateurres of the gods to whome ye Tempels weare dedicated.[81]

It is by the exercise of reason that 'the Ancients varied and composed their orders', producing 'a rare invention ... to be imitated'. Jones did imitate this invention, but it was in a masque set, not a building – the Roman Atrium for the first scene of *Albion's Triumph* (1632) (plate 4), a meticulously detailed architectural perspective.[82] Jones evidently did not think of architecture and masques as discontinuous; and this is quite logical, considering that each involves imitation, not only in being mimetic of nature, but in imitating prior works of art.

The way in which each structures its imitations increases the similarity. Yet another of Jones's notes discusses how Palladio has formulated his versions of the orders from a wide range of differing antique examples, with particular reference to the pedestals of columns:

> But in my opinio(n) Palladio Immitates ye Best Bacments of thes antiquities as ye Tempels of Pola, of Nerua, of Fortune, of Scicci, but

allwaes the libberty of composing wth reason is not taken awaye but who followes ye best of the ansientes cannot much earr.[83]

Reason, as we have seen, is the standard of nature, so again it seems that to follow the ancients is to be on the way to following Nature. But more pertinent here is that the architect's scope for invention is precisely delimited: at its widest it is 'the liberty of composing with reason'. When Jones talks of 'composing' he is referring to the constituent elements of the classical orders, each formal motif being susceptible of variation, and all together susceptible of different combinations and recombinations, subject to certain conventions or rules. 'Composing' is what the architect does with the basic formal vocabulary in order to produce his own inventions, and to realise a project, which may be an actual building or a paper project like Palladio's reconstructions of antique temples – or something in between like Jones's masque architecture. Since the formal language exists already only by virtue of the many authoritative 'compositions' made from it by the ancients, any use of it is bound to be a reuse. 'Composing' is tantamount to 'following'.

Jones's notion of 'composing' is illuminated by Vasari's history of classical architecture after antiquity. In the *Preface to the Lives* he follows its vicissitudes in the period of decline, between the era of Constantine and the mid thirteenth century, noting that alone of all the arts it kept up a certain competence:

> Architecture... maintained its excellence at a higher though not at the highest level. Nor is this a matter for surprise, since large buildings were almost entirely constructed of spoils, so that it was easy for the architects in great measure to imitate the old in making the new, since they had the former continually before their eyes.[84]

Vasari names a long series of buildings, from the Arch of Constantine to the Duomo of Pisa, which he sees as 'constructed of spoils'. He praises some of them, quite logically, since they carry the compositional method of classical architecture to its logical extreme. They are reconstituting the authoritative works of the ancients, not just figuratively but literally. Jones seems to have taken in Vasari's view of post-antique architecture as a literal remaking of the antique, since he used it to argue against Palladio in one of his notes.[85] And his sense of how it points up the fundamental but complex importance of 'composing' in architecture is seen in his design for Temple Bar. This is an imitation of the Arch of Constantine, and as if recognising Vasari's view of the Arch as 'constructed of spoils', Jones's project follows suit, incorporating sculptured panels derived from a variety of other sources.[86] Jones's imitation of a pastiche is logically also a pastiche, and self-

The theory and practice of imitation

Plate 4. Jones, A Roman atrium, for *Albion's Triumph*, Chatsworth

consciously reinforces the intrinsically imitative nature of architectural 'composing'.

It is through 'composing' in this sense that the masque designs are generated. Taking as their field of reference modern art – that is, the arts from the High Renaissance onwards seen as reviving the excellencies of antiquity – together with antique art as reproduced by modern artists, they treat this vast stock of motifs as a formal vocabulary, to be used in almost endless recombinations. The perspective provided by Vasari, like that we considered earlier provided by Armenini, helps to express the ambiguity of this enterprise. From one point of view the designs could be seen as 'constructed of spoils'. From another they could be seen as adopting the paradigm of invention underlying architectural classicism – of art as imitative 'composing' – and taking it to its logical conclusion in the genre of 'picture'. Certainly there is a parallel between the kind of minute attentiveness which Jones's architectural notes record, and the same methodical acuity displayed by his masque compositions. In annotating Palladio, he shows an extraordinary capacity for singling out and comparing tiny details, always in an appropriate general context; and the notes contain an elaborate network of cross-reference. Like Palladio – like any classical architect – he is acutely aware of parts, both analytically and synthetically. This comes out also in the masque designs, which often reveal a careful visual analysis of their sources, going beyond the need to rearrange visual 'spoils'. Armenini had written that imitation is nothing more than the practice of observation; Franciscus Junius took this further, and declared that imitation was essentially an analytical discipline.[87] This is certainly true of Jones, both as architectural thinker and masque designer, engaged in 'composing with reason'.

Imitation as teaching

Jones's self-characterisation as an imitator, in the motto which he discovered and inscribed in his Vitruvius, helps us to shake off the bugbear of 'originality' and appreciate how the masque designs are produced according to the same general principles as the architecture. And to see his copying in the masques in the context of 'imitation' is not only to understand them better as works in themselves, but also as a means to an end, that of learning, training himself (and, as we shall see, his public). The other known occurrence of the motto is in the Roman Sketchbook,[88] in which most of the material, both written and graphic, is secondhand.[89] It began as a notebook with a few illustrations, but came to include over the years numerous copies from prints, serving both for drawing practice and the compilation of a figurative vocabulary, but not essentially different from the material that is drafted into the masque designs; and the motto points up how this kind of copying is the same as learning.

Aristotle's account of mimesis had stressed that imitation was a means to knowledge, which was why it gave pleasure, although the fullest pleasure in knowledge could only be felt by the philosopher.[90] By stressing in the motto that learning is for him the exclusive pleasure, Jones identifies himself as a philosopher. So the claim made by inscribing the motto in the Roman Sketchbook is both self-effacing and proud: he learns by imitating other artists, but this learning is a philosophical enterprise. Plato's *Republic*, which he studied in Italian translation, made clear that philosophy was not confined to professional thinkers. The human soul has three parts, says Socrates: the aggressive, the appetitive, and 'if we were to call this third part desire of learning and love of wisdom (desiderio d'imparare & Philosopho), the name will not be applied inappropriately.'[91] The desire to learn is the true philosophical tendency; and, Socrates goes on, the man in whom it is uppermost experiences the highest of all pleasures.

Jones did also set himself to learn from professional philosophers.

Vitruvius had required the architect, among his manifold accomplishments, to be a 'diligent student of philosophy' so as to acquire moral disinterestedness and scientific insight. 'Philosophy then', comments Barbaro, 'is a help to virtuous behaviour, likewise an equal help with regard to acquiring knowledge of the truth ... '[92] Jones took this seriously. A passage which he seized on in Plutarch described the capacity of the philosophical mind to change its opinion and welcome the truth:

> *ne l'animo* che impara, e contempla solo le cose, non v'ha passione alcuna luoco che l'impedisca; anzi la parte irragionevole de l'animo vi stà quieta, ne si cura altramente; *Onde tosto* che la verità apparisce, è abbraciata volontieri de la ragione.
>
> in the mind which is disposed to learning and contemplation, no obstructive passion finds a place; indeed the irrational part of the mind remains still and unconcerned; so that as soon as truth appears reason freely embraces it.

Jones's marginal paraphrase concludes: 'as soo[n] / as truth appe/ars reason im/braseth it.'[93] The pattern of his own career, in which change and tentative exploration developed into certainty about what in an early court entertainment was called the 'truth of architecture',[94] and of art in general, could be seen as such a philosophical quest. His 'diligent study of philosophy' can be followed in his copies of Plato, Aristotle, Xenophon and Plutarch,[95] where certain sections are carefully annotated. He paid particular attention to the practice of philosophy itself, as exemplified by the figure of Socrates, especially the Socrates who was presented not only (as in Plato's dialogues) dramatically but also historically – in Xenophon's *Memorabilia* and Plutarch's *Moralia*. What drew him was the Socratic method, 'In what Socrates / was a midwife', as he writes in one of his notes, 'that arte' of asking questions, adopting the learner's stance in order to teach.[96] In a general sense Jones is doing the same thing. His imitativeness is a philosophical receptiveness.

It puts him in a position to teach others.[97] Jones's collaborator Jonson was quite explicit to their audience about the masques being both imitative and didactic. Jonson saw the masques as imitations of both nature and art – mimetic fictions in Aristotle's sense constructed through *imitatio* of prior works of art.[98] His poetry imitates a range of classical writers. In the famous late Renaissance debate about whether poets and artists should imitate one model or many,[99] he is obviously in the second camp. Jones's masque designs correspond to Jonson's poetry here except that they go beyond that debate, which seemed to have pre-empted the whole problem of *imitatio*. Jones does not follow many models: he follows every model – there is no limit to the range of artists whose work he uses. This puts him beyond the pale which the theoretical debates had marked out, and makes him look disreputably indiscriminate. But his peculiarly radical version of the practice of *imitatio* is the result of a peculiar didactic necessity – whereas Jonson can rely on their audience's familiarity with his poetic discourse and its cultural context, Jones has to teach the same audience the language of Renaissance art from scratch, before they can capably appreciate any specific usages of it.

Jones performs the role of the learner as teacher in a radically thorough way. Not only does he imitate all other artists, but he always imitates other artists. The indications are that no part of the masque designs is 'original' (except for certain scenes of local topography). This means that they represent nature wholly through imitating art: *mimesis* is effected wholly through *imitatio*.

The idea that art can stand in for nature as the object of imitation is associated with the idea that art can be seen as an alternative or a better nature. Jones would have been aware of a spectrum of views here, spread between positions which can roughly be identified with Aristotle and Plato. Palladio condemns any derogation from nature:

> that manner of building cannot but be blamed, which departing from that which the Nature of things teaches us, and from that simplicity which is perceived in the things created by her, making as it were another nature, departs from the true, good and beautiful method of building.[100]

In a spirit of puritanical Aristotelianism, Palladio seems to find the idea of making another nature perfectly scandalous. On the other hand, Jones's compatriot Sir Philip Sidney, inclined as a neo-Platonist and Calvinist to regard nature as imperfect and corrupt, writes in his *Apology for Poetry*:

> the poet ... doth grow in effect into another nature, in making things either better than Nature bringeth forth, or, quite anew, forms such as never were in Nature ... Her world is brazen, the poets only deliver a golden.[101]

Somewhere in between is Lomazzo, in the *Trattato della pittura*:

> all famous Inventors ... have ... shewed themselves subtile searchers out of the effectes of nature, being mooved thereunto by a speciall delight of often seeing, and continuall practizing that which they have preconceived. So that who so keepeth this order, shall unawares attaine to such an habite of practize, in lively expressing all *actions* and *gestures* best fitting his purpose, that it will become an other Nature.[102]

This passage comes at the beginning of the Second Book, 'Of Actions, Gestures . . . ' ('Moti' in Italian), and stresses the importance of motion in the workings of nature. This, notwithstanding the presence of the neo-Platonic concept of 'Idea', gives it an Aristotelian bias, compounded by Lomazzo's later example of a 'famous Inventor' – Cesare da Sesto – which suggests that Leonardoesque naturalism is the mode in which to create another nature. In short, Lomazzo expounds what may seem an almost inherently neo-Platonic doctrine in a very Aristotelian way, turning it into a virtual restatement of the theory of *mimesis*.

It has been said that Lomazzo's *Trattato* 'is to Jones the painter what the Palladio [*Quattro Libri*] is to Jones the architect'.[103] Since both view the relationship between art and nature, and the idea of art as another nature, in a decidedly Aristotelian perspective, the once received idea of Jones as a neo-Platonist tout court seems to be rightly under revision.[104] Looking from the theory of imitation implicit in his motto to his practice as a universal imitator of other artists' work, we may see him treating art as if it were nature. He addresses the corpus of European Renaissance art as if it were a whole new world of its own – which from the English point of view it precisely was – as if it constitutes a fundamental reality, which may then undergo the process of *mimesis* in the classic Aristotelian sense. His project involves not just the imitation, but the representation of art – opening up unexplored vistas of knowledge and experience to his compatriots.

Reform

Jones's representation of this new world of art is in accordance with Aristotle's recommendations about imitating the world of nature. These go far beyond the basic idea, from which the discussion in the *Poetics* develops, of mimesis as mimicry. Jones does not reproduce the literal actuality of the world of art, but as it 'ought to be', in Aristotle's words, 'for the ideal type must surpass the reality'.[105] One sign of this is his eclecticism – partly an eclecticism of style like that practised by Isaac Oliver in his drawings, or pursued by Tintoretto, or wrongly attributed to the Carracci[106] – but even more an eclecticism of content. The locus classicus here is the story of Zeuxis, taken out of Pliny and launched into the Renaissance theoretical tradition by Alberti's *De pictura*. Alberti, developing the Aristotelian argument that the painter imitates nature, contrasts Demetrius, 'who failed to obtain the highest praise because he was more devoted to representing the likeness of things than to beauty', with Zeuxis, who represented the beauty of Helen by selecting features from a number of beautiful women;[107] and the story was repeated over and over. Jones noted an earlier story in Xenophon, about Parrhasius, who agreed with Socrates that 'bautifull figu/res ar made /

by taking the / best of seueral / men . . . ,[108] and at the other end of the historical spectrum he was aware of Vasari's modern refinement of this idea into a stylistic doctrine:

> *La maniera* venne poi la piu bella, dall'havere messo in uso il frequente ritrarre le cose piu belle; & da quel piu bello o mani, o teste, o corpi, o gambe aggiugnerle insieme; & fare una figura di tutte quelle bellezze . . .

Changing Vasari's words from the historical to the demonstrative mode, from past to present, Jones paraphrases: 'gudd / manner comes by Copii/nge yᵉ fayrest thinges'.[109] He is working in this tradition, where an idealising eclecticism chimes in with Aristotelian criteria of imitation. He does not merely reproduce items from the repertory of Renaissance art, but selects and makes new combinations. Or else, when he does seem to resort to direct transcription, it always turns out that he is revising what he quotes. Either procedure, of eclectic reconstruction or revision, treats the world of art as an autonomous creation which, in the Aristotelian spirit of ideal imitation, can have its purposes admiringly but critically disclosed and carried to a more perfect completion.

Jones was a reformer as well as a propagandist. He was not engaged in simply importing continental art into England as if it were a range of aesthetic commodities. He actively mediated the Renaissance tradition, rather than present it neutrally as a historical panorama, criticising and revising it when he saw fit. Sixtus V, the model proposed by his friend Bolton, had been a reformer, whose works advertising the glory of the papacy had been carried out in a deliberated and highly organised way; the antique monuments which he restored, for example, were all surmounted with the symbols of Christianity – the Vatican obelisk with the cross, the columns of Trajan and Marcus Aurelius with the statues of Saints Peter and Paul. The combination of propaganda with discipline proved to be a pertinent exemplar for Jones. When in 1625 he used Sixtus's funeral catafalque, designed by the papal architect Fontana (plate 5), as the model for the catafalque of his own master James I (plate 6), he 'reformed' it radically. Fontana celebrated the works he had carried out for the Pope by representing them on the catafalque, either as part of its structure (making it an architectural pastiche) or in pictures attached to it. Jones followed this precedent, but instead of literally representing the projects he had executed as Surveyor of the King's Works (he was to do this on his own tomb)[110] he made the catafalque an embodiment of the architectural principles which had informed those projects. This simplified the design, and he simplified it further by taking it back closer to its original inspiration, the classic pattern of Bramante's Tempietto[111] (plate 7). These changes – the emphasis on inner

Plate 5. Domenico Fontana, Catafalque for Sixtus V, from B. Catani, *La Pompa Funerale di Papa Sisto il Quinto*, 1591, plate 24, British Library

Plate 6. Jones, Catafalque for James I, Worcester College, Oxford

principles replacing a display of externals, and the return to pure origins – came appropriately from an artist brought up in a Protestant culture.[112] The catafalque for James signals not only the end of a reign but the conclusion of Jones's first decade as Surveyor, and can be seen as a programmatic statement of his achievements and ideals. The inwardness of the statement shows how deeply these ideals are marked, culturally and aesthetically, by Protestantism – however unsympathetic he may have found it in some respects, and whatever his personal religion.

Summerson has presented Jones as undertaking in England a one-man reformation of Italian architecture, which in its own country 'was tired and going badly off the rails',[113] recalling it from the degeneracy of modern practice to the principles inherent in the theoretical tradition, and the pristine clarity of the antique as revived by the High Renaissance. The catafalque for James, a temporary structure existing on the border between architecture and scenography, is a signpost pointing the applicability of Summerson's thesis to the masque designs as well.

Their implicit tendency, as it emerges during the first decade of Jones's Surveyorship (the second of his stage designing), suggests the same reforming programme as his architecture: a critique of Mannerism. On the surface, their formal bias seems highly mannerist. They also conform to the general desire of mannerist art and thought to interpose other art between the artist and nature.[114] In the end they approach Vincenzio Danti's demand that the artist's procedure in representation shall be *imitare* rather than *ritrarre*, that he shall realise the latent perfectibility of things rather than depict their actual appearances.[115] But such a mannerist doctrine could be interpreted as sound Aristotelianism; and here Jones turns the tables. Much of the mannerist art he reproduces is treated below its own aesthetic pretensions, as if *it* contained defects which needed to be perfected. Judged wanting in 'gudd manner' (to use his Vasarian phrase) by the severe standards of an earlier classicism, it is brought back into line. This is especially true of his designs for architecture in the masques, and for decorative ornament. Even when there are no earlier classical models, as in the case of landscape, he implicitly refers to a notion of what such models might be, guided by the re-emerging classicism in contemporary European art. These areas will all be treated in detail in later chapters.

The artist as imitator

The ambitious plans for Jones which Bolton outlined – the project of introducing into England the 'elegant arts of the ancients' as revived by the Italian Renaissance – and Jones himself succinctly implied in his motto, committed him to a lifetime of imitation. This practice, documented in every area of his work, found its most extensive and public outlet in the court masques. As the masque designs show, it is a practice intrinsically fraught with ambivalence. What Bolton sees as serious employment of large scope and wide horizons (measured by 'the Alps'), Jones characterises more subjectively in terms of intellectual pleasure; and within Bolton's description there is the humorous shift between disparate functions of the art-god Mercury, from civilising enlightenment to knavish ingenuity. We have looked at the context and the reasons for this ambivalence, which may be summed up as the uncertain relationship between *mimesis* and *imitatio* in the work of the late Renaissance artist. Whether or not this problem was already endemic in antiquity – perhaps because of the uneasy relationship between Alexandrian and Athenian, as between Roman and Greek, culture – it was undoubtedly present for the modern artist from the later sixteenth century

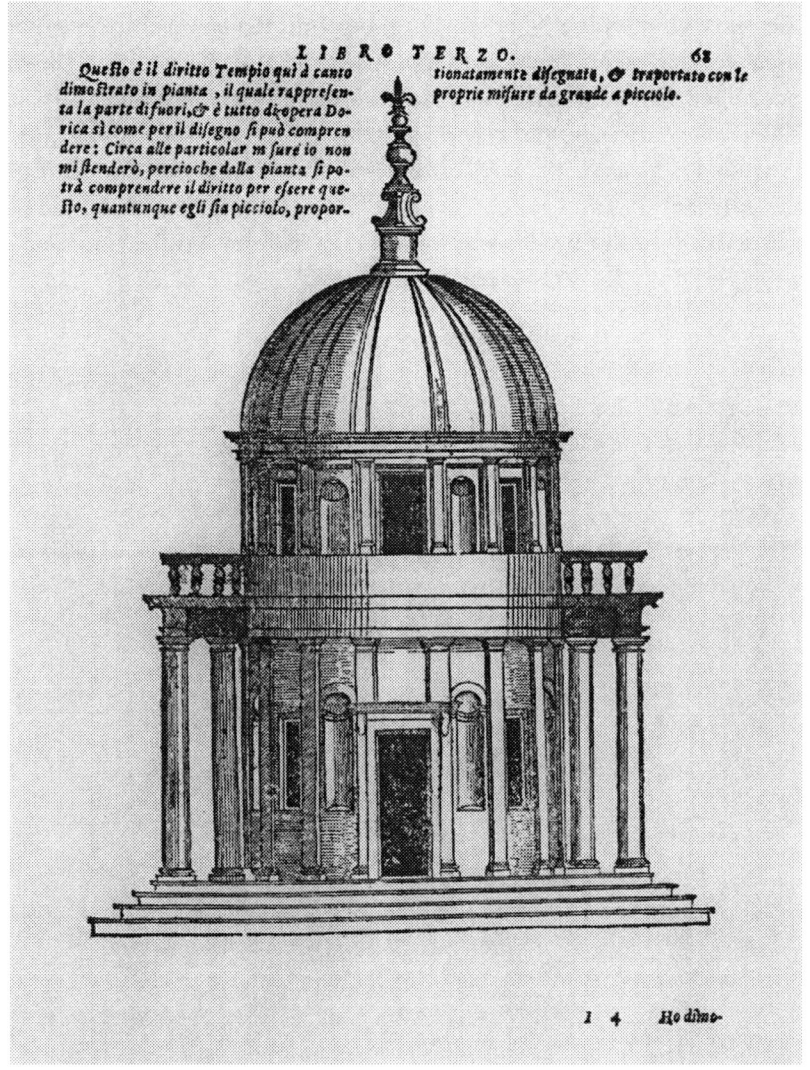

Plate 7. Donato Bramante, Tempietto di S. Pietro in Montorio, from Serlio, *Architettura*, 1619

onwards, and for Jones in particular. Vasari had posed, but not really discussed, the dilemma of the modern artist vis à vis his powerful predecessors; we have seen it spelt out by Armenini in imprecise but not uninformative terms, so as to suggest that, for the modern artist, representing the world necessarily involves imitating prior art.

Jones is both inside and outside this dilemma. His peculiar historical situation makes him both a European artist of his time and the belated protagonist of Renaissance art in England. In bringing together the two time-scales within which he is working, he continually produces effects of historical condensation. He is both a pioneer and a plagiarist, both a learner and a teacher. He promotes renaissance and reform simultaneously; one result is that mannerism and classicism coincide in his designs (and, as we shall see, this is a classicism which points both forward into the European seventeenth century and back to the High Renaissance). At one and the same time his work is both *mimesis* and *imitatio*, its material both nature and art. He is the perfect type of the artist as imitator.

2

The masques as pictures

English culture and its resistance

Jones's first modern biographer, J. A. Gotch, described him as having a 'mission' to England.¹ As we have seen, this kind of language was used of the English cultural situation during Jones's lifetime, when Rubens described Lord Arundel as 'one of the four evangelists . . . of our art'.² The idea of a mission suggests an analogy with the papal mission which tried to gain a foothold at Charles I's court – Jones's enemies were to see him in this context, and he was in effect a kind of one-man fifth column, while not in the way they imagined. Even so, the association of art with religion was not beside the point. Rubens combined painting and diplomacy in the service of the Catholic Habsburg governors of the Spanish Netherlands. Arundel's religious sympathies, while ostensibly transferred to the Church of England, probably matched his cultural sympathies all his life. And the Catholic Bolton, in recommending to Jones the cultural but not the religious example of Pope Sixtus V, suggests – precisely by his silence on this capital point – how art and religion are mixed up with each other. This unspoken relationship has a function in his brief text. By seeing the Alps as a boundary to be transgressed with ingenious secrecy, he shows that he is aware of obstacles to Jones's 'mission', and that these obstacles – since beyond the Alps lies the heartland of the Roman Church – have to do with religion.

To carry out the agenda Bolton sets for him, Jones has to do two things. He has to familiarise the English – that is, the privileged and influential minority who have access to the court masques – with a vast repertory of images, forms and styles which are still largely unknown to them. And, more fundamentally, he has to inculcate the idea that visual art is a meaningful language, a valid discourse in its own terms. Both objectives are difficult, and the difficulties had been created by the Reformation.³

Like other Protestant states, England had developed a culture wary of the visual arts. This wariness was in practice a variable response, depending on doctrinal differences and historical changes. Iconoclasm was not a simple, constant factor in the course of the Reformation, as was shown from the first in the contrast between Lutheran and Calvinist positions. Within the Calvinist Church of England there might still be differing interpretations of the commandment against idolatry.[4] And the overall success of the iconoclast cause by the third decade of the seventeenth century produced arguments for relaxing the Church's suspicion of religious imagery,[5] although such arguments might also be associated with the new, anti-Calvinist, Arminian theology of Laud and his supporters, who of course included Charles I. In the Caroline masques of the 1630s it may have seemed that the King appeared as an image of himself, to be revered and worshipped. In the end, the controversy around Charles's execution which centred on the apologia *Eikon Basilike* and Milton's *Eikonoklastes* showed the durability of the iconoclast debate,[6] and the dramatic revisions which had occurred within it.

When Jones began work as a court artist early in the reign of James I, and was given his charge by Bolton to transform English culture, that culture had received a deep but not uniform impression from Protestant iconoclasm. Calvin had overturned the traditional belief, stemming from Gregory the Great, that images could communicate divine truth to the illiterate; on the contrary, it was asserted, images drew the beholder away from God rather than towards Him. But the greatest Calvinist poet of Elizabethan England, Edmund Spenser, wrote completely against the grain of Calvin's teaching on this crucial point, using a rich structure of imagery to draw the reader's mind towards, among other things, the truth of Calvinist theology. While the English Reformation had severely checked or distorted the development of the visual arts, it had not always instilled the new mental attitudes which went along with the primacy of the Word.

The situation addressed by Jones had therefore its local uncertainties as well as its major underlying cause. The cause seems acknowledged by Bolton when he makes 'Statuaria' first of the arts on his agenda. In the classic usage of Pliny the word signifies sculpture in bronze, which, Pliny explains, was originally reserved for images of the gods (or the 'idols and images of the gods' as Philemon Holland puts it in his translation).[7] By leading off with his hope for a revival of the art of representing the divine, Bolton reverses the priorities of the Reformers, and implicitly identifies Protestant iconoclasm as a prime agent of England's artistic deprivation. It is the Reformation which stands at the head of the missing, or at least retarded, history of English Renaissance art, producing a dissociation between verbal and visual cultures. Jones not only has to fill in a history, but change a mentality.

This mentality has left its mark on the sparse English writings on art produced during Jones's lifetime. The paramount problem is the representation of God. Richard Haydocke, the pioneering translator of Lomazzo, felt he had to interrupt his author's discussion of how to paint God the Father. Lomazzo is debating whether God should be depicted with obscurity or clarity: 'I should rather thinke', he says, 'that... he ought to be represented with perfect cleere colours'; whereupon Haydocke interposes in the margin, 'And I that he should not be Painted at all'.[8] Henry Peacham, in *The Art of Drawing* (1606), expatiates on the same point:

> there be some things that ought to be free from the pencill, as the picture of God the father: or (as I have seene) the whole Trinitie painted in a glasse window...[9]

In the revised edition of his book, published as *The Gentleman's Exercise* in 1612, this discussion is rearranged and amplified, with various qualifications and nuances; he allows, for example, pictures of Christ as man. But he still takes a hard line on representing the Godhead, against Cardinal Bellarmine's claim that there are places in scripture which authorise it:

> But howsoever these and other places do seeme to make for the lawfulnes of it we are to hold it an impious thing, and not to be tolerated, as being expresly forbidden by the word of God, and giving occasion of the infinite errors in the Church.[10]

Such inhibitions compromised painting itself. Peacham begins *The Art of Drawing* not only with the assurance that painting is not ignoble but that it is not impious:

> Pictura, or painting in generall... we may find in the holy Scripture both allowed, and highly commended by the mouth of God himselfe...[11]

Two decades later, Edward Norgate in *Miniatura, or The Art of Limning* still feels himself to be up against this barrier, as he defends landscape painting in these terms:

> I owe much to this harmeles and honest Recreation, of all kinds of painting the most innocent, and which the Divill him selfe could never accuse of idolatry.

And there is still the need to speak up for his

> Art, which by Ignorance and *Bestie chi Parlano* is undeservedly traduced, as idolatrous, impious or impertinent.[12]

The touch of cosmopolitan impatience in Norgate's trenchant Italian phrase points to a continuing suspicion of visual art in English culture.

For Jones, the difficulties of this situation were most obviously played out in his long, close, but stormy relationship with Ben Jonson. As a learned court poet, but not a courtier, Jonson made assertive claims for his work, claims to which the inherent tendencies of English culture lent more support. He wrote:

> Picture is the invention of heaven: the most ancient, and most akinne to Nature. It is it selfe a silent worke ... Yet it doth so enter, and penetrate the inmost affection (being done by an excellent Artificer) as sometimes it orecomes the power of speech, and oratory.[13]

The operative word is 'sometimes'. Previously he had written:

> *Poetry*, and *Picture*, are Arts of a like nature; and both are busie about imitation ... Yet of the two, the Pen is more noble then the Pencill. For that can speake to the Understanding; the other, but to the Sense.[14]

Picture is mediated by sense, whereas poetry, which is verbal instead of sensuous and 'can speake', makes immediate contact with the mind – a typically Protestant contrast. Jonson, who was no religious radical and had been a Catholic, argues with the full support of Reformation culture behind him, without having to enlist it specifically. He assumes that the crucial function is language. 'Picture' is either 'silent', without language; or else, if it has a language, it is an inferior one. He had been arguing the second point ever since he began publishing the masques which he and Jones undertook together, diminishing in effect the high compliments he paid Jones in the same publications. It was quite logical for them to quarrel eventually, since Jonson represented the essential obduracy of English culture to Jones's whole enterprise.

Jonson's argument for the superiority of poetry to picture in the masques turns on a comparison of their relation to that of the soul and body. This was an established but questionable comparison; however, there is no question for Jonson that Jones's is 'the bodily part'.[15] Ironically, Jones's books contain ample evidence, in the form of annotation, of his intense interest in Plato's doctrine of the soul; and of his reflections on the problem of art's capacity to 'immitate the bauti / of the sowle'.[16] He worked carefully through Xenophon's account of conversations by Socrates with the painter Parrhasius and the sculptor Cliton, about the difficulty of representing the inner life through visual appearances. Jonson's reading took in the same passage, and he reports on it in the section of his *Discoveries* containing his ambivalent remarks on picture:

> *Socrates* taught *Parrhasius*, and *Clito* (two noble Statuaries) first to express manners by their looks in Imagery.[17]

Apart from the lapse of attention or memory in making Parrhasius a sculptor instead of a painter, Jonson gives a curiously impoverished summary of Xenophon's dialogue. Socrates questions both artists in his maieutic style, like a 'midwife' as Jones puts it, in order to elicit knowledge of their art which neither realised he possessed. Part of that knowledge concerns the representation of 'manners', that is, moral habits and dispositions, 'virtues and vises / expressed by y^e / face and gestur/es of me[n] . . . '[18] But the overall argument amounts to more than this. Given that art deals in visible appearances, and that the soul is invisible, still the artist may – Socrates makes them realise – represent the life of the soul through imitating outward appearances. His last words, to Clito, are, in Jones's version:

> A scultor must / express ye passi/ones of the mi/nde by the li/kenes of the / boddy.[19]

Socrates is not saying that this is an almost insuperable problem, but a possibility to be recognised and welcomed. Xenophon uses the word 'soul', which Ludovico Domenichi in Jones's text has rendered 'l'animo' (mind); but earlier Jones had translated this as 'soul'.[20] So the lesson of Socrates is how the soul can be represented through the medium of the body. Jonson's evasion of this crux in his version is wholly in keeping with his attitude to Jones as a visual artist: poetry is the art of the soul, picture only of the body. And this attitude is not untypical of Jonson's and Jones's contemporaries, with their rhetorical and literary education and legacy of suspicion against images.

In such a culture the doctrine of *ut pictura poesis* was bound to have a bias different from what it had in Italy. Jonson gives the conventional formulation:

> It was excellently said of *Plutarch*, *Poetry* was a speaking Picture, and *Picture* a mute Poesie . . . Yet of the two, the Pen is more noble, then the Pencill.[21]

The equation is not equal. Writing as a painter, Norgate, who is describing the abilities requisite for history painting, makes an open-minded reference to the topic:

> there must be in the workman a prompt and ready hand, and Invention (easier to tell then teach), well read in story, and something of the Poet, (whereof they say painting is a silent species) besides the observance and Imitation of those excellent Italian Masters . . . Raphael, da Vinci, Perin del Vago . . . [22]

His relaxed and mildly speculative tone contrasts with Jonson's terse, classicising, legislative discourse, which simply endorses the concept of 'mute poesy' and puts it in its (inferior) place. Jonson's style is a wonderful aesthetic construction; but a certain woodenness in his remorselessly literary neo-classicism is revealed when, at the end of his passage on 'picture', he gives a list of Italian masters equivalent to Norgate's:

> There liv'd in this latter Age six famous Painters in *Italy*: who were excellent, and emulous of the Ancients: *Raphael de Vrbino, Michel Angelo Buonarota, Titian, Antonie of Correggio, Sebastian of Venice, Iulio Romano*, and *Andrea Sartorio*.[23]

He stumbles by announcing six painters and naming seven; his inattention is unsurprising, since he is simply excerpting from Possevino's *Bibliotheca Selecta* information which appears to mean little to him.[24] Norgate knows what such names mean; yet Jonson is a much more authoritative and typical representative of the culture from which they both come.

In such a culture 'mute poesy' is somewhat at risk; to be mute is to be at a disadvantage. So the comparison is not a vehicle for expressing the possibility of fluid, developing, mutual relations between 'picture' and 'poesy' as it was in Italy, much less a pointer towards new forms of consciousness. In order to become a potential metaphor for painting, poetry would have to abdicate its supremacy and autonomy. This is what Jones was up against. To have one's work thought of as silent poetry is not to have it welcomed with a new receptiveness, but rather to have it thought of as somehow disabled. The baffled, bookish spectator who compared the wings of one of Jones's perspective sets to 'partitions, much resembling the desks or studies in a library'[25] was unconsciously revealing his atavistic point of reference.

Jones won his way against this kind of inertia because of the enabling potential of his chief vehicle, the masque. We have characterised it as an early kind of *Gesamtkunstwerk*, a combination of music, dance, text and visual spectacle. Inherent in this situation was the possibility of contention, as well as harmony, among the component arts, and of one striving for primacy over the others. In Wagnerian music drama the music tends to dominate and to appropriate to itself the other arts, taking over their functions as well as performing its own. This was the kind of situation which Ben Jonson tried to bring about with the masque, to make it seem a predominantly literary form. It was he who took charge of publishing the masques. The very concept of publication means that the text can appear in its own character while the other component arts, if they are to figure, have to lose their proper characters and be textualised. Designs can be represented by engravings, choreography by diagrams, and music in notation – and so they are in many continental festival books – but Jonson eschewed these aids[26] and represented all the other aspects of the masques (if at all) in carefully written verbal descriptions, assimilating them to his own medium. However, although his strategy succeeded with posterity, so that Jonson's texts have come to be thought of almost as dramatic scripts, contemporaries knew better. In performance, the masques were far too complex to have seemed simple triumphs of poetry, and if they were to work at all Jonson had to collaborate closely with others, especially Jones, who was not only designer but producer. In practice he was obliged to lend his assistance to the very art which he found, in theory, inferior to his own, to lend it a voice and soul. The combination of 'speaking picture' with 'mute poesy' can only have worked to Jones's advantage.

Speaking through picture

Apart from the 'muteness' supposedly intrinsic to his art, Jones never figured in public as a very verbal character. He took seriously Vitruvius's injunction 'that the Architect should be a man of letters', and Barbaro's comment, 'So it is needful to read, and what he reads turn over in his mind'[27] – as the marginal notes in his books show. These notes, and the longer ones in the Roman Sketchbook, show that flair for individual expression which is shared by every contemporary of Shakespeare; but it is significant that he left no extended piece of writing – the study of Stonehenge remained in note form, and it was his pupil Webb rather than Jones himself who seems to have projected a treatise on architecture.[28] And the annotations are private, not public, utterances. One of them is revealing of Jones's attitude to artists expounding and justifying their work in public. It concerns a story in Plutarch:

> come avenne di due *architettori in Athene*, chiamati per fare un lavoro publico, che volendo discutersi quale di loro fusse piu eccellente maestro; l'uno, che era molto acconcio parlator e sapea ben dimostrare l'intention sua, con una oratione premeditata recò il popolo a fare elettione di se, cosi seppe ben dirli quello, che d'intorno a quella materia s'haveva à fare; l'altro ch'era assai piu eccellente maestro, ma inetto à sapere accopiare due parole insieme, ò Athenesi, disse quello tutto, che costui ha cosi attamente ragionato, io sono per farlovi vedere con l'opra in effetto.

> (as happened in Athens with two architects, summoned to carry out a public commission, and wishing to debate which of them was the more excellent master; one, who was a very capable speaker and knew exactly how to expound his ideas, by a prepared speech got the people to choose him, as he was so skilful at telling them how he would deal

with the project; the other, who was a much more excellent master, but incompetent at putting two words together, said: Athenians, everything which that man has talked about so ably I would show you with the actual work itself.

Jones's note sums this up tersely: 'of too Athenia[n] / architectes. the / on could spe/ake. the other / could doe yᵉ thinge'.[29]

But there is a logic in this compounded silence. By becoming a writer Jones would have clouded his overall purpose, and by refraining he preserved its clarity. That clarity is emphasised in the moment of crisis, the quarrel with Jonson, which is also a quarrel with the excessive literariness of English culture. D. J. Gordon has shown that the proscenium of *Albion's Triumph* (1632), the first masque after the break, with its symbolic figures of Theory and Practice (plate 8), is Jones's argument against his abandoned colleague.[30] And the full force of the retort lies not just in the concepts represented but in the medium of representation, painting. Paolo Pino had long since suggested that painting was a language unto itself, and not translatable into words.[31] Jones for his part demonstrates quite simply that words are not essential to the production of a discourse, and refers implicitly to a whole body of discourse produced by non-verbal means – his own designs. To imply is to say without saying, which is of course the point: painting *does* speak mutely, it speaks *because* it is mute.

To reinforce this idea, Jones permits one pointed utterance at the beginning of the text (written by Aurelian Townshend, probably under his close supervision). The action opens with the descent of 'Mercury, the messenger of Jove', to announce the coming triumph of the Emperor Albanactus (Charles I), whose heroic virtues are 'infinite'. He makes his message brief, declaring that the triumph itself will be a visible demonstration making words unnecessary: 'We speak in acts, and scorn words' trifling scenes.'[32] The self-conscious play on notions of speaking and enacting, and the tone of aphoristic authority, make this into a general statement about meaning in the masque, following close after Jones's pictured statement on the proscenium. Under the guise of Mercury the mediator – the role which Bolton had assigned to him on the threshold of his career, and which he takes up again at the beginning of this new phase – Jones declares that the new visual discourse he is introducing into England (Albion in the masque) is not a language of words, but a more potent language of deeds or acts. The god's 'embassage' is welcomed by a chorus of poets, from their duly subordinate position.[33] Masques were always full of political allusions, and Jones is simply extending this practice into the politics of culture, as those courtiers who were on the same wavelength as him – a growing number by this time, including the King – would have recognised.

Plate 8. Jones, Proscenium, for *Albion's Triumph*, Chatsworth

Jonson for one knew exactly what Jones was on about (he had probably heard it all before). In his *Expostulation with Inigo Jones* he rebuts with outrage the idea that the eyes alone can be organs of understanding; or that the visual element in the masques can be intelligible in its own right without the aid of a text.[34]

Jones could risk such a radical statement because for the last quarter-century his pictorial discourse had been, as it were, underwritten by Jonson. The spectators of the masques, for most of whom reading was the paradigm of interpretation, were able to read Jones's designs with the help of Jonson's texts, which sometimes expounded the spectacle directly and always accompanied it suggestively. Working in this secure context, Jones proceeded to acquaint them with unfamiliar advances in the 'language' of art, some so unfamiliar as to force them to rethink their ideas about this 'language', to the extent of seeing that it was *sui generis* and not able to be read as words are read. An enlarged knowledge of the new art of the Renaissance involved for the English a new conception of art itself, and of how it worked; which in turn led to a new way of looking at the world.

These new perceptions were brought about by Jones's use of perspective, which, Roy Strong has suggested, radically changed his public's sense of vision.[35] Most of them had been conditioned by the non-realist aesthetic of Elizabethan painting, where the representation of space deferred to bold two-dimensional design, as if the intricate researches of the Italian Quattrocento into linear perspective had never taken place. This aesthetic was prepotently exemplified in the numerous portraits of the Queen, becoming by association the style of majesty, and sharing the authority of the monarchy; and that style's tendency to abstraction was reinforced by the doctrine of representing monarchs according to abstract principles.[36] The greatest painter of the age, Hilliard, brought out its more creative potential. In a painting such as the *Young Man among Roses* (plate 9), notionally discrete planes of the picture tend to coincide: the rose bushes 'imprint' themselves on the receptive surfaces of the youth's clothing (the black cloak, the white hose) and become fused with his figure – producing the same fusion of terms as occurs in a poetic metaphor. With such sophisticated aesthetic gratifications Hilliard encouraged his sitters' tendency to look at art and the world without benefit of perspective. His pupil Oliver began to turn the tide as early as the 1590s, using realistic modelling with chiaroscuro in his limned portraits and linear perspective in his avant-garde presentation drawings. But the perspective in Oliver's drawings has a self-conscious mannerist finesse which takes for granted a knowledge of norms that only a few connoisseurs would have had. It was left to Jones, in his set designs, to take the courtiers in effect through the history of perspective since the fifteenth century.

Very gradually they acquired what Franciscus Junius called 'eruditos oculos',[37] began to look with new eyes. The old conventions of pictorial space went on flourishing in Jacobean painting. The spectacular retardataire full-lengths from Redlynch date from as late as 1615,[38] although admittedly Jones's most thoroughgoing perspectives only begin to appear at about this time. One especially ironic throwback is Paul van Somer's portrait of James I in about 1620[39] (plate 10). The King stands in front of Jones's new Banqueting House, imagined as complete although still under construction, the foreground and background images being pressed together à la Hilliard, and the point emphasised by the inscription on an intervening window, 'Dieu et mon droit', making the building part of a metaphor of divine right. There is a contradiction between the meaning of Jones's revolutionary new structure and the antiquated composition into which it is drafted. Van Somer's deference to the conservative tendencies in English taste shows what an uphill battle Jones had in bringing about a 'rebirth of pictorial space'.

The masques as pictures

Plate 9. Nicholas Hilliard, Young man among roses,
Victoria and Albert Museum

The masque as pittura *and* storia

He made his impact in the end because he was not simply a lone voice crying in the wilderness, however loudly. He was able to marshal powerful forces, comprising countless European artists of the past and present. The strategy of reduplicating the work of others was a means of bringing it into action, reanimating it to new effect. A good example of this effect is the way he enlisted the great art collections of the Whitehall group, bringing them literally onto the public stage so as to enlarge their influence. In *Albion's*

Plate 10. Paul van Somer, James I, Royal Collection

Plate 11. Andrea Mantegna, Triumph of Julius Caesar, Royal Collection

Triumph he made a grand scenic tableau out of the Arundel Marbles, as a setting for a pastiche of Mantegna's *Triumph of Caesar*, which had only just arrived in the royal collection[40] (plate 11). Often he takes very small or reticent items from the collections and gives them a new impact by magnifying them; the Albani drawing used for *Coelum Britannicum* (plates 1–2) is a case in point. Another is the Elsheimer landscape background used in *Luminalia* (plates 123–5); Elsheimer's tiny pictures were strongly represented in the Arundel collection.[41] An analogy from Jones's architecture is the design for Temple Bar (plate 12), where the circular reliefs are magnified versions of Roman medals – he had recently been going through Charles I's antique coin collection.[42] In all this we see the reverse of what Charles I had Peter Oliver do with the royal collection, that is, paint miniature versions of some of its masterpieces.[43] This is treating works of art as the Elizabethans had treated their loved ones, producing small, intimate representations which emphasise the sense of personal attachment and possession. Jones's way was exactly the opposite: not to miniaturise and make private but to magnify and publicise.

But the masque scenes were not only vehicles for staging other works of art: they were works of art in themselves. Jones was very specific about this, and made the point clearly in 1632, at the start of the new era of his own ascendancy, after Jonson's dismissal. Describing the proscenium and opening scene of *Tempe Restored* (the companion piece to *Albion's Triumph*) he wrote:

> lest I should be too long in the description of the frame, I will go to the picture itself; and indeed these shows are nothing else but pictures with light and motion.[44]

The casual tone suggests that the idea of the masques as 'pictures' may have taken shape gradually, that Jones may not always have seen his design work in such a specific and systematic way. But evidence to the contrary comes from Jonson. In the text of *The Masque of Beauty* (1608), which was only their third collaboration, he has a description of the main scene, which he thought well conceived but imperfectly executed:

> The Painters, I must needs say, (not to belie them) lent small colour to any, to attribute much of the spirit of these things to their pen'cills. But that must not be imputed a crime either to the inuention, or designe.[45]

Here he is criticising not Jones, but the assistants who actually painted the sets, following the master's drawings. The deficiency was in 'colour'. that is, in the material realisation of ideas conceived by the poet and given form by the designer. Jonson's terminology comes from Lodovico Dolce's *Dialogo della pittura* (1557), which divides painting into three parts: *invenzione, disegno, colorito*.[46] While making a critical judgment in this case, he is obviously categorising masque scenes in general as *pittura* – the point Jones reiterates in 1632.

Jonson's motives for acknowledging the masque as a kind of *pittura* are opportunistic. In the division of labour among invention, design and colour he wants to appropriate the primary role of inventor, and put Jones the designer in second place. He had already staked his claim in the text of their first masque to be published, *Hymenaei* (1606). There he had made a distinction between the 'outward' and 'inward parts' of the masque, the 'body' and the 'soul'.[47] The soul is the invention, the originating concept of the whole work, which is articulated by the poet; the body is the visual presentation, the inferior province of the designer. Jonson is pressing into service a distinction familiar in Italian art theory of the sixteenth century, between poetry and painting:

Plate 12. Jones, Temple Bar, RIBA

> Poets mainly imitate what is inward . . . and painters mainly imitate what is outward.
>
> it seems that there is as much difference between poetry and painting as between the soul and the body.
>
> painting is called silent poetry, and poetry a speaking picture, and the former must be acknowledged the body, the latter the soul . . . [48]

However self-interested Jonson's position, his categories are clear: he identifies Jones as *pittore* to his own *poeta*, and the masque scenes as *pittura*. His pretensions were to be ironically confounded when Jones confirmed that the masques were '*nothing else* but pictures . . .'

The habit of seeing stage scenery not just as a mixed product to which painting contributes but as, overall, a mode of painting in itself comes out of sixteenth-century Italy. Vasari's schema in the *Lives* comprises only the three major arts of painting, sculpture and architecture, but his narrative makes clear in practice that stage design is to be included among the *arti del disegno*. Its genesis comes between architecture and painting, as he relates in such lives as those of Peruzzi and Bastiano da Sangallo, but in the end he sees it as an art which represents architecture while itself being a 'branch of painting'.[49] Serlio's interpretation of the Vitruvian scenic types shows one, the Satyric Scene, as purely pictorial; and later, in the 1620s, Giulio Mancini includes the scenes of pastoral plays in his account of landscape painting.[50]

The general view of painting and its development which is taken by Italian theorists implicitly points forward to Jones's idea of masques as 'pictures'. The leading writers on painting – Alberti, Vasari and Lomazzo – were all in his library; he annotated the latter two, and even translated passages from Lomazzo into the Roman Sketchbook.[51] These writers come to constitute a tradition, in which certain pictorial qualities are given the highest priority: complexity of composition, grandeur of scale, intellectualisation of subject-matter, and the greatest possible degree of realism. Alberti's insistence on the primacy of the *historia* – the elaborate, dramatically externalised, multiplex figure composition – was confirmed in Vasari's survey of the achievements of Italian painting, with the implication that these 'great subjects of art' were best executed on a large scale.[52] By the time of Lomazzo, the intellectualising tendency which is implicit in Alberti and evident in the practice of central Italian artists has been codified – 'historical' painting can be seen as a depiction of 'forms' or concepts.[53] The stage is set for Jones's grand masque tableaux, where extraordinary visual resources are devoted to representing not just complex formations of persons and events but elaborate moral, political and philosophical allegories.

The logical step from paintings to stage-pictures, a kind of abstraction in reverse, is finally substantiated by the increased possibilities for realism. As Jones says, these pictures have 'light and motion'; and in the figurative domain representational constraints disappear, since the figures do not need to be represented, being presented *ad vivum*. Both Lomazzo and Vasari point in this direction. Lomazzo has nothing original on stage design; but his whole conception of representation in painting points logically towards bringing the two together as Jones does. For Lomazzo the best kind of painting is that which represents nature most closely and completely, and its hero is Leonardo. He sees his own master Gaudenzio Ferrari as the heir to this naturalistic tradition, and particularly praises his Crucifixion at the Sacro Monte of Varallo where (as in all the tableaux at Varallo) painting moves into sculpture.[54] Jones's masques, which in painted scenes partly constructed in relief deploy real people, carry this illusionistic naturalism a step further, and could be seen as a hyper-realisation of Lomazzo's ideal of painting.[55] Vasari's view of painting in the *Lives*, also attentively studied by Jones, had contained similar implications. Vasari requires that a successful composition shall not seem merely painted but have the appearance of three-dimensionality and be 'living and truthful'. He insists that the goal towards which painting has developed is *vivacità*.[56] He particularly mentions Leonardo, who made his figures move and breathe; Correggio, whose works are more lively than the living; and Parmigianino (an artist very important to Jones), whose figures are so alive that one feels one can sense the beating of their pulses.[57] The logical outcome of Vasari's history of painting would be that in the end it should literally come to life, as it did in the *tableaux vivants* of the baroque theatre. Jones sets himself in this context when he speaks of his 'shows' as 'pictures with light and motion'.

To us, the equation of theatre and picture is an archaic cliché; but we must remember that Jones was daringly initiating a historical cycle which, over three centuries later, we now take to be concluded. It was an exacting view of his work he was proposing. To assert that the masques are pictures is to ask the spectators to put aside or reconsider ways of viewing them which may have seemed more obvious. Because the action at times moved out of the proscenium frame into the hall, and the masquers eventually danced with chosen spectators, they were not continuously contained within a separate world of art. And because most spectators sat sideways on to the stage, they could not scan and interpret the perspective as comfortably as the privileged group who enjoyed a frontal view. By putting the point about 'pictures' Jones is demanding a more sophisticated response than he had tacitly done in the past when requiring an understanding of perspective. What is called for is a more advanced notion of what a picture is, of an organised but also dynamic representation which includes its own boundaries and may move in and out of them – a notion, that is, which is properly baroque. This is the time, just after the break with Jonson, when Jones is virtually going it alone with poet-collaborators who are partly his mouthpieces, and he seems to step up his efforts and also his demands. Increasingly he seems to leave the more detailed technical execution of the masques to John Webb; and the descriptions in the published texts now evoke effects rather than causes, not wondrous feats of scenic engineering so much as beautiful visual compositions. The masques are described as if they were pictures.[58]

Jones delegated the execution of his stage-pictures to assistants who followed his designs, but this in no way derogated from his office as painter, since the original 'idea' was always his, and according to the most advanced tendencies in the theoretical tradition, the invention of the 'idea' was the painter's essential function.[59] And the practical possibility of putting one's best efforts into the 'intermediate' phase of drawing had been remarked by Vasari, in the case of Giulio Romano:

> si puo affermare, che Giulio esprimesse sempre meglio i suoi concetti ne' disegni, che nell'operare, ò nelle pitture: vedendosi in quelli piu vivacità, fierezza, & affetto.
>
> it can be affirmed that Giulio always expressed his ideas better in drawings, than when working them up, or in the finished paintings, showing in the former more liveliness, boldness and feeling.

Jones made a note on this, 'Julio expressed his / Conceyt better in / desine the[n] in collors',[60] perhaps thinking of himself; certainly the tenor of the observation applies to him, in that his energies went into the conception of his stage-pictures through drawings.

It was as a 'picture-maker' that Jones had started his career.[61] His earliest designs for the theatre and for architecture are conceived as paintings rather than drawings.[62] As he learned to draw more expertly, he occasionally revealed a growing talent for painting, which presumably he had neither time nor scope to develop systematically: the pen and watercolour design for a torchbearer of 1613, and the wash copy of an Elsheimer night-piece of 1638, are both beautiful images which seem to have been dashed off.[63] His most elaborate surviving masque drawing, the copy of Albani's Hercules-as-Atlas (plate 1), is directly connected with a classic problem for painters, propounded by Philostratus and quoted by Franciscus Junius.[64] The changeover from 'making' pictures in an empirical sense to 'picture-making' on the grand scale of the masques, from the act of painting to the practice of *pittura*, necessitated an economy of effort. His work now concentrated on conception rather than execution – to use Dolce's categories, on invention and design rather than colour. But he still kept in touch with the craft of painting; and throughout his life he made the sorts of drawings that a painter might make, unconnected with any specific projects – for exercise, study or experiment.[65]

Jones's view of his work on the masques as picture-making was borne out by the Italian theoretical tradition and given substance by his continuous practice as a graphic artist. It was also sanctioned by antiquity. Daniele Barbaro, in reproducing Vitruvius's description of the three types of stage scene used by the ancients, calls one of them a 'show' which is realised as a 'picture';[66] Jones uses the same wording when he writes, 'these shows are nothing else but pictures . . . ' He read carefully in Barbaro's edition of Vitruvius the account of how decorative mural painting originated in antiquity. After an initial, quasi-abstract phase, it began to develop in a realistic style, and the largest spaces were decorated with versions of the three types of stage scenery, 'painted wth ye Prospective of Sceanes', as Jones noted in the margin.[67] These included not just settings (buildings and landscapes) but figures as well.[68] Barbaro assigns this kind of painting the name 'scaenographia',[69] says he has written more about it elsewhere, and gives it pride of place in his study of perspective, published two years later. There he treats it as the very type of perspectival representation. He insists on its fundamental utility to 'Pittori, Scultori, & Architetti'; but his discussion lays most stress on its pictorial possibilities, on the sensuously realistic effects of colour, light and shade, and atmosphere in combination with accurate perspective construction.[70] The painterly emphasis comes appositely from a sixteenth-century Venetian writer; but at the same time Barbaro traces 'scenographia' back to classical Athens, seeing it as a neglected antique art in need of revival.[71] This neo-classical line of argument, developed from Vitruvius, which assimilates scene design to monumental decorative painting,[72] provides unquestionable authority for Jones when he makes the same assimilation.

When he came to write something himself about monumental painting, he preferred Alberti's term *historia*.[73] An important passage in the Roman Sketchbook, written almost immediately after his return from Italy in January 1615, when he was reflecting on the whole experience, reveals him thinking about the genre of *historia* – 'istoria' or 'storia' in contemporary Italian, or 'storry' as he calls it:

> As in dessigne first on Sttudies the partes of the boddy of man as Eyes noses mouthes Eares and So of the rest to bee practicke in the partes Sepperat ear on comm to put them togeathear to maak a hoole figgure and cloath y^t and consequently a hoole Storry wth all ye ornamentes
>
> So in Architecture on must Studdy the Partes as loges Entranses Haales chambers Staires doures windoues. and then adorne them wth collums. Cornishes. sfondati. Stattues. Paintings. Compartimentes . . .[74]

The consideration of 'Storry', by way of analogy, is subordinate to that of architecture. But the overall impersonality of the syntactic construction, the closeness of the parallel, and the detailed information rather over-insistently rehearsed in both cases suggest at the least a wish or hankering on Jones's part to see himself as a potential practitioner of 'Storry' as well as architecture. And the fact that the Roman Sketchbook contains many exercises 'in dessigne', exactly those 'Sttudies' of 'the partes of the boddy' which are said to be necessary steps to the composition of 'a hoole Storry', reinforces the suggestion that his aims embraced 'Storry' as well as architecture.

His encounter with the monumental *storie* which entered the collection of Charles I – the Raphael cartoons, the Mantegna *Triumph*, Tintoretto's

Washing of the Feet – would have been a further stimulus. The Mantegna canvases may originally have been used for court entertainments at Mantua; the Tintoretto had as its background one of Serlio's stage sets, often used by Jones, and so confirmed the possibility of crossing the frontier between painting and theatre.[75] When Rubens's allegories were installed in the ceiling of the Banqueting House in 1635, they must have seemed close in scale and content to the masque scenes presented year after year in the same place. Jones's supposed involvement in the ceiling programme[76] can scarcely be doubted: the devising of programmes for large-scale pictures had become his métier.

The acquisition of all these masterpieces during the 1620s and 1630s inspired not just emulation but rivalry. In *Salmacida Spolia* (1640), the last masque ever to be presented, Jones invited comparison with Rubens and Van Dyck. The Whitehall ceiling had been a tribute to High Renaissance Venice and Paolo Veronese, and Van Dyck resumed the same theme in his designs for the Garter tapestries in 1638.[77] Taking this cue as a challenge, Jones made the last scene of his masque a pastiche of Veronese's *Marriage at Cana* (plates 53–4), doubtless recalling not only its magnificence of composition and scale but its setting in a Palladian interior, akin to his own neo-Palladian Banqueting House, for which the projects of Rubens and Van Dyck had been designed. In one grand, compendious tableau he claims his due by making a summation of his lifelong enterprise: the naturalisation in England of Renaissance art through the medium of its most powerful genre, the monumental *historia*.

Salmacida Spolia is about power and civilisation: its programme appeals to the critics and opponents of the King, who 'seeks by all means to reduce tempestuous and turbulent natures into a sweet calm of civil concord'.[78] In the event the civilising power of Jones's designs was to take hold in a way denied to the King's policies. More fortunate than Reynolds in a later age striving to enlarge the possibilities of English art by introducing history painting into the narrow confines of portraiture, Jones had, in the Stuart masque, a vehicle of much more generous scope and larger effect. He used it to its fullest capacity, building up an oeuvre which memorably constituted what was for him the most important *historia* of all, the history of art itself.

3

Architecture

'Architecture' explained

Jones has been famous to posterity as an architect, and it is obvious that his buildings made a revolution in English architecture. But for the first decade of his employment at the Stuart court he put up no buildings to speak of. He made what seemed two false starts as an architect before being safely launched – the first in 1608 for Robert Cecil, Earl of Salisbury, the second in 1610 as Surveyor of Prince Henry's Works. For Salisbury he produced two ambitious designs, for the New Exchange and the tower of St Paul's, but neither was executed; the most he did was to intervene in the south front of Hatfield House. For Prince Henry he became a kind of architectural administrator, while two foreigners, Salomon de Caus and Costantino de' Servi, actually carried out new projects to do with the gardens of Richmond Palace. Both patrons meanwhile entrusted Jones with the design of masques and entertainments, so that ironically his architectural ambitions had to satisfy themselves in the design of scenic architecture rather than the 'real thing'.

The irony would have been less acute for Jones than to us, with our modern empiricist notions of what is 'real' and what not. Summerson, who presents Jones the architect as a precursor of neo-classicism, views the architectural inventions he made for the theatre in these early, tentative years as 'nonsense'.[1] Jones would not have thought in this way. From the start, a major point of reference was the text of Vitruvius, which he read and annotated in Daniele Barbaro's Italian edition. Vitruvius begins by stating that architecture embraces many arts and disciplines, over which it exercises its own mastery by combining skill in craftsmanship with technological know-how, *fabrica* with *ratiocinatio*.[2] Barbaro translates these terms into Italian as 'fabrica' and 'discorso', and in his commentary they become identified with the concepts of practice and theory. He expatiates fervently on the idea that architecture is not a simple art but a kind of meta-discipline, a 'science' akin to philosophy or mathematics. It can only come from the marriage of 'discorso' and 'fabrica': he reverses the order of Vitruvius, making 'discorso' the first (and the male) principle. He condemns any view of architecture as a mere practice: it is not enough 'to be nominated Architect by this or that prince' and, instead of being able to explain the principles underlying your work, simply to point to 'such-and-such a palazzo or church'.[3] Barbaro pours scorn on any empirical definition of architecture which restricts it to built projects.

Vitruvius treated stage design as a part of architecture. Of the three conventional types of Roman scene, two were wholly architectural. In his Fifth Book, on public buildings, he devotes several chapters to the design of theatres, including as a matter of course the scenery. Jones wrote numerous annotations on these chapters, many of them early in his career. Vitruvius required stage scenes, granted the prerogatives and limits of illusionism, to be rational and realistic. He has a long cautionary anecdote about the Greek Apaturius of Alabanda, who designed an architectural stage set for the theatre of Tralles. This was a great success with the citizens, until the mathematician Licymnius pointed out that it showed one range of buildings rising on top of another, against all logic and structural plausibility. Having no defence against this criticism, Apaturius had to redesign the scene 'to resemble reality'. Jones summarised this story in the margin. He took the point that stage design, being a part of architecture, should follow the rationale of architecture, observe the same 'decorum' as he put it.[4]

His overall view of the relationship is recorded by his pupil John Webb. After the Restoration Webb petitioned Charles II for the Surveyorship, claiming that by order of the King's father he had been trained to succeed Jones in the post: 'That hee was brought up by his unckle Mr Inigo Jones upon his late Majestyes comand in the study of Architecture, as well as that wch relates to building as for Masques, Tryumphs and the like.' In a later petition Webb reminded the King of the occasional work he had been employed in: he had not only designed the new building at Greenwich Palace but also 'At Whitehall hee made yor Theater, and thereby discovered much of the Scenicall Art, wch to others than himselfe was before much unknowne . . . ' Webb's education as an architect necessarily included 'the Scenicall Art'.[5]

In the Vitruvian tradition there is a sense in which stage design comes before other architectural activities. Vitruvius uses the preface to his seventh book to review the largely monographic writings on architecture which preceded his own comprehensive treatise. The earliest of these was by Agatharcus of Athens, describing the stage set he designed for a tragedy by Aeschylus. He was followed by Democritus and Anaxagoras, who wrote on the method of designing perspective scenery. Only later came books on the classical orders and on actual buildings. Again, Jones annotated this passage early in his career, observing how stage design preceded building in the architectural literature of antiquity.[6] Renaissance Vitruvian authors confirmed that this might not be a random pattern. Serlio, whom Jones also began to study in these early years, ordered his treatise so that, while Books III and IV covered antiquity and the orders, the first two books dealt with geometry and perspective; and Book II on perspective culminated in the treatment of theatre and stage design. In his introduction to this book Serlio argues that skill in perspective is essential for the architect, perspective and architecture being necessarily interrelated. As proof of this, he writes, 'let us briefly consider the Architects of our age, in which good Architecture has begun to flourish'. Bramante began as a painter, expert in perspective, before moving on to architecture. Raphael, Giulio Romano, Peruzzi and Serlio himself (he adds in a modest tone) all followed suit. Mastery of perspective, most publicly shown in stage design (and here he cites Girolamo Genga, court architect to the Duke of Urbino), is a necessary preparation for the complete mastery of architecture.[7]

It is Barbaro, in his commentary on Vitruvius, who develops this argument most fully, going about it in an idiosyncratic way. According to Vitruvius, that part of architectural design which he calls *dispositio* (the arrangement of details and their effect) should be approached under three categories: *ichnographia* (plan), *orthographia* (elevation), and *scaenographia* (perspective). Barbaro rejects the last term as an error in the text, and insists that it should read *sciographia* (section). Jones followed his comments carefully, annotating and paraphrasing; but on a later reading decided he was wrong: 'Barbaro is deceeued for Vitruvious plainly cales it / sceenografia wch is the front and side of a building draune in prospectiue.'[8] However, having expelled the concept of *scaenographia* from the Vitruvian text here, Barbaro reintroduces it elsewhere. When Vitruvius writes that the architect must be 'eruditus geometria', Barbaro expands the implication and interpolates the phrase 'non ignorante della prospettiva'. A few sentences later when a knowledge of optics is required he translates the word 'opticen' as 'Prospettiva'. His commentary expatiates on the possibilities of perspective representation, which includes scene-painting, 'from which it takes its name, and is called Scaenographia (Scenografia)'.[9] The contested term reappears under his own proprietorial sponsorship.

Having taken *scaenographia* away from Vitruvius, reasserted its origins in the theatre, and pushed it back into the limelight, Barbaro reinforces his procedure in a later passage. Vitruvius begins his sixth book, on the construction of private houses, by discussing how environmental conditions, which are variable, may interact with the rules of harmonious architectural design, which should be constant. He urges the architect, while calculating the symmetries of the design first, to be prepared to adapt them to the necessities of the site. If he needs to sacrifice strict symmetry in the objective sense, he must use skilful judgment to produce the *appearance* of a harmonious structure. Vitruvius compares this requisite expertise in optical deception to the effect of illusionistic painting. Here the manuscript tradition is divided between alternative readings. Modern editors read 'in cenis pictis', 'in painted dining-rooms'; Barbaro chose the alternative reading 'scenis', 'in painted scenes'. His Vitruvius makes scene-painting the model for the crucial operation of realising ideally designed buildings in the material world. He presses home the lesson in his commentary: 'Et qui si vede quanto sia necessaria la prospettiva allo Architetto . . . ' Jones took careful note: 'great creditte ['glory' struck out] to / the Architecte / whe[n] beinge / forced to goe fro[m] / the simitri noth/ing is taken / fro[m] / the bauti of the / aspecte. / therfor prospe/ctive is / ness/esary'.[10] Barbaro's conclusion, echoed by Jones, is far-reaching: *scaenographia* is not only a province of architecture, and an essential preparation for the architect, it is a fundamental element of architectural design.

It was not until 1615 that, fresh from the Italian journey and installed as Surveyor of the King's Works, Jones began his work as an architect in the fullest sense. Seven years later, the completion of the Banqueting House advertised his maturity, and on the site of royal power appeared as a manifesto of the definitive arrival of Renaissance classicism in England. But long before this Jones the masque designer was representing himself as an architect, and rightly so in the Vitruvian context which he was trying to transplant. One of the first things he set about was to publicise the very concept of the 'architect', which was relatively new to England, the Renaissance concept of an individual with overall responsibility for a project, guaranteed by creative and intellectual authority. And if people were to be made to understand that in designing buildings theoretical mastery should precede practical skills, it was quite logical for Jones to claim the status of 'architect' before he had much building to his credit – in a way it reinforced his point.

Significantly then, the most obvious references to Jones as an architect were made in the printed texts of the masques which he designed, and which in a simplistic view of the matter could seem to be diverting him from architecture in the first place. His appointment as Surveyor to Prince Henry (9 May 1610), which as it turned out was to be short-lived and relatively unproductive, nonetheless gave a special point to such references. Several months earlier, for *Prince Henry's Barriers*, Jones had displayed his first thoroughgoing work of *scaenographia* in Barbaro's sense – a practicable, architectural perspective stage set, exemplifying what Jonson's text called the 'truth of architecture'. With *Tethys' Festival*, the masque presented by Queen Anne on 6 June 1610 to mark her son's creation as Prince of Wales, Samuel Daniel's printed text followed this up in a frankly didactic spirit, by spelling out at length the features of one spectacular ensemble of scenographic architecture. This was the principal scene of the masque, when the Queen and her ladies made their appearance. Daniel introduces it as a 'scene, which I will . . . describe, in the language of the architector who contrived it, and speaks in his own mestier to such as are understanders and lovers of that design'.[11] The words 'architector' and 'mestier', one Greek and the other Italian, intrude themselves as unfamiliar terms, provoking the reader to 'understand' their meanings, as the spectators of the masque had been put to 'understand' the unusual visual language – the language of 'architecture' in the Renaissance sense – of the scene presented to their eyes.

The words can be glossed from Barbaro's Vitruvius. In commenting on Vitruvius's initial definition of architecture, Barbaro adds its etymology. It comes from a Greek word of two parts (the word *architector* which he does not trouble to mention): the first means 'principal' or 'chief'; the second 'craftsman' or 'artificer'. But there is one qualification to be made: 'Et però dice Platone, che lo Architetto non fa mestieri alcuno, mà e soprastante à quelli, che gli fanno' – the architect does not work at any particular trade, but superintends those who do.[12] So Jones has Daniel use the word 'architector' to bring out the full meaning of his office, and the word 'mestier' (which on the surface gives an Italianate flavour) ironically to emphasise that it is not a mere craft but a superior calling, requiring him to direct and oversee (as his official title of Surveyor denotes).

Barbaro invokes the authority of Plato; in the margin Jones noted the precise reference, which is to one of the lesser-known dialogues. This is the *Politicus* or *Statesman*; in the Italian translation Jones used the title is significantly translated as *Il Regno*, which could mean 'rulership', but literally means 'the kingdom'.[13] Plato does begin by assimilating the idea of statesmanship to that of kingship; and in order to illustrate how it is a theoretical science which nonetheless has a practical application, he compares the king to the architect, who is not a workman himself, but brings knowledge to bear in directing a group of workmen to carry out his aims.[14] This characterisation of the architect is typical of the Greek philosophers Jones read. A little later in Barbaro's text he noted a reference to Xenophon, recounting a conversation between Socrates and the gifted young aristocrat Euthydemus, who had collected an extraordinarily large library. Socrates asks him what vocation in life this thirst for knowledge is driving him towards, naming suitably exalted professions such as physician, astronomer, or statesmen, and including the architect, 'since he must be very fully equipped with wise precepts'.[15] Renaissance writers on the arts were aware of the prestige of the architect in Greek culture, summed up by Aristotle's metaphor 'architectonic' to describe the 'master arts', those areas of knowledge to which all others are subordinate.[16]

Ben Jonson ridiculed Jones for taking this metaphor literally; but the later, Vitruvian tradition encouraged just such an interpretation. By requiring the architect to be competent in the knowledge proper to many other professions – medicine, mathematics, astronomy, music, and so on – Vitruvius virtually represented him as the 'master artist', challenging other paradigms of masterly versatility, such as the philosopher, the orator or the statesman. Ostensibly his claim had a degree of modesty, since he formulated it by disagreeing with his predecessor Pythius, who had wanted the architect to be not merely competent but expert in all the other fields. But beginning with Alberti's *De re aedificatoria* the Renaissance read more ambition into Vitruvius than he had actually expressed.[17] For the first sentence of his first chapter, which defined architecture, Daniele Barbaro accepted a manuscript reading (rejected by modern editors) which made architecture not only comprehend all the other arts but judge them as well. This licensed him to assert triumphantly that 'the proper station of architecture is to be close to wisdom, and to dwell amidst all the arts like heroic virtue' – a claim soon repeated, with the addition that architecture is 'queen' of the arts.[18] As a magnate of the Venetian Republic, Barbaro owed nobody the deference which Vitruvius continually pays the Emperor, and he confers on the discipline he is expounding an intellectual power analogous to his own social position. Here was the starting-point for Jones's view of architecture, which therefore began at a rather high pitch. His notes show him joining in the debate between Vitruvius and Pythius, arguing against Vitruvius and taking Pythius more seriously. When Vitruvius settles for a limit to the architect's knowledge, and admits it must be inferior to the higher intellectual attainments of the mathematician, Jones pointedly disagrees: 'meethinke that / Vitruuious might / as well prefer the / gramarian to y^e / philosofer as the / mathematitien to / the Architect'.[19] This is not just personal conceit, as Jonson would have it, but the voice of Renaissance Vitruvianism revising Vitruvius.

For Jones then, the concept of the 'architector' which Daniel uses to represent him in his new role as Surveyor to Prince Henry is a very powerful one. Just how powerful is indicated by Barbaro's appeal to Plato in his politically élitist vein. Jones was exceptionally sensitive to any mention of architecture in the classical authors he studied, especially the philosophers Plato, Aristotle, Xenophon and Plutarch. For example, when his text of Plutarch's essay on the *Timaeus* describes the soul as 'architetto principale' of the body, he underlines the phrase and sketches a pointing hand in the margin.[20] When Plato compared the architect to the king he was mainly illustrating a relationship between knowledge and its application; but Jones would also have read this as conferring a kind of regality on the architect. The association is made by the actual text where he figures as the 'architector': as 'the 'Royall maske' it was published in the same volume as the account of Henry's ceremonial creation as Prince of Wales. Alongside the 'High and mightie Prince' the 'architector' implicitly assumes his rightful intellectual and artistic sovereignty.[21]

Within the text his special authority is demonstrated through language. Daniel had heralded a passage 'in the language of the architector . . . who speaks in his own mestier to such as are understanders . . . ' What follows is a lengthy description which freely uses the terminology of classical architecture. Vitruvius had warned that architectural writing could not have the sympathetically engaging qualities of historical narrative or poetic drama, since the unaccustomed technical vocabulary needed to be offset by crisp explanations. Jones noted: 'in architectre yᵉ / wordes of artt ar / har[d]ly understood'; and repeated the recommendation 'fewe and cleear / sentenses'.[22] But what he does in *Tethys' Festival* is use 'the words of art' so as to make them more familiar, while relying on Daniel's literary skill to provide an attractive context. Alberti had criticised the Latin style of Vitruvius as impure and awkward, and set out to write about architecture with Ciceronian elegance.[23] Jones and Daniel use the text of a masque, where imaginative persuasion is all-important, to devise a new kind of Vitruvian discourse, which can enlist a narrative and poetic style to make the vocabulary of architecture amenable.

Not all Jones's collaborators in this period were prepared to adopt 'the language of the architector'. Campion in *The Lords' Masque* (1613) gave him his due with that one reservation:

> Master Inigo Jones . . . in all . . . the workmanship which belonged to the whole invention showed extraordinary industry and skill; which if it be not as lively expressed in writing as it appeared in view, rob him not of his due, but lay the blame on my want of right apprehending his instructions for the adoring of his art.[24]

Beyond the standard rhetoric of compliment, Campion implies he was pressed to adopt certain descriptive techniques and refused to do so; this suggests how insistent Jones was to have his work put across in the appropriate vocabulary. Jonson, no doubt even more chary of 'instructions', became increasingly laconic in describing Jones's increasingly eloquent scenic architecture, such as the palace in *Oberon* (1611). But Chapman in the *Memorable Masque* (1613) was an effective literary partner, describing the Temple of Honour – a centralised, classical structure – in such precise

Plate 13. Jones, Archway, Chatsworth

detail that its source can be identified, and advertising Jones as 'our Kingdomes most Artfull and ingenious *Architect*'.[25]

Much later, in the 1630s, when this role was taken for granted, and he had the ascendancy over all his collaborators, Jones still took care that the masque architecture was described in detail. This suggests how important he thought it. In the early days it was partly a surrogate, but also a means of study and experiment. For the courtiers it provided a grounding in the formal language, both visual and verbal, of the Renaissance architectural tradition. Even when the Banqueting House and other works were there for all to see, the masques supplemented Jones's built oeuvre, helping to provide a context for it and mediate its extraordinary impact.

Theory and style

Jones's earliest designs for scenic architecture are related to the arches and pageants of sixteenth-century festivals, of which there was a large literature combining verbal descriptions with illustrative prints. A recent home-grown example was Stephen Harrison's *Arches of Triumph*, the record of James I's entry into London in 1604. The commentary by Ben Jonson saw the arches

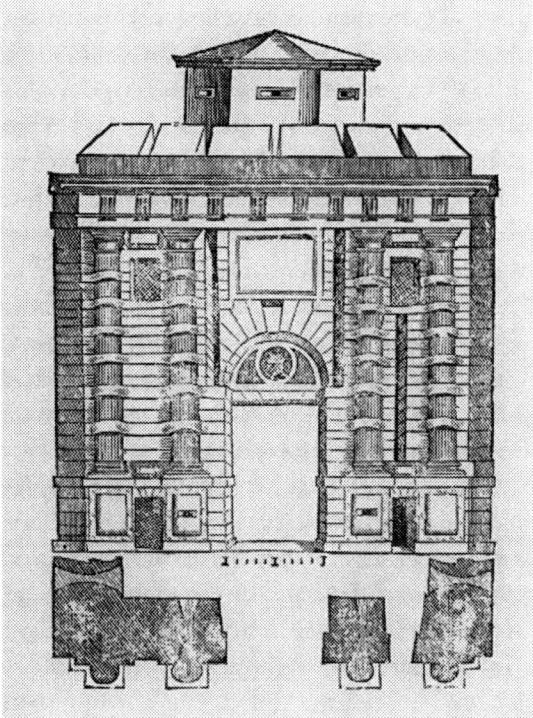

Plate 14. Serlio, Perspective construction, from *Architettura*, 1619

Plate 15. Serlio, City gate, from *Architettura*, 1619

in Albertian terms, the separate features of each being 'with that generall harmonie so connexed, and disposed, as no one little part can be missing to the illustration of the whole'.[26] In fact the arches are teeming farragos of infelicitous detail, their chaos emphasised by a busy, rebarbative Flemish mannerist style. Jones's inventions of this kind at once set higher standards, and really do measure up to Alberti's criterion. This is because, understanding the relationship between style and theory, he chooses his models carefully. An arch designed for one of Salisbury's entertainments derives fron Jean Martin's arches for Henri II's Paris entry of 1549;[27] and this kind of refined French classicism was to appear again in the early masques.

But it would be wrong to suggest that Jones simply copied such things from the festival books. Apart from displaying the best models, he was also interested in designing on his own account. Another arch design, probably an arch-corridor through which knights made their entry for a barriers (plate 13), is treated as an exercise in composition, combining various motifs from Serlio. The basic scheme is the outline of an archway from Serlio's Second Book, which, being a perspective exercise, is virtually bare of detail except for the features of the Doric order and the rustication of the arches (plate 14); the detail is supplied mainly from a design of a fortified city gate in the Seventh Book (plate 15), with minor details coming from elsewhere in Serlio.[28] The arrow slits seem to introduce a discordant note and make the battlemented parapet (which Serlio says is for the deployment of artillery) look mock-medieval. This is the synthesis of medieval and classical styles which Jones developed as a special architectural metaphor for Prince Henry's martial festivals (which are discussed below). But this romantic-military style is underpinned by a careful discipline: given that the drawing is not to scale and somewhat loosely sketched, the proportions seem carefully considered; the rustication mediates between the medieval and classical elements in the composition, which is drawn together by the Doric order, which Serlio, elaborating on Vitruvius, associates with masculine strength and military prowess.[29]

At the same time as he mixes styles to devise a theatrical metaphor, Jones shows his fundamental commitment to theory. Although this is scarcely the design of a purist it uses Serlio with a discrimination not found in English architecture to date, and foreshadows those refined pastiches of Serlio which Jones was to produce in his much later designs for gateways.[30]

Jones read Serlio differently from the builders of Elizabethan and Jacobean houses, not only using him as a pattern book but attending to the theoretical context and appreciating its fundamental importance. In this way he came to an understanding of the necessary relationship between style and theory, which he was able to pass on by example in the masques.

Reworking Bramante

Having been to Italy, and convinced of the importance of that kind of experience, Jones also read the treatises as records of real buildings, ancient and modern. It was with reference to Serlio and Palladio that he began to make imaginary reworkings of actual buildings. The one that fascinated him most was Bramante's Tempietto. In the treatises Bramante has a dual character. Palladio praises him as the rediscoverer of classical architecture, for which reason 'it seems right to find a place for his works among those of the ancients';[31] and so the Tempietto makes an honorary appearance in the Fourth Book on antique temples. Serlio had also placed Bramante's work in his Third Book, *Delle Antichità* (plate 7), but as well as its classical authenticity he praises its inventiveness, its capacity for what is 'bella' and 'artificiosa'.[32] Jones came to accept this idea of Bramante as a touchstone of High Renaissance classicism. This is how he uses him in designing the catafalque for James I's funeral in 1625, where (as we have seen) he corrects his model, Domenico Fontana's catafalque for Sixtus V (plates 5–6), by the standards of *its* model, which is Bramante's Tempietto.[33] Much earlier, in

Plate 16. Jones, Temple of Apollo, Chatsworth

Plate 17. Bramante, Tempietto, from L. Sirigatti, *Prospettiva*, 1625, British Library

1611 for the masque *Oberon*, he produced an elegant Frenchified variant of the Tempietto which implies an appreciation of the finesse of its scale and proportions (plate 22). But the *Oberon* drawing also shows an acute sense of the Tempietto as what Arnaldo Bruschi calls a *spettacolo*: the palace of Oberon framed in an archway of rocks recalls the initial view (in Vitruvian parlance the 'aspect') of the Tempietto framed by the gate into the cortile of S. Pietro in Montorio.[34] A much later drawing continues these well-informed variations on Bramante. It is inscribed 'The Temple of Apollo' (plate 16), and reproduces the Tempietto as illustrated in Lorenzo Sirigatti's perspective treatise (plate 17), but in a clearing surrounded by trees.[35] This is more Bramantesque than it may at first seem, since the landscape setting paraphrases the loggia which Bramante intended to build around the Tempietto but never executed – the plan is given in Serlio.[36] Jones the masque designer knows his Bramante well, and is especially sensitive to those aspects of his work which cannot be subsumed under the rubric of classicism.

Another of Bramante's most renowned ideas is reworked in Jones's design for 'A Throne' (plate 18), possibly connected with one of Salisbury's entertainments. This is the exedra of the Belvedere courtyard, illustrated in

Plate 18. Jones, A Throne, Chatsworth

Serlio (plate 19), who singles it out as an 'inventione'.[37] In Jones's lifetime the actual structure no longer existed, but the idea lived on, and versions of it (especially the concave-convex staircase) had passed into the repertoire of sixteenth-century architecture, painting and scenography.[38] In this tradition Jones's version looks like an extreme mutation. He has literally made a travesty of the original – Serlio uses the interesting notion of architectural travesty in the *Libro Straordinario*[39] – in much the same way as Italian churches were travestied for grand celebrations, dressed with fabrics and covered in lights. But he is only reinterpreting a theatricality which is intrinsic to the original. Serlio remarks that it 'has the form of a theatre';[40] but as a theatre to be looked at rather than looked from it has a self-conscious quality. The part played in it by perspective illusion is shown in Serlio's print, where the front pairs of pilasters look like stage-wings, and serve to mask and magnify the distance back to the hemicycle. Jones paraphrases this with the muffling and dissolving effects of his draperies and lights, so that the depth of the hemicycle is rendered uncertain and illusionistically magnified by the diminution of the pilasters of the throne niche, which looks farther away than it actually is. This is Bramante travestied, but by no means misunderstood.

It was Jones's experience of the theatre which schooled him to appreciate the Bramante who was not the figure canonised by Palladio. Serlio praises

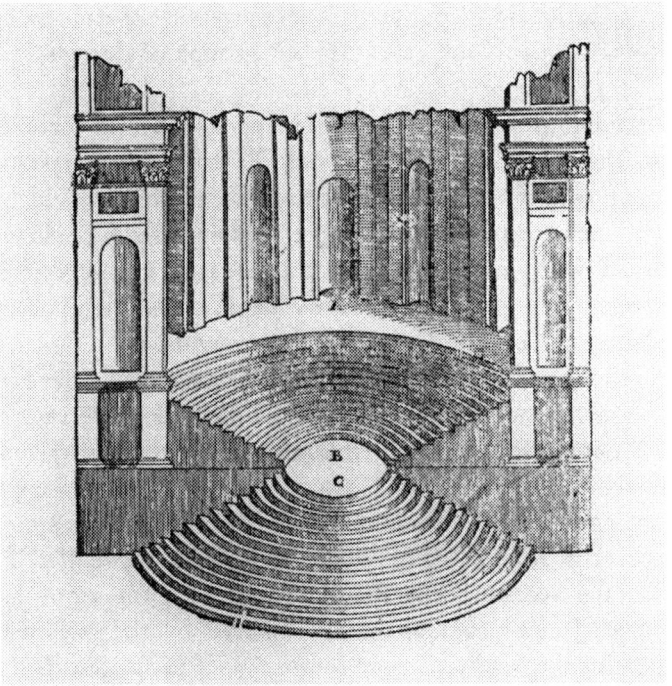

Plate 19. Bramante, Exedra of the Belvedere, from Serlio, *Architettura*, 1619

the 'artificiosa architettura' of another project, the Belvedere spiral staircase, where the orders are so ingeniously superimposed that 'one cannot see where one order finishes and another begins'.[41] This kind of valuation is relevant to the exedra which Jones paraphrased; and may recall the choir of Bramante's Santa Maria presso S. Satiro, where perspective foreshortening and the use of directed light produce a famous illusionistic effect. The perceptions which were sharpened by stage design helped Jones to take a more complex view of Bramante than he might otherwise, as a student of the classical tradition, have done; and we may see this as indicative of the function served by the masques in his architectural studies and propaganda.

Prince Henry's Barriers *and the 'truth of architecture'*

It is around the time of his appointment as Surveyor to Prince Henry that Jones announces himself as 'architector'. But since these are the years when he has much more to do designing masques than buildings, it is from his masque designs that we may gain some insight into the tendency of his architectural thinking. Here for the first time there are drawings of stage architecture which can be associated with specific productions, and interpreted with the aid of the texts. There are two set-designs for *Prince Henry's Barriers* (1610), and two different groups of designs for *Oberon* (1611).

These productions were brought into being by a trio of forceful figures: the patron, the poet, and the designer. Prince Henry, now officially recognised as heir to the throne, wanted to present himself in a highly salient political role. Ben Jonson, a much more formed artistic personality than Jones, worked with his patron and collaborator in a cooperative but individual way. And Jones, moderately experienced stage-designer and nascent architect, appears both ambitious and tentative.

The ambivalence of Jones's position at this stage of his development is suggested in the first scene of *Prince Henry's Barriers* (plate 169), where he makes a self-quotation: for Merlin's tomb he uses the funeral monument he had recently designed for Lady Cotton, based on Roman sarcophagi seen in France the year before.[42] Given its provenance, this comes appropriately into the scene of Roman ruins which represents the Fallen House of Chivalry. In the second scene (plate 170), where the ruins have been partly restored, Jones's sarcophagus is replaced by the one invented by Michelangelo for the Medici Chapel tombs,[43] as if to suggest its degenerate or imperfect quality in comparison with a masterpiece. To include his own work in a scene of classical ruins suggests diffidence; but it could also seem aspiring and ambitious. More than once Jones used architectural self-quotation in the masques to make assessments of his own work; but whereas the later quotation of the Banqueting House in *Time Vindicated* (1623)[44] (plate 35) stresses achievement, the quotation of the Cotton tomb here speaks more tentatively of ambition and hope.

The *Barriers* had an Arthurian text about the revival of chivalry. James I is hailed as a second King Arthur who has brought back the united Britain of his glorious predecessor. Prince Henry is Meliadus, a figure from Arthurian romance; in the hellenised form Moeliades his name is an anagram of 'Miles a deo', 'God's knight', and he is to restore the ruined House of Chivalry. The main speakers are the Lady of the Lake, Arthur and Merlin.

It was Prince Henry who had wanted an Arthurian entertainment. Jonson largely despised Arthurian romance, and his text explicitly refrains from presenting its romance material romantically; nor does it give any countenance to Arthurian story as historical fact. It is treated as legend, and therefore being fictional it can more readily be moralised and idealised. Jonson manages this characteristically by classicising the material, assimilating the factitious anciency of Arthurian myth to the authentic antiquity of Greece and Rome. So he begins by having the Lady of the Lake rise from the waters on her 'silver feet' exactly like the 'silver-footed' sea nymph Thetis of Homer; and at the centre of the action is a storiated shield presented to Meliadus by the Lady, which recalls the shield of Achilles given by Thetis in the Iliad, and Virgil's imitation of it in the Aeneid.[45]

In the event Jonson's presentation of medieval romance in a context of classical allusion serves the Prince's turn well. Henry shows himself, in contrast to his peace-loving father, as the champion of militant Protestantism, and a compelling literary pattern for this attitude had been established by Spenser's Protestant epic *The Faerie Queene*, where with the help of Arthur knights of romance struggle against evil by striving to practise the virtues defined by Aristotle. Jonson's emphases are different, but he reproduces the Spenserian conflation of cultures, and characterises the Prince as a paragon of Christian chivalry who is also an antique hero.

He also gives a suggestive lead to Jones, who can represent the synthesis of Christian and pagan virtue, of medievalism and antiquity, in architectural terms. Jonson spends a lot of time bringing out the significance of Jones's two sets, the ruined House of Chivalry and the gloriously restored St George's Portico. His stress on architecture as a metaphor is summed up in the Lady of the Lake's lament for the passing of the House of Chivalry:

> More truth of *architecture* there was blaz'd
> Than liv'd in all the ignorant *Gothes* have raz'd,[46]

where the word 'blazed', taken from heraldry, reinforces the idea of architecture as a descriptive, demonstrative medium, which can manifest moral values. Jones's designs accord with this idea of architecture as a morally demonstrative discourse; he agreed with Daniele Barbaro, whose comparison of the architect to the orator made him write an approving note in the margin of his Vitruvius.[47] So the designs need to be *read*, exactly as the text does with them.

Alongside the classicising tendency of the text Jones shows Arthurian Britain as Roman Britain, but this is probably because unlike Jonson he believed this to be historically the case (his tendency to see the British past generally in Roman terms comes out in his later belief that Stonehenge was a Roman temple).[48] And just as he tends to see Arthur more historically than Jonson does, he also sees classical antiquity more historically, not just as a timeless ideal. So by representing Roman architecture in a partly historicist spirit instead of with Jonson's strict idealism he gives a more tolerant, nuanced version of the conflation of chivalric and classical values. He had been studying Roman remains in France only a few months beforehand; and whether or not he had been to Rome during his first visit to Italy a decade ago, he was familiar with the visual documentation of its ancient monuments. He gives a sense of ancient Rome in its historical contingency. A disadvantage is that his scenes look crowded: they have been called a 'jumble'.[49] But to read them patiently is to discover the broad spans of meaning that have been packed into them.

They expound visually on two major themes in Jonson's text. The first is that of revival. The revival of chivalry by Henry/Meliadus is expressed in architectural terms as a progress from ruin to restoration. This can be followed in two buildings, one from France and one from Rome – the Piliers de Tutelle and the Torre delle Milizie (which, although medieval, was regarded as antique); both are identifiable, although Jones depicts neither literally. The Tutelles, which he may have seen on his French visit the year before, had been reconstructed in a print of Jacques Androuet du Cerceau[50] (plate 171). In the first scene it is shown ruined and with a lesser order than in fact it had, the Ionic; in the second it is restored intact with the order upgraded to the proper Corinthian. The Torre delle Milizie is so ruinous in the first scene as to be almost unrecognisable (in the right foreground); in the second it is copied from a topographical etching by van Nieulandt[51] (plate 172), but the proportions are adjusted, the masonry graduated regularly, and the fenestration rationalised – all along classicising lines. In both cases the restoration is partly archaeological and partly ideological, historical actuality shading into idealising symbolism.

The same move between history and symbolism is seen in Jones's treatment of the second major theme, which Jonson calls 'mixture' or 'union', referring to James's combination of England and Scotland under one crown into Great Britain:

> Here are kingdomes mixt
> And nations joyn'd ...
> and in them combin'd
> A union, that shall never be declin'd.[52]

Jones expresses these ideas in architectural paraphrase, especially in the structure he has invented to be the seat of revived chivalry, St George's Portico. It is mixed in type, form and style. It seems a compound of three building types: a triumphal arch (the front), a temple or church (the main body) and a portico (the roofed colonnade beyond). If we try to deduce the plan, we get two conflicting results: the exterior suggests a hexagonal, centralised structure, while the interior is planned on a longitudinal axis, like a basilica. And in style it extends over a whole spectrum: from late antique or early Christian, through Romanesque to Gothic and Renaissance.

Although this tripartite architectural conceit seems to sacrifice history to symbolism, it is no mere flight of fancy. There is an antique precedent for its mixture of types – a Roman monument which is portico, temple and triumphal arch all in one. Modern archaeology refers to it non-committally as Janus Quadrifrons; but the prints of Roman remains published in the sixteenth and seventeenth centuries often record its ambivalent character[53] (plate 174). Serlio tries to clear this up:

> In Rome there are many ancient Tryumphant Arches, among the which, this Building, by the greatest number, is accounted for a Tryumphant Arch: yet by the knowledge that men have of it, it is thought to be a Porticus, or a Gallery, like unto a Burse or Exchange for Marchants . . . This Porticus . . . in ancient times was called, the Temple of Janus . . .[54]

Serlio also illustrates the medieval superstructure which gave the building a stylistically mixed character. Jones's typological invention is not fantasy but imitation, based on historical scholarship.

The ambivalence of plan looks towards modern rather than ancient architectural history. It rehearses the major dilemma of church design in the Renaissance, between centralised and longitudinal planning.[55] In effect Jones represents the fusion of both kinds of plan achieved by certain sixteenth-century architects, especially his admired Palladio;[56] and uses the visual conjunction of bell-towers and dome, as a means of suggesting such a fusion on the skyline, which Palladio took over from Venetian Renaissance architecture. A related problem which Jones recapitulates here is the adaptation of an appropriate classical system to the church façade. He tries out Alberti's prototype solution, the application of the triumphal arch scheme.[57] Each of these design exercises is worked through only in scenographic shorthand; but this kind of serious play or architectural thinking aloud was to bear fruit in 1623 when he had to design the Queen's Chapel.[58]

Finally, the mixture or spectrum of styles mediates between past and present, and shows the process of renewal which has produced St George's Portico. What is renewed is what was lost in the ruin of the House of Chivalry, what Jonson's text calls the 'truth of architecture'. For Jonson, truth is to be found in antiquity, and the renewal of truth must come from the revival of antiquity. Jones's design makes the same point, but it also expounds an equally vital point which Jonson leaves unsaid: it locates truth not only in antiquity but in Christianity. Instead of simply leaping from the classical to the neo-classical, it performs a more complex feat of historical condensation: it moves from antiquity to Renaissance classicism via the intervening phases of architecture: palaeo-Christian, Romanesque and Gothic. Through this series of styles it represents the revival of antiquity as a renewal of Christianity.

The cue for this idea came from Jones's principal model. Any church or cathedral built over different periods could be seen as a metaphor of historical change; but the conceit of a building which condensed disparate elements into a unitary structure was found in two designs close at hand.

The stage designs of Inigo Jones

Plate 20. Remigio Cantagallina after Giulio Parigi, Palazzo della Fama, from
Il giudizio di Paride, 1608, Victoria and Albert Museum

One was Giulio Parigi's *Palazzo della Fama* (plate 20), which is an image of fame resulting from the passage of time: a neo-classical portico supports a medieval tower; Jones had already adapted this, compacting it further, for his House of Fame (plate 21) in *The Masque of Queens* (1609). The other is Domenico Fontana's catafalque for Sixtus V, which combines all the Pope's building works into one structure; Jones was to use it for King James's funeral in 1625 (plates 5–6). Parigi's hybrid mixes styles and types in order to represent the process of history. Fontana's, by compacting many Roman monuments into one, does something similar but more ambitious, to celebrate a programme of architectural renewal. St George's Portico combines both objectives into one: it relates a history which culminates in a renewal. But in summing up the 'truth of architecture' with a Christian import it closely follows Fontana's synoptic memorial to Pope Sixtus.

There were wider lessons for Jones in the story Fontana had recorded there. The Sixtine *renovatio Romae*, of which Fontana was the executant, had effected a striking transformation of the city. It realised the ambitions of earlier Popes, such as Julius II, to associate the revived glories of ancient Rome – revived through Renaissance classical architecture – with the triumph of the Christian Church. The great coup was the removal and re-erection of the Vatican obelisk, surmounted by the cross, to become the

Architecture

Plate 21. Jones, The House of Fame, for *The Masque of Queens*, Chatsworth

focus of the piazza in front of the new St Peter's. Fontana described this tremendous feat of engineering, along with his other works for the Pope, in a book which Jones studied.[59] Sixtus achieved his aims through a kind of visionary flexibility: where he could not rebuild, he would set Fontana to modernise or recompose the urban fabric. St George's Portico is reminiscent of one of these projects, the replanning of the Lateran complex. The twin pointed towers come from the façade of S. Giovanni in Laterano, which Fontana had modernised by adding a classical portico. The combination of a round with a pointed Gothic arch is found on the tabernacle over the main altar. And the colonnaded interior suggests an early Christian basilica such as S. Giovanni.[60] Jones would have been interested in S. Giovanni and Fontana's work on it, since in 1608 he had been commissioned to modernise a similarly venerable metropolitan cathedral, St Paul's. Here, in his imaginary church of revived British chivalry, St George's, he rehearses the association of the neo-antique with early Christianity which was the key to Fontana's renewal of Sixtine Rome.

The accompanying context of grand planning is also glimpsed in Jones's design, which is articulated on a perspective scheme, its converging lines actually marked on the stage floor. Sixtus had reorganised the city as if it were a stage set, opening vistas focussed on monuments; and Jones's perspective vista is in that spirit. We recall that the Sixtine programme had been recommended to him by Edmund Bolton only three years before, as a pattern for his artistic ambitions. Bolton was dedicating Bordino's poem on the Pope's achievements, in which architecture and truth, especially religious truth, are emphatically linked. There of course religious truth means the truth of Catholicism. That Jones has adapted the revivalist ideology of the counter-Reformation papacy to the uses of 'God's knight', the fiercely Protestant Henry, shows a determination to follow on his own terms the demanding path Bolton had pointed out.

As well as showing his ambition to restore 'true' architecture to Britain, Jones's designs for the *Barriers* also suggest a hesitation or division in approach. Their crowded multiplicity of forms, which pertinently illustrate the political theme of 'mixture', on the level of Jones's own art pose a question. Was the 'truth of architecture' to be found in an empirical and historical study of the classical heritage, or in a theoretical interpretation of it which gave priority to underlying principles? The obvious answer would be: in both – and the interdependence of archaeology and theory, of a historicist and a more doctrinal conception of classicism, is central to the growth of Renaissance architecture. But Jones's recapitulation of such problems is of unprecedented importance in the context of English culture, both for himself and his public. We see here how his emergence as a Palladian by the 1620s was preceded by conflicts and choices, and that his revisionist critique of Italian architecture evolved from an exploration of problems which was partly done, especially earlier on, in the masques.

Jacobean romanticism reassessed

Oberon the Fairy Prince (1611), as its title suggests, is another entertainment set in Spenserian Britain. The figure of Oberon comes from the popular romance *Huon of Bordeaux*; the English translation had been reprinted in 1601.[61] He is the son of Julius Caesar and the Lady of the Secret Isle, so he provides Prince Henry with another role which combines a classical and a medieval identity, a synthesis of antique heroism and Christian chivalry. As before, the composite role of the virtuous British prince is associated with King James's union of the English and Scottish crowns to form the new Great Britain, a symbolic map of which appears on the curtain before the masque begins.[62] Once again Jones takes up these themes from the text, and makes an essay in what may be called synthetic architecture, but the result is more confident than his corresponding design of the year before.

This is because before he worked out his 'synthetic' design for Oberon's Palace, which mixes forms and styles in a self-consciously metaphoric way (plate 23), Jones produced an earlier design which is much more stylistically unified[63] (plate 22). It is very French in feeling, and recalls that he had been looking at architecture in France eighteen months before: the guest of honour was to be the French ambassador extraordinary sent to ratify a new treaty (although in the event he arrived too late to attend the masque).[64] It is also pertinent that Jones's palace employs motifs from the château of Anet (plate 24), a striking example of Renaissance architecture used to create a mythological role for a great personage – Diane de Poitiers in the role of the goddess Diana. Jones copies the sculptural group over the gateway of Anet, and draws on a view of the 'fontaine d'Anet' published by the antiquarian Gabriele Simeoni[65] (plate 25). Jones may have taken over the imagery as well as the method of Anet because Diana could be seen as a British goddess: in the traditional British history she was worshipped by Brut the founder of Britain.[66] There would certainly be a compliment to James (as Arthur) watching the masque, since he was devoted to hunting, and in the *Basilicon Doron* had commended it to Henry as 'the most honourable and noblest' of princely sports.[67] But whatever the meanings of the mythology its original French accent is retained; and although the matrix onto which the Anet motifs are grafted is by origin Italian – it could be described summarily as Serlio's Bramante's Tempietto[68] (plate 7) – the whole emerges with a French character.

Proportional relationships, as well as style, hold the design together. Its geometry appears to have been carefully plotted. There is a partially visible network of diagonal lines marked on the drawing which regulates the placing of the figures in relation to the building; for example, the putti with javelins point them along two lines which intersect at the mid-point of the central arch. But there are also traces of a network of horizontal and vertical lines which, as well as helping to articulate the design, reveal a system of proportions. The design broadly follows a Vitruvian formula for circular temples, which ordains that the height of the dome should be half the diameter of the whole structure.[69] The notional diameter of the circular pavilion is twice that of the drum of the dome. The first diameter is equal to the distance from the base of the columns to the underside of the cornice, the second to the distance from the bottom of the drum to the top of the dome. In other words, each of the main parts of the building is inscribed in a square, and the sides of the squares are in the ratio 2 : 1. Jones seems to be using as a module the height of the column shafts excluding the bases and capitals: this is equal to the side of the smaller square (or the radius of the larger circle);

The stage designs of Inigo Jones

Plate 22. Jones, Palace within a Cavern, for *Oberon*, Chatsworth

it is also twice the height of the three equal zones in which the figures appear.

These figures add a complementary dimension to the whole concept. The architecture, realised inwardly through proportion, is also externalised through the action of the figure sculpture: the view of the palace standing on its slender columns with the encompassing rock 'at bay' is dramatised by the image of the stag standing serenely in the centre of the hunt. The figures gesture diagonally across the rectilinear proportional grid; the scheme of simple proportional relationships supplies a rational framework for the play of cohesive linear tensions across the structure. The former suggests the influence of Palladio; the latter, that of Jones's colleague in Prince Henry's works, Salomon de Caus. His grotto and fountain designs of this period, published in *Les Raisons des forces mouvantes* (1615), adumbrate the idea of structures realised through an interplay of linear forces – in his case jets of water, often produced by sculpted figures which literally moved (plate 26) (just like Jones's models here, the Anet sculptures, which were automata).[70] Jones has adapted de Caus's idea of linear forces to purely architectural design, generating through the relations of his figures an abstract version of de Caus's *forces mouvantes*, a version informed by a quasi-Palladian

Plate 23. Jones, Oberon's Palace, for *Oberon*, Chatsworth

mathematical harmony. This very individual experiment is worked through with scrupulous care.

Because the first project for Oberon's Palace is such a careful exercise in design, and homogeneous in style, the second version, which returns to the metaphor of stylistic and typological synthesis or 'mixture' used in St George's Portico, holds together rather better than that did. It is composed from very diverse sources – parts are from du Cerceau (the turrets from Anet, the terms from the Château de Madrid), parts from Serlio (the windows and the ground floor), parts from Bramante's Tempietto via Serlio (plate 7) (the dome and drum, and what Jones calls 'the bace of the finishing' and 'the Cartuses' above the turrets).[71] The result is a mixture of French Renaissance château, Italian palazzo and Elizabethan prodigy house; but the mixture is methodical and theoretically informed. The scheme of the elevation is derived from the châteaux shown in du Cerceau's *Les plus excellents Bastiments de France*, some of which Jones would have been able to see in 1609. Du Cerceau's elevations show buildings rising up from actual rock (Blois, Amboise) or heavily rusticated basements (Verneuil, Valléry, the Louvre) towards airy skylines accentuated by efflorescent window surrounds, tall decorated chimneys, cupolas and attenuated finials (Chambord, Chantilly, Chenonceau, Anet) (plate 27). The theme of an ascent from foundations of primitive roughness to heights of civilised

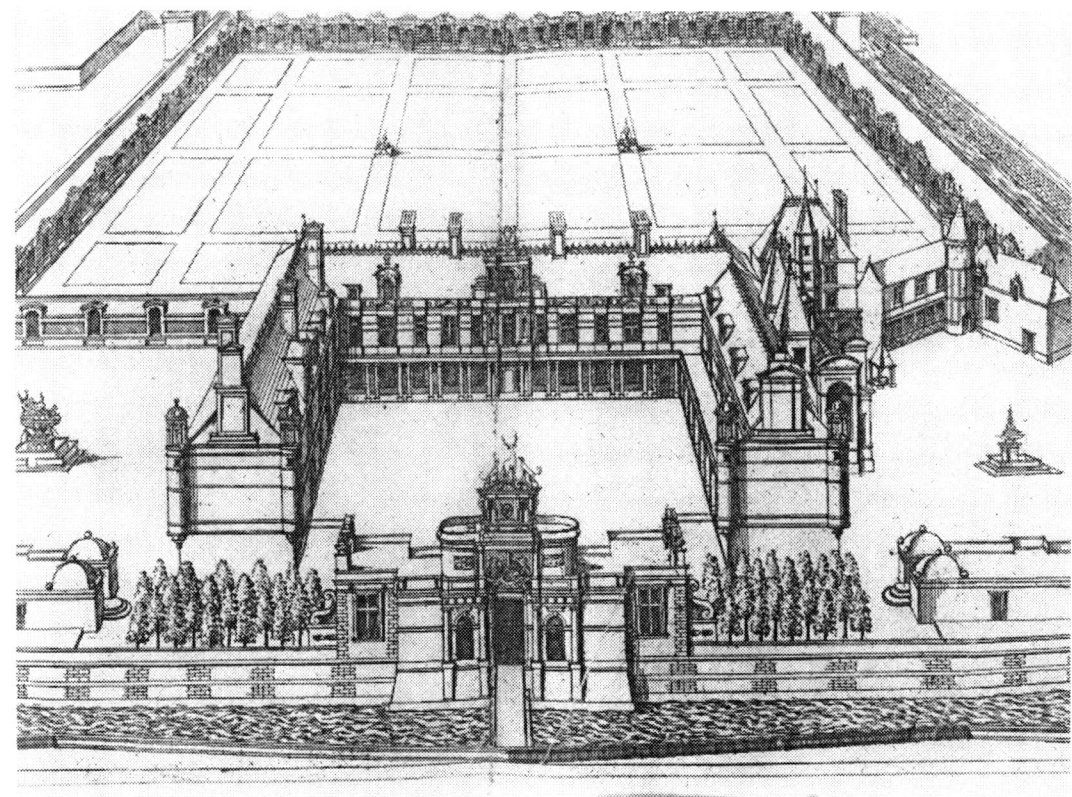

Plate 24. Philibert de l'Orme, Gateway of the château of Anet, from J. A. du Cerceau, *Les plus excellents bastiments de France*, 1609, Bodleian Library

delicacy paraphrases the action of the masque, which begins with a scene of disorderly satyrs and moves in stages towards the appearance of Prince Oberon – from the natural to the civilised. The complementary theme is the rapprochement of different styles, romantically primitivist neo-Gothic and classical, which expresses the duality of Oberon's virtue, at once chivalric and antique.

These methodically constructed architectural metaphors are brought together by a shared infrastructure of Vitruvian theory. The common factor is the Doric order. The ascent from nature to civilisation is rendered through an upward progression, or more precisely an emergence, of the orders: from natural rock and pre-Tuscan 'rustic-work' through Tuscan to Doric. The windows which occur on the way up are in a transitional order which Serlio calls 'Dorico bastardo';[72] and the rustication becomes less rough and more refined at each stage. The union of different styles is rationalised through the 'civilising' Doric order which emerges: the battlements, in relation to the pilasters below, are rhythmically spaced as if they were part of a primitive version of a Doric entablature, as Jones confirms in his notes by using the

Plate 25. Fountain of Anet, from G. Simeoni, *Les Illustres Observations Antiques*, 1558, British Library

phrase 'freec with battlement'; and the same kind of 'proto-Doric' or 'quasi-Tuscan'[73] air is given to the colonettes which have been added to the turrets and which thus draw them into the building's overall system of orders. In the same way the picturesque chimneys are made to look like Doric pilasters crowned by excerpts of an entablature.

Doric is theoretically 'right' from both points of view. Firstly, it is associated with pastoral, and so appropriate to Oberon as prince over all the pastoral characters in the antimasque, who are recruited from Virgil's *Eclogues*.[74] Secondly, Serlio (modernising Vitruvius) associates it with virile, soldierly figures such as St George, 'with the strength to risk their lives for the Christian faith',[75] and so it is the order to express Prince Henry's ideal of Christian chivalry. As Jones writes, paraphrasing Serlio, 'The Ansients dedicated This Dorricke Order T[o] most Roboustious good[s] / Cristians too Saintes o[f] The like nature'.

Jones's design has been seen as part of a trend in English architecture of this period towards a romantic neo-medievalism. But it is more than just symptomatic. To propound an eclectic synthesis of different styles in the way he does, on a carefully plotted classicising matrix, is to review self-consciously the constitution of contemporary English architecture – which had quite unproblematically accommodated French and Italian influences alongside medieval survivals and daring transformations of the medieval tradition.[76] He is rehearsing the eclectic character of English architecture in

Plate 26. Salomon de Caus, Grotto design, from *Les Raisons des forces mouvantes*, 1615, Bodleian Library

a way which amounts to a questioning of that character. As well as seeing him here as a 'Jacobean romantic' one could relate this design to a whole context of sixteenth-century European classicism where a conflation of the Tuscan and Doric orders, combined with rustication (and even late Gothicism) defined a scope for numerous buildings.[77] As with the designs for the *Barriers*, two different attitudes to architecture, and especially to classicism, are being canvassed simultaneously: a tolerant historicism and a potential commitment to Vitruvian theory. But in this later design his direction seems clearer. His use of the classical orders as a vehicle for his romantically expressive metaphors hints not so much at a celebration of Jacobean architecture as at a potential reform of it.

Architecture

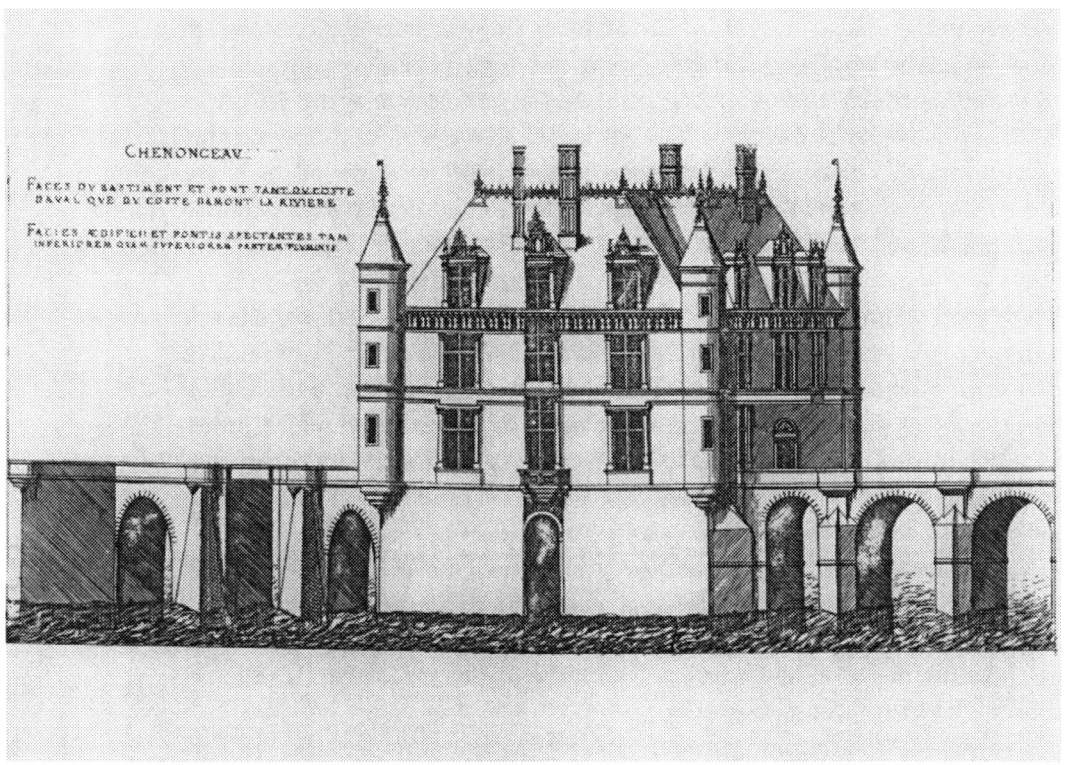

Plate 27. Château of Chenonceau, from J. A. du Cerceau, *Les plus excellents bastiments de France*, 1609

Reform requires power. The view of architecture which is shown here – that it has its material origins in the rude strength of nature which it then refines and transcends – takes its meaning from the concept of hierarchy. The dome which surmounts the palace symbolises the authority of Prince Oberon over his wild inferiors, although that authority is said to be persuasive and not coercive, to work 'by the sweetnesse of his sway, / And not by force'.[18] Jones was to bring about his architectural reformation as the King's Surveyor (as he was now, but for too short a time, the Prince's Surveyor). But the power he wielded was complemented by the persuasive propaganda of the masque designs.

Imagining the classical city

Jones's return from Italy, and the architectural commissions he then received from Lord Arundel, were soon followed by his succession to the Surveyorship. The task of presiding over the King's Works involved not only putting up individual royal buildings but concern with the form and functioning of the urban environment. Probably as a consequence of this, the scenes of architecture which he designs for the masques show an enlarged conception of what architecture is all about. From now on, instead of the unitary architectural constructions which dominate the first decade of the masques, there is an emphasis on the urban perspective sets which, following the descriptions of Vitruvius and the realisations of them by artists of the High Renaissance, were published as models by Serlio and developed in Italian scenography of the sixteenth century. A design which illustrates this transition while it was still in progress is the second scene of the *Barriers* (plate 170), where the meanings of Jones's architecture are both condensed into the single structure of St George's Portico and spelt out in the extended perspective which surrounds it. This duplication of means, part of the uncertainty of the design, does however point in the direction which Jones is taking, towards what might be called the unitary perspective set. As finally developed in the Caroline masques, this is the kind of set which adumbrates the concept, central to Renaissance architecture, of the ideal city.

Meanwhile, in the years immediately following the Italian journey, the spectators of the masques are gradually introduced to the idea that a new architecture means a new city, and vice versa. Long before Jones is able to demonstrate this idea on the ground, with the piazza at Covent Garden, he communicates it through stage design.

The earliest architectural perspective surviving from this period is for *The Vision of Delight* (1617). It is described in Jonson's text simply as 'a street in perspective of fair building'[79] (plate 28). The design looks careless; it is not drawn in correct perspective (although there may have been a more finished drawing which was) and is a mélange of buildings and styles. But as a composition it carefully conflates three precedents: Serlio's Comic and Tragic Scenes (plates 29–30) and a handsome chiaroscuro woodcut recording the set designed in 1560 by the Sienese artist Bartolomeo Neroni, called Riccio, for a play of the Accademia degli Intronati[80] (plate 31). Riccio shows how Serlio's fascinating but stilted prototypes can be turned into a real set design. Jones has made a careful pastiche of these sources which ends up looking broadly composed and miscellaneous. The explanation is that this set was for the antimasque, where the leading characters are Delight, Night, Phant'sy and Wonder, and their theme is the recreative power of the imagination, which may produce bizarre incoherence or ideal beauty. So Jones's architecture is offered self-consciously, to be perceived as a product of imagination, where order and disorder mingle: the regular classical *palazzi* in the foreground clash suggestively with the vernacular townscape beyond them. The general idea originates with Riccio, whose design represents classicism as a ruling style; Jones's paraphrase introduces ambiguity. His design speaks of what we would call the pleasure of architecture, placing the Italianate townscape in inverted commas, and showing

Plate 28. Jones, A Street in Perspective, for *The Vision of Delight*, Chatsworth

classicism as an ideal but not exclusive option. It inculcates a lesson about the authority of classical architecture, but also appeals more broadly to the mentality for which architecture in general has meaning.

In the context of Jones's built work this design can be related to that immediate post-Italian phase which has been called 'transitional',[81] during which he designs tall, narrow town-houses on a similar scale to the scenic *palazzi* here, which are classicising insertions into the vernacular fabric of London. They are in a largely Italian but not yet Palladian style, and characterised by ornamental balconies called 'pergulars', like that on the second *palazzo* to the right. In fact a masque drawing of this period – for *The Masque of Augurs* (1622), which contained one of these urban street perspectives – has on the verso a plan and elevation for just such a house.[82] No doubt the stylistic standards set by these houses were out of all proportion to their sparse presences in a London still largely medieval. In this scene for *The Vision of Delight* Jones can give them a pre-eminence which will reinforce their message: what would the city look like if there were more houses like this? The necessity of such reinforcement is shown by

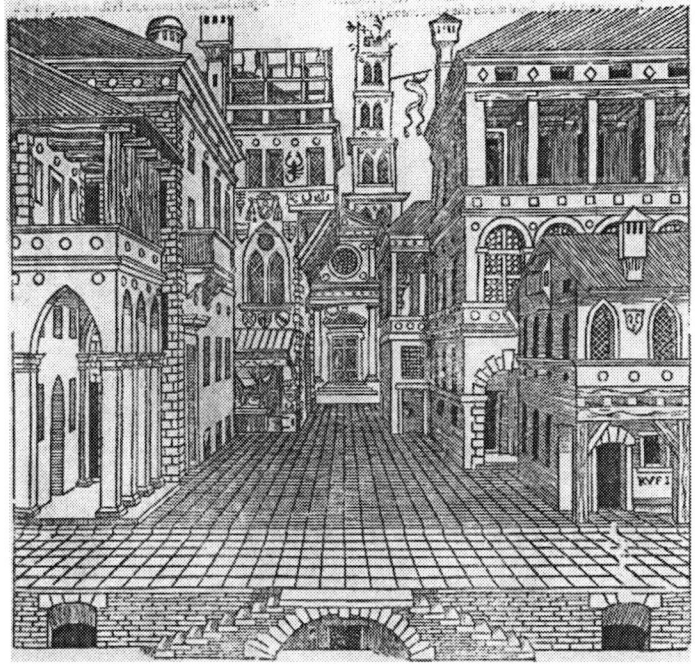

Plate 29. Serlio, Comic Scene, from *Architettura*, 1560

Plate 30. Serlio, Tragic Scene, from *Architettura*, 1560

Architecture

Plate 31. Bartolomeo Neroni called Riccio, Design for *L'Ortensio*, Victoria and Albert Museum

John Smythson's partly uncomprehending drawings of Jonesian houses from his London visit of 1619[83] – if even an architect could misread them they clearly needed all the help they could get.

A perspective composition which shows a complementary aspect of the relation between Jones's buildings and his scenic architecture of this period is the drawing inscribed 'Cupid's Pallas' (plate 32), possibly for a masque of the 1620s.[84] The masque presumably concerned the power of love: the design represents this in terms of the power of architecture. Here, the features which Smythson misses in his drawings of the town-houses, careful proportioning and exactitude of classical detail, are clearly seen, only this time in a grander context. The drawing is ambiguous: the same building forms each side of the street vista or rather piazza, but whereas on the left it looks overbearingly lofty, on the right it is drawn on a smaller scale, compatible with the 'Pallas' beyond; the emphasis swings between monumentality and proportional harmony. Its relation to the grand design for the Star Chamber (1617) has been noted by Summerson, and to the more subtly articulated Queen's House by Harris and Higgott; the 'Pallas' itself has connexions with the Prince's Lodging at Newmarket (1619).[85] Jones is drawing together several of his own projects into an ideal ensemble which

Plate 32. Jones, Cupid's Palace, Chatsworth

makes an exposition of their transforming powers. The general form of the ensemble echoes a famous predecessor: the giant order and the overall plan recall Michelangelo's Piazza del Campidoglio,[86] and suggest a very powerful fantasy about recreating the city at its centre.

The architecture of the world

'Cupid's Pallas' contains in embryo what I have called the unitary perspective set, that is, a set which uses the street vista of Serlio but abolishes its architectural variety, substituting usually two basic architectural units, one for the background and one repeated in pairs for the wings. The first surviving design of this type is 'The House of Oceanus', intended for *Neptune's Triumph for the Return of Albion* (1624), and when that was

Architecture

Plate 33. Jones, Proscenium and Standing Scene, for *Artenice*, Chatsworth

cancelled used for the reworking of it as *The Fortunate Isles and Their Union* (1625).[87] Thereafter Jones developed the type in the masques of Charles I's reign, and its architectonic discipline underlies all his set designs for the Caroline masques.

To point up the process by which all Jones's masque scenes become in a sense scenes of architecture it helps to look at what seems an awkward exception. For the first of the pastoral plays performed by Charles's new queen, Henrietta Maria, and her ladies, *Artenice* (1626), Jones designed a basic set or 'standing scene' (plate 33) which appropriately uses Serlio's Satyric Scene (plate 95) but inappropriately mixes in motifs from the Comic and Tragic Scenes[88] (plates 29–30). The mélange does not have the thematic justification that it does in *The Vision of Delight*, although a rationale for it can be found in the text. It combines several of the locales of the play – a village, the house of Artenice's father, a ruined château, a temple – together in one set, and composes them into a Serlian street vista as if they constituted a single scene.[89] This oddity is the Queen's doing: she was used to the scenographic style of the Hôtel de Bourgogne, which used old-fashioned simultaneous settings schematised according to 'modern' perspective methods,[90] and she must have ordered Jones to follow that convention. The awkwardness of the result suggests how much this went against the grain, although while obeying the Queen's insensitive command Jones has made efforts to bring some discipline into the proceedings. For the proscenium he uses the Doric order, appropriate to pastoral, but in a very forceful version (adapted from Riccio, plate 31) which frames the scene firmly. And the building on the left which is copied from Serlio's Comic Scene has been restyled from Gothic to classical and had its proportions rationalised, so the three storeys are in the ratio 2 : 2 : 1. These moves intimate a reassertion of those rational architectonic values which the aesthetically conservative Queen had momentarily forced the King's Surveyor to put aside.

Jones went on expounding these values in the masque designs, and the Queen came to accept them, while retaining her French tastes. For the third of her pastoral plays, *Florimène*, performed almost a decade later in 1635, he designed a standing scene which is demonstrably French in its visual idiom, while constructed on a latent but firm architectural framework (plate 97). The scheme of the landscape is borrowed from the frontispiece of Guarini's *Pastor Fido* (plate 98) (itself derived from Serlio's Satyric Scene) but the space is amplified and the trees and rustic buildings replaced by more monumental equivalents taken from Callot etchings.[91] The result affirms subtly that there can be an architecture of landscape, and this point is incidentally emphasised by the survival of a drawing showing the wings for *Florimène*, their utterly symmetrical forms revealing the matrix on which the pastoral landscape is constructed.[92] Similarly the proscenium, largely composed of figurative ornament of French derivation[93] (plates 133–4), is in outline based on the proscenium of Riccio's Intronati set (plate 31), a thoroughly architectonic conception which gives a latent but strong definition to Jones's design. The sense of an architecture immanent even in compositions of landscape and ornament is typical of Jones's later masque designs, and appreciable eventually, it would seem, by the Queen.

Henrietta Maria is a good case of Jones's effect as a teacher. Through the yearly routine of the masque performances – the King's on Twelfth Night, the Queen's on Shrove Tuesday – she came to absorb the lessons of Jones's scenography, and grew accustomed to that rational architectonic conception of the visible world to which she had seemed a stranger at the time of *Artenice*. The two masques of 1632 illustrate this attitude. In the King's masque, *Albion's Triumph*, the first scene is a perspective of Composite colonnades (plate 4). Jones's careful drawing has lines scored along the entablatures above the columns and the steps below them, each set of lines being produced to their respective vanishing points. In the Queen's masque, *Tempe Restored*, the corresponding scene is a perspective of garden pavilions[94] (plate 34). This is less elevated architecture, and the order – the

Plate 34. Jones, The Vale of Tempe, for *Tempe Restored*, Chatsworth

'feminine' Ionic – lower down the scale. Nonetheless the structures are morphologically similar, and the same sets of lines are incised along their entablatures and bases. Each scene is discernibly constructed on the same kind of ideal Platonic grid, as if in some underlying sense each were the *same* scene. This kind of relationship between appearances and reality points to a fundamental tendency of the Renaissance Vitruvian tradition, the idea that architecture could express the underlying harmony of the universe. The Queen was in her way a Platonist, as her most ambitious theatrical venture, *The Shepherds' Paradise* (1633), demonstrated. *Tempe Restored* has a neo-Platonic programme, attributed to Jones, which suggests he did not see his scenic architecture as a mere adjunct to the ideological content of the masques, but was prepared to use that content for his own ends, to instil a more inward understanding of classical architectural principles.

Renaissance architecture revised

Jones's eventual Palladianism has been seen as inseparable from a neo-Platonist philosophical position, which 'viewed architecture . . . as an

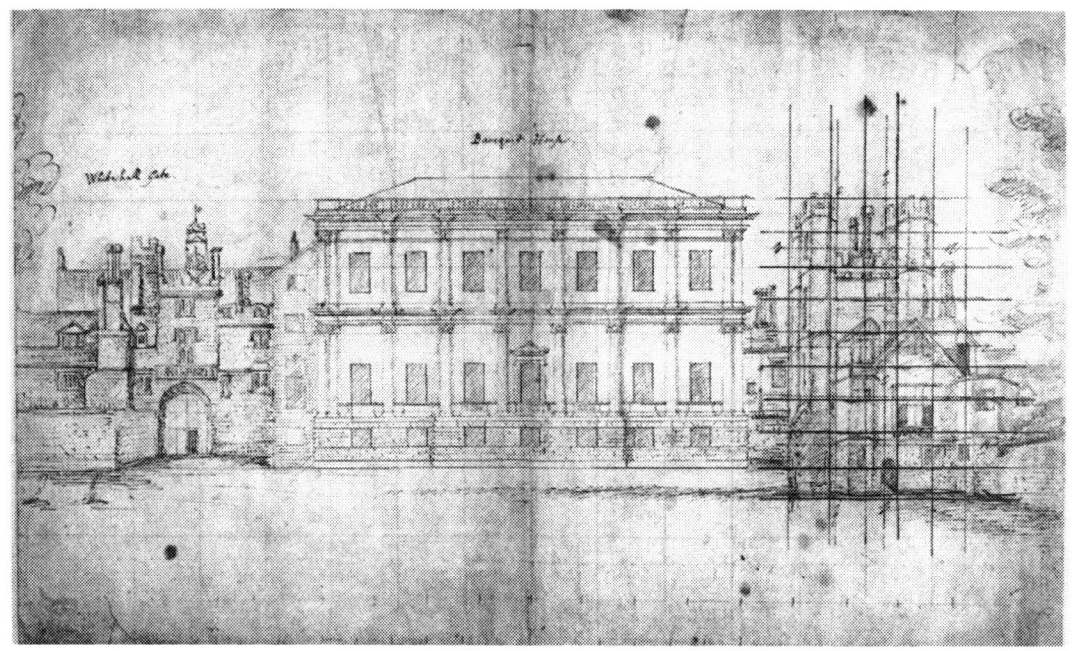

Plate 35. Jones, Whitehall Banqueting House, for *Time Vindicated*, Chatsworth

opportunity, if not an obligation, to echo the structuring of the universe . . . to reawaken man to the reality of deeper truth than lies in the world of appearances'.[95] More recently this has been challenged by Gordon Higgott, who shows that Jones was an attentive reader of the text of Vitruvius rather than an absolute devotee of some kind of idealist Vitruvianism, acknowledging that visual appearances played their part in the achievement of harmoniously proportioned architecture.[96] This new emphasis may recall Daniele Barbaro's concept of *scaenographia*, and suggest how fictive architecture could plausibly be used not just to advertise a repertory of forms but to demonstrate principles. Any historical knowledge of classical architecture needs to be complemented by a theoretical critique of its manifold formal possibilities. Such a critique becomes an implicit element in the masque designs of the 1620s and 1630s. Their instructive exhibition of the forms of Renaissance classicism is informed by Jones's neo-Palladian revision of the whole tradition. One way in which he did this was to display his own buildings on the stage in a context which pointed up their special qualities. So the first scene of *Time Vindicated* (1623) is 'a prospective of Whitehall, with the Banqueting House'[97] (plate 35), rehearsing the startling sight of the unprecedented Palladian hall (in which the performance was taking place) inserted into the medieval and Tudor fabric of Whitehall Palace. The whole view is painstakingly composed, with the Banqueting

Plate 36. Jones, English Houses with London and the Thames afar off, for *Britannia Triumphans*, Chatsworth

House significantly at the centre. Whereas the older buildings are rendered in topographical detail and drawn in perspective, the new one appears as if in an elevation drawing, suggesting that its classical symmetry demands the more abstract mode of representation, and constitutes a standard.[98]

In a later design, for *Britannia Triumphans* (1637), Jones applies this standard to his own earlier work. The first scene of the masque shows 'English houses of the old and newer forms . . . and afar off a prospect of the city of London'[99] (plate 36). The distant prospect has at its centre St Paul's Cathedral, the object of Jones's carefully meditated classical renovations. In the foreground is a Serlian street of houses which does seem to contain one or two examples of timber framed buildings with medieval windows, mixed in with houses of a more modern classical style, but the distinction is hard to make. In spite of features such as gabled roofs all the houses are classically proportioned in their fenestration and the relation of their storeys, whether they have classical detailing, like columns and pediments, or not. In general they resemble Jones's town houses of the 'transitional' period, the ones alluded to in *The Vision of Delight*. Their mixed style, like that of the classically remodelled medieval cathedral, is certainly appropriate for the first scene, where Action opposes Imposture under the motto 'Medio Tutissima', so the architecture serves as a metaphor for the Aristotelian middle way. But whereas the style of *mediocritas* is inevitable and just for St Paul's, it is now out of date for Jones's independent work; and in so far as this drawing reviews the pre-Palladian houses and identifies them in a relativistic spirit as 'English', in that they mingle old and new, it makes a logical judgment on them – they are superseded.[100]

Most of the masque architecture is not of course Jones's own work in that sense but adapted from the inventions of other artists. By following the process of adaptation we can actually see Jones formulating his architectural critiques, correcting his sources according to his own principles before showing them to the masque spectators. This is his normal procedure for the masques of the 1630s, which form a series of object lessons in the most rigorous standards of classical design. A case in point is *Albion's Triumph*. The first scene, 'a Roman atrium' (plate 4), is copied from *Il Tempio della Pace* (plate 37), Giulio Parigi's design for the final intermedio of *Il giudizio di Paride* (1608).[101] Apart from clarifying the forms of the architecture and adjusting the proportions Jones has corrected Parigi's use of the Composite order with a Doric frieze. Instead he has substituted a frieze of masks and consoles which he thought could properly be associated with the Composite according to antique precedent, this being provided by a marble fragment in Lord Arundel's collection[102] (plate 3). The third scene of the masque is an amphitheatre which seems to have been copied without alteration from du Cerceau[103] (plates 38–9). But a closer look reveals that, as well as again adjusting the proportions (so that the height of the interior space defined by the arcades is equal to its diameter), Jones has simplified the main arches of the arcading, which were articulated in a retardataire Quattrocento style of distressing impropriety.

One of the artists Jones drew on repeatedly in this period was Callot. His etchings teemed with ideas for costumes and dramatic figuration, but they also offered a range of architectural forms which were equally lively. One composition derived entirely from Callot is the background of the first scene of *The Triumph of Peace* (1634), which the text calls 'the Forum or Piazza of Peace'[104] (plate 40). The phrase 'forum or piazza' is a formula used in Barbaro's Vitruvius, which suggests Jones's habitual frame of reference;[105] the alternative names are also appropriate because his design has an Italianate vernacular quality combined with a classical rectitude. Comparing the finished conception with the sources shows how this dual effect has been arrived at. The larger buildings to left and right come from two of Callot's commedia dell'arte prints, the *Capitano Spagnuolo* (plate 41) and *Pantalone*. The city-gate or archway in the centre of the background is from a print in

Plate 37. Cantagallina after Parigi, Tempio della Pace, from *Il giudizio di Paride*, 1608, Victoria and Albert Museum

the *Small Passion* (plate 55). To the right of the arch, the church with its tower and the adjacent building are from *The Fair at Impruneta*. The buildings to the left are from *The Punishments*.[106]

None of these buildings has been copied literally: all have been revised. Take, for example, the large building on the left. The irrationality of scale in the relation of the balustraded portico to the house has been adjusted. The proportions have been simplified in a way which is made clear by a system of sill-cornices and string-courses. The irregular attic is omitted. Equally in the buildings of the background forms have been simplified, proportions adjusted, fenestration rationalised. The variety and vivacity of Callot's architecture is still there, but a classical discipline subtly informs the whole composition.

The habit of both welcoming and reforming the inventions of other artists is most clearly seen in Jones's dealings with Hans Vredeman de Vries. His engravings of architectural perspectives and ornament had a far-reaching influence on Renaissance architecture in northern Europe, including England. But whereas the designers of Elizabethan and Jacobean houses

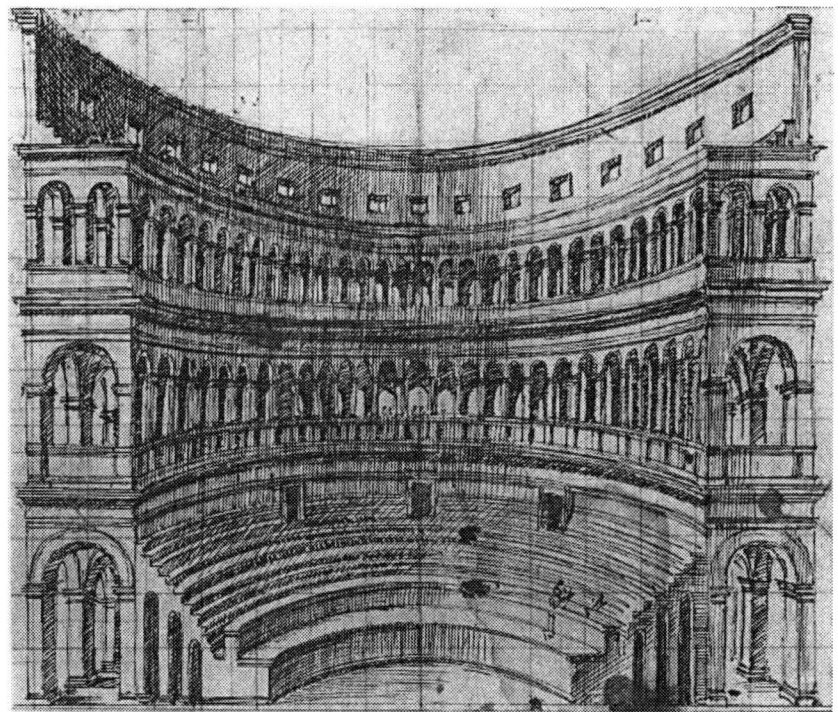

Plate 38. Jones, An Amphitheatre, for *Albion's Triumph*, Chatsworth

reproduced his work uncritically, having no theoretical framework in which to assess his very idiosyncratic versions of classical forms, Jones, when adapting his perspectives for the masques, corrected their architectural grammar with remorseless consistency. A typical example is the drawing inscribed 'A Pallas' (plate 42), which may be a design for the Cockpit-in-Court theatre. This uses two prints in Vredeman's *Perspective* (plate 43), combined with, and corrected in the light of, the architectural background of a painting by Federico Barocci, which has a version of Bramante's Tempietto[107] (plate 44). The scheme of two partly glimpsed colonnades framing a monumental gateway, together with the gateway itself, are taken from Vredeman. But the Italian artist provides a correctly used Doric order for the colonnades, and a Bramantesque standard by which to correct the gateway. So the obsessively recurring blind arches, the incorrect Ionic order, the irregular superimposition of the columns, the gratuitously quaint obelisk finials above the pediment – all that has been unsparingly revised.

We can see Jones working out a revision of this kind in the first design for the Temple of Diana in *Florimène* (plate 45). It derives from an Ionic portico by Vredeman de Vries (plate 46), with the plan adapted and the order corrected by reference to Scamozzi (Jones had already used Scamozzi's

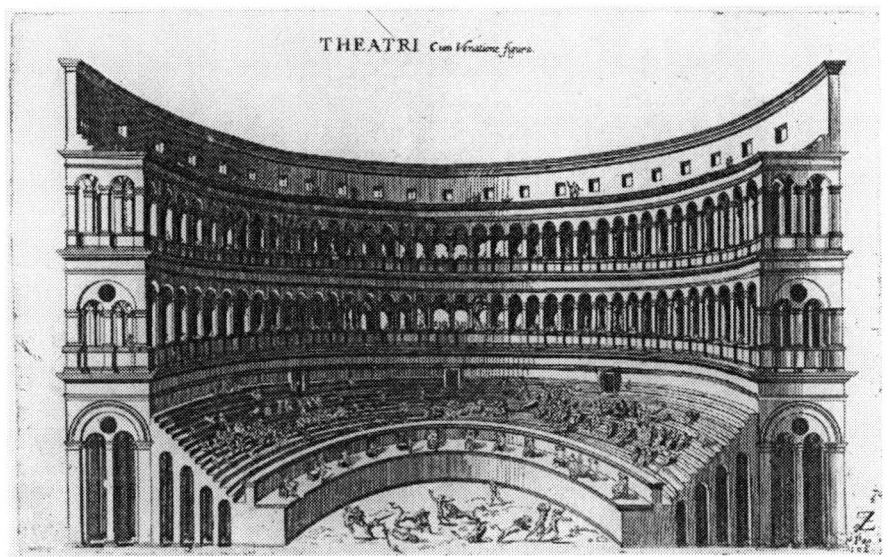

Plate 39. Amphitheatre, from O. Panvinio, *De Ludis Circensibus*, 1600, British Library

Ionic on the façade of the Banqueting House).[108] The drawing suggests the design had got into difficulties, mainly by trying to apply a complete Ionic entablature to the interior. Instead of starting afresh Jones has written next to the entablature 'only an Architraue / and yᵉ Celing in / squares', instructing an assistant how the revision is to be carried through.

Written instructions like this appear on his designs for buildings, assuming a thorough knowledge of the classical vocabulary in those who worked under him, and suggesting a practice of diffusing this knowledge impartially through both buildings and stage designs. The design for the second appearance of the Temple of Diana in *Florimène* ('for no scene but that of the pastoral was twice seen') is actually drawn by an assistant (plate 47). It starts as a copy of Labacco's reconstruction of the Temple of Jupiter Stator[109] (plate 48), but the Corinthian order has been appropriately changed to Ionic, the proportions of the columns altered, and the intercolumniation adjusted according to a formula from Scamozzi.[110] The delegation of this task to an intermediary only confirms that the grammar of the classical orders is to be punctiliously observed and communicated.

Above all it is Vredeman de Vries's distortion of the orders which seems, in Jones's response to his work, to cry out for correction. A scene for the Palace of Fame in *Britannia Triumphans* shows a classical peristyle: the basic unit is derived from another plate in the *Perspective*[111] (plates 49–50). In that plate the entablatures of the Doric and Ionic orders are both wrong, but the most glaring solecism is that the volute of the Ionic capital has been turned

Plate 40. Jones, The Forum or Piazza of Peace, for
The Triumph of Peace, Chatsworth

sideways so as to face the spectator. Jones has turned it back the right way, and what at first looks like a squiggle at the top of his drawing is a rapid sketch of the volute in correct side view. He has made other improvements as well. By contrast, in a stage design which is almost contemporaneous, Stefano della Bella has copied the identical motif in a wholly uncritical spirit, reproducing those features which Jones corrects.[112]

The 'Flemish Vitruvius' was by no means Vitruvian enough for Jones. He was a fertile source of ideas, but his inventions had always to be purged of their improprieties and barbarisms. The comparison with Stefano della Bella, formed in the Tuscan late mannerist tradition of Giulio Parigi, points up Jones's individual attitude to stage design. Through its representations of architecture it was a means of instilling true classical principles.

Decorum and pleasure

If this makes Jones seem doctrinaire, a kind of evangelical puritan of architecture, then the emphasis is not wholly misplaced. At the same time, the masques exhibit many different architectural styles and types, and not only because they are the province of what Jonson in *The Vision of Delight* called 'Phant'sy', and permissive to the imagination. Jones and his contemporaries were acutely aware – as Vitruvius had been – of the principle of decorum, an

Plate 41. Jacques Callot, Capitano Spagnuolo, British Museum

aesthetic doctrine with an obvious social basis. So a style proper for the houses of citizens would not do for the palaces of kings. By extension, the severer demands of what Jones called 'sollid architecture' could be relaxed for garden buildings or interior decoration.[113] There is a whole system, in fact a hierarchy, of relationships between style and function. In Jones's stage design there is an awareness of the same relationships, given that the function of certain architectural styles or types may be to represent the themes of the stage action as well as the social character of a situation.

In the drawing we have just been considering, for the Palace of Fame, the stylistic incoherence of the palace itself has a decorum associated with its thematic function. It is copied from Giulio Parigi's *Palazzo della Fama*[114] (plate 20), which represents the idea that Fame brings the past into the present – so stylistically it combines past and present, medieval and modern. Jones had already adapted Parigi's idea for the House of Fame in *The Masque of Queens* (1609) (plate 21), where he had more or less turned the design inside out, condensing the conceit into the single form of the hexagonal tower, with the upper storey medieval and the lower modern. He

Plate 42. Jones, A Palace, Chatsworth

had to simplify the structure because at that period his stage technology was unequal to it – Parigi's palace had risen from the stage floor.[115] Now for *Britannia Triumphans* nearly thirty years later he can reproduce the scenic marvels of the Florentine theatre, and so the original form of the palace is restored, making thematic sense through a more evident stylistic incoherence. Since its function is symbolic not realistic it can appropriately accommodate implausibility. Even so Jones has adjusted its proportions, to make it fit in better with the classical peristyle.

The nuances of architectural decorum in the social sense can be seen in the differences between the productions Jones designed for the King or Queen in the 1630s. Decorum explains the contrast already noted between the opening scenes of the masques of 1632 – the grand palace of *Albion's Triumph*, its Composite order associated with Roman imperium, and the more informal garden architecture of *Tempe Restored*, with the 'feminine' Ionic order. An even wider contrast is that between the King's masques and the Queen's pastoral plays. The architectural register of the pastorals is typified by the 'standing scenes', landscape compositions including appropriately rural architecture, although this could vary from the villa of *The Shepherds' Paradise* to the cottages of *Florimène*. And the scene changes

Plate 43. Jan Vredeman de Vries, Perspective construction, from *Perspective*, 1605

in each play introduce a varied spectrum of buildings, from temples to farmhouses. The point is that the decorum of pastoral is never dissociated from the decorum of royalty, which Jones had come to envisage in terms of the principles of classicism. So for the First Intermedium in *Florimène* he copies a farm building in Tuscan vernacular style from a print by Tempesta, but adjusts the proportions and the fenestration to give it a more symmetrical look.[116] He makes similar alterations to buildings which are copied from engravings for *The Shepherds' Paradise*.[117] All this pastoral architecture is endowed with an innate classicism, which shows through its 'various forms'.[118]

It is this interaction between the authority of classicism and the principle of decorum which accounts for the scenic architecture of Jones's most mature period as a designer, the 1630s. The interaction was fruitful, because at a time when his personal study of the Renaissance architectural tradition had led him to adopt a definitive position – his mind was, as it were, made up – he could go on communicating to his far less instructed public the historical repertory of forms and styles in terms of which his position made sense. He could also go on enlarging his own studies. In his motto, 'Altro diletto che imparar non trovo', learning and pleasure are said to be synonymous. The architectural variety which decorum licensed in the masques was one form of pleasurable instruction. It ordained a system of

Plate 44. Agostino Carracci after Federigo Barocci, Aeneas fleeing Troy

differences which was meaningful in principle but could appear gratuitous and therefore enjoyable. For Serlio and Vasari the great joy of scenic architecture was its variety of forms, an idea taken up by Shakespeare when he has Prospero detailing

> The cloud-capped towers, the gorgeous palaces,
> The solemn temples . . . [119]

So the spectators of Jones's masques, to which Shakespeare must have been alluding, are taught those pleasures of architecture which reside in differences – while being supplied with a more refined typology than Prospero's epithets suggest.

Variety could be shown in two ways, either within a single scene, or in the succession of different scenes. When Serlio and Vasari praised it, they were referring to the 'wealth of invention' which could be displayed in a single perspective set. The phrase is Vasari's, and he used it in praise of Peruzzi, Serlio's master,[120] whose designs Serlio drew on when he published his models for the Tragic, Comic and Satyric Scenes. At least once in his later years Jones turned aside from his refined reworkings of the uniform

Architecture

Plate 45. Jones, the Temple of Diana, for *Florimène*, Chatsworth

Plate 46. Vredeman de Vries, Ionic portico, from *Perspective*, 1605

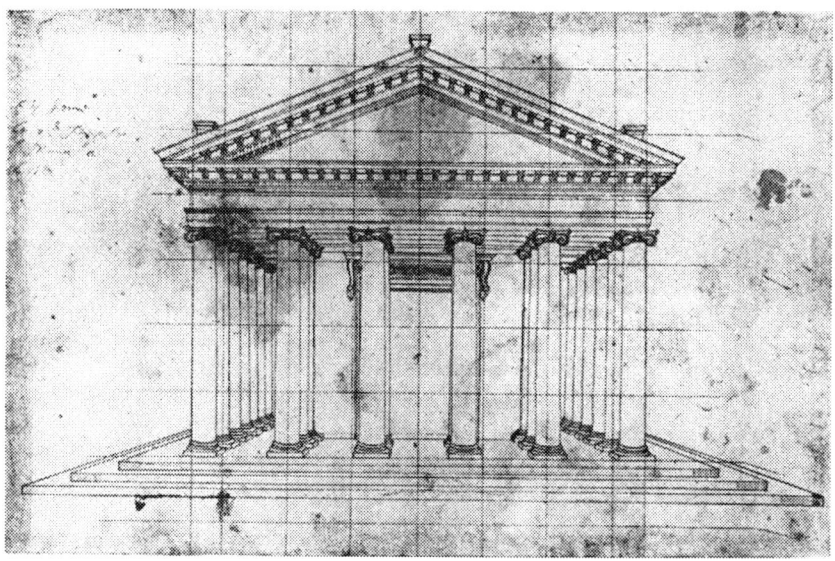

Plate 47. Jones (?), The Second Temple of Diana, for *Florimène*, Chatsworth

architectural sets of Giulio Parigi to make a design in the Serlian mode. This is the drawing inscribed 'The Tragick . . . scene' which probably belongs to the later 1630s (plate 51). Daniele Barbaro, following Vitruvius, had identified the Tragic Scene as the seminal scenic type, going back to the first recorded perspective scene design in the Greek theatre; and while Jones's drawing is evidently intended for a production, it also has a theoretical dimension.[121] Its various parts are selected from a range of predecessors, mainly Serlio's Tragic Scene (plate 30), the Riccio Intronati set (plate 31), and G. B. Aleotti's much later Scena Tragica (plate 52), another theoretical project used for an actual production, which owes a lot to both Serlio and Riccio.[122] By recomposing and continuing this genealogy Jones essays a contribution to a classic tradition. He changes the spatial emphasis of his models from deep recession into distance to greater breadth, and cues this with the reclining figures on the proscenium frieze and the 'leaning' cartouches. He also achieves a consistent solution to the problem of reconciling variety of architecture with the classical grandeur required by the decorum of tragedy. Serlio is miscellaneous in every way; Aleotti provides a variety of building types with a uniform pomposity of style. Jones takes a hint from Riccio's Comic Scene which establishes a determining norm of classicism in the foreground and can then put the other vernacular architecture in perspective both literally and metaphorically. So using perspective as an ideological framework he has a Palladian foreground, a medieval/vernacular middleground, and a background which combines the two around a dominant feature, the monumental archway he had borrowed

Plate 48. Antonio Labacco, Temple of Jupiter Stator, from *Architettura*, 1569, Bodleian Library

from Vredeman de Vries and rationalised (plates 42–3). The dignity proper to the Tragic Scene is made compatible with a 'wealth of invention'.

Jones's exemplars of architectural variety are often northern artists resident in Italy who regard the Italian scene as just that, a scene, and in the role of delighted onlookers represent it in a deliberately picturesque way. Two favourites were the Netherlanders Paul Bril and Willem van Nieulandt. But the Italianised northerner who most appealed was Callot. In his etchings the sense of being a rapt spectator of the Italian scene is conveyed highly self-consciously; the architecture is sometimes frankly arranged as a theatrical setting. One of Callot's characteristic procedures is to elaborate such an ensemble and then use it not as a setting but as a distant background for one figure who is excerpted from it and made to loom in the foreground. His prints of commedia dell'arte characters treat the theatre like this – the chosen character is in the foreground but the audience and stage in the background (plate 41). Jones, in his first scene for *Britannia Triumphans* (plate 36), paraphrases this device in purely architectural terms: the street of

Plate 49. Jones, The Palace of Fame, for *Britannia Triumphans*, Chatsworth

'English houses' which really belongs in the overall London scene is placed on a stage of its own in the foreground, while London becomes a distant prospect. The buildings do not formally resemble Callot's, but the composition has an intrinsically Callotesque quality which piquantly focusses and refocusses the architecture, to be relished by the spectator's gaze.

The lesson of the master

The demonstrative power of Jones's scenic architecture reaches a high point with the last scene of what was to be the last masque ever presented, *Salmacida Spolia* (1640). Later in the same year he was still designing plays, but this was the last of those opportunities for extravagant display which only a masque could offer. There is no reason to suppose that he regarded *Salmacida Spolia* as a swan song; its magnificence can be explained by the fact that it was an unusually important project. It was a double masque for both the King and Queen; and it was trying to make an impressive appeal for political sympathy in an atmosphere of crisis. In the event, while few found it sympathetic, it was judged on its own terms impressive.[123]

Plate 50. Vredeman de Vries, Courtyard, from *Perspective*, 1605

The final scene comprises heaven and earth in a way which had become conventional in European court entertainments. The most recent example of such a cosmic panorama had been *Le nozze degli dei*, performed at Florence in 1637, and the designs by Alfonso Parigi were drawn upon by Jones for *Salmacida Spolia*. But Jones's finale avoids the conventional tendency of Parigi's symbolic localities and represents earthly reality in characteristically specific form, as a city; and this city, while being an ideal construction, has its own sort of particularity. It is described by Davenant, who wrote the text of the masque:

> the scene was changed into magnificent buildings composed of several selected pieces of architecture. In the furthest part was a bridge over a river, where many people, coaches, horses, and such like, were seen to pass to and fro. Beyond this on the shore were buildings in prospective, which shooting far from the eye showed as the suburbs of a great city.[124]

Although the only surviving drawing of the whole scene, by John Webb[125] (plate 53), is faulty in its perspective, it shows the contrast between the 'magnificent . . . architecture' of the 'great city' and the 'buildings' of its 'suburbs'. This contrast is implicit in the provenance of Jones's imagery.

His 'several selected pieces of architecture' have literally been selected from Veronese and Callot. The identical ranges of classical colonnades in the

Plate 51. Jones, The Tragic Scene, Chatsworth

foreground are taken from G. B. Vanni's engraving of *The Marriage at Cana* (plate 54); and the two less homogeneous structures in front of the bridge from Callot's etching *Christ Presented to the People* (plate 55) which Jones had already used for the Forum of Peace.[126] The background (plate 56) is derived from views of the Isola Tiberina and its bridges by van Nieulandt[127] (plates 57–8). Jones's bridge is an idealised reworking of the Ponte Rotto, with features from the Ponte Cestio and Ponte Fabricio (Ponte Quattro Capi); and the 'suburbs' seen through it are the cluster of buildings on the right bank of the Tiber beyond the Ponte Fabricio.

These various motifs are organised to form a strong stylistic contrast, analogous to that between the 'city' and its 'suburbs'. The ideal Palladian idiom of Veronese's pictorial architecture literally puts in perspective the more idiosyncratic style of the buildings from Callot. This effect is immediately repeated in the background. The bridge is Palladianised, translated from an item of topography into a neo-antique reconstruction; and the congested view of houses on the foreshore is recomposed in the more relaxed manner of Callot's *Diverse Vedute*.[128] The bridge becomes an imposing frame for the lively, miscellaneous townscape, and again Palladian classicism puts in perspective the vivacious but uncanonical style of Callot. The two artists' inventions, frequently resorted to by Jones, had taken on

Architecture

Plate 52. Oliviero Gatti after G. B. Aleotti, Scena Tragica del Teatro di Ferrara

such definite but distinct characters in the architectural discourse of the masque designs that here they can produce meaning through a stylistic dialogue. From this dialogue Palladianism emerges in the ascendant.

It matters that this ascendancy is displayed, in the way the composition is articulated, as an inclusion, an encompassment, an embrace. The title of *Salmacida Spolia* refers to the Greek colonisation of Asia Minor, and alludes to the victory of civility over barbarism won by gracious persuasion rather than force. In the masque Charles I as the wise ruler Philogenes graciously pacifies the 'turbulent natures' of his dissident subjects into 'a sweet calm of civil concord'.[129] Jones uses his architecture (as he had often before) metaphorically, to represent this benign contest: the animated, populist spirit of Callot, who stands in for the 'beloved people' of the text, is harmoniously contained by the suave grandeur of Palladio who was, in Jones's reading of the Renaissance tradition, the Prince of Architects. The relationship is obviously one of supremacy and subordination, but the contrast is made without disdain. Two drawings for parts of the background survive in Jones's own hand. One is for the Palladian bridge and one for the higgledy-piggledy 'suburbs' which it frames,[130] but both are executed with equal care. The promulgation of stylistic purity in a context of the widest aesthetic sympathies had always characterised Jones's architectural pedagogy in the masque designs.

Plate 53. John Webb after Jones, The Suburbs of a Great City, for *Salmacida Spolia*, Chatsworth

However the vision of an ideal city realised here forces the political issue more sharply. The 'eight persons richly attired' on the central cloud machine represent the celestial spheres,[131] and evoke the idea, central to the Renaissance tradition, of classical architecture as a means of manifesting the harmonious constitution of the cosmos. But, closer to home, the design seems to allude to grandiose projects for the 'great city' which was Charles's capital, particularly the rebuilding of Whitehall Palace in a monumental classical vein and the replacement of the damaged medieval fabric of London Bridge with a new bridge in antique Roman style.[132] Seen in this light the design shows Westminster and the City in allusively schematic form, and plots the new projects onto this scheme. The four parts of the composition stand for four parts of an itinerary: Whitehall, the Strand, London Bridge, the City. The Palladian colonnades in their abstract magnificence stand for an imagined new Whitehall, and the irregular structures from Callot which come next for the aristocratic mansions along the route from Whitehall to the City, whose eclectic architectural idiom would be outfaced by a new palace. The bridge is a new London Bridge in the new royal style, and the buildings seen through it the medieval City on the bank of the Thames. By calling them 'the suburbs of a great city' Jones coolly suggests that the new seat of royal power would itself be a metropolis of overpowering magnitude, relegating the City to its margin.[133] This is not total fantasy. The bridge, if

Plate 54. G. B. Vanni after Paolo Veronese, The Marriage at Cana

built, would have been another of those interventions in the fabric of the City by which royal authority symbolically framed and contained its subjects; other examples are Jones's renovations of St Paul's, which cast a classical embrace round the old medieval cathedral, and the project for Temple Bar, which for royal entries would have presented the City through a Roman imperial triumphal arch.[134]

Davenant's poetic text for the masque tries to clarify this uneasy relationship between persuasion and coercion. The chorus sings finally to the King and Queen of the desired effect of royal authority:

> All that are harsh, all that are rude,
> Are by your harmony subdued;
> Yet so into obedience wrought,
> As if not forced to it but taught.[135]

The idea of a potent harmony by which recalcitrance or ignorance can be 'taught' receives much less substantiation from Charles's politics than from Jones's architecture. The lines could stand as a motto for his work as an architect, extended through the insistently 'delightful teaching' of the

Plate 55. Callot, Christ Presented to the People, from *La Petite passion*

Plate 56. Jones, Design for Bridge, for *Salmacida Spolia*, Chatsworth

Plate 57. Willem van Nieulandt, Ponte Quattro Capi

Plate 58. Van Nieulandt, Isola Tiberina and Ponte Quattro Capi (detail)

masque designs. That work depended on the power of the crown, but the architect was to prove more successful than the king.

The aesthetic medium of Jones's great metaphoric tableau was to leave a more lasting imprint than the political message. As so often before, the medium constituted a message in its own right. Here it received the maximum of attention because the final scene of the masque was reserved until the King and Queen had concluded their dances and were 'seated under the state' as spectators. Normally one or other would be involved in the masque for its entire duration; but this being a double masque and the Queen pregnant, it was arranged that both should retire from the action before the conclusion, which they watched from their privileged vantage-point. Jones was able to show his spectacular finale to a plenary gathering of the court, and he clearly took advantage of this unusual situation, its atmosphere heightened by political crisis, to design something that would be, in Jonson's phrase, 'impressing and lasting' in their imaginations. Certainly his lessons in the theory and practice of architecture were to be more enduring than King Charles's in the theory and practice of monarchy.

Thirty-five years had passed since Jones's first masque in 1605. During that time he had taught himself to be a classical architect and the Stuart court to appreciate the tradition which gave his work meaning. The two enterprises are closely related, and the story of both is implicitly told in the masque designs. That narrative complements the evidence of Jones's actual building projects, especially as many of them are lost or altered, or remained unrealised; and it provides one chapter that would otherwise be missing, on his prehistory as an architect. In mediating between his built oeuvre and the privileged but often uninstructed public to whom that was addressed, the designs played a crucial part in defining his legacy to succeeding ages. Jones's role in English architecture has perhaps been distorted by the neo-Palladians' appropriation of him in the eighteenth century, offering a view of him as a rigorous purist. But the way in which his ideas were communicated partly through the court masques suggests a different emphasis. The masque was a dramatic form in only a partial sense, but it was certainly a highly theatrical one, and by staging his architectural principles Jones was presenting them in a context of argument and dialectic, a context which was litigious rather than simply legislative. The treatise which his disciple John Webb planned but never wrote might have given his master's work a far more prescriptive character. Instead of any such system we have Jones's private, informal, fragmentary writings – the marginalia and the sketchbook – and the masque designs, the informal substitute for a Jonesian *cours d'architecture*. In the end, the fact that Jones represented rather than codified his ideas on architecture makes him seem a very English figure.

4

Figures

The bodily part

In keeping with his idea of the masques as pictures, Jones treated his costume designs for the masquers as exercises in figuration. The theoretical context for this was first articulated by Jonson, although he did it by the way, in the course of a programmatic exposition of his own importance in their collaboration. Anxious to define the poet's primacy, Jonson produced a subordinate but suggestive categorisation of Jones as an artist.

This is in his first published text of a masque, *Hymenaei* (1606), which begins with a preface or manifesto:

> It is a noble and just advantage, that the things subjected to *understanding* have of those which are objected to *sense*, that the one sort are but momentarie, and meerely taking; the other impressing, and lasting: Else the glorie of all these *solemnities* had perish'd like a blaze, and gone out, in the *beholders* eyes. So short-liv'd are the *bodies* of all things, in comparison of their *soules*. And, though *bodies* oft-times have the ill luck to be sensually preferr'd, they find afterwards, the good fortune (when *soules* live) to be utterly forgotten. This it is hath made the most royall *Princes*, and greatest *persons* (who are commonly the *personators* of these *actions*) not onely studious of riches, and magnificence in the outward celebration, or shew: (which rightly becomes them) but curious after the most high, and heartie *inventions*, to furnish the inward parts: (and those grounded upon *antiquitie*, and solide *learnings*) which, though their *voyce* be taught to sound to present occasions, their *sense*, or doth, or should always lay hold on more remov'd *mysteries*. And, howsoever some may squemishly crie out, that all endevour of *learning*, and *sharpnesse* in these transitorie

devices especially, where it steps beyond their little, or (let me not wrong 'hem) no braine at all, is superfluous; I am contented, these fastidious *stomachs* should leave my full tables, and enjoy at home, their cleane emptie trenchers, fittest for such ayrie tastes: where perhaps a few *Italian* herbs, pick'd up, and made into a *sallade*, may find sweeter acceptance, than all, the most nourishing, and sound meates of the world.[1]

Jonson distinguishes the separate strains in the make-up of this hybrid genre: the 'outward' and the 'inward parts', the body and the soul. The soul is the poetry and the 'invention', the intellectual conception which gives rise to it and to the whole work. This endures, while the body, that is, the visual presentation, perishes. As we have seen, the distinction comes from Italian art theory of the sixteenth century, where the relationship of poetry and painting is compared to that of the soul and body.[2] Into this ready-made *paragone* Jonson implicitly fits himself and Jones, although no names are named. But in his next published text, *The Masques of Blackness and Beauty* (1608), he designates the other's role explicitly. After describing the set and costumes and the entire disposition of the first scene in *The Masque of Blackness*, and before coming to his own poetic text, he sums up: 'So much for the bodily part. Which was of master YNIGO JONES his designe and act.'[3] The soul-poet puts the body-painter in his place.

By using the term 'designe' Jonson at least suggests that he sees Jones as a painter in a somewhat intellectualised sense. He repeats the term later in the same text, when explaining how he thought the main scene of *The Masque of Beauty* well conceived but imperfectly executed: 'The Painters, I must needs say, (not to belie them) lent small colour to any, to attribute much of the spirit of these things to their pen'cills. But that must not be imputed a crime either to the invention, or designe.'[4] This criticism of Jones's assistants absolves the designer himself from blame, and puts him in the company of the inventor, above the level of unreliable artisans. We have already noted that Jonson's categories come from Lodovico Dolce's *Dialogo della pittura* (1557), which names the three parts of painting as invention, design, and colour. For Dolce, *disegno* is the process of giving visible form to the painter's inventions, and he does this through drawing. But instead of merely reproducing natural appearances, *disegno* consists in perfecting the imperfections of nature,[5] so it uses a manual aptitude and a sensuous medium to rise to the level of the ideal. The scheme which Jonson uses therefore assigns Jones an ambivalent middle position, dependent on the poet for the originating concept of the work, the *invenzione*, but himself giving form to ideas which are to be realised by subordinates.

The concepts which Jonson appropriated from Cinquecento art theory to put Jones in his place were not innately docile instruments. The soul/body analogy from the *paragone* literature was reversible, as Jones would have known. Its bias had been intelligently challenged by Leonardo, as Lomazzo reported: 'poetry is like the shadow of painting, and the shadow cannot exist without the body that casts it, which is none other than painting herself...'[6] And the concept of *disegno*, used in a relatively empirical sense by the Venetian Dolce, took on a more metaphysical meaning in the context of later central Italian thought. Quite possibly Jonson was introduced to Dolce's theory of painting by Jones. If so, his use of it to reinforce his own theory of the masque, which made the designer secondary and the poet not just supreme but transcendent, was to be ironically confounded. Jonson probably did not know that the concept of 'design', which he used so magisterially in 1608, had by then much more power than it was accorded by Dolce in the old-fashioned usage of fifty years before. As Jones's career progressed, he arrogated this conceptual power to his increasingly dominant role in their relationship, the balance of which was shifting. When Jonson was finally cast off in 1631, he fulminated satirically against 'Omnipotent Design', and with reason. But leaving aside Jonson's effrontery and the poetic justice which overtook it, we have still to consider the more suggestive aspect of his characterisation of Jones as the artist of the 'body' articulating his ideas through 'design'.

Representing the body: disegno *and* maniera

There actually is a benign sense enfolded in this characterisation. The *paragone* literature, written mostly by humanist critics, which classified *pittura* as body-art rather than soul-art, was complemented by the treatises written by artists, which claimed that painting was an art of the body in a more positive sense. The fundamental discipline for the painter was *disegno*, and the elements of *disegno* consisted in learning to represent the human body. Moreover, *disegno* was fundamental to all the arts – architecture, just as much as painting or sculpture; all were based on figuration. Jones's studies made him familiar with this doctrine.

Apart from the theoretical centrality of figuration to his oeuvre, figure drawing was part of Jones's working routine from an early stage. It was always required by masques, for sets and proscenia but especially for costumes. Later it was needed for schemes of interior decoration, in the Queen's House for example, and for statuary, as on the west front of the remodelled St Paul's Cathedral. Eventually, what may be called pure figure drawing makes a significant appearance in his work, in the later 1630s and 1640s. This is puzzling, because in theory it should have been there from the first; long before it appears there is a theoretical space reserved for it, waiting to be populated.

Jones's ideas about figuration were formed early in his career by his reading of Vasari. The one volume of his copy of the *Lives* which has survived is the first volume of the Third Part. This is the volume which gives Vasari's definitive view of modern art, to which Jones's notes indicate his close attention. One annotation succinctly sums up his general attitude: 'on must beeginn / beetimes to learne / ye good principles',[7] and the style of his handwriting in some notes shows that he did in fact study Vasari from an early stage. In the *Proemio* he has marked a passage in which Vasari expounds those qualities which, while present in the art of the 'eccellenti maestri' of the Quattrocento, were only brought to perfection by their successors, the artists of his third period, or as we would say the High Renaissance. The qualities are 'regola, ordine, misura, disegno e maniera', and Jones has marked Vasari's description of the last two:

> *Disegno* was the imitation of the most beautiful aspects of nature in all figures, whether sculpted or painted – a capacity which comes from having a hand and intellect able to reproduce everything that the eye sees on a level surface ...
>
> *Maniera* then reached its finest pitch from the practice of constantly portraying the most beautiful things, and joining together these superlative hands, heads, torsos and legs, so as to make a complete figure of all those fine features ...[8]

Opposite the two terms underlined, Jones has written brief notes in the margin:

what desine is / To Imitate ye best of / nature

gudd / manner coms by Copii/nge ye fayrest thinges

His terse paraphrases suggest a determination to learn 'good principles' of figuration from Vasari, although this response to the text produces a complication, as we shall see.

Vasari's first concept sums up the whole Florentine tradition of *disegno*, with its two basic ideas. One of these is the equal emphasis on 'hand' and 'intellect': design is conceptualisation as well as manual delineation. The other is that the objects of design are 'figures', and their interrelationships. The second idea goes back, in the literature, to Alberti's *De pictura* (also in Jones's library), although it could be deduced by anyone familiar with Florentine and central Italian art, as Jones was. It was an idea which stayed with him through his career.

Much earlier in the *Lives*, in the introductory essay on painting, Vasari has stressed the intellectual aspect of *disegno*. He declares the common affiliation of all the arts to 'design, father of our three arts, architecture, sculpture and painting ...'⁹ The power to conceptualise, to conceive, is the power of generation. Previously, he had called *disegno* 'mother of each one of these arts...'¹⁰ This was in a book debating the primacy of painting or sculpture, edited by Benedetto Varchi, which included contributions by contemporary Florentine artists; several besides Vasari stressed that all the arts stemmed from *disegno*. Varchi himself pushed this doctrine to its logical conclusion:

> I would say then, arguing along strictly philosophical lines, that I consider, indeed I take it as certain, that sculpture and painting are substantially a single art, and in consequence the one is as noble as the other ... Now it is generally acknowledged that not only do they have a common end, that is, an artistic imitation of nature, but also a common beginning, that is, design ...¹¹

When Vasari later switches his metaphor, asserting *disegno* to be not just mother but father of the arts, he is affirming this insistence on its intellectual role by enlisting the conventional association of masculinity and mental power. As for design as a manual practice, he has two sorts of advice to give, about acquiring skill and, beyond that, style. Representational skill comes from copying relief sculpture, casts from life or the antique, or figures modelled in clay, and then moving on to life studies, the drawing of the nude. This must be supplemented by the study of anatomy. The knowledge thus gained of the body from the inside and the outside ensures that the artist can draw the contours of his figures perfectly. This is where representational competence shades into a beautiful style, a *bella maniera*. Figures which are rendered with the assurance springing from thorough knowledge will for that very reason, says Vasari, display 'buona grazia e bella maniera'. But in the next sentence he takes this back, or at least implies it is not enough:

> For whoever studies good paintings and sculptures, and at the same time looks with understanding at the live model, must necessarily have acquired a good manner in art.¹²

Life study must be supplemented by the study of art.

According to Vasari then, the study of drawing has two complementary aspects, one practical and the other historical. Skill or competence comes from following an empirical pedagogic method which, by implication, applies in all cases and at all times, and has presumably been handed down unchanged (for at least an appreciable number of generations). Style comes from a critical study of the history of art, recognising and adopting what is best in a changing process (or progress, as Vasari would have it). In reality, the distinction between skill and style cannot be strictly preserved, since the highest competence takes on the quality of good style. In practice, *disegno* cannot be conceived of without *maniera*, which brings us back to the passage Jones annotated. This forms part of the major historical section of the *Lives*. By contrast, the essay on painting which contains the advice on drawing practice occurs in an introductory section, where Vasari discusses materials, technique and method. In that introduction the main emphasis – concerned with copying models, life drawing and anatomy – is on learning to acquire graphic competence. In the part Jones annotated the emphasis is on achieved artistic progress, through advances in style. Vasari writes in the past tense, although he sometimes shifts into the present – not illogically, since his exposition of historical advances implicitly details the sound methods which led to them. However, although the parts paraphrased by Jones are in the past tense, he translates them into the present. He is evidently reading Vasari's history as an exposition of method.

The character or bias of the method Jones is reading out of Vasari is indicated by the parallel words 'best' and 'fayrest', which translate the identical concept in the original: 'il piu bello'/'le piu belle'. These highlight the studious representation not of natural appearances but only of what is fit in nature to be represented, what approaches perfection. This involves remaking the figures or bodies which nature has made. Vasari's assumption to this effect derives authority from its allusion to the famous story of Zeuxis, who composed a Helen from the most beautiful features of various women.[13] Jones himself wrote in the margin of another of his books, 'bautifull figu/res ar made / by taking the / best of seueral / men . . .', paraphrasing no less an authority than Socrates.[14] It is not surprising then to find him reading Vasari's concept of *disegno* with a notable bias towards the overlapping concept of *maniera*. And, as we shall see, Jones's figurative drawings, especially his costume designs for the masques, show him approaching the practice of design through the idea of *maniera*.

This approach, given the order of Vasari's treatment, starts strictly speaking from the wrong end. But apart from this deviation, caused by Jones's peculiar historical circumstances, he took in the central tenets of Vasari's doctrine of *disegno*: the tendency to assimilate the arts to each other, and to base them all on the discipline of figuration.

The Vitruvian body

Within this context, Jones's branching out into architecture from stage design (seen by Vasari as both a pictorial and an architectural discipline) made unexceptionable sense; both belonged to the 'arts of design', with their roots in figuration. There was also a complementary context in which architecture was linked to figuration, was in effect a figurative art in its own right – the tradition of Renaissance Vitruvianism. In his discussion of building types, Vitruvius gave priority to the temples of the gods, implying that the temple-plan was an ideal for other buildings to follow. This, he declared in a doctrine that became famous, 'must have an exact proportion worked out after the fashion of the members of the finely-shaped human body', which Jones paraphrased in the margin of his copy: 'the boddi of man well/ proporsioned Is the/ paterne for proport/ion in buildinges'.[15]

Renaissance architects and theorists were deeply impressed by the Vitruvian analogy between building and body and often developed it in their own ways. The architectural writers whom Jones studied repeat and elaborate Vitruvius's arguments in the context of Christian belief. Daniele Barbaro in his tireless commentary is a great repeater of Vitruvius, and quite capable of forecasting a point before his author makes it, such as Vitruvius's reminder that the architect's terms of mensuration are taken from the human body – thus giving it greater prominence than it had in the original.[16] That kind of repetition becomes tantamount to a new reading; but an even greater change comes in the shift of the religious context. Barbaro not only makes the conventional paraphrase of pagan temple into Christian church, but assumes a Christian Aristotelian view of nature and its chief glory, man, made in the image and likeness of God:

> Nature, our instructor, teaches us how we are to proceed in the planning of buildings: for she requires that we learn the ratios of the proportions that we have to use in the structure of temples from nowhere else than that sacred temple made in the image and likeness of God, which is man – in whose make-up all the other wonders of nature are comprised.[17]

Barbaro follows Vitruvius in using the concept of *compositione* (Lat. *compositio*) to refer to the well-proportioned structure of the body, as well as that of the temple; and I shall return to this concept later.

Lomazzo too transposes Vitruvius's arguments into a Christian culture. As with Barbaro, repetition in itself can amount to a new reading. Lomazzo, before blindness confined him to literary pursuits, had been primarily a painter, and it is as a painter that he reads Vitruvius. Although his treatise deals with 'Painting, Sculpture and Architecture', the parts on architecture are written from a painter's point of view. So in Book I, writing on proportion, he deals successively with the proportions of figures and the proportions of columns, following the association of the two made by Vitruvius:

> Wherefore, we may be bolde, to represent any columne after the similitude of mans body, which is the perfectest of all Gods creatures; and so shall it neither exceede, nor be defective: and so consequently will all the partes which are reduced unto these proportions, proove exceeding beautifull . . . [18]

This corresponds with the Christian humanist tone of Barbaro, proper to the temperate religious climate of Venice, but elsewhere Lomazzo, in keeping with the hispanised, counter-Reformation atmosphere of his own Milan, is more fervent. He actually extends the Vitruvian doctrine of proportion in a chapter on 'Howe The Measures Of Ships, Temples And Other Things Were First Drawne From the Imitation Of Man's Bodie', the crux being an argument that the proportions of the Ark were based on the human form, by a divine revelation to Noah.[19] His ultimate emphasis is that skill in proportion comes from knowledge conferred by divine grace, which makes men 'worthy to ascend into heavenly glory, living by means of good works, and in the fear of God, with whose name I conclude these remarks on proportion'.[20] At this point Lomazzo's English translator, Richard Haydocke, recoiled (not for the first time) like the good Protestant he was, perhaps at the ambiguous mention of 'good works' and the somewhat too buoyant theology of grace. He ends his version of the chapter with the sentence before, commenting on 'the proportionable agreement and admirable harmony of the partes of man's body':

> *Whereas therefore every one of us carrieth about him a modell of these proportions, let us not thinke the time lost, which is spent in learning how to know our selves.*[21]

The new stress (these are Haydocke's italics) on self-examination rather than self-forgetfulness as part of an apologia for the arts, and sober philosophical humanism rather than baroque religiosity, suggests how Lomazzo's elaboration of the Vitruvian doctrine of architecture as a 'body-art' came to be read in a Protestant culture. Jones, whatever his personal religion, was culturally a Protestant, and his mature architectural style is not out of keeping with Haydocke's sobered-up version of Lomazzo on proportion. But underlying that sober architecture there is still the Vitruvian idea of bodily representation.

Further extensions of this idea are found in other writers. Alberti, as befits a pioneer making a fresh start on the business of writing an architectural treatise, takes the idea back to a more basic form than it had in Vitruvius:

> The most expert Artists among the Ancients, as we have observed elsewhere, were of Opinion, that an Edifice was like an Animal, so that in the Formation of it we ought to imitate Nature.[22]

Alberti seems to arrive at this point by making an Aristotelian deduction from Vitruvius: there is an analogy with the *Poetics*, where Aristotle says that a poem is like a natural organism.[23] Alberti's expansion of the concept of the bodily into that of the organic is accompanied by a tendency to deduce new metaphors from the body analogy itself. So on the topic of architectural ornament he writes:

> We should erect our Building naked, and let it be quite compleated before we dress it with Ornaments, which should always be our last Work...[24]

Alberti's opening out, at the beginning of the Renaissance architectural tradition, of the Vitruvian analogy to the concept of the organic and to the transformations of metaphor, was to be extremely influential.

All the principal writers Jones read on architecture followed Alberti's lead. Daniele Barbaro compared the architect drawing a cross-section to a physician, because he can show the anatomy of a building.[25] Vasari, describing the qualities of a well-proportioned building, said that it should 'represent' the human body both as a whole and in all its parts. The façade should have the symmetry of the human face, the door placed like the mouth, the windows like the eyes, and so on. Vasari develops the comparison in elaborate detail: staircases, for example, are the arms and legs of the building.[26] In effect, this is an allegorisation of the original Vitruvian analogy (pointing towards a conception like Spenser's House of Alma), animating it far beyond an abstract doctrine of proportion.

Palladio, discussing the planning of palaces and villas, compared their lay-out to that of the human body, some parts of which are noble, some mean and ugly, but all of which need each other. Implicit here is Menenius's fable of the body politic from Livy.[27] God, Palladio continues, has created the body in such a way as to solve the architect's planning problem:

> as the Blessed Creator has ordered our members, so that the most beautiful are in places most exposed to view, and the less decent hidden; so too in building...

Jones annotated this passage: 'Comparason to a mans boddi // the most butifule partes of mans boddy most exposed to sight. so in building'.[28] For Palladio the unpresentable parts are 'less decent' and 'hidden': he not only politicises but sexualises the body-building. We are not accustomed to seeing Palladio's architecture, nor that of his disciple Jones, with these associations, perhaps because they have been caught and extracted by the filter of neo-classicism. It should therefore be stressed that by the late Renaissance the Vitruvian body analogy did not remain only an abstract doctrine but had a proliferating life as a powerful metaphor.

Design and 'story'

For Jones, the Vitruvian idea of architecture as bodily representation was closely linked to the Vasarian idea of *disegno* as a fundamentally figurative discipline. He writes a personal manifesto to this effect in the Roman Sketchbook, as he looks back over his journey to Italy, the climax of a decade of work, and considers what he has learnt:

> Thursday ye 19 January 1614 [i.e. 1615]
>
> As in dessigne first on Studies the partes of the boddy of man as Eyes noses mouthes Eares and so of the rest to bee practicke in the partes sepperat can on comm to put them toggethear to maak a hoole figgur [and cloath yt] and consequently a hoole Storry wth all ye ornamentes
>
> So in Architecture on must Studdy the Partes as loges Entranses Haales Chambers Staires doures windoues, and [then] adorrne them wth colloms Cornishes sfondati. Stattues. paintings. Compartimentes ...

The terms of the comparison are derived from Alberti, writer of the first Renaissance text on painting as well as architecture. In both arts he had stressed the relation between parts and whole, whether in a building (which as we saw he likened to an organism) or in an *historia*, the kind of dramatic, complex figurative narration which he held to be the painter's highest project (what Jones calls a 'Storry'). Jones's first paragraph is spelling out further Alberti's key concept of *compositio*:

> Composition is that procedure in painting whereby the parts are composed together in a picture. The great work of the painter is the *historia*; parts of the *historia* are the bodies, part of the body is the member, and part of the member is a surface.[29]

Surfaces are composed into members, members into bodies, bodies into the total *historia*. In this analysis the central concept is obviously the body, and we get what looks like an implicit extension of Vitruvius: that is, just as a good body is the paradigm for a good building, so it is for a good *historia*.

Jones's account of the construction of a *storia* (to return to the Italian vernacular term) updates Alberti in two ways. Firstly, he substitutes Vasari's concept of *disegno* ('dessigne') for Alberti's concept of *compositio*. This seems to present no problem, since Vasari's exposition of design, which begins his essay on painting, is obviously descended from Alberti's treatise. He too stresses the relation between parts and whole, both in the works of nature (especially the bodies of humans and animals) and in works of art, and the final goal of his discussion is the 'invenzione delle storie'.[30] Secondly, Jones follows Vasari's lead in detailing the parts of the body which go 'to maak a hoole figgur', which Alberti had always referred to simply as 'members'. But whereas Vasari had kept to a certain level of generality in his detailing of the body, referring to 'hands, heads, torsos, legs', Jones goes into more minute detail, with his 'Eyes noses mouthes Eares and so of the rest . . . ' This emphasis on facial features reflects the academic drawing manuals which were beginning to be published in the early seventeenth century and which Jones used for drawing practice. A typical example is Odoardo Fialetti's *Tutte le parti Del Corpo Humano diviso in piu pezzi* (1608), which begins with pages of eyes, ears, noses and mouths, before going on to larger matters (and eventually to whole compositions).[31] True to his motto about learning inscribed on an earlier page of the Roman Sketchbook, Jones here implies that for him the most elementary graphic tasks have priority in practice as well as theory.

The drawing manuals had their origin in the circle of the Carracci, as part of a movement to re-educate artists in the rational classicism of the High Renaissance after the wayward figural and compositional deformations of Mannerism.[32] To someone such as Jones, who was learning the whole Renaissance tradition backwards, as it were, from a position historically and geographically beyond it, they could be seen as a late realisation of Alberti's programme for learning to construct *storie*. He therefore implicitly associates the Carraccian manuals with Alberti under the umbrella of Vasarian *disegno*, a concept which could be said to mediate historically between them. But this sturdy and plausible historical condensation harbours a problem, which is that in Vasari the idea of *disegno* is bound up with the idea of *maniera*, in a way it could not be for either Alberti or the Carracci. Certainly Alberti in his writing and the Carracci in their painting display the idealist strain which persists in central Italian art and is compatible with an equally persistent naturalism. But Vasari – at least in Jones's reading of him – insists that the representation of nature is a means to the production of beauty. It seems then there is a difficulty lurking in Jones's account of 'dessigne' and its basic function in the composing of *storie*.

The figure in the 'story'

This matters because Jones did put his knowledge of figuration to use in the invention of 'historical' compositions, analogous to the architectural projects he constructed. Each of the masques was 'a hoole Storry', including not just painted figures but real ones. Some of these were the most powerful figures in the state, so the masque could appropriately be assimilated to the most powerful genre in the Italian tradition of painting, the monumental *storia*. In this context, the costume designs for the masquers become not just clothes arranged on dummies but figure drawings in their own right, and this is how Jones treated them, as studies towards the figures in the perfected composition. The fact that the perfected composition was a performance, and the final figurations the masquers themselves as they appeared *ad vivum*, simply reinforces this way of thinking. If, as Vasari insisted, the goal towards which modern painting had developed was *vivacità*,[33] then Jones's theatrical tableaux could be seen as taking the next logical step in that direction.

Given the peculiarity of the mode in which he practised the art of 'storry', his study and practice of 'dessigne' also took on a peculiar character. Unlike the Italian artists whom he tried to emulate, he was far from well grounded in the representational and especially figurative disciplines which Vasari took for granted. Evidently Jones had received some instruction, but beyond a certain point he had to teach himself.[34] Using his regular tasks of designing court entertainments as a means of self-education, he especially took costume design as an opportunity to practise figure drawing. This basic training was a way of disciplining not only himself but also the entire organisation of his 'pictures'. The principal figures in these pictures were real people, and very exalted people with wills of their own. His only way of retaining as much control as possible over the total conception was, in his costume studies, to ensure the acceptance of his ideas by representing the courtiers to themselves as appealingly as possible. Therefore, in order to economise his own efforts at self-instruction and to maximise his influence over the patrons who were both the subjects and the materials of his grand compositions, he took a strategic short-cut: he approached the practice of *disegno* through the acquisition of *maniera*.

Jones had extracted two lessons from Vasari: 'what design is, to imitate the best of nature' and, next in order, that 'good manner comes by copying the fairest things'. The second dictum is very much his own reading of the text. The term used by Vasari, which Jones translates as 'copying', is 'ritrarre'. Vasari's contemporary Vincenzio Danti explains that it means the replication of natural appearances (as distinct from 'imitare', a representation which perfects the imperfections of nature).[35] Jones's very literal rendering of the word tends to narrow its meaning, as if it refers not to nature, or to both nature and art, but only to art; and this of course is in keeping with the direction of his work. In practice, he conflated the programme which he read from Vasari, and set out 'to imitate the best of nature' precisely 'by copying the fairest things'. To him, 'the fairest things' were to be found in the figurative repertory of the Renaissance tradition, drawn both from antique sculpture and from the modern art which Vasari had praised. This was most accessible through the work of Cinquecento print-makers, expertly inaugurated (according to Vasari) in the circle of

Raphael, the supreme painter, by Marcantonio Raimondi. In his life of Marcantonio, whom he judged the first in both senses among Italian engravers, Vasari wrote that his legacy was 'the benefit that northerners have had from seeing, by way of prints, the styles of Italian art (le maniere d'Italia) ... '[36] Jones's use of Marcantonio and the prints of his successors amply confirms this. Vasari also relates admiringly how Marcantonio began his career, by imitating the prints of Dürer so closely that his versions were taken for the originals.[37] This association of innovation with imitation is also entirely pertinent to Jones, whose imitations of Marcantonio, and of the *maniera* of Raphael as mediated by him, are the basis for his first essays in figurative design, which were to introduce the Stuart courtiers, through masques, to the 'maniere d'Italia'.

From the start, Jones's costume drawings, for all their romantically elaborate attire, are based on classicising figurative designs. A drawing for a Naiad in *Tethys' Festival* (1610), who has sea-shells in her hair and seaweed hanging from her shoulders (plate 59), is derived from an image of Temperance (plate 60), one of a series of Virtues engraved by Marcantonio after Raphael.[38] Jones has thinned and elongated Raphael's sturdy, sculptural figure, transposing her into a mannerist key, but the original figurative matrix is still there. A contemporary drawing for a squire in a tilt (plate 61), one of the chivalric entertainments closely related to the masque, is taken from another print by Marcantonio, of David with the head of Goliath[39] (plate 62). This is after Francia, whom Vasari had praised as a precursor of the 'new, living beauty' in modern painting, to be perfected later by Raphael.[40] The image is clearly based on antique sculpture. Its late Quattrocento style furnishes the classical body with an aesthetic glamour which translates perfectly into the courtly social style of its new context. Apart from altering the pose of one arm for practical purposes, Jones reproduces the figure intact.

Vasari had said that *maniera* was perfected by using a principle of selection, composing the best features of various figures into a new figure which would be even more beautiful. Jones himself had written that in practice figuration was a matter of making parts into a whole. Many of his costume drawings combine features from different figures, and the most striking examples bear out Vasari's advice, since they are carefully composed from models of considerable distinction. Jones's best-known image, often reproduced, is the design for a Fiery Spirit (plate 63) in *The Lords' Masque* (1613). This is a composite of two figures from antique sculpture: the younger of two fauns from a bas-relief (plate 64), and the Apollo Belvedere[41] (plate 65). The basic idea, with suggestions for the costume, is provided by the faun, who is carrying a torch (Jones's Spirit is a torchbearer). This figure is part of a composition representing a complex of interrelated movements,

Plate 59. Jones, Naiad, for *Tethys' Festival*, Chatsworth

Plate 60. Marcantonio Raimondi after Raphael, Temperance

and it therefore strains emphatically in one direction. Jones re-poses it with reference to the Apollo, with its more moderate representation of movement, its stability as a free-standing figure, and its authority as a 'classic' masterpiece. The final form incorporates a conflict between stability and motion, the conceit of fire being introduced via certain subtle figural attenuations, such as the slimmer legs and feet and the sharpened profile. This beautiful design best demonstrates how Jones, along the lines recommended by Vasari, cultivated *maniera*.

A comparable design of the same period is for another torchbearer, this time an American Indian (plate 66), in *The Memorable Masque* (1613). Here

Plate 61. Jones, Page Bearing a Helmet, Chatsworth

Plate 62. Marcantonio after Francesco Francia, David with the Head of Goliath

the basic idea comes from an engraving after Mantegna (plate 67). His figure represents *La Servitù*,[42] and Jones has not only freed it from its bonds – the ball and chain on the ankles and the yoke on the shoulder, which is changed into a torch and held aloft – but from the constraints of Mantegna's style, which Vasari had characterised as sometimes 'sharp' and 'dry'.[43] In keeping with the theme of the noble savage or natural man, he has amplified the form of the body, given it a more 'heroic', athletic bulk. His models are partly the faun from the bas-relief again and partly a figure of a nude warrior, engraved after Raphael.[44] This reworking of Mantegna in a High Renaissance style to produce a neo-antique figure is another of Jones's most striking compositions and another good instance of his *maniera*.

These last two examples can be usefully compared with others from the

Plate 63. Jones, A Fiery Spirit, for *The Lords' Masque*, Chatsworth

1630s, when the assurance which they display became routine. After the partnership with Jonson was dissolved, and Jones took full control of the masques, he used the occasions they provided to augment the efficiency of his figurative design. It was at this stage that he seems to have felt confident enough to extend his interest in figure drawing beyond the bounds of expediency, into areas which in theory he ought to have explored during the preceding twenty-five years, but which he seems to have passed by. In one direction, he returns to the elements of figuration, to the analytical exercises which his note of 1615 in the Roman Sketchbook had taken to be essential; in another direction, he produces more and more drawings which seem gratuitous and experimental.

A sheet associated with *Albion's Triumph* (1632), the first masque produced after Jonson had been dispensed with, shows the proliferation of Jones's figure drawings beyond the masque. It contains a costume design for

Plate 64. Marcantonio, Two Fauns carrying a Child

Plate 65. A. V., Apollo Belvedere

Charles I as the emperor Albanactus (plate 68). The figure is composed from two similar images on Roman bas-reliefs, both engraved by Marcantonio. One is of Trajan, being crowned by Victory, from the Arch of Constantine (plate 69); the other is from a well-known sarcophagus, showing a lion-hunt[45] (plate 70). This follows Jones's normal practice; what is unusual is the more freely drawn figure on the left, adapted from one of the *ignudi* on the Sistine ceiling, as engraved by Adamo Scultori[46] (plate 71). It has nothing to do with *Albion's Triumph*, but its proximity to the other figure is symbiotic, reinforcing the point that Jones saw the masques as complex figurative projects, and also revealing the widening range of his figure studies.

There are similar sheets of the 1630s which bring together costume designs and apparently irrelevant figure drawings. One which opens up a further vista contains a costume design for *The Triumph of Peace* (1634), together with a number of related and unrelated heads[47] (plate 72). One of these is replicated (in reverse) on a page of the Roman Sketchbook, where it is marked with a grid of lines (plate 73). These show it to be derived from the drawing manual of Odoardo Fialetti, which contains examples of how to draw the head in foreshortening with the aid of simple linear schematisations (plate 74). Another of Fialetti's heads turns up in the costume design itself.[48]

These links between Jones's mature costume drawings and the most elementary exercises in figuration, which he could be expected to have progressed through years before, show him in a new phase of self-education.

By now Jones had mastered his craft as a stage designer. This meant that his study of figure drawing, which had necessarily coincided with learning to design not only costumes but acceptable roles for the courtiers, could be pursued in a more independent way. He added many new drawings to the Roman Sketchbook: some are exercises from the drawing manuals; some are careful copies after Raphael and his school; some are analyses of small-scale compositions by Parmigianino, or monumental *storie*, such as Michelangelo's *Last Judgment*.[49] In the same period he filled sheet after sheet with drawings of heads, apparently in pursuit of what Vasari had praised as one of Raphael's unique effects, 'il dono della grazia delle teste' – 'the gifte of the / grace in heddes' as he translated.[50] But the original impulse for all this new activity and diversity springs from the 'bodily part' of the masques, and the special figurative discipline which Jones practised in his costume designs for the masquers.

The antimasque

Designing for antimasquers (as for all the speaking, singing or dancing roles apart from the masquers themselves) also involved Jones in building up a figurative repertory. Even though the characters and roles might be invented by the poet, especially under Jonson's régime, it fell to the designer (who was also the producer) to give them concrete visual form in the first place; and he had much more scope to set his own stamp on these realisations than when designing for the masquers. Masquers were important people who had to be represented according to a courtly decorum. Their costumes were often replicas of that worn by the principal, royal masquer, who might have to be consulted about every detail. We have seen how Jones turned these social constraints to artistic advantage. With the antimasquers, usually professional performers, there were no such constraints, so that the designer had much more freedom. This might be curtailed in the event by the sheer burden of work for a particular production: in *Albion's Triumph*, for example, Jones had to design the staffage of a triumphal procession, and some of his efforts are rather economical. But in general the creative scope was there, and he took advantage of it.

His surviving designs for antimasque characters may seem to add up to nothing more than a huge miscellany. This is to be expected since, from the beginning, the keynote of the antimasque is diversity. In the main masque repetition, with variation, was the ruling principle. So the roles designed for

Plate 66. Jones, An Indian, for *The Memorable Masque*, Chatsworth

Plate 67. Adamo Scultori after Mantegna, Allegory of Servitude, British Museum

Prince Henry in the entertainments of 1610–11, Meliadus and Oberon, are essentially similar; and if he had lived a whole series of such roles would probably have resulted, like those devised for his brother Charles in the 1630s. In the antimasque the assumed stability of monarchic power is set off by disorder and multiplicity, passing phenomena which, because they cannot prevail, are there to be aestheticised and subjected to admonitory interpretation. So the apparently gratuitous variety of the antimasque acquires meaning in the dominant context of the masque as a whole.

To see Jones's antimasque figures in this context and relate them to the Italianising figurative programme of his designs for the masquers, one has to examine the concept of the antimasque itself. This is not easy, since the nature of the antimasque was never settled: ideas of it differed between one poet and another, and between designer and poet eventually, in the quarrel between Jones and Jonson. Even Jonson, who explored the masque genre

Plate 68. Jones, Albanactus: Preliminary Sketch, for
Albion's Triumph, Chatsworth

seriously over a long period, never worked out a definitive form for the antimasque, although he did have decided views on its function.

Jonson expounded his idea of the antimasque in the preface to *The Masque of Queens* (1609). He begins by invoking the principle of decorum, the necessity of fitting his theme to the high rank of the masquers, led by Queen Anne, 'that the Nobilyty of the Invention should be answerable to the dignity of theyr persons'. Therefore, he goes on, 'I chose the Argument, to be, *A Celebration of honorable, & true Fame, bred out of Vertue*: obseruing that rule of the best *Artist*, to suffer no obiect of delight to passe w'hout his mixture of profit, & example.'[51] In associating the Horatian 'rules' of delightful teaching and decorum with the power of the Queen he

Figures

Plate 69. Marcantonio, Trajan between Rome and Victory

Plate 70. Marcantonio, Lion Hunt

Plate 71. Adamo Scultori after Michelangelo, Ignudo from the Sistine Ceiling, British Museum

fortifies his own theoretical position – which includes, by implication, Horace's Aristotelian insistence on poetry as rational mimesis. He continues:

> And because her Matie (best knowing, that a principall part of life in these *Spectacles* lay in they^r variety) had commaunded mee to think on some *Daunce*, or shew, that might præcede hers, and haue the place of a foyle, or false-*Masque;* I was carefull to decline not only from others, but mine owne stepps in that kind, since the last yeare [margin: In the

Plate 72. Jones, The Sons of Peace, for
The Triumph of Peace, Chatsworth

Masque at my *L. Hading.* wedding] I had an *Anti-Masque* of Boyes: and therefore, now, deuis'd that twelue Women, in the habite of *Haggs*, or Witches, sustayning the persons of *Ignorance, Suspicion, Credulity,* &c. the opposites to good *Fame*, should fill that part; not as a *masque*, but a spectacle of strangenesse, producing multiplicity of Gesture, and not vnaptly sorting w^{t}th the current, and whole fall of the Deuise.⁵²

Jonson's argument here gives the antimasque generic authority and formal identity. Authority comes from both Queen and poet, opportunely associated, from the royal command and the poet's knowing anticipation of it. Identity is determined by its difference from the main masque – it contrasts, or opposes, or even counterfeits. The exact nature of this difference is never clearly defined, and the imprecision links up with the impartial 'variety' which was all that the Queen is supposed to have wanted. Jonson forcefully counters this aestheticising impartiality by reintroducing the principle of

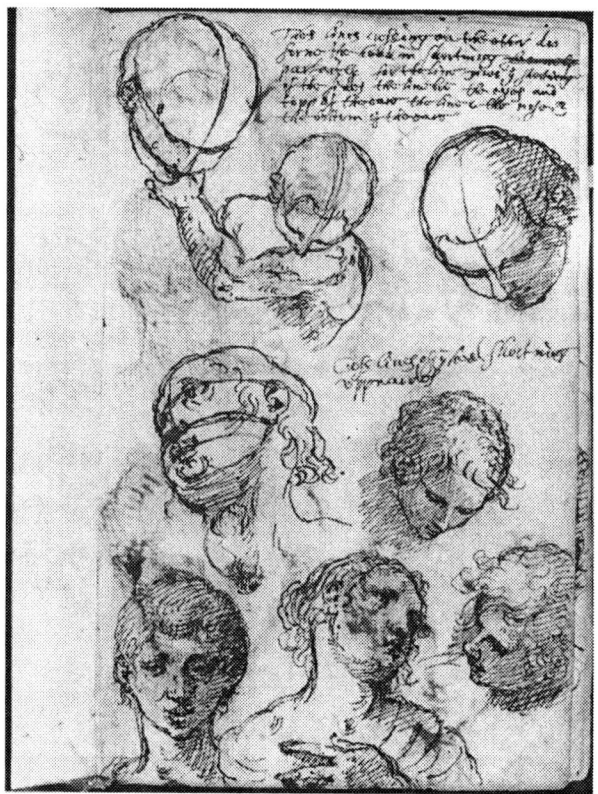

Plate 73. Jones, Sketches of heads, from the *Roman Sketchbook*, Chatsworth

decorum: the 'spectacle of strangeness' is to be appropriate to the invention, 'sorting with . . . the device'. But his whole statement betrays a potential conflict between the will to 'variety' and the 'rules' of poetic mimesis.

Over the next few years, Jonson took two different but overlapping approaches to the antimasque, sometimes experimenting diversely and sometimes trying to develop it along a straight line. On one hand he tried out different kinds of antimasque, changing from classicising or mythological scenarios to modern, topical ones, and from poetry to prose. *Pleasure Reconciled to Virtue* (1618), which was presented again as *For the Honour of Wales*, had a different antimasque each time: the earlier in two scenes, with Comus 'god of cheer and the belly' followed by Hercules and the pigmies, the later a burlesque of comic Welshmen. On the other hand Jonson tried to work out a serviceable format which could be adapted to any occasion. The standard here was set by *Love Restored* (1612), where the antimasque self-consciously reflects on the masque genre in a sustained episode of prose comedy. This virtuoso piece, which became a model for several later

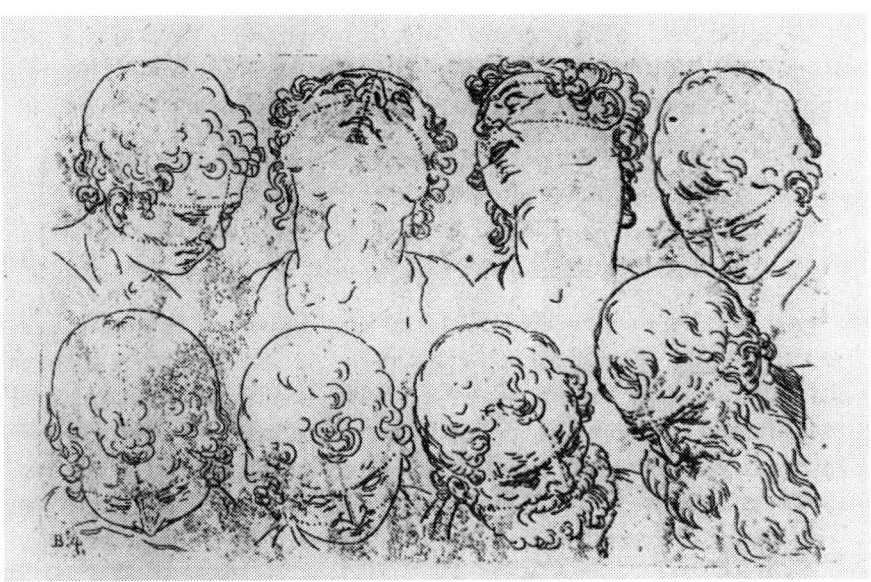

Plate 74. Odoardo Fialetti, Heads in foreshortening, from *Il vero modo et ordine*, 1608, British Library

antimasques, draws on Jonson's experience as a writer of comedy for the theatre. It also reflects Italian example. In Italy the court entertainment which corresponded to the English masque was the performance of a comedy interspersed with *intermedi*. Jonson could be seen as condensing this mixed, diffuse and prolix format into a neater, binary, through-composed structure.

In so far as the Jonsonian antimasque becomes a comic episode, its generic 'rules' become those of comedy. Jonson's view of these is expounded in the dedications, prologues and inductions of his plays. His leading ideas are straightforward: the aim of comedy, which is 'to profit, and delight', is achieved through an imitation of human life or, more broadly, of nature. Both concepts, mimesis and nature, are crucial. Comedy does not present the truth direct 'but things (like truths) well fain'd'; it is a representation. But it represents nature; as Jonson writes of himself, 'Hee is loth to make Nature afraid in his *Playes*, like those that beget *Tales*, *Tempests*, and such-like *Drolleries*', dismissing the preternatural happenings of Shakespearean romance. And he condemns 'Playes: wherein, now, the Concupiscence of Daunces, and Antickes so raigneth, as to runne away from Nature, and be afraid of her, is the onely point of art that tickles the *Spectators*.'[53]

Such a doctrine seems inimical to the form which Jonson had characterised as 'a spectacle of strangeness'; but it is reiterated in one of his own antimasques. This is the antimasque to *The Masque of Augurs* (1622), a piece of broad city comedy including an absurd character called Vangoose, 'a rare Artist... and a Projector of Masques'.[54] He stages an antimasque of his own for the other characters, enthusiastically defending it against their criticism:

> O Sir, all de better, vor an Antick-maske, de more absurd it be, and vrom de purpose, it be ever all de better. If it goe from de *Nature* of de ting, it is de more *Art*: for deare is *Art*, and deere is *Nature*; you sall see. Hochos-pochos, Paucos palabros.[55]

Knowing spectators could have taken this as a parody of Jones, with his cosmopolitan affectations. More to the point, Jonson satirises a doctrine (which he may be attributing, justly or unjustly, to his collaborator): that the antimasque is licensed to depart from nature, and dispense with the rationalising constraints of Aristotelian mimesis. In place of the strong stress which he himself placed on nature, the 'rare Artist' (who is partly an anti-self and partly a caricature of his difficult partner) puts the stress on representation.

This criticism would have more force if all Jonson's own antimasques were in a mode which could be seen as realist, however heightened by comic theatricality. But the model established by *Love Restored* and followed in other works beside *The Masque of Augurs* is challenged by another model, which seems to shrug off the obligation of imitating nature. This appears in *The Vision of Delight* (1617), which, as the title suggests, self-consciously takes as its theme the 'insubstantial pageant' of the masque experience, the pleasure given by its unreal or imagined spectacles. The action is initiated by Delight, the pleasure principle, who introduces Night, goddess of dreams and visions, who in turn introduces Phant'sy, the principle of imagination. In the psychology underlying Jonson's allegory, *phantasia* is the faculty which mediates the evidence of the senses to reason and understanding.[56] It may do this more or less accurately, depending on the proper use of its peculiar power, which is to fragment and combine the sensory images it receives. So by producing false syntheses it may disfigure or counterfeit the forms of nature. Jonson's Phant'sy, licensed here to 'Create ... forms' for the pleasure of the spectators, launches into a long speech describing bizarre, comic monstrosities in the tradition of Bosch; and this is followed by a danced 'Anti-masque of *Phantasmes*'.[57] Stephen Orgel describes the speech as a 'verbal antimasque':[58] it rivals the bizarre ballet which comes after. And as a tour de force of poetic surrealism it appears to go against the author's own doctrine of representation.

Jonson's surrealist antimasque could be defended, as a mimesis of the workings of the human mind; but the energy with which it represents the mind's power to flout nature makes the defence shaky. The concept of Phant'sy breaks with the realist strain in his own theory of the antimasque, and fits into a different tradition of thought which he had previously resisted. This comes from the Italian court entertainments which he professed to despise, and continues through the rival poets who occasionally broke his virtual monopoly of masque writing for the court – Daniel, Campion and Chapman. This tradition frankly accepts the 'unnatural' or surreal aspects of the masque, and thematises the special turns of consciousness and modes of perception which it calls into play. So Campion generates the action of his *Lords' Masque* (1613) from the initial appearance of Mania (madness) and her displacement by the allied but benign figure of Entheus (poetic fury). Chapman constructs the antimasque of his *Memorable Masque* (1613) around the figure of Capriccio, who represents the arbitrary power of the mind to change or recreate reality. Jonson's Phant'sy is evidently a close relative.

Chapman's Capriccio was the first attempt to personify the spirit of this new sub-genre – the antimasque. The figure is closely based on Ripa, whose characterisation emphasises concepts such as extraordinariness, changeability, variety and *phantasia*.[59] In the procession before the performance Capriccio rode in a chariot covered with decorations 'all composed à la grotesca'.[60] Grotesques are the aesthetic equivalent of those unnatural recombinations of natural forms produced by *phantasia*, which Ripa says is the source of Capriccio's eccentricities. Jonson condemned grotesques, agreeing with Vitruvius: 'he complaines of their painting *Chimaera's*, by the vulgar unaptly called *Grottesque*: Saying, that men who were borne truly to study, and emulate nature, did nothing but make monsters against nature; which *Horace* so laught at'.[61] Jones by contrast was interested in grotesques, and also prepared to use 'capriccio' as a term of approval in his comments on architecture. So in emulating Chapman's Capriccio in his own figure of Phant'sy Jonson seemed to be adopting a point of view indulgent to ideas he normally found intolerable.

By being both proprietorial and adventurous, wanting to make any new developments his own, he got into a fix. The form of the antimasque as he evolved it therefore incorporated a conflict, between fidelity to an Aristotelian imitation of nature, as exemplified in his own comic drama, and a self-conscious openness to the workings of *phantasia* or imagination. Jonson's attempt to project this conflict onto his difficult relationship with Jones suggests his inability to resolve it in his own work. It was inherited by the poets who succeeded him as Jones's collaborators in the 1630s, but for those less strenuous souls it ceased to be problematic. In Shirley's *Triumph of Peace* (1634), for example, the figure of Fancy is 'sole presenter of the antimasques';[62] but these, as well as parading bizarre and grotesque creations, also accommodate more prosaic comedy or satire. Fantasy and realism have come to coexist.

Antimasquers

In Jones's designs for antimasquers, and for others who played histrionic roles in the action of the masques, this coexistence of realism and fantasy seems to be there from the beginning. It was in his interest not only to learn the figurative canon established by Vasari's authoritative account of Italian art, but to practise as many types of figuration as possible, so as to build up a knowledge of the whole history, past and present, Italian and extra-Italian, which gave meaning to Vasari's preferences. In so far as he saw the masques as 'pictures with light and motion', the authorities whom he read for guidance offered a potentially catholic approach to figurative representation. The writer he most consulted was Lomazzo. The very lay-out of Lomazzo's treatise seems to anticipate the order of Jones's priorities as a figurative designer for the masques. The first book deals with the proportions of figures, and the second largely with what the English translator calls 'Actions and Gestures' and Lomazzo simply 'moti', motions or movements. This order corresponds to Jones's main concerns, firstly with the sober and graceful figures of the masquers, secondly with the animated or often agitated figures of the antimasquers. As for the composition of figures into *storie*, Lomazzo reinforces the traditional recommendation from Alberti onwards of variety – in body type, age, sex, nationality, attitude, and every appropriate aspect of the figural ensemble.[63] Variety was exactly the criterion the Queen had invoked when she ordered Jonson to bring the antimasque into being. However, it was Jones who was readier to fulfil the spirit of her command.

The extent of Jones's eclecticism, and its relationship to Jonson's less eclectic approach to the antimasque, can be gauged by comparing two of their collaborative works. When Jonson wrote new antimasques for the repeat performance of *Pleasure Reconciled to Virtue*, Jones sketched one of his new designs next to a drawing for the original production. The earlier design is for Hercules' bowl-bearer, who appeared with Comus in the first of the original antimasques, and Jones has appropriately adapted it from an engraving by Marcantonio of a Bacchanalian scene on an antique sarcophagus.[64] The later one is for a pair of Welsh dancers, in an antimasque for the second production; this is derived from a sixteenth-century German print,[65] the alien, outdated costumes condescendingly suggesting the foreignness and provinciality of the Welsh (whose speech also is guyed in the dialogue). On the same sheet antique and modern figures rub shoulders, which is in order: Jones is simply following Jonson in his more experimental vein, since the rewritten version is deliberately far from the original. By comparison, the same wide disparity in the designs for *Oberon* (1611) goes against Jonson's concept of the production. Jones's drawing for the satyrs in the antimasque (plate 75) is again derived from a print of an antique scene by Marcantonio (plate 76).[66] There is also a design for the fays or fairies who, while they appeared in the main masque, had roles akin to those of the antimasquers: they wear sixteenth-century or medieval dress, with fantastic additions such as bats' wings or animal headgear.[67] Since Jonson planned this masque as a serious pastiche of a Greek satyr-play, the classicising design for the satyrs is appropriate, the quaint medievalising design for the fays not at all. It may accord with the inclinations of the chief masquer, Prince Henry, but scarcely with the poet's plan.

Jonson's eventual burlesque of Jones as Vangoose, the ludicrous 'Projector' of antimasques, indicates that he found this range of inventiveness a denial of true art. Vangoose is made to pour scorn on the very idea of imitating nature: 'Now, me vould bring in some dainty new ting, dat never vas, nor never sall be, in de *rebus natura* . . .'[68] The broadness of the satire screens an attempt to pass off as common sense what is really theoretical polemic. Jonson must have been aware of perfectly respectable neo-Platonic arguments against his own Aristotelian position that art is strictly confined to the imitation of nature. Recent Italian critics had elaborated out of Plato's *Sophist* a distinction between 'eikastic' and 'phantastic' imitation: 'The first imitates things which exist: the second feigns things which are non-existent.'[69] This explanation comes from Gregorio Comanini's *Il Figino* (1591), a text with which Jones at least had some acquaintance.[70] In effect, Jonson's Vangoose is a satire on the concept of phantastic imitation, and Jones's tolerance of it. Another character asks: 'what *Hans Flutterkin* is this . . . doe's build or frame Castles in the Aire?'[71] One of Jones's later antimasques has exactly such a motif, 'a great city sustained by a rainbow'. This city in the air is inhabited by Sleep and his sons, one of whom is Phantaste, 'the presenter . . . of anything that may be imagined'.[72]

But rather than realising Jonson's worst fears, Jones seems to be following an intelligible line of his own. Although his thinking about phantasy and the antimasque can only be deduced from his actual designs and from comments made on other, related topics, a coherent view does emerge. A helpful passage in the Roman Sketchbook is that about 'capricious ornaments', by which he means the inventive, irrational architectural ornament deriving from Michelangelo, which boldly composes disparate formal motifs together. He argues that these should only be used in interiors or gardens, while architectural exteriors should be 'masculine and unaffected'; and reinforces the point with an analogy:

> as outwardly euery wyse ma[n] carrieth a grauiti in Publicke Places, whear ther is nothing els looked for, & yt inwardly hath his Immaginacy set free, and sumetimes licenciously flying out . . .[73]

Plate 75. Jones, Satyrs, for *Oberon*, Chatsworth

The series of oppositions set up in this argument – between outer and inner, public and private, masculine and feminine, wisdom and imagination, gravity and licence – has suggestive implications for all Jones's work, not just his architecture. The concept of 'Immaginacy' is especially powerful, and linked with the notion of the 'Cappresious' points towards the characterisations of the antimasque by Jonson and Chapman as the domain of Capriccio or Phant'sy. A view of the antimasque could be extrapolated from this brief discussion, seeing it as an area where imaginative licence is properly permitted, but an area contained by and subordinate to the commanding wisdom of the main masque.

Such a view is supplemented by Jones's contemporary Franciscus Junius, in his treatise written for Lord Arundel, *The Painting of the Ancients*. Through his First Book he argues insistently that the power of imitation in art must be assisted by the power of phantasy. He appeals to the authority of a range of classical writers, and cites Plato's distinction between eikastic and phantastic imitation:

Plate 76. Marcantonio, Satyrs abducting
a Nymph

the first medleth onely with things seene, whilest they are set before our eyes; the other on the contrary studieth also to expresse things prefigured only and represented by the phantasie.[74]

Junius advises that the artist's faculty of phantasy should be exercised and refined; time must be devoted to 'the nurturing of Imagination'.[75] He is so voluble and enthusiastic on this subject that his eventual reaction comes as a surprise. Checks must be placed on phantasy; and the artist must not 'by a malepart wantonnesse of his vainly conceited wit devise all kind of monstrous and prodigious Images of things not knowne in nature . . . '[76] In the end the argument comes back to the Aristotelian sanction endorsed by Jonson, the discipline of the natural. But instead of treating the concept of phantasy with Jonson's awkward ambivalence, Junius has opened it out so sympathetically as to provide a context for the force which Jones calls 'Immaginacy', and shed potential light on how this force is released and disciplined in his antimasques.

What keeps Jones's designs for antimasquers from being mere fantasies in a bad sense, slight or insubstantial, is that they, like the designs for masquers, are treated as exercises in figuration. However scattered their sources, Jones

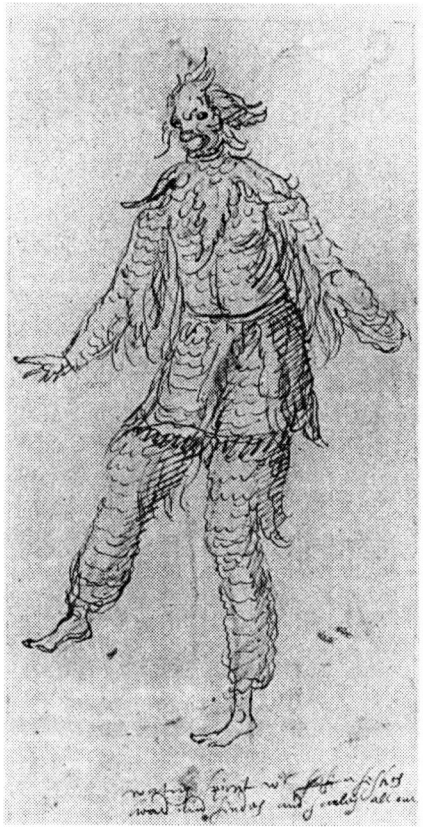

Plate 77. Jones, A Watery Spirit, for
The Temple of Love, Chatsworth

reworks them in his individual way, and brings each figure into relation with the group it is to belong to. Queen Henrietta Maria's masque of 1635, *The Temple of Love*, has an antimasque of elemental spirits, and the Queen herself may have intervened in the design. Two of the spirits are based on drawings by or after Daniel Rabel (plates 77–80), chief designer of court ballets for Louis XIII, the Queen's brother.[77] Whatever pressure there was on him to use these French designs, Jones appropriates them in an active way. They are essentially designs for costume and choreography: the colours and the poses make their points, but the drawing is very meagre. The figures which Jones selects are redrawn in lively, vigorous detail, and re-posed to show their roles in his own ensemble. As a result his figures express a sense of dramatically stylised physical movement far more forcefully than those of Rabel, the specialist in ballet design. A third design, for an Airy Spirit (plate 81), is taken from a remoter source, but one closer to Jones's personal

Plate 78. Daniel Rabel, Entrée des Sorcières et des Monstres, from *Ballet du château de Bicêtre*, 1632, Paris, Bibliothèque Nationale

interests, the engravings of the reliefs on Trajan's Column. In the Roman Sketchbook he had transcribed details of imperial military dress from the Column reliefs; on this occasion an image of a barbarian sparks off a different, novel idea. From a battle scene he has excerpted a figure of a Sarmatian cavalryman with arms outstretched (plate 82, far left), paraphrasing the tiny plates of his armour into a suit of feathers, and his attitude into a movement between running and flying.[78] The context could scarcely be farther from the French ballet designs, but the striking pose of the antique figure lends appropriate contrast to the whole group, and fits into its range of dramatically differentiated concepts.

Such unpredictable associations of images suggest the freedom stimulated by antimasque design. At the same time Jones came to rely often on a familiar stock of material where an exceptional range of figure imagery had already been compiled or devised by other artists. The artists he most often turned to were Cesare Vecellio and Jacques Callot, the first a workaday standby, the second an uncommon stimulus.

Vecellio's *Habiti Antichi e Moderni di Tutto il Mondo* (the expanded second edition came out in 1598) was the most comprehensive and celebrated of the wave of costume books published in the later sixteenth century. Its images presented a conspectus of the nations of Europe, with their antitype, the Turkish empire; and ranged further into north Africa, Asia, America, and even the Arctic. Lomazzo had complained that many artists in composing *storie* 'sinned' by making errors in costume,[79] and Jones

Plate 79. Jones, An Earthy Spirit, for *The Temple of Love*, Chatsworth

was careful to observe this requirement of decorum. Vecellio presented his book as a work of research rather than imagination, based on the information of paintings, sculptures and written texts; and some of the captions refer to sources in antique sculpture or medieval painting.[80] As a result the woodcut figures are not stylistically uniform throughout; but there is an overall effort to assimilate them to a generalised figurative style which, given Vecellio's situation in fin-de-siècle Venice, could be described as conservative late mannerism. Jones was attentive not only to Vecellio's costumes but to the stylistic accentuation of his figures, which he did not always merely transcribe: at times he would redraw them, changing the figurative concept by shifting the idiom. A design for a Polish knight, evidently intended for a courtier in a barriers, is redrawn in this way, to make the figure younger and more graceful; and a preliminary sketch, with the right arm and right leg in different positions, shows the redrawing

Plate 80. Rabel, Entrée des Gelés, from *Ballet de la douairière de Billebahaut*, 1626, Paris, Bibliothèque Nationale

in progress.[81] Conversely, a later design for 'a porter laden' in *Britannia Triumphans* (plate 83) paraphrases Vecellio's image of a Venetian *facchino* (plate 84) with his heroic physique into a less mannerist style, making the figure look 'realistically' stocky and plebeian.[82]

Callot's etchings provided Jones with an unparalleled variety of ideas for antimasquers. Two of the titles for his suites of prints, *Capricci* and *Fantaisies*, suggest how his work chimed in with that tendency of the antimasque to which Jones was sympathetic and Jonson ambivalent or hostile; and the discovery of Callot seems to have coincided with Jonson's departure. His repertory of figures questions simplistic notions of the normal or the natural, comprising grotesque dwarfs, hysterical commedia dell'arte characters, and a social typology slipping below the expected levels of nobles, bourgeois and peasants to gypsies and beggars. The width of the spectrum, stretching far into the 'unnatural', is what Jonson reprehended but for once recognised when he made Phant'sy the presiding spirit of the antimasque. Acknowledging Callot's coverage of that 'fantastic' terrain, Jones then supplemented the main parts of his repertory from the work of other artists. Along with the commedia dell'arte characters he used a set of engravings of masquerade figures by Jacques de Gheyn II; the grotesques were supplemented with the Bosch-like anonymous woodcuts of *Les songes drolatiques de Pantagruel*;[83] and to the images of different ranks of society

Plate 81. Jones, An Airy Spirit, for *The Temple of Love*, Chatsworth

he sometimes added sixteenth-century German prints showing citizens or peasants at their recreations.

The fullest surviving collection of Jones's antimasquer designs is for *Britannia Triumphans* (1638), and here the influence of Callotesque figuration can be most clearly seen. The antimasques comprised a *ballet à entrées* in the French fashion, so that many of the figures are shown dancing, or at least gesticulating, spiritedly. Only one or two may be directly derived from Callot,[84] but the overall liveliness of the poses bears his imprint. In Callot's work the sometimes manic vivacity of the figures is matched by the animation of his graphic style, which his mastery of the etching medium sharply conveys (plate 85). A similar animation is manifest in Jones's preliminary sketches for some of these figures, where a free, bold, quick pen technique, dealing adeptly with foreshortenings and complexities of pose, projects a sense of excited movement (plate 86). This matching of graphic and figural gesture re-enacts Callot's quintessential strength, not as pastiche

Plate 82. Scene from Trajan's Column, from Chacón, *Historia Utriusque Belli Dacici*, 1576, British Library

but as a kind of role-playing. In the finished designs, where much more detail can be read, it becomes apparent how the figurative models used by Jones have been modified in the direction of Callot's style. A design for 'a crier of mouse traps' (plate 87) is derived from two German prints of dancing couples, by Hans Sebald Beham and Aldegrever[85] (plates 88–9). A similar design of a man playing a gridiron (plate 90) combines Aldegrever's male dancer with a masquerader by Jacques de Gheyn II[86] (plate 91). In both cases Jones attenuates the original figure types, which are physically bulky and heavy in their movements, and makes them look thinner and taller. As a result their dancing postures look more sprightly, less earthbound. Their new commedia dell'arte hats indicate the tendency of the changes: Jones has restyled the figures with reference to Callot.

The antimasques of the 1630s for which these figures were designed might seem to have realised Jonson's fears, in that they became balletic episodes in the French style not always too obviously 'sorting with the current, and whole fall of the device'. But if his worst fear was that the 'rare Artist' his collaborator would forsake nature, and abandon mimesis for *phantasia*, he was to be proved wrong. Jones of course understood the enterprise of

Plate 83. Jones, A Porter Laden, for *Britannia Triumphans*, Chatsworth

mimesis in his own way. Designing for antimasques had always allowed him to diversify his figurative skills; designing for ballets gave him a new kind of opportunity to extend them. Performers whose expression was confined to gesture and movement made little sense in the context of spoken drama, which was Jonson's paradigm for the antimasque, and much more in the context of 'picture', which was Jones's. The brief of the painter as defined by the Italian Renaissance tradition, to convey narrative and dramatic themes through the representation of the figure, could now be carried out more fully. While the productions still contained a wealth of prose and poetic dialogue, spoken or sung, the silence of the masquers, ordained by the decorum of courtly behaviour, was now matched by a silence of the anti-masquers, due to the new emphasis on dance and mime. The first silence had offered models of graceful composure, and the chance to work economically

Plate 84. Cesare Vecellio, Facchino

at the graphic qualities given priority by Vasari, approaching *disegno* through *maniera*; the second added the challenge of a more demonstrative language of the body, and a new stimulus to the practice of 'design' in its most basic sense, the technique of figure drawing and the conduct of narrative through the figure.

Plate 85. Callot, The Two Pantaloons, British Museum

Plate 86. Jones, Antimasque Characters, for *Britannia Triumphans*, Chatsworth

Plate 87. Jones, A Crier of Mouse Traps, for *Britannia Triumphans*, Chatsworth

Figures

Plate 88. Hans Sebald Beham, Dancing Couple

Plate 89. Albrecht Aldegrever, Dancing Couple

Plate 90. Jones, A Man with Gridiron and Shoe Horn, for *Britannia Triumphans*, Chatsworth

Figures

Plate 91. Jacques de Gheyn II, Masquerade figures,
Theatre Museum

5

Landscape

The first landscape

The first image that Jones ever presented to his court audience was a landscape, painted on the curtain before *The Masque of Blackness* (1605). Jonson describes it in his published text:

> First, for the *Scene*, was drawne a *Landtschape*, consisting of small woods, and here and there a void place fill'd with huntings; which falling, an artificiall sea was seene to shoote forth, as if it flowed to the land ... The *Masquers* were placed in a great concaue shell like mother of pearle ... [1]

Both the hunting scene and the great sea-shell are derived from the Florentine festival tradition, the first from a curtain painted by Federigo Zuccaro for a comedy celebrating Francesco de' Medici's first marriage in 1565, and the second from a joust for his second marriage in 1579.[2] It was the combination of both that would have struck the English courtiers of 1605, at the outset of Jones and Jonson's long series of masques, the startling transition from land to sea, a kind of montage which expresses the idea of Great Britain as a sea-empire. But the landscape on its own makes an aesthetic statement, and one implying even more than the magnificent inauguration of a court theatre which would come to rival the Medici.

This statement does not depend on the novelty of the image, which is quite unoriginal – the courtiers would not have known this, but they would at least have found it familiar. The idea, derived from Zuccaro's curtain which Jonson and Jones could only have read about, was probably realised by copying one of Antonio Tempesta's hunting prints, much resorted to by Jones, and later used for the interior decoration of the fourth Earl of

Pembroke's newly rebuilt Wilton House. When the courtiers, including the young Pembroke,[3] looked at Jones's curtain, they would have been reminded of the tapestries which covered the walls of their houses and which often used landscape motifs, including scenes of their characteristic recreation, hunting. In this respect the curtain has a topical point. The masque was being presented by the Queen to the King. So as to indulge in public her passion for the arts, which her husband did not share, she had spent a huge amount of his money.[4] His passion, the hunting field, had to be abandoned for the Christmas festivities,[5] of which the masque formed the climax. So the hunting scene appears as a tactful compliment to the King, who has deferred from his own pleasure to the Queen's.

Jones's statement is bound up with Queen Anne's visual compliment, to which it adds an invitation or demand. That is, he tries to get the courtiers to read the curtain aesthetically, not just as a topical allusion. The difficulty of separating these perceptions in his historical context is neatly illustrated by Henry Peacham. Writing 'Of Lant-Skip' in 1612, he lists 'the fairest and most beautifull Landtskips in the world', ending with 'the countrey about Roiston',[6] which everyone knew was King James's favourite hunting place; the flattery is at least appropriate in a drawing manual republished as *The Gentleman's Exercise* and aimed at the gentry class. Jones, much more adventurous, uses the necessary flattery as a means to a less prosaic end. By making the courtiers view familiar imagery of the countryside and country sports in a special, new setting he is trying to induce them to see it as art. It is as if one of the tapestries, half utilitarian and half decorative, which formed the background of their domestic lives, is being set up as an object of scrutiny in its own right, requiring a new sort of attention.[7] He presents them with the new concept of landscape.

Jonson's published text stresses the novelty of the concept by not attempting to anglicise the spelling. In the quarto of 1608 it is 'Landtschape'; in the folio of 1616, to which he devoted so much care, he has the word printed in Gothic type,[8] as if to represent its foreign, northern European origins – this is a new kind of painting, yet to be naturalised in England. Jonson gives a clear textual image of what was to be Jones's ultimate enterprise in the masques, the transferral of a new art into England, here beginning with the newest pictorial genre, which was evolving towards its 'classic' mode at the very moment when *The Masque of Blackness* appeared.

Contemporary writers on art tell the story behind Jonson's self-conscious use of the word (which had first appeared in an English printed text only ten years before).[9] Edward Norgate, writing much later (certainly after the 1620s), still hesitates between the spellings 'Lanscape' and 'Landscape', and calls it 'an art so new in England, and so lately come a shore, as all the language within our four seas cannot find it a name, but a borrowed one... '¹⁰ Peacham, whose drawing book had its first edition the year after *Blackness* was produced, writes:

> Landtskip is a Dutch word, & it is as much as wee should say in English landship, or expressing of the land by hills, woodes, Castles, seas, valleys, ruines, hanging rocks, Citties, Townes, &c. as farre as may be shewed within our Horizon.[11]

To define the word he keeps up the idea of a language, sliding metaphorically from 'say' to 'expressing', and suggesting that landscape has a vocabulary, some of the main items of which he lists. Later, Norgate pursues a similar metaphor: 'the best in that kind that ever I saw speake Dutch, viz. Paulo Brill ... and his Contemporary, Adam Elshamer, termed by the Italians *Diavolo per gli cose piccole*'.[12] We seem to have a surfeit of languages here – Dutch, German (by implication, for Elsheimer), Italian – but the comment is less confusing than it looks. Norgate sees landscape as a northern pictorial 'language' which has become intelligible in Italy. And so he continues in the same vein in his definition of the landscape vocabulary as

> nothing but a picture of *Gli belle Vedute*, or beautifull prospect of Feilds, Cities, Rivers, Castles, Mountaines, Trees or what soever delightfull view the Eye takes pleasure in, nothing more in Art or Nature affording soe great variety and beautie as beholding the farre distant Mountaines and strange scituation of ancient Castles... most of which have been very well designed after the life by Peter Brugell of Antwerp.[13]

What becomes clear is that Peacham and Norgate are not describing what we would call 'Dutch' landscape painting at all, if by that we understand the naturalistic art which arose in Holland in the early seventeenth century. The pictorial vocabulary which they detail is that of the School of Antwerp, reaching its apogee in Brueghel and later naturalised in Rome by Paul Bril. Norgate's singling out of Elsheimer, the Venetianised German who associated with the Flemish Bril in Rome, does imply a more nuanced history of landscape, in which 'Dutch' stands for not just 'Netherlandish' but 'Northern', and the importance of Rome as the crucible in which the genre was Italianised, before being redirected north, is stressed. But this history is contradicted by his general history of the genre; and the similarity of that to what Peacham was writing in 1606 gives us the simplistic notion of landscape which the average English gentleman interested in the arts would have entertained not only at the outset of Jones's masque productions but for quite a while afterwards.

What Jones is showing the courtly spectators of his masque curtain is something more up-to-date. It sounds from the description like one of the wooded landscapes of a modern Antwerp painter such as Coninxloo or Vinckboons, whose style was being transmitted to England by Isaac Oliver.[14] The same style, derived from little known aspects of Brueghel the elder's oeuvre, appears in Italy in the prints of Tempesta, probably by way of his Flemish master Stradano (van der Straet).[15] So if Jones copied a Tempesta print he would have produced something stylistically unfamiliar to all except the few connoisseurs who kept up with the more recherché work which Oliver produced beside his portraits. The majority of the courtiers would be looking at familiar imagery, presented in an unusual way and rendered in an unfamiliarly advanced style. The implied invitation to new ways of looking and to an enlarged conception of art is of course the keynote for all Jones's succeeding masque designs.

One change in thinking about landscape which coincides with the first phase of Jones's masque productions can be traced through the two editions of Peacham's manual of drawing for the gentry. In the first edition of 1606, called *The Art of Drawing*, landscape is said to be 'among those things which we call *Parerga* [a term from Pliny], which are additions or adiuncts rather of ornament, than otherwise necessary . . . ' It is secondary, marginal: 'Seldome is it drawne by it selfe, but in respect & for the sake of some thing els.' But in the new edition of 1612, now entitled *The Gentleman's Exercise*, Peacham no longer sees landscape as necessarily peripheral:

> If it be not drawne by it selfe or for the owne sake, but in respect, and for the sake of some thing else: it falleth out among those things which we call *Parerga* . . . [16]

Evidently the new climate of interest in the arts, promoted by the Queen and Prince Henry, of which Jones's masques were such a vital manifestation, has produced a shift in understanding of the new genre. The change is expressed at exactly the point where Jones's efforts were focussed, the point where the potential patrons of a new English art are being offered advice and instruction in the latest developments by someone who professes to be abreast of them. Peacham of course was an amateur artist and a populariser; Jones on the contrary really was abreast of everything new. Peacham is perhaps articulating a shift in taste which is being brought about by various factors, but by Jones above all.

Prospects and 'Prospective'

The ambivalence which Peacham reveals in the concept of 'landscape', as meaning a representation which can be either accessory or autonomous, is implicitly present in the way Jones uses landscape to inaugurate his masques. The principal scene of *Blackness*, revealed when the landscape curtain is drawn aside, is the maritime equivalent of a landscape, a seascape. At least, that is how the spectators were meant to see it, as the description suggests:

> an artificiall sea was seene to shoote forth, as if it flowed to the land, raysed with waues, which seemed to move, and in some places the billow to breake, as imitating that orderly disorder, which is common in nature.
>
> The *Masquers* were placed in a great concaue shell ... These thus presented, the *Scene* behind, seemed a vast sea (and vnited with this that flowed forth) from the termination, or *horizon* of which (being the leuell of the *State*, which was placed in the vpper end of the hall) was drawne, by the lines of *Prospectiue*, the whole worke shooting downewards, from the eye; which *decorum* made it more conspicuous, and caught the eye a farre off with a wandring beauty. To which was added an obscure and cloudy night-piece, that made the whole set of.[17]

The 'seeming' of the maritime scene is partly contrived by stage machinery, but ultimately by painting; it is not just a pageant (the name given to a large, detached scenic unit) but a picture, just as the preceding landscape had been.

Jones makes a point of this. The surviving manuscript of the masque, associated with the production in 1605 and so preceding by three years the quarto text from which the description is quoted, contains practically none of it, only the barest references to the 'artificiall sea' and the 'entire concave shell'.[18] When Jonson amplified the description for publication he must have had Jones at his elbow. The phraseology is mostly his own ('shooting' seems a favourite metaphor),[19] but he must have needed Jones's prompting to help explain the novel use of perspective. The explanation is not easy to follow – Jonson's syntax almost falters in trying to represent the new pictorial syntax – and suggests an anxiety that a new mode of scenic representation should be properly recorded, expounded and valued. Since the innovation derives from Jones, the anxiously intricate description of it must be motivated by him.

The anxiety is to get the courtiers to read the scene in a particular way. The landscape which precedes it is a cue. It sets up a series of related oppositions to define the spectators' view. It is associated with the King; what follows is a setting for the Queen. It represents land; what follows is a representation of the sea. It is a picture in two dimensions; what follows is meant to be seen as a picture in three dimensions.

Why did Jones use the genre of landscape from which to deduce the conventions of perspective, in this first attempt to restructure his audience's habits of seeing? Precisely I think because of its shifting, enlarging scope, because it was on the way from being a mere background or setting to becoming a representation of all nature, a genre which could include everything. In one sense Jones's visual sequence seems to run this history backwards, since his first picture shows landscape in its own right and his second relegates it to a mere background: the sea in the distance and the 'obscure and cloudy night-piece', that is, the night sky with clouds, moon and stars.[20] But in another sense the second 'picture', the tableau vivant of the masquers, for all its allegorical panoply and staffage, is just as much a seascape as the first is a landscape, just as extensive, varied and inclusive a 'prospect', to use the contemporary word that will encompass both. Its status as a 'prospect' is implied in the statement that it 'was drawne, by the lines of *Prospectiue*': contemporary English writers often assimilated the Italian word for perspective, 'prospettiva', to the English 'prospect', so making the concepts of perspective and landscape view overlap.[21] This is not merely an impertinent confusion, since landscape could demonstrate the workings of perspective more fully than other kinds of painting, showing, for example, the use of aerial as well as linear perspective. Jonson's description here implies the overlap of the two concepts: the technical phrase (surely supplied by Jones) 'termination, or *horizon*' comes from discussions of perspective – Paolo Pino, for example, uses the phrase 'origionte o termine'; but the term 'horizon' also belongs in writing about landscape, and is used and explained by Karel van Mander, who published the first full discussion of the genre in 1604.[22]

The alliance of landscape and perspective in Jones's first masque was a logical gambit, but probably too taxing for the Jacobean courtiers. They were not familiar enough with conventions of landscape to use it as an aid to perspective vision. Nor were they offered more than an imperfect point of view from which to see Jones's scenic compositions, let alone revise their habits of seeing. The description says that the horizon of the scene was 'the leuell of the *State*', that is, only the King and anyone close to him had a perfect view of the perspective. This 'decorum' would have made the view of the generality of courtiers more difficult, although the description fudges the issue by talking eloquently about the view of a generalised 'eye'. In fact this description, published three years after the event, and not in the manuscript version of the masque, probably needs to be seen as a retrospective account of Jones's intentions, which could only be fully realised in Jonson's prose (and even that is put under strain). His attempt to use landscape, with its new possibilities, as a seminal motif, an aid for showing the courtiers how to picture the world in terms of perspective, proved too ambitious an enterprise for one masque.

From scenic to pictorial landscape: defining nature

To change ingrained habits of vision Jones needed to adopt new forms of scenic representation, which could be assimilated to the new forms of pictorial representation – new at least in England – which he was striving to advertise. Whereas the landscape curtain which commenced *The Masque of Blackness* showed the most modern kind of painting, the 'great concaue shell' containing the masquers which it revealed was basically an old-fashioned structure, the sort of device which was by now of some antiquity in the history of the theatre. Jones had tried to make it part of a picture, a seascape structured by the conventions of linear perspective. His failure in the eyes of the court is recorded by Dudley Carleton, who was knowledgeable about the arts, and no doubt sensitive to innovation. His comments on the main tableau are initially approving: 'The presentation of the masque at the first drawing of the traverse was very fair . . . ' But he saw nothing new; on the contrary, he refers to 'the Queen's Maske . . . or rather her Pageant', picking on the outmoded scenic machinery.[23] Apparently it was not going to be easy for Jones to use the theatre to make pictures. But the incoherence between his pictorial and theatrical means was to be gradually resolved as the masque productions progressed. Eventually the landscape which he can only represent superficially would become, as the Italians said, *praticabile*, spatially viable; the masquers would inhabit and animate it. For this to happen, for pictorial space to be realised as scenic space so that a mise en scène can then look like a picture, Jones has to develop his stage technology; and these mechanical advances will involve changes in his representation of space in general and landscape in particular.

This rapprochement between Jones's pictorial and scenic resources, which makes him able to 'stage' landscapes, crucially involves a more radical use of perspective to define space. He had created the conditions for this in his first masque, by abandoning the old-fashioned method of scenic units dispersed around the hall in favour of a unitary setting, positioned and structured according to the rules of perspective. But by making his principal stage set (the 'great . . . shell') a variant of a pageant machine he reactivated familiar habits of vision and negated the effect of the perspective. So long as the masque sets used what were essentially sophisticated pageant machines – like the floating island in *The Masque of Beauty* (1608) or the revolving sphere in *The Haddington Masque* (1607) – they were resistant to articulation and revision in perspective terms. They were in consequence imperfect vehicles for staging landscape. Several years after *Blackness* Jones designed an entertainment for the Earl of Salisbury at Theobalds, to mark the handing over of the house to King James. The main scene was '*a glorious place, figuring the* Lararium, *or seat of the household-gods . . . Within, as farder off, in* Landtschap, *were seene clouds riding . . .* '[24] Once again, in the Folio, Jonson uses Gothic type for the exotic term 'Landtschap'; but it obviously signifies much less than it does when applied to the curtain for *Blackness*. Although it denotes a comparable novelty, describing the context which the natural world provides for the action, it refers to a mere background, which can be perceived as that and no more. No doubt Salisbury's entertainment was on a much more reduced scale than a court masque, and elaborate scenery was out of the question. But the point is that the court masques were no more scenically advanced than this modest domestic production, as yet.

It may have been Queen Anne who was the real devotee of floating islands, revolving thrones, and all that other retardataire paraphernalia, since the first surviving design for a thoroughgoing perspective set comes in a commission for Prince Henry – St George's Portico in *Prince Henry's Barriers* (1610). Although this is largely an architectural design, it is related to the ruin scenes which not surprisingly figured in the work of contemporary Roman landscapists, and it contains traces of the *vedute* of Paul Bril and his pupil Willem van Nieulandt, in which architecture and landscape meet.[25] The first 'pure' landscape perspective seems to occur in *The Lords' Masque* of 1613. Campion's description runs:

> the scene was divided into two parts . . . the lower part being first discovered . . . there appeared a wood in perspective, the innermost part being of relieve or whole round, the rest painted. On the left hand from the seat was a cave, and on the right a thicket . . . [26]

The scheme resembles that for St George's Portico, which in the left foreground has Merlin's tomb, from which he emerges, and on the right Chivalry's cave, each being assimilated into the general vista of Roman ruins. But Campion's description implies (as does the action which follows) that the wood, although logically it is the inclusive motif of the entire scene, is viewed in practice not as an overall milieu but as one in a series of scenic items. Quite possibly Jones meant the ensemble to be viewed as a landscape, but Campion (who was not his regular collaborator), and probably most spectators, saw it in old-fashioned terms as a collection of scenic units which happened to be ordered in a perspective scheme. Such an irrational conception of perspective, as a device for ordering different scenic locales rather than for representing space realistically, was quite familiar at the time, and it persisted in the French theatre until the next decade.[27] Campion's plot, which has Orpheus emerging from the thicket on the right to argue with Mania coming from the cave on the left, scarcely helps, since it divides the scene symbolically and resists a unitary view of it. In fact, his thicket and cave are not far in advance of medieval 'mansions', like the Bower of Flora and the House of Night in his earlier *Lord Hay's Masque* (1607).[28] Jones the innovator had a lot to contend with. The difficulty which some of his earliest spectators had in 'reading' perspective may have been overcome by now; but the root of that disability, the old habit of viewing masque sets as aggregations of discrete parts – the habit which Jones and Jonson had turned their backs on in 1605 – seems not to have wholly disappeared.

A parallel problem occurs in the development of landscape. If landscape, according to the standard characterisation given by Peacham and Norgate, is to have a wide sweep and include all the features of the natural scene, it must nevertheless be structured and circumscribed in order to be intelligible as a representation. Karel van Mander warns against 'showing . . . too many things', which will 'prevent the achievement of harmony'. He recommends the example of Italian artists such as Titian, whose landscapes are rationally ordered by single-point perspective.[29] Sir Henry Wotton in *The Elements of Architecture* (1624), transposing the concept of landscape into a discussion of the natural 'prospect' which the architect will choose to be visible from a house, condemns 'vaste and indefinite viewes'.[30] Again, intelligibility requires definition.

In place of a diffuse multiplicity, the new scenography requires unity, the new landscape clarity. This is the direction in which Jones is moving, as his scenic resources and his pictorial aims gradually converge to facilitate the representation of landscape in the masques. His progress is not only to be discerned visually, as the designs evolve beyond the aesthetic conservatism of his audience, but can be tracked through the texts of the masques too. For another problem in the landscape tradition, as we have seen, is how to conceptualise its subject, nature – is it a background against which the human world defines itself, or is it the principle of all life, the universal milieu? – and this is a problem actually discussed in some of the masques Jones designed. These discussions signpost his way, since they cannot but influence the accompanying designs. A masque like *Oberon* (1611), which is actually about nature (in its relation to civilisation), is going to make the picturing of nature in the theatre a notably self-conscious activity.

The problem of nature is also illustrated by another production of 1613, Chapman's *Memorable Masque*. The set was a rock, a very old-fashioned motif, as the poet jokingly admits in the opening speech. On one side is the Temple of Honour. 'On the other side of the rock grew a grove, in whose utmost part appeared a vast, withered, and hollow tree; being the bare receptacle of the baboonery', that is, the baboons who dance the antimasque.[31] Again there is a symbolic contrast of localities, between the arts of civilisation and the rudeness of wild nature. The masquers are Virginian princes, which raises familiar questions about the noble savage and the life lived according to nature. The rock symbolises a neutral concept of 'the natural', which can either raise itself to the level of cultivated humanity or sink towards the bestial. 'Nature' is ambivalent, and its representation is therefore problematic.

This debate about nature receives its classic articulation in a 'masque' which stands to one side of the court tradition, Milton's *Comus*. By that time (1634) it was no longer a live issue for Jones and the poets he worked with; in the Caroline court different ideological debates had come to the fore. But in the court masques of twenty years before it certainly affected the development of Jones's repertory of designs. If the representation of nature was problematic, and if landscape was in the most general sense the representation of nature, then it could not be drafted directly into Jones's scenography.

There is one group of designs from the earlier period which show this problem being worked through. The various drawings for the set of *Oberon* (1611) seem to relate to two different versions of the masque, and the difference between the first project and the second shows a revision of Jones's original conception. The crux is the scene-change from the 'dark rock', which is the habitat of the satyrs in the antimasque, to the 'bright and glorious palace' of Oberon, the Fairy Prince, the wildness of nature giving way to civilisation. The idea Jones arrived at was to show the palace growing out of the rock, as if the rude materiality of nature is susceptible of being formed, refined and idealised through human artistry.[32] To make the transition visually plausible and produce a continuum from nature to art, he designed the rock not just as a scenic unit in the old-fashioned pageant style (like the sort of thing called for in the *The Memorable Masque* or *The Haddington Masque*)[33] but as something between that and a landscape (plate 92). The process can be gauged by looking at one of the illustrations to an account of a French court entertainment of 1573, the *Ballet des provinces de la France*.[34] There, an old-style pageant rock is shown against a rocky, mountainous landscape background (plate 93). Jones has fused the two conventions, assimilating the scenic image to the pictorial one. The result looks like a stylised excerpt from one of the mountain landscapes of the Brueghel tradition, or a theatrical adaptation of the rock and mountain prints of Jones's contemporary Goltzius.[35] To see how the design is moving tentatively towards the Antwerp landscape style we can compare it with a later design, for 'A Mountainous Valley' (plate 94), which combines the backgrounds of two landscape etchings by Paul Bril (plates 120, 127), and turns out like a more naturalistic version of the *Oberon* rock scene.

The later design is for a back shutter, part of the elaborate system of moveable side wings and back flats which Jones's theatre gradually perfected, whereas the *Oberon* design is for a *scena ductilis*, or relatively simple pair of flats at the front of the stage. Comparison of the two demonstrates how the development of Jones's stage machinery facilitated the pictorialisation of his imagery of nature. As the process goes forward, the kind of commentary which the texts make on scenery alters correspondingly. Comments which stress the ingenious contrivance of scenic effects give way to what are in

Plate 92. Jones, Scene of Rocks, for *Oberon*, Chatsworth

fact pictorial descriptions, as if the writers are actually viewing pictures and not theatrical scenes. Campion's comment, 'there appeared a wood in perspective, the innermost part being of relieve or whole round, the rest painted',[36] is typical of the earlier kind of commentary, which reveals how things work and invites admiration for the designer's Dedalus-like skill. Twenty years later, this is Townshend in the text of *Tempe Restored*:

> Then the scene is changed into an oriental sky such as appears at the sun rising, and afar off is seen a landscape and a calm sea, which did terminate the horizon; in the hither part was a haven with a citadel, and opposite to that were broken grounds and craggy rocks.[37]

He is, in effect, describing a landscape painting; and this is not untypical. The word 'landscape' occurs frequently when the Caroline masque poets are writing about scenery, as a familiar term in those pictorialising descriptions which are by then the norm. Jones himself is very much behind these descriptions, giving cues to his audiences, and it would seem by now that when he represented the natural world in his masques he wished it to be understood that he was exhibiting landscapes.

What has become in the meantime of the problematic ambivalence of the concept of nature? It is difficult to say. But certainly the move from

Plate 93. Rock pageant, for *Ballet des provinces de la France*, British Library

Plate 94. Jones, A Mountainous Valley, Chatsworth

the scenic to the pictorial, from the stress on ingenious contrivances and operations in the earlier Jacobean masques to the new stress on harmonious visual effects in the Caroline masques, seems to be accompanied by a shift in the content of the masques, in the issues which are dealt with. The Caroline masques, with their sophisticated machinery, are able to show contrary aspects of nature in a 'natural' way, not crowded into a single scenic tableau but sequentially, storms succeeding fair weather, for example.[38] But these newly complex resources are used to represent a simpler concept of nature. It ceases to be problematic and figures merely instrumentally. Whereas the Jacobean masques treat nature as a philosophical issue, the Caroline masques treat it as a symbolic system – they present the natural world in a frankly aestheticised fashion, as if it were a neo-Platonic veil covering higher realities. In this context, *Comus* can be seen not only as a kind of homage on Milton's part to the masque genre, which it undoubtedly is, but a sharp critique of a certain philosophical complacency in the Caroline masques – since it turns on a passionate debate about what nature is, and what moral and political injunctions nature lays on human beings. The court masque of the 1630s had closed down this kind of debate, perhaps because both the

King and Queen had an interest in maintaining an unproblematic idea of nature – Henrietta Maria because of her preoccupation with neo-Platonism, Charles I because of his attempt to consolidate a political order undisturbed by serious divisions (as Milton showed, debates about nature turn into debates about politics).

Jones's response to this changing ideological climate is difficult to gauge. Unfortunately there is a gap in the design record of almost ten years, between *Oberon* (1611) and *Pan's Anniversary* (1620), from which no drawings of natural scenery survive. When they reappear in the 1620s they are fully articulated landscapes. From their format and composition we can deduce, if not the cause, at least the vehicle of Jones's changed representations of nature. He has evidently been thinking about Vitruvius's scenic types, and especially the last of these, the Satyric Scene.

The Satyric Scene

Vitruvius's three types of stage scene are arranged in a hierarchy, with the Satyric Scene at the bottom. It is rustic rather than urban, and it shows the countryside in its wild, uncultivated aspect (plate 95). Even so, Vitruvius indicates, its various features are subject to a kind of informal organisation. In Daniele Barbaro's version, which Jones used, this is made clear:

> the Satyric Scenes are decorated with trees, and caves, and mountains, and other rustic and rural features, arranged as in landscaping (in forma di giardini).[39]

The countryside is viewed as a natural garden, a landscape. Barbaro uses the word 'paese' (landscape) in his commentary on this passage: 'la scena era di verdure, d'acque, di paesi di lontani colorita'.[40] This association of the Satyric Scene with landscape is authorised by Vitruvius, and simply draws out an implication in his chapter on mural painting, where he says that outdoor places were decorated with motifs taken from the three types of stage scene ('painted / wth ye Prospectiue / of Sceanes' Jones notes), while walkways were painted with motifs from gardening and the countryside:

> ne i luoghi aperti ... disegnarono le fronti delle Scene all' usanza Tragica, overo Comica, overo Satirica: ma ne i luoghi da passeggiare per essere gli spacii lunghi si diedero ad ornarli di varietà di giardini esprimendo le imagini di certe proprietà di paesi: perche dipingono i porti, le Promontore, i Liti, i fiumi, le fonti, gli tratte delle acque, i tempii, i boschi sacri, i monti, le pecore, i pastori ...[41]
>
> in outdoor places ... they depicted stage settings in the Tragic or Comic or Satyric modes: but places for walking, because of their

finissima seta di variati colori, le ripe & i sassi copiosi de diuerse conche marine, di limache & altri animaletti, di tronchi di coralli di piu colori, di matre perle, & di granchi marini inserti ne i sassi, con tanta diuersità di cose belle : che a uolerle scriuere tutte : io farei troppo lungo in questa parte. Io non dirò de i Satiri : delle Ninfe, delle Sirene, & diuersi monstri o animali strani, fatti con tal artificio, che acconci sopra gli huomini & fanciulli secondo la grandezza loro, & quelli andando & mouendosi secondo la sua natura, rappresentauano essi animali uiui. Et se non ch'io farei troppo prolisso : io narrarei gli habiti superbi di alcuni pastori, fatti di ricchi drappi d'oro & di seta, foderati di finissime pelle d'animali seluatici. Direi anchora de i uestimenti d'alcuni pescatori, liquali non furono men ricchi de gli altri, le reti de iquali erano di fila d'oro fino, & d'altri suoi strumenti tutti dorati. Direi di alcune pastorelle & Ninfe, gli habiti delle quali sprezzauano l'Auaritia. Ma io lasarò tutte queste cose ne gli intelletti de i giudiciosi Architetti : liquali faranno sempre di queste cose, quando trouaranno simili padroni conformi alle lor uoglie : & gli dono piena licenza, con larga mano, di operare tutto quello che uorranno.

Plate 95. Serlio, Satyric Scene, from *Architettura*, 1560

length, were decorated with a variety of landscape scenery, images depicting the character of certain localities: for they paint ports, promontories, shores, rivers, springs, straits, temples, sacred groves, mountains, cattle, shepherds...

Jones summarises in the margin: 'in wakying / plases. landscip'. This is the decorative style closest to the Satyric Scene, using motifs from landscape gardening. The list of motifs contains a further implication, which Barbaro draws out for himself. In his earlier commentary on the Satyric Scene he suggests how it is applicable to the modern theatre: 'The Satyric had forest and woodland motifs suitable for shepherds and nymphs, and similar things...'[42] In other words it is suitable for pastoral drama, a burgeoning form in sixteenth-century Italy.[43]

This triple association – of the Satyric Scene, landscape and pastoral – is backed up by other treatises which Jones read. Alberti, following Vitruvius, has a chapter in *Dell'architettura* on mural painting, where he compares painting to poetry and divides both into three types, in descending order of importance. Behind this is presumably the rhetorical distinction, transferred to poetry, between high, middle and low styles; but Alberti's description suggests that he has in the forefront of his mind the Vitruvian hierarchy of scenic types:

> The type that portrays the great deeds of great men, worthy of memory, differs from that which describes the habits of private citizens, and again from that depicting the life of the peasants... the last mentioned will be suitable for gardens, for it is the most pleasing of all.
>
> Our minds are cheered beyond measure by the sight of paintings depicting the delightful countryside, harbours, fishing, hunting, swimming, the games of shepherds...[44]

The same sequence of ideas occurs in Barbaro's Vitruvius: 'the life of the peasants... gardens... the delightful countryside... the games of shepherds' – the Satyric Scene, landscape, pastoral.

Finally Serlio, who actually published well-known designs for the Vitruvian Scenes, gives a list of motifs for the Satyric Scene – 'trees, rocks, hills, mountains, grasses, flowers, and fountains'[45] – which conflates Vitruvius's description of the Scene with his description of landscape painting. And he actually undertakes to explain how scenery designed for satyr-plays in antiquity may be reasonably adapted for modern pastoral drama. His argument is rather tortuous, but the gist of it is that a setting suitable for the unbridled, instinctual lives of satyrs can also be a context for the uncouth directness of 'la gente rustica'. He insists that such scenery can be beautiful, even extravagantly splendid; and describes a magnificent example devised by Girolamo Genga, court architect to the Duke of Urbino.[46]

The adaptation of the Satyric Scene to pastoral, a mode in which the natural life is represented self-consciously, becoming a metaphor for exploring the private and public concerns of a sophisticated audience, makes the representation of nature a means to an end, so that questions about 'nature' itself may be bypassed. And the closer pastoral scene-design comes to landscape painting the more it will take on an aesthetic character in which natural appearances are idealised, calculated to engage the spectator in an experience of pure beauty. Alberti's stress on the pleasure of landscape, and Serlio's on the luxurious beauty of scenes which imitate and surpass nature, are consonant here. Given these modern readings of Vitruvius, to which Jones must have paid attention, we begin to understand how landscape became an important element in his scenic repertory, superseding less developed representations of nature where interesting problems were somewhat awkwardly canvassed through the older scenic tradition.

Jones's view of landscape painting: the case of Paul Bril

The Satyric Scene, reinterpreted in modern Vitruvian theory, offered Jones a matrix on which the pictorial conventions of landscape painting could be reconciled with the practical demands of scene-design. This formulation necessarily begs a question, since who was to say what the pictorial conventions of landscape painting were? To begin with, it had no rules. Belonging among the lowest genres, and associated with Pliny's idea of *parerga*, it seemed to escape the legislative gaze. The fact that this humble and marginal kind of painting had become during the sixteenth century a genre in its own right seems not to have mattered: it was still considered unworthy of regulation. To be more precise, the criticism seemed to be that it was innately unsusceptible of regulation, being associated with Flemish empiricism rather than Italian idealism. The famous dismissal by Michelangelo[47] suggests that it is beyond consideration. Paolo Pino declares it is an art which would have no point in the Italian context:[48] in theory it does not exist.

Landscape painting therefore, at the beginning of the seventeenth century when Jones began his career, existed as a set of practices, or rather sets of practices associated with different traditions, the chief being the Venetian and the Flemish. During the decades when he was designing his masques, and incorporating an increasing number of landscape scenes into them, these practices were diversifying and changing dramatically, especially (as far as his own interests were concerned) in Rome. They were also, because of their remarkable success in the hands of masters such as Paul Bril, Annibale Carracci, Elsheimer and Rubens, being drawn within the pale of Italian theory. By the time Baglione appeared in print as the new Vasari in 1642, landscape painting had a history and was susceptible of theorisation.

The pivotal figure in the acknowledged constellation of Roman landscape artists was Annibale Carracci. That he was Italian was not irrelevant. But more important was the historical prestige which accrued to the artist who had revived the values of classicism, after the steep decline, during the later sixteenth century, from the achievements of the High Renaissance. By going back to school with Raphael almost a century after his demise, Annibale restored the classical style which the master's first followers had in their own time transmuted and traduced. Just as Perino del Vaga, among the original *garzoni*, had evolved a monumental decorative idiom by abstracting from the figure style of Raphael, so Annibale, by a more complex process of extrapolation, arrived at a 'Raphaelesque' landscape. Donald Posner sees this as a result of the painting of the Farnese Gallery: 'The system of surface and space construction, and of figural interrelationships, that Annibale had deduced from Raphael has . . . been extended to encompass and monumentalize inanimate nature.'[49] Alongside these researches Posner detects a study of the only significant landscape paintings which survive from the school of Raphael, Polidoro's frescoes in S. Silvestro.[50]

Annibale derived a complementary ability from the main corpus of High Renaissance painting, growing out of the Venetian tradition. His early work shows the influence of Muziano, a seminal artist who was evolving an almost 'pure' landscape out of the given possibilities of Venetian painting. And, in general, his Bolognese origins placed him between the spheres of Rome and Venice. His 'ideal' landscape was to combine natural verisimilitude with classical structure.

Such at least are the assumptions of those commentators who praise Annibale's landscapes throughout the seventeenth century. The assumptions emerge in judgments made on another of the leading Roman landscapists of this period, whose work figures extensively in Jones's designs – Paul Bril. Jones's use of Bril suggests a strong interest in his work, and in order to try and see how contemporary landscape painting would have looked to Jones, an artist who was both connoisseur and theorist, aesthete and classicist, it may help to examine how Italian writers judged Bril by criteria derived from their valuation of the 'classic' Annibale Carracci.

The crux of the story is Bril's change of style, occurring over a long period of residence in Rome, from his earlier Antwerp manner to a more simple, monumental proto-classicism which has come to be recognised as anticipating the mature classicism of Claude. It now seems that one contributor to this change was his friend Elsheimer, but the figure singled out in the accounts of contemporaries is Annibale. Baglione summed this up in 1642:

> he refashioned his early, Flemish style (maniera Fiamenga), making very great progress after having seen the beautiful landscapes of Annibale Carracci and copied those of Titian, that exceptional painter; with the sound judgment thus acquired he changed his manner, and devoted himself to a better practice in art, approaching closer to nature (al naturale), and to the good Italian style (buona maniera Italiana) . . . [51]

What Baglione means here by the 'buona maniera Italiana' can be inferred from the paintings he has been praising, the frescoes of the seasons in the Casino Rospigliosi, which announce Bril's new 'Italian style'. It unites classical composition with closeness to nature, the legacy of Titian; and Annibale is its modern representative.

The 'maniera Fiamenga' is expounded in Giulio Mancini's earlier, unpublished observations of the 1620s:

> from his long sojourn in Italy, seeing the works of the Carracci, he abandoned that laboured Flemish style of landscape, moving closer to the truth (al vero), and not placing the horizon as high as the Flemish habitually do, with the result that their landscape is rather a theatrical spectacle (maestà scenica) than a view of the countryside (prospetto di paese).[52]

This can be filled out from Baldinucci who, although writing much later (published 1688), appears to be giving substantially the same account (he is referring to Paul and his brother Matthias together):

> their scheme of colour . . . was beautiful, but of their own contrivance, and consequently resembled the truth up to a certain point and no further; thus they could be praised rather for a beautiful method of constructing landscapes than for a perfect representation of real landscapes (perfetta imitazione de' veri paesi).[53]

Conventionalised rather than naturalistic colour, an arbitrarily high point of view, an overall sense of construction rather than observation – these are the drawbacks of the Flemish style in the standard Italian view. They are certainly characteristics which can still be seen in the early work of Paul Bril.

The criteria invoked in judgment appear simple and straightforward: 'il naturale', 'il vero' – nature and truth. But the straightforwardness lies in their engaging ideological effrontery rather than in the concepts themselves. Do they embody a demand for naturalism? Up to a point they do, and Baglione's invocation of Titian supports this. But his simultaneous appeal to the 'buona maniera Italiana', the classicism of Annibale, complicates the issue. The complexities are best expressed in the final phrase used by Baldinucci in his final retelling of the story, 'una perfetta imitazione de' veri paesi'. The Aristotelian concept of imitation, especially in this historical context, implies not just a copy of the appearances of the natural world but an implicit acknowledgement of its informing intelligence, a realism compatible with idealisation,[54] 'il naturale' represented as 'il vero'. Looking back to Mancini's critique, which reads like the original source of Baldinucci's, we may say he is praising Bril not for giving up artifice in favour of naturalism but for moving from a convention which saw landscape as an aesthetic construction to one which strove for the *appearance* of truth to nature, where the concept of 'truth' reconciles the real with the ideal.

There is no evidence to show that Jones was in the least familiar with this received Italian interpretation of Bril's development, which never saw print until 1642. He must have had a general awareness of the reputation of Annibale, one of whose pupils, Francesco Albani, was invited to England by Charles I;[55] and, as we have seen, Jones made a careful copy of one of Albani's figure drawings (plates 1–2). But whether he knew of Annibale's landscapes as touchstones for new developments in that genre, we do not know. He was last in Rome in 1614, about the time when Bril's style was changing, but with so much to see he may have missed that at the time. Edward Norgate knew Bril well, and could have passed on news of his work, but whether he was in contact with Bril in the earlier or later period is uncertain. It is doubtful whether during the 1620s and 30s Jones had a proper chance to catch up, from faraway London, with developments in the Roman school. English collections contained pictures by Bril, probably in his earlier manner, and by other Antwerp artists down to Jan Brueghel. Charles I had pictures by the Italianate Dutch painters Breenbergh and Poelenburgh, whose work was Italian in subject-matter, but had not internalised Annibale's classicism or even Bril's. Probably the most advanced Roman landscapist with whom Jones was familiar was Elsheimer, represented in the collection of Lord Arundel, and highly esteemed by Rubens, the greatest living landscape painter in northern Europe.[56]

Jones's possible ignorance of the 'classical' Bril, and of the specific historical tendencies which produced in the career of one exemplary landscape painter a transition from Flemish mannerism to Italian classicism, did not prevent him from handling Bril's work in an uncannily instructive way. When he reproduces excerpts from Bril's compositions, always from the first period of the 'maniera Fiamenga', he revises them according to classicising criteria analogous to those which the Italian writers saw Bril applying to his own earlier work. Jones corrects Bril in the same spirit as Bril was seen in hindsight, by Mancini and Baglione, to have corrected himself. In this curious replica of the pattern of Bril's career as it was construed by the Italian critics, Jones stands in for Annibale Carracci. This is not surprising. Posner sees Annibale as applying an inner architectural discipline to landscape; and Jones, architect above all, certainly did the same to all his stage scenes, including landscapes. He is also comparable to Annibale in being, as it were, a re-classiciser, a member of that generation of European artists who around 1600 turned back to the High Renaissance. In Jones's case this 'second classicism' was a notion, since England had never fully experienced the original classicising epoch, but it was a powerful notion, and was provided with a prehistory within the long series of masque designs. It is in the designs that the supersession of mannerism by new classicism, which had never yet properly happened in English art, is enacted. In the field of landscape this is demonstrated through Jones's use of Bril – which can be shown to be typical of his dealings with the other landscape artists he drafted into his stage-pictures.

Staging the Satyric Scene: landscape as architecture

Vitruvius's prototype of scenic landscape, the Satyric Scene, was thus used by Jones not only as a vehicle for the display of landscape compositions taken from the mannerist pictorial tradition but as a framework on which those compositions could be corrected and classicised. Some of the changes he made were necessitated by exigencies of staging. An example would be lowering the horizon: Mancini required it for the sake of 'truth'; Jones had to do it anyway, to open up the sky and accommodate the cloud machines which came to figure in his productions. The staging of the Satyric Scene itself involved certain constraints, and those problems themselves had to be solved before it could be used for ulterior purposes.

Jones's designs include two versions of the Satyric Scene made for its own sake, a decade apart; the first is tentative, the second much more assured. The difficulties of composition, which become apparent in comparing the two, can be traced back through Serlio to Vitruvius. A late Renaissance stage designer, reading the descriptions of the Tragic, Comic and Satyric Scenes in Vitruvius, would probably have felt that the last presented different problems of construction from the other two, but would have received no hint from his author about how to overcome them. Bastiano da Sangallo suggests this in the drawings he made of the three Scenes on the relevant page of his Vitruvius. The first two are articulated as street vistas, and fitted very precisely into the margin of the text; but the Satyric Scene spreads asymmetrically from the margin across the bottom of the page, and its much looser definition makes it a far less viable solution, if it can be called a solution at all.[57] Serlio's woodcut, which as the only realisation to be published must have been widely consulted, is no more practicable, since he suggests nothing about how its pictorial effects of wild disarray can be reproduced on the stage. But his sequence of three illustrations does bring out an implication in the Vitruvian text which was to prove fruitful. The Tragic Scene, Vitruvius said, consisted of noble buildings, the Comic of more ordinary buildings, the Satyric of 'trees, caves, mountains and other country features'.[58] That is, his determining concept is architecture, and the Scenes are on a descending architectural scale, so that the Satyric is to be understood as nature's architecture, or urban architecture manqué. Serlio brings this out by including rustic huts in his design, and by composing it as a parody of the urban street vistas of the first two, as if it is striving to be architecture but can only be a demeaned and deranged version of that ideal. Here then is the answer to the stage designer: to realise the Satyric Scene, both as a pictorial composition and a practicable construction, as a variant of the other two Scenes – on an implicit architectural substructure based on the same physical substructure of regular scenic wings.[59]

Again the exigencies of stage practice produce a quite material explanation of Jones's treatment of landscape. If, in order to be put feasibly on the stage, landscape has to be 'architecturally' articulated in a physical sense, this means, for example, that mannerist compositional schemes like Bril's will have to be rationalised. So do we need aesthetic explanations, in terms of classicism, of Jones's changes to his sources? I think a closer look at these changes will show that we do.

Jones went about using the Satyric Scene to adapt pictorial landscape for the stage in three ways. He produced his own versions of the Scene for pastoral plays put on by Queen Henrietta Maria. He used it in some earlier masques as a loose framework onto which he grafted landscape designs by other artists. And in the later masques he took over an already existing adaptation of it – the schematisation worked out in Florence by Buontalenti and Giulio Parigi – and performed certain variations on that.

Pastoral scenes and Vitruvian landscape

Jones's first 'pastoral sceane' as he called it was for *Artenice*, a French pastoral acted by Henrietta Maria and her ladies on Shrove Tuesday, 1626. His design (plate 33) actually conflates parts of all three of Serlio's Scenes,[60] in an attempt to show different locales of the action simultaneously: the Queen seems to have ordered a kind of setting she would have been used to in France, a *décor simultané* arranged in perspective[61] – a convention which straddled the old stage design and the new. This forced Jones to regress to a convention he had originally turned his back on, where the set is a collection of discrete scenic items – with the added irrationality of perspective being

Plate 96. Jones, Sketch for Scene 1 of *The Shepherds' Paradise*, Chatsworth

used to organise not only space but time as well. He cannot have felt comfortable with this commission. He tries to give some visual unity by using the 'capanne alla rustica' among trees which feature in Serlio's third Scene. But where Serlio has few huts and many trees Jones reverses the proportions, leaving out most of the trees – which only makes a naive exposé of the architectural substructure of Serlio's design. A preferable solution appears in a design made seven years later (plate 96), for *The Shepherds' Paradise* (1633).[62] This time the trees predominate over the buildings, as in Serlio, although Serlio's factitiously messy composition is clarified. The drawing is sketched so freely that the buildings seem swallowed up in the trees, scarcely distinguishable from them. This carries an idea implicit in Serlio to its logical conclusion – not just buildings in landscape, but architecture absorbed *into* landscape. Landscape with an internalised, intrinsic architecture – this was to be Jones's successful formula.

It is fully realised in another version of the Satyric Scene (plate 97), made for a later French pastoral, *Florimène*, in 1635. It is worked out by careful adaptation from a number of sources.[63] The composition is based on another artist's reworking of Serlio – the engraved frontispiece to Guarini's *Pastor Fido* (plate 98), omitting the river-god Alpheus, and the temple.[64] But in reproducing all the other motifs in their exact relations in the engraving

Plate 97. Jones, Proscenium and Standing Scene, for *Florimène*, Chatsworth

Jones has amplified the spatial scheme and changed the forms. The trees are enlarged, the cottages replaced by handsomer buildings taken from Callot prints, and their relative dimensions more nicely adjusted. The new cottages, which Jones has altered where necessary, are architecturally more lucid and legible, and this helps to clarify the massing of the amplified tree-forms. The result is a successful realisation of the possibilities of the Satyric Scene – an architecture of natural forms and natural space. No doubt Jones would have seen it not just in relation to Serlio but in the context of antiquity, as a Vitruvian exercise, parallel to his own reconstruction of the Tragic Scene (plate 51) in the neo-antique vocabulary of Palladianism.

Between each act of *Florimène* was an 'intermedium' devoted to one of the seasons. For each of these the wings of the basic set remained, while the back shutter changed into a series of seasonal landscapes. Two of these are taken from a set of etchings of the months by Antonio Tempesta, and one from a similar set of prints after Bril.[65] In each case Jones has simplified the original mannerist compositions. This is an expedient in that these background landscapes are scenes of relieve, and cannot be over-complex; but Jones still leaves a lot of detail in his drawings, and his alterations seem to have an aesthetic motive, to make these landscapes accord with the broad conception of his main scene. For 'Summer' he reworks the background of Tempesta's

Plate 98. Frontispiece to B. Guarini, *Il Pastor Fido*, 1602, Bodleian Library

Giugno into a more compact and spacious composition, the horizon lowered just as Mancini would have wanted. 'Autumn' (plate 99) is a bold simplification of Bril's *September*. *October* (plate 100), eliminating all the figures and buildings and opening up the space. Bril's composition goes back to a drawing of 1598, and was then reworked in his proto-classical style for a fresco in the Casino Rospigliosi, dated c. 1613. Jones is using a print by Aegidius Sadeler which conflates motifs from both the drawing and the fresco;[66] it dates from 1615, and by returning in part to the drawing it gives an inadequate impression of Bril's development by 1615. Jones's version looks like a ruthless correction of the retardataire mannerist print by the standards of the classical fresco. In fact this is most unlikely, but the point is that Jones's simplification of Sadeler by classicising criteria of his own reveals the classicising Bril whom Sadeler had misrepresented. By pursuing a parallel path – in his radical effort to recover 'Vitruvian' landscape – Jones brings to light for his audience the 'real' Bril (the Bril aiming for 'il naturale' and 'il vero') and the progressive tendencies in the Roman landscape school.

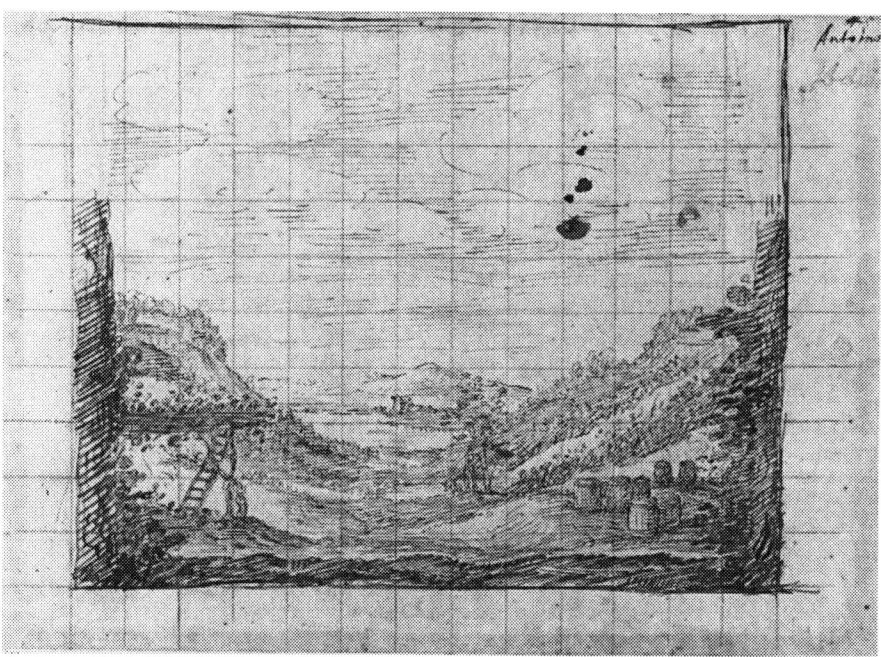

Plate 99. Jones, The Fourth Intermedium: Autumn, for *Florimène*, Chatsworth

Mannerist landscape classicised: Jones and Tempesta

Jones made freer reference to the Satyric Scene when designing for pastoral masques, or masques with landscape settings. There is a group of designs which are connected with *Pan's Anniversary, or The Shepherd's Holiday*, a masque for King James's birthday in 1620. Jonson gives the scene simply as 'Arcadia', and all these designs, which are vistas of trees and mountains, might be thought of as Arcadian landscapes.[67] Jones has composed them from the hunting prints of Tempesta, many of which have mythological themes. The hero of these Arcadian settings, which recall the curtain of *The Masque of Blackness*, is King James the hunter, celebrated in one of the 'hymns' of his birthday masque: '*Of Pan we sing, the best of Hunters*, Pan'.[68] The theme is taken up in *Time Vindicated* (1623), where in the final scene, a wood presided over by Diana, the Chorus sings to the masquers,

> *Turne Hunters then,*
>   *agen.*
> *Hunting it is the noblest exercise,*
> *Makes men laborious, active, wise . . .*

But they must follow the example of the King, who is not bloodthirsty but loves peace:

Plate 100. Aegidius Sadeler after Paul Bril, September. October

But strike the enemies of Man;
Kill vices if you can:
They are your wildest beasts.
And when they thickest fall, you make the Gods true feasts.[69]

This is the strain of idealising symbolism which was to flourish in the Caroline masques, such as *Albion's Triumph*. Instead of the simple compliment to James implied in the *Blackness* landscape, his royal pastimes are being allegorised and mythologised.

But in the first place, whatever their symbolic context, these Arcadian hunting scenes presumably had to look plausible to the King, who knew how to recognise good hunting country. In this practical sense James I must have been an exacting connoisseur of landscape, just as his son was in the aesthetic sense. Jones's designs provide the requisite terrain, described in a later masque as 'a woody landscape with low grounds proper for hunting'.[70] But they also make aesthetic capital out of the occasion by experimenting with the composition of broad, spacious stage landscapes, more ambitious in conception than the Serlian prototype.

These experiments can be followed through Jones's adaptations of Tempesta. The latter, although Florentine by origin, had been taught by the Fleming Stradano, and collaborated in the Vatican with Matthias Bril.[71] His

Plate 101. Jones, Back Shutter, Chatsworth

landscapes are in a late sixteenth-century Flemish style, characterised by asymmetrical construction and strong diagonal recessions. Jones excerpts, condenses and recomposes them to produce notably different effects.

In a design which Orgel and Strong suggest is for a back shutter (plate 101) he adapts Tempesta's *Death of Adonis*[72] (plate 102). He treats its mannerist scheme as if it could be imagined as one half of a more symmetrical composition. He reproduces the salient motifs in the four distinct planes of Tempesta's scheme, but condenses the space between the foreground and the middleground, thus tightening up the pattern of recessions (interrupted by Venus's chariot in the original) and making it correspond to the left hand half of his own composition. The result is an equal variety of forms with a more ample spatial organisation and an inherent, but not overstressed, symmetry.

It could be argued that these changes are made from practical necessity. If the design were not for a back shutter but an entire set (which is quite possible) with two pairs of wings, then there would be no choice but to recast Tempesta's motifs into a symmetrical pattern. But if we look at a related design, *Back Shutter for a Landscape* (plate 103), aesthetic demands reassert themselves. The drawing is inscribed 'shutter of this scene',[73] and it has the kind of asymmetry that only a back shutter, painted on one

Plate 102. Antonio Tempesta, Death of Adonis, Victoria and Albert Museum

continuous plane, could accommodate. It is composed from two separate Tempesta backgrounds, the left side from a *Gazelle Hunt* (plate 104) and the right from *Diana and Callisto*[74] (plate 105). To balance the high peak on the left, a similar feature from a Paul Bril etching of 1590 (plate 120) has been drafted in. Again, the picturesque variety of Tempesta's forms is retained, but they are recomposed in a very different spirit. Jones's asymmetries are embraced within a broad, binary structure which derives its logic from the fixed sequence of stage-wings which are implied in front of the scene depicted – although it is physically at the limit of the stage it is visually a continuation of it, and the rational amplitude of the stage space is suggested in the lay-out of the composition.

What Jones has done with Tempesta in these two cases is typical. In order to adapt the available repertory of landscape imagery to the physical and technical structure of his theatre he was forced to revise its mannerist spatial conventions, which were for his purposes wholly impractical. But his response was not only on the level of external necessity. The fact that he had to provide ample space for movement, and work with a rigidly regular scenic matrix, could be turned to aesthetic advantage. By using the physical qualities of his given stage scope – the amplitude and regularity – as a model for the composition of landscape, Jones produced landscape designs which advanced beyond the limits of the mannerist artists whose work he used,

Plate 103. Jones, Back Shutter for a Landscape, Chatsworth

made in fact advances analogous to those being made by the new classicising painters of the Roman school. In making mannerist landscape scenically practicable he also made it classical.

Tempesta's multitudinous etchings almost amount to a résumé of mannerist landscape schemes. A final example of Jones's revisions will help to emphasise the view, implicit in his practice, that every mannerist landscape is a classical landscape manqué. The unidentified *Forest Scene*[75] (plate 106) is much later than the Arcadian scenes of c. 1620, but it is composed by the same method. The left side is taken from Tempesta's *Narcissus* (plate 107) and the right side is a condensed excerpt from a *Stag Hunt*[76] (plate 108). On the left Jones has also added a passage from the same Bril etching as before (plate 120). Whereas the left-hand motifs are excerpted from the exactly corresponding planes in their respective sources, the group of trees on the right has been promoted from the middleground in Tempesta's scheme to the foreground in Jones's. To adjust the overall tonality, he has shaded the principal tree, which Tempesta had lit strongly. Details like this reveal the remorselessly analytical eye with which Jones dissected these compositions so as to make them serve his needs. These needs

Landscape

Plate 104. Tempesta, Gazelle Hunt, Victoria and Albert Museum

Plate 105. Tempesta, Diana and Callisto

Plate 106. Jones, Forest Scene, Chatsworth

were in the first place utterly practical – patterns had to be found which would fit his stage – but in the course of ensuring that the show went on he simultaneously pursued aesthetic researches, schooled himself in the ways of landscape composition, and exhibited the results, with a determination no less resolute.

Florentine patterns

Jones's reworkings of Tempesta for scenic purposes seem to belong to the masques of the 1620s, although he used this method for back shutter designs in later years as well.[77] But for the Caroline masques of the 1630s, when his stage technology reached its most sophisticated development, he resorted for his set designs to the Florentine scenographers who had first perfected the technology which he had now caught up with, and who had been publishing records of their productions which provided scenic patterns for the new kind of theatre. It was Bernardo Buontalenti who had made the Medici court theatre the wonder of Europe; but more influential for Jones was his successor Giulio Parigi, the first stage designer to publish his work systematically.[78] Giulio was unusual, in that his work in the theatre was not

Landscape

Plate 107. Tempesta, Narcissus, Victoria and Albert Museum

Plate 108. Tempesta, Stag Hunt, Victoria and Albert Museum

an offshoot of the activity of someone who was first and foremost an architect; he differed in this from most of his confrères at European courts. His great talent was for landscape drawing: according to Baldinucci, he taught his pupils 'un bello, e nuovo modo di toccare di penna vaghissimi paesi'.[79] And the distinctive style of his landscape drawings is certainly discernible in his stage designs.

Following the example set by Buontalenti for the famous *intermedi* of 1589, Giulio published a wide variety of scenic types. In practice, Renaissance designers had never confined themselves to the three types of Vitruvius, making for example their own realisations of the hell and heaven scenes that they inherited from the medieval theatre. But they were powerfully affected by the underlying idea of the Vitruvian typology – that stage scenes were works of architecture, and represented reality as structured architecturally, ranging from the architecture of man to that of nature. Buontalenti's designs are based on this premise, but he adds an overriding idea which did not figure in Serlio's visualisations of Vitruvius, that of symmetry. His scenes worked through an elaborate structure of perspective wings, and instead of trying to mask their artificial regularity with a more wayward, 'natural' pictorial overlay, he embraces it and raises it to the power of metaphor, presenting a universe spectacularly articulated through the master-idea of symmetry. Since he was, like Vitruvius, basically an architect and mechanician, his practice can be seen as a kind of ultra-Vitruvianism. This is the scenographic legacy of Buontalenti the architect/engineer to Parigi the landscape artist.

The contrast between them must not be overstated. Buontalenti was perfectly capable of concealing his art as well as displaying it, and of grafting secondary picturesque irregularities into his set designs; and his famous cloud machines gave the actual productions a proto-baroque, mouvementé appearance. Giulio, in turn, did not reject the ruling concept of symmetry in favour of a more painterly approach. His sets have more pictorial variety, and they open up the background more and exploit its visual possibilities, but they persevere with Buontalenti's highly symmetrical schemes. His landscape sets are no exception. Indeed, it looks as if the style of his landscape drawings, declared so novel by Baldinucci, was influenced by Buontalentian scenography. He articulates rocks and trees in thin vertical segments as if they had to be fitted onto stage wings; this is a persistent idiosyncrasy, which is copied by his pupils, and recurs in their etchings of his landscape scenes for the theatre.[80] In this respect there is a similarity between Giulio's drawings and those of his pupil Remigio Cantagallina, and between both and Cantagallina's prints of Giulio's stage designs. The pictorialism of Giulio's stage landscapes has already, therefore, submitted to the prepotent dictates of Buontalenti's example.

Buontalenti had designed a version of the Satyric Scene for the third *intermedio* of 1589, *Apollo slays the Python*, where the symmetries of the perspective are stressed, in the published engraving of the scene, by the actors spaced carefully alongside the tree wings.[81] Giulio followed this example sometimes more closely, sometimes less. Callot's etching of his production of *La liberazione di Tirreno* (1617) shows an utterly regimented perspective of tree wings, whereas Cantagallina's of the basic set, representing Mount Ida, for *Il giudizio di Paride* (1608), shows a much freer organisation[82] (plate 109). Jones used the Mount Ida design for the first scene of *Chloridia* (1631) (plate 110). Jonson's text uses the word 'Land-shape' of Jones's scene,[83] and the print he is adapting is much closer to the informality of Giulio's landscape drawings than to the ultra-regimentation of the Buontalentian scenic style. Nonetheless it shows that segmented verticality which is a sign of Buontalenti's influence, the forms prefabricated on a scenic pattern – and this is the aspect which Jones changes. He rounds out the forms and works them closer together, counteracting the effect of meagre, attenuated height and of many separate accents. In fact, a second drawing exaggerates the effects of roundness and bulk to an inept degree,[84] but at least it emphasises the tendency of Jones's revisions. He accepts Giulio's pictorialising scenography and rejects the scenic mannerism of his pictorial style.

Jones was quite ready to use the Florentine schematisation of the Satyric Scene for his own stage, while judging it to be from a pictorial point of view unsatisfactory. The same critique of the pictorial values of the Buontalentian style had been made by an earlier artist. When Agostino Carracci made an engraving of the third *intermedio* of 1589 (as he did also of the first) he similarly rounded out the forms and broke down the excessively vertical emphases;[85] he revised the tree forms, for example, towards the style of Muziano, whose Venetianising manner had influenced the early landscapes of his brother Annibale. Jones is, presumably without knowing it, doing the same in turn to Parigi (and again, moving in the same direction as the Roman landscapists).

In Giulio Parigi, unique combination of stage designer and landscape artist, Jones found a uniquely useful guide to the staging of landscape. As a practitioner of both arts, Giulio was experienced in remodelling mannerist landscape compositions into scenically viable schemes on a symmetrical matrix. Jones both followed his example and copied his work, but did neither uncritically. The practical lessons he learnt were the means to an end – a classicising revision of the landscape tradition – which lay beyond the horizon of Florentine art. Jones copied Parigi in the interests of being aesthetically more progressive.

The stage designs of Inigo Jones

Plate 109. Cantagallina after Parigi, Scene of Mount Ida, from *Il giudizio di Paride*, 1608, British Museum

Scenes and pictures

Aside from his two (surviving) attempts to reinvent the Satyric Scene from first principles – which constitute a special case – Jones worked at the rapprochement of stage scenery and landscape from two different, in fact opposite, directions. He started from pictures (such as Tempesta's or Bril's) and made them viable as scenes, or he started from preformed scenes (such as Parigi's) and made them more pictorial. In his many landscape scenes of the 1630s both approaches are often combined. A typical design is *Scene 1: A Grove* for *The Temple of Love* (1635)[86] (plate 111). The tree wings are adapted from a scheme by Giulio Parigi's son Alfonso[87] (plate 112). His scenic style is more painterly than his father's, as far as one can tell from his own etching of the design: Jones's drawing does, however, soften the idiosyncrasies of Alfonso's etching style, subduing some of its heavy linear gestures, and lightening in parts its dark tonality. The back shutter is excerpted from the background of a Tempesta print showing a palace and its gardens[88] (plate 113), but redrawn in a symmetrical form to regularise its

Plate 110. Jones, Scene 1: A Landscape, for *Chloridia*, Chatsworth

mannerist skewness. Jones condenses the space in Alfonso's scheme in order to compose together the separately derived parts of his new design. Each part is adjusted in the light of the other: the passage from Tempesta rationalised in accord with the symmetry of Alfonso's scheme, which is in turn cued to the pictorial values of Tempesta, including his different tonality.

This reciprocal adjustment between foreground and background – the two visual zones corresponding to the physical distinction between wings and back shutter – in which scenic schemes are rendered more pictorial and pictures made viably scenic, becomes Jones's standard method for the composition of stage landscapes. It can best be observed in a whole series of designs for one production, *The Shepherds' Paradise*, a pastoral performed by the Queen and her ladies in 1633. There is a design for the basic set or 'standing scene'; another for the first scene in which that is varied, mainly by replacing the back shutter; and finally a sequence of other backgrounds – back shutters or scenes of relieve – which were used for scene-changes.

The standing scene[89] (plate 114) uses a scheme of four pairs of tree wings, the first pair more bulky and darkly shaded, the rest with smaller trees rising from mounds or hillocks – this is the standard Parigian formula, as adapted by Alfonso from Giulio's example in *Il giudizio di Paride*. The back shutter shows a villa resembling one of the Spanish king's country palaces,

Plate 111. Jones, Scene 1: A Grove, for *The Temple of Love*, Chatsworth

such as the Pardo or the Buen Retiro, with a formal garden in front and woods and mountains behind – all lined up symmetrically on a central axis, which is actually marked on the drawing as a guideline.

This design is varied for the opening scene of the play[90] (plate 115). One tree wing is replaced by a temple portico, and the back shutter is changed. The background composition is no longer symmetrical, part of it being copied from a print after Pieter Stievens,[91] one of the mannerist artists employed by Rudolf II. But its picturesque irregularities are visually contained by the symmetrical wing pattern. There are designs for five other alternative backgrounds, mostly symmetrical in composition, derived from *vedute* or landscapes by various artists. Sometimes their symmetry is given in the source, such as with the adaptation of Callot's *Grand Parterre de Nancy*,[92] sometimes not; but if not, Jones extrapolates a symmetrical version of the motif from the original. Two of these are derived from an engraving in Bril's series of months, *Maius. Junius*[93] (plate 116). For *Love's Cabinet*[94] (plate 117) Jones takes the summer house on a mount, clears away the trees in front, and turns it to give a clear, frontal, symmetrical view. For *A Prospect of Trees and Houses*[95] (plate 118) he takes the villa in the distance, enlarges the façade from three bays to five, and again turns it to give a frontal view, placing it in the exact centre of the composition. As in the case of the print

Plate 112. Alfonso Parigi, Sbarco di Venere, from *La Flora*, 1628, British Library

Plate 113. Tempesta, Palace Garden, Victoria and Albert Museum

Plate 114. Jones, Proscenium and Standing Scene, for *The Shepherds' Paradise*, Chatsworth

used for *Florimène*, the engraving had given a false account of Bril, being based on a much earlier drawing of which he had already produced a classicising revision for the Casino Rospigliosi frescoes.[96] As before, Jones rectifies the misrepresentation, by revealing a new 'classical' Bril within the earlier 'mannerist' Bril. These pictorial backgrounds for *The Shepherds' Paradise* remain picturesque but acquire a discipline in keeping with the ordered foreground scheme.

The foregrounds in turn take on a certain picturesque dishevelment, as seen in the pair of tree wings flanking *A Prospect of Trees and Houses* (or the similar pair in *A Garden*).[97] Since the tree wings were painted on a symmetrical matrix, their forms could be varied without the risk of disorder. It was the backgrounds, painted as it were on a single blank canvas, where a premissed licence had to be checked. The interplay between foreground and background worked within material constraints, but was brought about by visual means. One may wonder how successful this visual interplay was in practice, that is, in the eyes of Jones's assembled spectators.

The two large designs for *The Shepherds' Paradise* suggest opposite answers. The drawing for the standing scene (including the proscenium) is all of a piece. Jones's rather free pen technique literally draws the various parts of the scene together, so that its symmetry becomes perceptible but

Plate 115. Jones, A Palace in Trees, for *The Shepherds' Paradise*, Chatsworth

covert. The realisation of a beautiful prospect with an order below the surface fits this neo-Platonic play; and the symbols of an eye and a flaming heart prominent on the proscenium suggest the neo-Platonic theme of visible beauty arousing a love of invisible beauty. It is a theme pertinent not only to this play but to all the masques of the 1630s as well; and it suggests an underlying motive for Jones's efforts to coordinate the disparately derived elements of his landscape designs (and of all his stage-pictures). The logical goal (for a classicist like Jones, working within the neo-Platonising context of the Caroline masques) would be to make a landscape, as an assemblage of the various items of the Serlian/Vitruvian model, into a totality, a single image which will focus the spectator's eye decisively on an ideal beauty within or beyond that image itself. In this context classicism is a means to a neo-Platonic end: the achievement of a composition so unified as to have the force of an image,[98] truth revealed in a single, intense *coup d'œil*.

This could be called the theoretical answer to the question propounded earlier. The practical answer is given by the other large design for *The Shepherds' Paradise* (plate 115). This is probably a working pattern for the scene painters, since it is larger than Jones's *vue d'ensemble*,[99] and it makes the separate parts of the scenic fabric discernible. Jones's pen drawing is used for the delineation of discrete items in the composition, instead of having the

Plate 116. Sadeler after Bril, Maius. Junius

'overall' effect of the first design. It may be that many spectators saw such a scene in this quasi-analytic way, rather than with the synthetic view of the first design.

If this was so it may have been no bad thing. Given that landscape was a relatively new genre, many of the Stuart courtiers would not have had very clear ideas about it. They would probably tend to see it as a kind of idealised topography. Jones did introduce topographical views into his productions, such as the new Banqueting House in *Time Vindicated* and Somerset House in *Artenice*,[100] but as well as having personal and local references these tended to have a symbolic dimension as well. But it is noticeable that the majority of the landscape scenes eschew not only familiar views in the real world but also preordained views from the world of art. He never reproduces any of his models literally, even the schemes of Giulio Parigi, which lend themselves to literal copying. In fact he uses Giulio's basic scheme as an analytical device, a means for dissecting and reworking the compositions of other artists. There are drawings for separate tree wings, perhaps part of a repertory or kit, which show that, although he combined these basic units according to a pattern or convention derived from Parigi, he copied them from any artist but Parigi. One is taken from Bril (plates 119–20), another from a landscape by Muziano[101] (plates 121–2).

Landscape

Plate 117. Jones, Love's Cabinet, for *The Shepherds' Paradise*, Chatsworth

Plate 118. Jones, A Prospect of Trees and Houses, for *The Shepherds' Paradise*, Chatsworth

Jones seems to have had a compulsion to analyse and recompose landscape compositions, not to take them literally at all.

Obviously in doing this he was teaching himself new things: the compulsion, in general, is his self-declared compulsion to learn. But he was also, consciously or not, teaching his audience. They were at an elementary

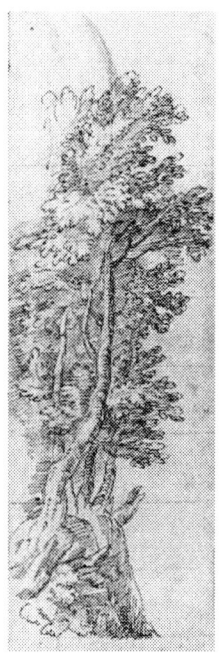 

Plate 119.
Jones, Tree Wing,
Chatsworth

Plate 120. Bril, Landscape

stage in their understanding of landscape. They were certainly not up to the conceptual sophistication of the Italian connoisseurs and critics for whom Mancini spoke when he reproved Flemish painters for providing 'una Maestà scenica che prospetto di paese' (a theatrical spectacle rather than a view of the countryside).[102] He was attacking the treatment of landscape as a pictorial construction in favour of representing views from nature. Of course what he called 'prospetto di paese' was nothing of the sort: it was a representational convention which concealed its own compositional artifices, made them seem inevitable and natural. In Mancini's argument classicism masquerades as naturalism. What the English public needed to learn was how to avoid Mancini's fallacy in the form in which it might present itself to much less advanced observers. They had too little, not too much, appreciation of landscape as artifice. They needed precisely to learn how landscape could be, not a literal prospect, but 'una Maestà scenica'. Jones's masques were the ideal vehicle for inculcating this lesson. As they watched them, they could acquire a sense of landscape as a pictorial construction, as art above all.

Jones's lesson moreover is twofold, rehearsing two successive phases in the history of landscape simultaneously. He conveys the Flemish mannerist

Landscape

Plate 121. Jones, Tree Wing, Chatsworth

Plate 122. Cornelis Cort after Girolamo Muziano, St Onuphrius in a Landscape, British Museum

sense of landscape as a pictorial construction, but also the Italian classical sense of landscape as a harmonious, natural ensemble.

Bril and Elsheimer

By the time of his very late masques, towards the end of the 1630s, these two phases seem to assume in his work their 'correct' historical relationship. He catches up, as it were, with the history of landscape painting in Italy: the idea of landscape as a construction becomes subsumed in, or at least subordinated to, the idea of landscape as a harmonious composition in which art conceals itself – a view, a unified image of the natural world.

This is especially true in the first two scenes of *Luminalia* (1638). The text records the Queen's command to Jones 'to make a new subject of a masque for herself, that with high and hearty invention might give occasion for variety of scenes, strange apparitions, songs, music, and dancing of several kinds, from whence doth result the true pleasure peculiar to our English masques...'[103] This reads like an apologia for the new kind of masque which

Jones had developed after the dismissal of Jonson, and the phrase 'high and hearty invention' echoes Jonson's own apologia for the then new Jacobean masque in the text of *Hymenaei* over thirty years before.[104] At the end of the piece Jones staged a ballet in mid-air, the dancers performing on a cloud machine, 'which apparition ... was much admired, being a thing not before attempted in the air'.[105] But this newly ambitious spectacle, whatever 'variety' it gave 'occasion' for, was thematically disciplined and unified, 'the invention consisting of darkness and light'.[106] This simple idea is reflected in the title and subtitle, *Luminalia: The Queen's Festival of Light*, characterising the subject in terms which are abstract and aesthetic. Jonson, and the poets who succeeded him, were accustomed to describe the 'invention' of a masque in moral and allegorical terms: this bold stress on the aesthetic is something new. It is associated with a boldly simple philosophical conceit, of Henrietta Maria as 'the queen of brightness'.[107] As darkness gives way to light at the centre of the masque, 'Hesperus asks Aurora why the sun is so long in coming ... Aurora answers that her brother the sun hath for this time given up his charge of lightening the hemisphere to a terrestrial beauty, in whom intellectual and corporeal brightness are joined ... '[108] This is the Queen, idealised as a neo-Platonic demi-goddess, who provides the rationale for Jones's 'Festival of Light'.

The theme of darkness and light is represented, as so often in the Queen's masques, in a series of landscape designs. Designs for only the first two, scenes of darkness, survive, but their relationship shows Jones's developed view of the Italianate landscape tradition. One is based on Elsheimer and the other on Bril, and the use to which Jones puts each artist's work suggests a relative evaluation of each in the history of landscape.

The opening 'scene of night' is a perspective of trees, with a background taken from Goudt's engraving of Elsheimer's *Flight into Egypt*[109] (plates 123–5). It is described as

> a scene all of darkness, the nearer part woody, and farther off more open, with a calm river, that took the shadows of the trees by the light of the moon, that appeared shining in the river, there being no more light to lighten the whole scene than served to distinguish the several grounds that seemed to run in from the eye.[110]

The key element in the design – in that it determines the lighting of the whole scene – is the excerpt from Elsheimer. The verbal description (which no doubt comes from Jones) suggests a grasp of the essential principle of Elsheimer's composition, as an 'invention consisting of darkness and light'. It also suggests an imaginative response to Elsheimer, and to that tendency in his work. Jones may have known of Rubens's admiration for Elsheimer, and of the pastiche he had made of *The Flight into Egypt*.[111] He would certainly have seen Lord Arundel's Elsheimers and known of the importance they had for their owner: when Hollar etched a series of views of Arundel's beloved country retreat at Albury, he imitated Elsheimer's landscape style, strongly suggesting that Elsheimer was for Arundel *the* landscape artist par excellence.[112] That Jones sympathised with this preference is shown by his small wash drawing for the background of the *Luminalia* scene – it is one of the liveliest and most beautiful of all his masque designs, and the most spirited landscape drawing he has left us. It is a tacit homage to Elsheimer, and its freedom of technique paradoxically suggests that Jones, probably with the stimulus of the pictures collected by Arundel and the excellent engravings of Goudt, has brought the artist's achievement into a decisive focus.

Jones arranged that the first scene of *Luminalia* should appear to the spectators as a self-sufficient picture,[113] simply to be looked at for some time before the action of the masque started. As a picture it is unprecedented in Jones's work. It combines two diverse principles of pictorial unity, one older and one more modern, but neither yet fully established in English painting. The older is the system of linear perspective, worked out in the Quattrocento, which Jones had been using now for thirty years and more; the newer is the tenebrism of Caravaggio, which had been taken up in the early Seicento by many painters, including Elsheimer. Caravaggio's introduction of light as a principle of unity in pictorial composition has been seen by Longhi as a revolutionary move, posing a challenge to the rule of perspective.[114] Jones's stage-picture, as the drawing and the textual description together make clear, combines both these principles in a deliberate fashion. In effect, it re-enacts a crucial moment of change in the recent history of Italian art, and intimates, beyond the conflict expounded by Longhi, a new 'classical' reconciliation between perspectivism and tenebrism.

In his design light and perspective complement each other. Instead of the two main light sources in Elsheimer (the moon and the fire), Jones, by excerpting from the original, has confined himself to one (although the reflection of the moon in the water preserves the notion of a complexity in the lighting scheme). This means that the perspective can reinforce the effect of the light, rationalising the impalpable (what the text calls the 'immaterial').[115] And this visual exposition replicates the programme expounded in the text of the masque. The moon, the luminary of Night (who appears in the opening scene), is the benign antithesis of Henrietta Maria, who appears at the climax as a substitute for the sun-god, as 'queen of brightness'. The idea of the Queen as a neo-Platonic deity, the personification of Oneness and Brightness, is anticipated in Jones's first scene, where the landscape is unified through a rational principle of light.

Plate 123. Jones, Scene 1: Night, for *Luminalia*, Chatsworth

Plate 124. Jones, Back Shutter for Scene 1: Night, for *Luminalia*, Chatsworth

Plate 125. Hendrik Goudt after Adam Elsheimer, Flight into Egypt, British Museum

The philosophical stimulus of neo-Platonism and the aesthetic stimulus of Elsheimer's seminal oeuvre combine in *Luminalia* to prompt Jones's most interesting experiment in landscape composition – the experiment of seeing how far a scenic fabrication of various parts (both physically and formally) can be turned into a single image. His idealising simplification of Elsheimer, the great proto-naturalist of the seventeenth century, seems to fall far short of Mancini's demand that the fabrication of landscapes ('Maestà scenica') should give way to the naturalistic observation of them ('prospetto di paese'). But once we recognise that Mancini, like the critics who succeed him, is covertly demanding a classicising or idealising naturalism, such as that of Annibale Carracci or the later Bril, then Jones's design begins to look much closer to the requirements of that critical tradition. Mancini's contrast traces a shift from an analytic to a synthetic concept of landscape, and this is the direction in which Jones's designs have been moving.

This is confirmed by his use of Paul Bril in the second scene of *Luminalia*. The 'scene of night' inspired by Elsheimer gives way to the 'City

Plate 126. Webb after Jones, The City of Sleep, for *Luminalia*, Chatsworth

of Sleep', which appears in a 'strange prospect of chimeras'.[116] This scene is an antimasque, associated with the irrational side of the night experience, which in Scene 1 was introduced with majestic solemnity. *The City of Sleep*[117] (plate 126) appears hovering on a rainbow. It is concocted from various buildings in two etchings by Bril[118] (plates 120, 127), which are typical of his earliest, most 'Flemish' landscape manner. The surviving drawing is ineptly sketched by John Webb, as if Jones himself saw no need to attend personally to these details. The buildings are copied from Bril without any alteration. This literal use of early Bril to suggest irrationality and fantasy intimates a retrospective judgment on the early Italianate Flemish landscape tradition. The 'scenic', piecemeal style of arbitrary fantasy, of which he was the protagonist, is viewed in contrast to the newer style of Elsheimer and found wanting. Jones's two contrasting designs constitute a bare summary of the history of early Seicento landscape painting, comparable in succinctness to that of Mancini, but presumably the outcome of his own independent observations.

Jones's experiments with landscape composition may seem limited by their data, none of which was more recent than the first decade of the seventeenth century (Elsheimer's *Flight into Egypt* belongs to 1609). Admittedly he will have seen some newer works as they entered English collections in the 1620s and 30s; and he will have been attentive to Van Dyck's use of Venetian landscape in the settings of his portraits. But it was the principles he applied to his data which mattered, principles deduced from his individual study of the development of landscape in the light of the Italian

Plate 127. Bril, Landscape

Renaissance tradition. Their classicising tendency chimed with the most advanced developments in Rome, the capital of modern art, and ensured that the landscape tableaux which he exhibited to the spectators of his masques had an essentially contemporary quality.

6

Ornament

The proscenium arch: function and meaning

For Jones himself, the term 'ornament' had two main senses. It referred to those formal or morphological features which were proper to each of the classical orders, and differentiated them from each other, such as the volute of the Ionic capital, or the rhythmic repetition of metopes and triglyphs (which might sometimes appear in paraphrase) in the Doric frieze. It also meant any kind of adornment, not only in architecture, but along the whole spectrum of the arts. In his stage design both kinds of ornament are present. As he refines his understanding of classical architecture, he represents it on the stage with rigorous attention to the formal grammar of the orders. So, in the text of *Britannia Triumphans* (1638), we read at one point, 'the whole scene was changed into a peristylium of two orders, Doric and Ionic, with their several ornaments'; and Jones's drawing for this scene (plate 49) shows him redrafting and correcting so as to get the 'several ornaments' exactly right.[1] And ornament in the wider sense obviously plays a major role in the festive entertainments he designed – in the more fanciful architecture that was admitted in stage-furniture such as thrones, chariots and ships, and in costume. But the best place to study Jones's approach to ornament is on his proscenium arches, those complex constructions, part-architecture and part-painting, where both kinds of ornament meet. In fact he came to refer to the proscenium simply as 'the ornament'. Here we see him systematically working out a language of ornament which will form part of the comprehensive discourse of the masque designs, complementing the other new visual languages evolved from his aesthetic researches and communicated to his audiences.

Before discussing the proscenium as a field of ornament we have to look at it as a structure, and consider its function in the late Renaissance theatre.

Its formal origins lie in the Roman theatre as described by Vitruvius – or at least that is what Palladio implies in his reconstruction of the Vitruvian theatre, the Teatro Olimpico. Jones will have been familiar with the Teatro Olimpico from his earliest visit to Italy around 1600, and whatever his opinion of its historical accuracy, it was a definitive point of reference for thinking about the relation of the modern theatre to that of antiquity. By reintroducing the Roman *frons scenae* not only as an architectural setting for dramatic action but as a frame for modern perspective scenery, Palladio implies that the modern proscenium derives from the central element of the Roman *frons scenae*, the *porta regia*. This locates it in the tradition of classical architecture, and gives it a pedigree going back to antiquity. A drawing by Jones's disciple, John Webb, shows that he agreed with Palladio; and we may suppose that Jones did too.[2]

But this Palladian history of the proscenium as an architectural form needs to be filled out by considering its practical function in the modern theatre. During the sixteenth century, stage machinery became more and more sophisticated, facilitating scenic transformations of startling ingenuity. These spectacular effects took on a preternatural character, as the causes which produced them became more thoroughly hidden and indiscernible. The proscenium constituted a limit between the visible and the invisible, helping to conceal the stage machinery and its workings, and to focus the spectators' attention within the defined space of the scenic action. By being both a screen and a frame, the proscenium enhanced, in fact it helped to constitute, the 'miraculous' spectacularity of the Cinquecento theatre.

The proscenium evolved a form which followed its function, while also self-consciously reflecting and elaborating on it. The medium of this self-consciousness was the painted figuration added to the basic architectural matrix. Two early examples illustrate the formal evolution from different angles. In 1548, when Henri II made his triumphal entry into Lyon, the Florentine community produced a comedy in his honour. The theatre and stage set were designed by Nannoccio, a former pupil of Andrea del Sarto and colleague of Vasari, now in the employ of the Cardinal of Tournon. In front of the set on either side he placed two guardian figures of heroes:

> Keeping watch over the prospettiva were two giant-size, painted figures, Samson on the right side and Hercules on the left, both positioned exactly over two wings ...[3]

Samson and Hercules have more than one symbolic meaning. Since the 'prospettiva' showed Florence, they may well be alluding to the King's heroic virtue and representing the hope that his power will protect Florentine interests. But their role within Nannoccio's theatre is to mark, forcibly as it were, the frontiers of his scenic spectacle: to rebut one sort of visual curiosity (about what Ben Jonson called 'art's hid causes') and compel another, to define the exact scope of the spectators' attention.

This relatively 'primitive' type of proscenium, using terminal figures rather than a complete arch (and the convention appears in later work, including that of Jones), nicely represents the elements of compulsion and restraint necessarily exercised by designers over their audiences in the development of the proscenium, and of Cinquecento scenography in general. The complementary proscenium type is found in 1565, during the wedding celebrations of Francesco de' Medici and Joanna of Austria, when Vasari set up a theatre in the Salone of the Palazzo Vecchio. He marked the limits of the stage by two Corinthian columns carrying an entablature, in the centre of which were the ducal arms.[4] Unlike Nannoccio's proscenium, Vasari's gives little away. The architecture speaks of festive grandeur and princely power in the most conventional manner. But it exerts its own aesthetic and visual control over the audience tacitly – except, that is, for one detail. On the front of the stage platform Vasari painted a feigned staircase, connecting the stage with the auditorium in appearance but not in practice. Here the crucial process of simultaneously inviting and rebuffing the spectators, and so determining the exact scope of their attention, instead of being writ, or figured, large, is expressed in a compact visual paradox.

Vasari cannot refrain, any more than his predecessor, from drawing attention to the apparatus of power manipulated by the artist, however much it subserves the power of the ruler. In each case the proscenium shows its determination of just what shall be visible; and this politics of vision relates to the monarchic politics of the French and Tuscan states. But in their formal means they are in complete contrast: one stressing a boundary not to be crossed, the other circumscribing an aperture for inspection; one using the more demonstrative language of figuration, the other the more abstract language of architecture. In its fully evolved form the Italian proscenium is a composite of these two types and their contradictory, but in practice necessarily complementary, possibilities.

The perfected form is first recorded in a design of 1560, by the Sienese painter Bartolomeo Neroni, called Riccio. This was for the performance of a comedy, Alessandro Piccolomini's *L'Ortensio*, by the Accademia degli Intronati before Cosimo I. It was published almost thirty years later (1589) in an impressive chiaroscuro woodcut by Andrea Andreani[5] (plate 31). This shows a perspective stage set and a proscenium together, the set being a rationalised and idealised version of a Sienese street, leading to the Duomo in the background. The proscenium is a monumental work of architecture, with two pilasters supporting an entablature, which carries the ducal arms in the centre surmounted by emblems of the Academy. The pilasters accommodate feigned sculptural figures: on either side Poetry and Comedy seated in niches, and standing on pedestals figures of Roman emperors identified by inscriptions as patrons of those arts. The order is Doric, enriched with modilions in the frieze; and the same order is continued into the idealised palazzi in the foreground of the scene. This may allude to the character of the Academy, or to comedy as a basically realistic genre; but it overpoweringly evokes that dour grandeur which is the architectural hallmark of the Medici domination of Tuscany in this period.

The theme of deference to political power is writ large on the proscenium, not only stylistically and emblematically, but in the poses of the figures: Poetry and Comedy, seated females, attend with downcast eyes to the assertive representations of the *princeps*. But the commandingly handsome structure also declares, in fact constitutes, the designer's power over the domain of visibility. The spectators, by being made to keep their distance (and the figures of emperors, like those of Nannoccio's heroes, seem to repel any untoward approach), are thereby positioned to enter optically into the distances of the perspective. Architecture and figuration join forces to describe a frontier, across which the visual experience of the spectators is mediated through a complex two-way mechanism of control. This is self-consciously emphasised by the motif of the curtain – that part of the *apparato* analogous to the proscenium, in both masking and presenting the scene – which is here rendered decoratively as an extension of the proscenium structure. It becomes a metaphor of the proscenium's function to hide and show at the same time.

Riccio's *apparato* for the Accademia degli Intronati remained in place until 1647, and Jones would have been able to study it when Lord Arundel's entourage stayed in Siena for the autumn of 1613.[6] He also had a copy of the Andreani print, and resorted to it in his own work almost incessantly: he seems to have regarded Riccio's design as a paradigm. This is understandable, not just because it was the first published print of a proscenium design, but also because it summed up decades of work on this quite new problem, and offered an authoritative solution. Its treatment of the proscenium as an architectural form is practical in a way that Palladio's was not to be, and more economically efficient in its deployment of figurative ornament. The only improvements, from Jones's point of view, were made by Buontalenti. His proscenia were not reproduced in prints, but described in detail in festival books. His contribution was to turn the symbolic discourse of the proscenium much more towards self-conscious reflection on the capacities and operations of the artist. In a typically Florentine way he makes the proscenium a meditation on the power of *disegno*.

For the opening of the Uffizi theatre in 1586 Buontalenti designed a proscenium flanked by 'due grandi e belle figure finte di marmo', each one holding a flaming torch and the instruments appropriate to their work, which identified them as Architecture and Perspective. Beyond them was revealed the architectural perspective of the scene, a view of Florence. The obverse of the artist's power was shown in an equally refined way: Buontalenti repeated Vasari's feigned staircase on the front of the stage platform, but added two crouching lions who appeared to ward off anyone who might approach.[7] For the celebrations of the marriage of Maria de' Medici in 1600, his proscenium had the Medici arms in the frieze accompanied by figures of Dignity and Magnanimity, but at the sides were figures of Theory and Practice, as the fundamental concepts for those wishing to master the 'mathematical arts' such as perspective.[8] Jones of course imitated these figures for a proscenium of his own in 1632. But he also responded in a general way to Buontalenti's sophistication of the proscenium from a means of mediating between scene and spectators to a medium of self-justification, where the discourse of politics could give place to the discourse of art.

Jones's proscenia

Jones's development of the proscenium in his own theatre had reached the same point of sophistication by the beginning of the 1630s, as we know through the abundance of documentation, both visual and textual, from that decade. He may have arrived at his characteristic type of proscenium earlier, but the evidence is too patchy to tell, with neither enough drawings nor enough descriptions in printed texts. What there are suggest a long period of tentative and then more confident experiment, as if in his own career he is rehearsing in condensed form the gradual evolution of the proscenium in sixteenth-century Italy.

Part of the trouble is that Ben Jonson's masque texts, unlike their Italian counterparts, waste little or no time over describing proscenium arches. The first reference to one, implying that it was a normal feature of the occasion, comes with the fourth production he and Jones worked on, the *Haddington Masque* of 1608. His description is revealing, and worth quoting at length (the first scene alludes to the family name of Lord Haddington's bride):

> The *scene* to this *Masque*, was a high, steepe, red cliffe, advancing it selfe into the cloudes, figuring the place, from whence . . . the honourable family of the RADCLIFFES first took their name . . . before which, on the two sides, were erected two *pilasters*, chardg'd with spoiles & *trophees*, of *love*, and his *mother*, consecrate to *marriage*: amongst which were old and young persons figur'd, bound with *roses*, the wedding garments, rocks, and spindles, hearts transfixt with arrowes, others flaming, *virgins* girdles, gyrlonds, and worlds of such

like; all wrought round and bold: and over-head two personages, *triumph* and *victory*, in flying postures, and twise as big as the life, in place of the arch, and holding a gyrlond of *myrtle* for the key. All which, with the *pillars*, seem'd to be of burnished gold, and emboss'd out of the metall.[9]

Jones's scenic design, as described by Jonson, seems at a more 'primitive' stage of development than that of his Italian contemporaries, or even predecessors. Apparently both the proscenium and the set are simultaneously visible, instead of one being a visual prelude to the other. This may be an effect of Jonson's description, which takes its cue from the emblematic significance of the set, and starts by decoding it into words. Having given verbal meaning priority, his rhetoric then expounds the proscenium point by point, as if its syntax consisted of a series of statements. Even though the description is unprecedentedly fulsome it does not faithfully represent the visual experience of apprehending Jones's overall design, or *apparato* as the Italians called it.

Of course Jonson's fidelity is otherwise engaged. The tendency of his description does reflect the way in which most of the Jacobean court would have 'read' what they saw before them: their reception would literally have been a reading, given their cultural predisposition to translate images into words. But if we turn Jonson's account back to front, we can see through the eyes of the few courtiers who were following what Jones was doing. He sums up, for example, 'All which, with the *pillars*, seem'd to be of burnished gold . . .' That is, the proscenium is a total structure, not just a sequence of signifying items: '*triumph* and *victory*' are 'in place of the arch . . . holding a gyrlond of *myrtle* for the key'. That is, the structure has a properly architectural syntax, which works consistently even when parts are paraphrased by figuration. The pilasters support the arch, and are not separate units as they seem at first.

Jonson's rather casual phrase, 'in place of the arch', suggests that even in these early years it was customary for Jones to use a proscenium arch. With the next year's production, *The Masque of Queens* (1609), Jonson makes the same assumption: 'he devis'd two eminent figures of *Honor*, & *Vertue*, for the *Arch*'.[10] The use in the *Haddington Masque* of flying Victories holding up a wreath suggests that these were roundheaded arches, like Roman triumphal arches. In two later productions, the *Somerset Masque* (1614) and *Lovers Made Men* (1617), the writers, Campion and Jonson, both refer to the proscenium as 'an Arch Triumphal'.[11] Neither of these was designed by Jones – the first was by Costantino de' Servi and the second by Nicholas Lanier – but they may reflect his example. He by then was probably experimenting with square or rectangular proscenia. Even in 1609 he was shifting between different possibilities. The print after Rosso Fiorentino which gave him the idea for the set and proscenium of *Queens* shows a roundheaded arch, but his surviving drawing of the set (plate 21) suggests a flattening of the upper section.[12]

Rereading Jonson's description for the *Haddington Masque* will not answer the question whether, in these early productions, Jones initially showed proscenium and set together. But a text of two years later, Daniel's *Tethys' Festival* (1610), suggests that he did. Daniel's description does not have to be unscrambled, and transposed from a verbal to a visual key. He makes a point (quite possibly in opposition to Jonson) of saying that he 'will describe' the spectacle 'in the language of the architector who contrived it, and speaks in his own mestier to such as are understanders and lovers of that design'. He tells us that the drawing aside of a curtain revealed the first scene, but also, at the same time, the proscenium. This consisted of two gigantic figures of sea-gods, Neptune and Nereus, standing on pedestals before two pilasters, which supported a frieze bearing other figures and a central compartment with the title of the masque. There was also a feigned drapery gathered in folds and hanging down beside the pilasters, obviously imitated from Riccio.[13] In fact all the formal features of the fully developed Italian proscenium type are present, yet there appears to be no clear conceptual distinction between proscenium and scene.

These were still early days in Jones's scenography. Even in Italy the proscenium was a relatively new species in the field of design. He has learned to deploy its formal vocabulary perfectly well; but his practice is haunted by vestiges of older design habits which Italian artists had by now refined out of their work. The most obvious is the convention of overbearing terminal figures set up to police the frontier between fiction and reality. Daniel's description of Neptune and Nereus is elaborate, and makes them loom large. In fact they are charged with uncomfortable political significance, alluding to a current problem which the masque addresses in coded terms that the audience would have understood. The English and Dutch had been in dispute over fishing rights in the North Sea. The dispute was now being settled, and the creation of Prince Henry as Prince of Wales – the occasion of this masque – was used by the States-General to send a conciliatory embassy.[14] But the situation had been awkward, and the masque assertively overstates the English case. Striving to represent the English position in the figuration of his proscenium, Jones has regressed to a primitive phase in the evolution of the scenic art.

Implicit in the history of the proscenium during the sixteenth century had been a contest between figuration and architecture. One resolution of this conflict had been propounded by Palladio in the Teatro Olimpico, which gave the primacy to architecture, on the authority of Roman antiquity. This may have been all very well for the Accademia Olimpica, but would not necessarily do for the court theatres which sponsored most of the new scenography. In practice the contest could always be accommodated, if not settled, by virtue of the fact that scenic architecture was always feigned, so that the contestants could meet each other on the terrain of painting – both figures and architecture were pictured. Jones's proscenia act out this conflict over the span of his career, their allegiance gradually shifting from figuration to architecture, as he himself becomes more and more of an architect (with a later move back towards figuration, after he had mastered the proscenium as an architectural form). The earlier emphasis on terminal figures is a case in point. In his second masque, *Hymenaei* (1606), he had used a kind of inner proscenium with gigantic figures of Hercules and Atlas holding up the sky.[15] The giant gods for *Tethys' Festival* provide the same kind of animistic theatrical thrill, even though they are supposed to be parts of an architectural scheme. In later years Jones could design a proscenium composed of terminal forms with figures in a less barnstorming vein. In *Neptune's Triumph* in 1624 (eventually performed in a different version the following year) he devised a proscenium of 'two erected pillars', dedicated to Neptune. Although these are politically charged, taking over Charles V's *impresa* of empire over the seas,[16] they make their point calmly, figuration being subordinated to architecture.

In theory, Jones's proscenia were always constructed as properly architectural forms which provided a 'ground', as he called it, for ornamental and symbolic figuration. Even in *The Haddington Masque*, where the pilasters are crowned by flying figures, these are 'in place of the arch', whose architecture is notionally present; and the sense of an architectural matrix under the figuration is always there. But in practice it took Jones a long time to conceive of the proscenium as a discrete structure, *sui generis* but with a basic architectual rationale. Even in the 1620s, when he had already spent over fifteen years in scenic design, he had not reached this point. This is shown by an elaborate drawing, probably of 1621, with a proscenium framing a scene of hunting[17] (plate 128). The hunt scene is quite lightly sketched in, while the proscenium is heavily worked with darker ink, and is a much more complex and spirited piece of drawing. Despite this strong graphic contrast, the proscenium is still drawn as if it were part of the scene; and its architectural basis seems to be eclipsed by the exuberant spread of ornament and figures. An even later design, for *Time Vindicated* (1623), again shows a proscenium drawn as continuous with the scene it encloses,[18] and not conceptually separate.

To us, for whom the proscenium arch is a cliché, Jones's difficulties in grasping the idea of it may provoke impatience. But we have to remember that he was rehearsing a very recent phase of the history of design, and making this the opportunity for, typically, complicating the issue so as to learn more – thinking, for example, of theatrical proscenia in relation to the problems of 'framing' monumental art, in frescoes, ceiling paintings, tapestries, and so on. However, by the 1630s his fully realised concept of the proscenium emerges, in which figures and ornament are subordinated to architecture. Significantly, the drawings from this decade show proscenium arches either as free-standing structures on their own, or else framing scenes which are stylistically homogeneous but formally discrete. The theory has not changed but the practice is quite different; and this is also reflected in the texts. In *Tethys' Festival* Daniel reports: 'the scene was discovered with these adornments', meaning the proscenium. In *Chloridia* (1631) Jonson first describes 'the ornament, which went about the *Scene*', and then the scene itself as revealed by the raising of the curtain.[19] The concepts seem almost identical – 'adornments' and 'ornament' – but the descriptions make clear that the first proscenium is auxiliary and over-figured, whereas the second is free-standing and architectonic.

Ornament in theory: the problem of grottesche

Jonson's phrase 'the ornament, which went about the *Scene*' becomes absolutely standard to describe Jones's proscenia throughout the 1630s, even though none of the masques after *Chloridia* was written by Jonson himself. Aurelian Townshend repeats it in the text of *Albion's Triumph* (1632), and thereafter it becomes a formula. The only significant variation in wording comes from Townshend in another masque of 1632, *Tempe Restored*, where he writes of 'the border serving for ornament to the scene'.[20] The word 'border', as well as recalling the original concept of a limit or frontier, reinforces the suggestions of 'ornament' – although the proscenium is now designed by Jones as a self-contained structure, it is still in the end subsidiary and peripheral, a contributory part of a greater whole. In order to understand this idea of the proscenium as 'ornament', it will be helpful to compare different but related uses of that word in a typical masque text of the 1630s, *Britannia Triumphans* (1638). This was by Davenant, who wrote all the masque texts from 1635 to 1640; and who, in his descriptions of the scenic designs, makes clear that he is following Jones's lead or even using Jones's own words. First, he refers to the proscenium as 'the ornament that enclosed the scene'. Then, after detailing the symbolic figures on it, he adds: 'Above these were other composed ornaments', making an implicit contrast between ornamental figuration and quasi-abstract ornamental forms made up with fanciful artifice. Later he describes the scene being 'changed into a peristylium of two orders, Doric and Ionic, with their several ornaments . . .'[21]

Plate 128. Jones, Proscenium and Hunt Scene, Chatsworth

The last usage obviously refers to the formal features which characterise the orders, and, in combination with more abstract qualities such as scale and proportion, constitute their respective identities. There is a potential contradiction in the idea of 'ornaments' being somehow intrinsic rather than ancillary; but the usage is standard and comes straight from the literature of architectural theory. However, its logical oddness sets off the other two usages in Davenant's text, which speak of 'ornaments', both figurative and artificial, borne by the proscenium, which is itself an 'ornament'. There is distinction and overlapping at the same time. It is as if the proscenium (like the orders) is in one sense constituted by the fact that it carries ornaments, and by the ornaments it carries, and in another sense an independent entity.

This ambivalence may be endemic to the proscenium as a form, especially when it is used for a masque, in which important action may take place both behind it (the appearance of the masquers) and in front of it (the dancing). It mediates between the scenic action and the audience, providing a frontier across which the transactions of representation and perception can take place; and on its own painted surface it mediates between 'picture' and architecture. This ambivalence registers in Jones's thinking about the proscenium even during the 1630s, when he had to all appearances mastered the form. In 1632 he refers to it as a 'frame' for the 'picture itself', which is the 'show' or scenic spectacle. By 1640 he is speaking of 'the work of this front, consisting of picture qualified with moral philosophy':[22] the proscenium is seen not just as a frame but as a picture proper. At the same time he can still use the word 'ornament' of it.

Luckily we can pursue Jones's thinking about ornament, since he made some lively and revealing notes on the topic in his Roman Sketchbook. To provide a context first of all for these notes, we need to look at the theory and practice of ornament inherited by Jones from his Italian predecessors. Leaving aside the ornaments of the orders – substantially a separate matter – we may begin with discussions of decorative ornament in the authors Jones studied, such as Serlio, Vasari and Lomazzo. They have an original point of reference in common. The agenda for these discussions had been set by Vitruvius, in his Seventh Book, dealing with the interior decoration of houses. His argument becomes polemical, so much so that Renaissance writers on ornament felt bound to take up a position towards it. Vitruvius's own position is this: painting is fictional representation, sometimes compounding fiction with illusionism, but it should always represent what is real, that which 'really exists or which can exist'; decorative painting is no exception to this rule, which is sanctioned by the practice of 'the ancients'.

A point especially pertinent to Jones is that Vitruvius will not even exempt scenic painting from the requirement of realistic representation, even though it could be thought to belong to the domain of fantasy. In fact, to exemplify the necessity of pictorial realism, he tells a long anecdote about the stage designer Apaturius, whose *scena* for the theatre of Tralles contained elements of illogical architectural fantasy, and who was forced to correct it 'so that it conformed to reality'.[23] Jones summarised this story in the margin of his copy; and other notes show he attended closely to its context, which connects stage design with decorative painting.

Vitruvius relates the progress of interior decoration in fresco from its simple beginnings. At first it replicated features of buildings themselves – feigning materials, such as marble, or architecture, such as cornices. This led on to more elaborate representations of architecture; to illusionistic paintings of the three types of stage scene, Tragic, Comic and Satyric; and to grand mythological subjects. This narration is used to bear down forcefully on modern decorative painting, against which Vitruvius makes a trenchant attack:

But those subjects which were copied from actual realities are scorned in these days of bad taste. We now have fresco paintings of monstrosities, rather than truthful representations of definite things. For instance, reeds are put in the place of columns, fluted appendages with curly leaves and volutes, instead of pediments, candelabra supporting representations of shrines, and on top of their pediments numerous tender stalks and volutes growing up from the roots and having human figures senselessly seated upon them; sometimes stalks having only half-length figures, some with human heads, others with the heads of animals.

Such things do not exist and cannot exist and never have existed.[24]

He is describing the paintings which, when rediscovered and imitated in the Renaissance, came to be called *grottesche*. Revived by the School of Raphael, with the authority of antiquarian research brilliantly brought to life by the technical virtuosity of Giovanni da Udine, they were popularised by artists and spread throughout Europe. But at the same time writers on art felt bound to acknowledge that Vitruvius had condemned them as unreal and irrational.

The full range of questions about ornament in the sixteenth century was by no means covered by the problem of grotesques; there were various other types of ornament. But discussions of that problem tended to raise issues about ornament in general, sometimes with the added emphasis of the dramatic tone in which Vitruvius had launched the controversy. In the broadest terms, the problem was about imitation. Renaissance theorists placed artists under a dual mandate, the imitation of nature and the imitation of the antique, the argument being that these aims were the same, since the ancients had been the supreme imitators of nature. But with grotesque ornament a conflict arose: antiquity pointed in opposite directions. Vitruvius was the only surviving writer on the topic, which tended to make his view canonical. On the other hand, the *grottesche* discovered in the Domus Aurea were the only considerable remnant of Roman painting. There was a clash of authority, between antique theory and antique practice; or, according to Vitruvius, between nature and the antique. In the event, *grottesche* were irresistible, given the fascinating beauty of the Domus Aurea frescoes, which can still be felt today, and the powerful recreation of their effects by Giovanni da Udine. Vasari testifies to this in his life of Giovanni: he and Raphael, at first sight of the frescoes, 'were both struck with amazement at the freshness, beauty and quality of those works . . . ' In the Vatican Logge, where he displayed his rediscovery of ancient stucco work alongside his skilful painting, he produced, says Vasari, 'the most beautiful, remarkable and excellent painting ever seen by human eyes'. There is no hint in this account of any problem of theory or doctrine; the emphasis is on Giovanni's revival of the decorative work of the ancients, whom he is said to have surpassed.[25]

Although Vasari's pragmatic tribute to Giovanni da Udine makes no mention of the Vitruvian denunciation of grotesques, he does not ignore it. His biographical narrative implicitly takes up the charge made by Vitruvius against grotesques, that they are unreal or irrational. Giovanni is seen to develop as a master of naturalistic painting, who first shows his talent as a child out hunting with his father, by drawing animals and birds. His early training is in the empirical atmosphere of Venice, from Giorgione; later, in the school of Raphael, he learns from a Flemish colleague to paint fruit, flowers and foliage; he also learns to paint landscape. The turning point for him, is the discovery of the Domus Aurea frescoes; to the study and recreation of them he devotes his career, with signal success. The modern master of grotesques has prepared for his life's work by learning to represent the natural world.

Of course this story does not answer the main point of the Vitruvian interdiction, that grotesques mix forms (from both nature and art) to produce unnatural hybrids. Nor is Vasari very exact in his use of the category 'nature'. To describe Giovanni's quickness in learning, he writes: 'he succeeded in copying convincingly, in a word, every natural object (tutte le cose naturali) – animals, fabrics, implements, vessels, landscapes, buildings and vegetation . . . '[26] It seems cavalier to sweep together all these, whether natural or artificial, as 'cose naturali'. The reason perhaps emerges in Vasari's other biography devoted to a specialist in grotesques, Morto da Feltre. This artist is presented as the precursor of Giovanni and the original pioneer in the whole field; Jones paraphrases Vasari in the margin of his copy: 'morto da feltre found / out agayne ye manner / of groteskes.'[27] The turning point of his biography is a hesitation between figure painting and grotesques: after going to see the cartoons of Leonardo and Michelangelo in Florence, he decides he cannot aspire to such work, 'wherefore he went back to working at his grotesques'.[28] In other words *grottesche* are seen as a lesser alternative to *storie*, to grand figurative compositions; and their content, as opposed to *figure*, can broadly be described as *cose naturali*. This leads to a perversely paradoxical reversal of the Vitruvian position. So Guicciardini can write of Cornelis Floris, who introduced grotesques into the Netherlands, as 'the first to bring into these countries from Italy the art of imitating grotesques naturally (al naturale)'.[29]

In characterising the range of Giovanni da Udine's subject-matter as 'tutte le cose naturali', Vasari not only stretches the category of 'nature' to generous proportions but also loosens the category 'grotesque', beginning to blur any strict distinction between *grottesche* proper and other kinds of ornament, which may give a similar effect of variety and fantasy without the hybridisation of forms. So he describes a frieze executed by Giovanni as 'pieno di festoni, di putti, di frutte, ed altre fantasie', where the 'fantasie' mentioned are no more than ordinary decorative motifs. And in the life of Donatello he says that the Cavalcanti Annunciation in Santa Croce has ornament 'alla grottesca', whereas the ornament is not grotesque at all, although it is imaginatively pseudo-antique.[30] In using the concept of grotesque flexibly, so that sometimes it has a specific meaning and sometimes overlaps or coincides with the general concept of ornament, Vasari reflects the practice of later generations of Cinquecento artists who, after the neo-classical purism of the school of Raphael, might mix grotesque and non-grotesque ornament together. Grotesque itself becomes hybridised.

The obvious place for this to happen was in festival design, as Vasari shows. A sequel to the life of Morto da Feltre is that of his follower in Florence, Andrea di Cosimo Feltrini, who first mingled figure painting with grotesques, composing them with greater order and in a more ample style, moving on from the *maniera* of the ancients. Vasari records his commissions for interior and exterior decoration (sgraffito façades), but especially his work on temporary festive structures for the weddings of Medici princes, and the triumphal entries of Leo X and Charles V.[31] This account of grotesque ornament being revived and modernised, and applied equally to house decoration and festival design is obviously pertinent to Jones's use of ornament; and his marginal notes show that he read these pages of Vasari attentively early in his career.

Vasari, despite his voracious interest in art as a practice above all, makes one concession to the theoretical bias of the Vitruvian doctrine of ornament. In the introductory section to the *Lives*, which he usually refers back to as the 'Theorica', he has a chapter about grotesques. He describes their fantastic and bizarre quality, but in an indulgent way, summing them up as 'cose senza alcuna regola'. He goes on: 'Thereafter they were subjected to rule, and on friezes and compartments had a most beautiful effect . . . '[32] This ought to mean that the introduction of 'regola' did away with the irrationality of grotesques; but the context rather suggests that they became not more rational but more regular. With his ambiguous use of the words 'regola' and 'regolate' Vasari appears to acknowledge a theoretical problem about grotesques while at the same time sliding away from it. This ambivalence is found in other Cinquecento writing on the topic, where it comes to seem almost endemic.

Serlio, the first writer to deal with decorative painting after the Renaissance efflorescence of *grottesche*, has the seeds of this ambivalence, although he follows a much stricter line than Vasari was to. Towards the end of his Fourth Book, on the five orders characterised as the chief ornaments of a building, he devotes a chapter to ornamental wall painting. This, he says, is a matter not for the painter's discretion but for the architect's supervisory control, and must be subject to 'regola'.[33] But Serlio is much less casual than Vasari about what 'regola' involves. There must be a logical relationship between wall surfaces and what is represented on them. Exterior walls may not have sky or landscape painted on them, since that would deny their solidity; interior walls may, since it is logical to feign openings through them onto the world outside. Façades may logically be painted with feigned marble, and feigned bronze statues in niches; or with motifs that could logically be attached to them, such as swags, festoons, shields and trophies. Walls of loggias or courtyards are permitted to show figures, animals, buildings –whatever can be viewed from them in reality. If your patron or painter wants, for example, a more colourful façade, says Serlio, then first of all represent feigned draperies, and on them you may reasonably paint whatever you please.[34]

Casuistical as this sounds, the underlying principles are serious. They are 'la ragione' and 'il vero'. The artist who abides by them 'will imitate the truth, in accordance with decorum', and his work will be 'worthy of praise by all those who know the true from the false'.[35] This is the language of Vitruvius. Evidently Serlio is adopting the principles of Vitruvius's critique of wall-painting and on them basing his instructions to modern architects and painters. At the same time he illustrates these principles with models of rational, truthful decoration, the chief one being the Sala delle Prospettive in the Farnesina by his own master, Baldassare Peruzzi. His discussion also evokes the Loggia di Psiche by Giulio Romano and Giovanni da Udine (which he takes to be by Raphael).[36] Altogether, the neo-antique 'authenticity' of the Raphaelesque decoration of the Farnesina fits in well with the rules he adduces from his antique authority. Serlio articulates a position, substantiated with both theoretical and practical content, which can be called neo-Vitruvian.

But when he comes specifically to grotesques, he abandons the Vitruvian line. They are 'molte bene, & commode'. He does betray some guilt by saying defensively that they can be used 'sensa riprensione alcuna', following the good example of the ancients. He evades dealing with the 'reprehension' of Vitruvius, which logically he should accept or confront, by fudging the definition of what grotesques are. He identifies

> la licentia che s'ha di far ciò che si vuole, come sariano fogliami, frondi, fiori, animali, uccelli figure di qualunque sorte, mescolate però con animali... Qualche fiata si può fare una figuretta finta di cameo, o altra cosa di simile materia, qualche tempietto, & altre architetture si posson mescolare con queste...[37]

the freedom there is to depict whatever one wants, such as foliage, fronds, flowers, animals, birds, figures of whatever kind, mixed however with animals . . . Sometimes a feigned cameo figure can be depicted, or some other object of a similar substance, a little temple and other pieces of architecture can be mixed in with these motifs . . .

Serlio's imprecise syntax, and the ambiguity of his explanatory term, 'mescolare', fall short of a precise description of grotesques. He does not pinpoint the exact relationship of the various motifs; 'mescolare' could refer to the blending of forms or simply the mixture of forms – and in any case he states that sometimes the motifs are separate or self-contained. In effect he is relaxing and enlarging the category 'grotesque' (as Vasari was to), perhaps reflecting a growing eclecticism in the decorative styles of the post-Raphael generation, and certainly allowing himself a contradictory response to the authority of Vitruvius, which he champions and evades at the same time.

Like Vasari also, Serlio cannot discuss decorative painting and ornament without moving on to festival and stage design; and the association is obviously pertinent to Jones's interests.

Coming after Serlio, and contemporaneous with Vasari, Daniele Barbaro was the most crucial of the authors Jones read on ornament in general and grotesques in particular. Since he studied the text of Vitruvius through Barbaro's Italian translation, the accompanying commentary was bound to make an impression. Barbaro, in characteristic Aristotelian vein, reinforces the case made by Vitruvius against grotesques, on the grounds that 'la pittura è una imitatione delle cose che sono, o che possono essere . . .' (painting is a representation of things which are, or which can be). He also attributes them to 'fantasia', the antithesis of reason. This is the faculty which in dreams produces similar confusions of natural species, similar monstrosities and unrealities. Grotesques, then, may be called the 'sogni della pittura'.[38] Barbaro is emphatically arguing on the side of Vitruvius, but the image is too suggestive to sit obediently inside the argument. We begin to sense the same ambivalence that other, less dutiful responses to the Vitruvian text had shown more openly. As Barbaro's commentary continues, it strays quite obviously from the path of neo-classical doctrine. He employs the conventional rhetorical strategy of saying he will not amplify Vitruvius's general remarks on painting, while going on to do precisely that. The art of painting, as he describes it, is frankly that practised in sixteenth-century Venice. The two subjects he dwells on are landscape and the female nude, recalling the archetypally Venetian Sleeping Venus of Giorgione and Titian. He praises sfumato and softness of outline, which persuade the eye to see what it does not see.[39] In one way this is perfectly in accord with Vitruvius, who requires convincing mimesis of the real world;

in another way, by stressing self-conscious pleasure in the processes of illusion, it exalts that gratuitous aestheticism which had been the initial object of his attack.

Lomazzo is the first writer to try to sort out the conflict between the Vitruvian doctrine of ornament and the neo-antique revival of *grottesche* by the school of Raphael. In the Sixth Book of his *Trattato*, a work which undertakes to be consistently systematic, he discusses the problems involved and reviews the treatment of them by his predecessors, Serlio and Barbaro. In Book VI he devotes a chapter to the 'Composizione de le grottesche' (XLIX); but his discussion of grotesques, and of the general problems of rationality and realism in painted ornament, effectively begins in the previous chapter, on the composition of friezes. The fact that he at once places questions of ornament within the confines of architecture and its schematic partition of space is significant of his overall approach. He is dealing with friezes as painted accessories to *istorie*; and although he lets the painter display 'ogni bizarria e stravaganza' in this auxiliary ornament, he insists that it is governed by 'ragione', 'legge' and 'regola'. The painter must imitate nature, and observe decorum – this latter being determined by the content and *maniera* of the principal picture.[40]

To subject the bizarre and extravagant to reason seems a tall order. Lomazzo does not pause over the looming contradiction, but goes straight on to make it appear plausible in practice. First, he gives rules for ornamenting the friezes of the five classical orders. For the fifth, Composite order, he requires that any figures in the frieze should follow the character of the order, that is, be composite in nature. This means 'composing' creatures such as birds with wings and tails of foliage, or using mythic creatures like tritons, sirens, harpies or sphinxes. This is not offered as a recommendation but stated as a law derived from the work of the ancients: 'In short, this frieze admitted no entire figure of a living creature, but every one was "composed" in different ways . . .'[41] The tone of unexceptionable authority is tacitly aimed against Vitruvius, whose prohibition of 'composed' forms is turned on its head. This tone carries on into the next part of Lomazzo's argument, where he deals with an objection; if ornaments in friezes are 'bizarrie del pittore', why is the painter limited in what he can represent? The answer is that since painting represents what is both natural and beautiful, if it departs arbitrarily from nature it will produce disorder and lose its beauty. Here, Lomazzo turns to, rather than away from, Vitruvius; and gives almost the same Aristotelian definition of painting,

> essendo la pittura una dimostrazione di tutte le cose che sono fatte e che si possono imaginar di potersi fare . . .[42]

painting being a display of everything that is created, and can be imagined as able to be created

The words of Vitruvius, in Barbaro's translation, and then in his editorial paraphrase, are:

> la pittura si fa imagine di quello che è, & puo esser ... la pittura è una imitazione delle cose, che sono, o che possono essere ... [43]

> by painting an image is made of what is, and can be ... painting is a representation of things which are, or which can be ...

Barbaro and Lomazzo are each nudging the text in a different direction. Barbaro, by using the term 'imitatione' in place of 'imagine', turns it into a strict Aristotelian pronouncement. Lomazzo, by stressing the role of imagination, tends to compromise the Vitruvian position he is arguing and leave it open to the 'bizarrie del pittore', the painter's licentious fantasies.

Lomazzo's argument is carefully handled but logically unstable, as it offers to accommodate concepts inimical to each other. In moving on to the actual topic of grotesques it begins to work more convincingly. At first it merely sets Barbaro and Serlio against each other as rival authorities. Barbaro had called grotesques 'sogni e chimere della pittura', unreal creations with no point. Serlio, on the other hand, had argued for their practical function, as legitimate ornament to fill otherwise empty subsidiary spaces in schemes of decoration. For Lomazzo's purposes, the second argument is more useful but less interesting. But here he adds a powerful hypothesis, or rather presumption, on his own part: grotesques are not meaningless – they constitute an entire pictorial language with its own raison d'être. It is an enigmatic language, a code, like Egyptian hieroglyphs, in which covert meanings can be expressed as they are in emblems and *imprese*. It is used alongside the more obvious, demonstrative language of monumental figurative painting, in the margins and borders of the *istoria*, to draw out the same ideas in a deliberately less accessible mode.[44]

This explanation of grotesques, probably derived from the antiquarian researches and speculations of Pirro Ligorio,[45] is historically implausible but extremely effective within Lomazzo's argument. It deals with Vitruvius's objection that grotesques are no more than arbitrary fabrications, deviations from reality. In justifying their idiosyncrasy, it reveals that they are covertly rational and realistic – they *are* systematic, and they *do* refer to reality. It follows that they are subject to rules of composition. There must be regard for symmetry and proportion in deploying the motifs within their spaces. There must also be 'verisimilitudine naturale' in representing them. For example, hybrid forms should be composed logically – it makes sense to put trees in place of columns because both will bear loads. The relative sizes of figures should be naturally plausible, and their relative positions should be naturally motivated. Lomazzo had already made the last point in the discussion of friezes, rejecting the unnaturalness of motifs such as children playing with snakes or wild animals. The demand for naturalism brings Lomazzo back again to a Vitruvian position; and in his lengthy denunciation of wrongly designed grotesques he sounds uncannily like Vitruvius denouncing the whole style in the first place.[46]

Lomazzo's idea of grotesques as a second language, a spirited but enigmatic gloss on the standard language of monumental figuration, is the most capable attempt by a sixteenth-century writer to confront the challenge posed by Vitruvius. He sums up his discussion by comparing the relationship of the two languages or discourses to that between prose and verse: grotesque ornament, with its mysterious stir of significance, translates the central tableau into a kind of poetry, drawing it off to the margins but expressing it more beautifully, 'convertendo l'istoria in favola'.[47]

Such a suggestive conclusion indicates both the power and the unsolved difficulties of Lomazzo's argument. He seems to be drifting towards aesthetic heresy, reversing the relative importance of the centre and the periphery. His discovery of grotesques as a sort of alternative (and not just subsidiary) discourse is reflected in the major volume of poems he published called *Le Grottesche* which, he explains, are so called not only for the range of subject matter and the pleasurable variety of invention but also because of 'the morality which they contain'.[48] In the end, his revision of Vitruvius does not settle the odd relationship he originally proposes between 'ragione' and 'bizarria'. This shows especially when he defines the quality which the painter of grotesques needs:

> in the devising of grotesques, more than in any other form of invention, you feel a certain frenzy and a natural strangeness (natural bizarria) ... for this both natural inspiration and artifice (furia naturale ed arte) have to work together jointly.[49]

This is an ingenious move, appropriating the Vitruvian criterion of the 'natural' to describe the working of the individual artist's imagination, which is after all a part of nature. Fantasy, instead of being an affront to nature, becomes an expression of it; and art, which in Vitruvius's account abetted the unreality of grotesques, becomes instead a check or discipline on natural energies. Nature and art cooperate in the production of grotesques, 'furia naturale ed arte'. Lomazzo preserves the framework in which Vitruvius had set up the discussion, but alters or stretches some of the concepts involved. It is not obvious, for example, that the concept of 'nature' has the elasticity he demands of it. At one moment it figures in Aristotelian guise, with reference to the idea of art as a mimesis of reality, at another in Platonic guise, with reference to the idea of the artist as singularly and arbitrarily inspired. A phrase such as 'natural bizarria' tugs in two directions. Lomazzo needs, and has, a touch of 'furia naturale' on his own account to hold this argument together.

Jones on ornament

Jones studied Lomazzo's treatise with sustained attention; and clearly Lomazzo's discussion of grotesques had important implications for his own use of ornament, especially on the proscenium arches of his masques and plays. The fact that he used grotesques sparingly makes no difference. Lomazzo implies that instead of being an eccentricity they are the paradigm of all ornament, because they can use any motif; the potential scope of 'la grottesca' is universal,

> per ciò che lei sola nell'arte sono concessi sacrifici, trofei, istromenti, gradi concavi, conversi, in giro e pendenti e rilevati; et oltre di ciò tutti gli animali, fogliami, arbori, figure, uccelli, sassi, monti, fiumi, campi, cieli, tempeste, saette, tuoni, frondi, fiori, frutti, lucerne, candelieri accesi, chimere, mostri et, in somma, tutto quello che si può trovare et imaginare.[50]

> because it alone in the realm of art is granted sacrifices, trophies, instruments, flights of steps concave, convex, round, both overhanging and ascending; and furthermore all kinds of animals, foliage, trees, figures, birds, rocks, mountains, rivers, fields, skies, tempests, lightnings, thunders, fronds, flowers, fruits, lamps, lighted candelabra, chimeras, monsters and, in short, everything that can be discovered and imagined.

The final formula recalls Vitruvius's definition of the subject-matter of painting, so that grotesques become the paradigm of *pittura* in general. Lomazzo's discussion takes on the widest application; and it certainly applies to Jones, who took up the idea of ornament as complementary to *storia*, an alternative language into which the grand propositions of *storia* could be more subtly translated. This is how his proscenia and the grand tableaux of the masques are gradually developed in relation to each other, as complementary forms of discourse.

His view of ornament, including the problems raised by the debate over grotesques, is documented both in designs and in words: in drawings for proscenia and for interior decoration, mostly from the 1630s, and in some notes made in the Roman Sketchbook early in 1615, just after his return from Italy. A useful way into these notes is provided by a text dating from

1613, not long before Jones set out for Italy. This is the *Memorable Masque* of George Chapman, produced to celebrate the wedding of Princess Elizabeth to the Elector Palatine. Chapman was a friend and admirer of Jones, who designed the masque, and his description of the designs details them with what sounds like great fidelity; it can only have been worked out in close collaboration with Jones. The masquers, from the Inns of Court, rode in procession to Whitehall. Some were in chariots, decorated in two distinct styles. Firstly came

> two cars triumphal, adorned with great mask-heads, festoons, scrolls, and antic leaves, every part enriched with silver and gold.
>
> The last chariot, which was most of all adorned, had his whole frame filled with moulded work, mixed all with paintings and glittering scarfings of silver, over which was cast a canopy of gold borne up with antic figures, and all composed *à la grotesca*. Before this, in the seat of it as the charioteer, was advanced a strange person, and as strangely habited, half French, half Swiss, his name Capriccio... [51]

The first chariots have straightforward neo-antique ornament. The last one is ornamented with grotesques. It emerges that there is a point in the stylistic contrast, which becomes a symbolic motif leading into the action of the masque.

The earlier two chariots carry the musicians, who in the masque represent the priests of Phoebus, the Phoebades. The later one carries Eunomia, goddess of honour, and Plutus, god of wealth; but the special accentuation of its ornament comes from the figure of Capriccio, who is the leading character in the antimasque. The key to his character is given by one of his speeches:

> A man must be a second Proteus, and turn himself into all shapes, like Ulysses, to wind through the straits of this pinching vale of misery.[52]

Capriccio enacts the idea of gratuitous change or metamorphosis; and that idea has been symbolised in advance by the grotesque ornament on his chariot. This could suggest a purist Vitruvian rejection of grotesques, but the context rather suggests a tolerance for them. The grotesques of Capriccio's chariot work as a metaphor, but they also form part of the overall antique style which Jones's designs match to Chapman's learned, neo-classical text. They evoke a knowledge of Vitruvian doctrine in a humorous, self-conscious spirit; and the allegiance implied is to the richness of antiquity in general, rather than to one narrow school of thought.

Jones's flexible attitude towards 'capriccio' in antique art comes out in a marginal note inserted in his Palladio. He is writing less than two years later, and reflecting on his recent Italian travels. He had been struck by the variety of texture in the materials of ancient Roman building, instancing the baths at Baia:

> lik wise at yᵉ Thearmi at Baia . . . for yᵉ Romans varried thes things according to thear Cappriccio mingling on wiᵗʰ an other. so yt sheaud well.⁵³

'Capriccio' here is not just whim or wilfulness but the exercise of aesthetic choice to produce effects which satisfy on pragmatic rather than doctrinal grounds. It seems a flighty word to use about the ancient Romans, but that gesture or affectation suggests the breadth of Jones's sympathies, and the habit of seeing antiquity through modern Italian eyes.

At this point in his career, about to take up his new responsibilities as Surveyor of the King's Works, Jones is just as willing to admit 'Capriccio' into architecture as into stage design. But his tolerance included reservations and qualifications. The notes in the Roman Sketchbook show him working out his attitude to what he called 'capricious ornaments'. There are three notes which bear on this topic. Two are dated 19 and 20 January 1614 [i.e. 1615] and were written just after his return to England from Italy. The other is undated, and could have been written around the same time or, more likely, earlier in Italy. It is probably the earliest, since it is untroubled by the questions which make the other notes more complicated. Jones heads it 'of Charriotes and Poops of anticke shipes', which makes it sound like antiquarian research; but it becomes clear that he is thinking of neo-antique structures for stage or festival design:

> thear formes ar uarried according to the Subject ether rich or Playne Cap[r]iccious or Sodo and soumtimes Comp[o]sed of Rock or vaines or cloudes sheles and such leyke . . .

The idea of 'formes' which are 'Capriccious' is explained by contrast to 'Sodo' (solid) and by association with 'Composed': they are constructed of decoratively varied parts. Jones goes on:

> but the ordinary forme is most in imitatio[n] of gouldsmiths worke and ornamentes of Architectur as Cornishmentes terme Cartouses of seuerall kynds quadraturs for storietti scroules sfinckes harpyes mask heads of all kyndes . . .

The list of 'ornamentes of architecture' is quite promiscuous, mixing ornament intrinsic to the orders with auxiliary ornament, and simple forms with hybrid forms or grotesques. It seems to come to an arbitrary halt, as if it could go on indefinitely; and its rhetoric resembles the manic breathlessness of Lucky's tirade in *Waiting for Godot*. On the whole, Jones's description, which continues for over a page, is worked out in an orderly way, and it emphasises the principle of decorum: the parts of the structure, however varied, should be appropriate to the deity or person it conveys. But the mention of ornament seems to release an indefinite stream of words, as if the pleasure of rehearsing the rich variety of motifs can only be curtailed with difficulty. Jones's fervid writing takes on the 'capricious' or 'grotesque' style.

The note dated '19 January 1614' breaks out even more into this style. Jones is comparing 'design' (he means the general concept of *disegno*, with particular reference to painting) and architecture. The analogy turns on Alberti's concept of 'compositio', the building up of parts into the whole:

> As in dessigne first on Sttudies the partes of the boddy of man as Eyees noses mouthes Eares and so of the rest to bee practicke in the partes sepperat ear on comm to put them toggethear to maak a hoole figgure (and cloath yt) and consequently a hoole Storry wth all ye ornamentes
>
> So in Architecture on must Studdy the Partes as loges Entranses Haales Chambers Staires doures windoues. and then adorrne them wth colloms Cornishes sfondati. stattues. Paintings. Compartimentes. quadraturs. Cartochi tearmi festoni armes. Emprese. massquati folliami. Vasi. harpis. Puttini. scarfinges Stratsi. Scroules. bacementes. balustri Risialti. lions, or eagls claues, conuerted in to folliami. sattires serpentes victories, or angels, antike heads in shells. Cherrubins heads wi^th winges. heades of beastes. Pedistals. Cornucopias. basketes of fruites. trofees. Juels. and agates medalie. draperies. frontispices Broken. and Composed

This is an unabashed essay in verbal *grottesche*. Jones covers the page as if it were a blank wall with a wonderful variety of ornament, promiscuously mingling motifs in a hybrid language of English and Italian. There is no distinction between different modes of ornament: intrinsic or auxiliary, major or minor, carved or painted, simple or grotesque. The careful scheme of the analogy between design and architecture, which is the ostensible structure of the piece, is swamped by a plethora of ornament – the attitude to which seems utterly undiscriminating.

After this outburst Jones added a last small paragraph, a coda of repentance. As he poured out his stream of exotic words his handwriting had started to run off the straight. Afterwards he noticed this, and wrote in neat straight lines:

> nooate
>
> I must euer remember to Curbe ye deffette of wrighting and drauinge awrye upwards to ye right hande and rather sinn in the contrary

By displacing the blame onto his handwriting he reproaches himself for the pleasurable excess just committed.[54]

Jones was not unique in his 'sin', whatever idiosyncratic guilt he may have felt at momentarily straying from the straight and narrow path of truth, reason, rule and decorum towards the temptations of insubordination and eclecticism. His Protestant mentality merely made him uneasily sensitive to a problem which his Italian colleagues handled more briskly. His freewheeling list of ornamental motifs fits into an accepted convention. Such lists were a standard rhetorical means of representing the ornamental vocabulary of Cinquecento art in all its breadth and variety. We have already seen this rhetoric used by Serlio, and by Lomazzo, whose enthusiastic account of grotesque ornament as a universal language throws intellectual caution and theoretical scruple to the winds.

But someone who began as a Protestant and ended as a strictly observant classicist necessarily sought more consistency and certainty than his Italian authors seemed to care about. A close comparison can be made with Jones's contemporary Scamozzi, just deceased, who had talked with him earlier in Venice and who was preparing his architectural treatise for the press at much the same time as Jones was writing these notes. Scamozzi is almost unique among practising artists in not only repeating Vitruvius's prohibition of grotesques but explicitly approving it. In their place he recommends simple and unadulterated ornament. He gives two engraved examples to illustrate what he means. One is very fussily designed, and goes against the spirit of his recommendation; but the other contains grotesque motifs, and clearly contravenes it. To adorn ceilings he recommends following the ancients, and begins to list a repertory of possible motifs:

> si possono ornare con compartimenti legati con Cartelle, Mascare, Festoni, e tallhor con girari di fogliami, Arabeschi & intagli: fraponendovi alcune Storie, Puttini, & animali . . . [55]
>
> they can be decorated with linked compartments, with placards, masks, festoons, and sometimes with rinceaux, arabesques and carvings: interspersed with narratives, putti, and animals . . .

Scamozzi's long sentence is articulated into the 'compartimenti legati' which he recommends to the designer; but his orderly syntax is in danger of being swamped by the multiplying vocabulary of ornament which generates its familiar, hectic rhetorical momentum.

Scamozzi, easily the stuffiest writer Jones would have read on the subject, shows how difficult it is in the end to think through the problems of ornament in a completely rigorous way. But Jones himself made a determined effort to do so. After detailing the endlessly pleasurable possibilities of ornament in his note of 19 January, he wrote another note the following day to sort out the questions he had raised. It is an essay in speculation but also in self-discipline, and although dated 'friday ye 20 January 1614' it is written on the page before the earlier note, as if it had to acquire priority:

> In all inuencions of C[a]ppresious ornamentes on must first designe ye Ground, or ye thing plaine, as yt is for youse, and on that, uarry it, addorne yt. Compose yt wth deccorum according to the youse, and ye order yt is of, as in the Cartouses I haue of Tarquinnio Ligustri of Vitterbo.
> and to saie true all thes Composed ornamentes the wch Procced out of ye aboundance of dessignes, and wear brought in by Mihill Angell and his followers, in my oppignion do not well in sollid Architecture and ye facciati of houses, but in gardens loggis, stucco or ornaments of chimnies peeces, or the innerparts of houses thes composisiones ar of neccesety to be youshed: for as outwar[d]ly euery wyse ma[n] carrieth a grauiti in Publicke Places, whear ther is nothing els looked for, y[e]t inwardly hath his Immaginacy set free, and sumetimes licenciously flying out, as nature hirsealf dooth often tymes Strauagantly, to dellight, amase us sumtimes moufe us to laughter, Sumtimes to Contemplatio[n] and horror, So in architecture ye outward ornamentes oft to be, Sollid, proporsionable according to the rulles, masculine and unaffected
> whears within the Cimeras youshed by the ansientes the varried and Compoced ornamentes both of the house yt Sealf and the moueables within it ar most commendable

The earlier note had stopped inconclusively on the word 'composed', as if at a stumbling-block, and that concept now becomes the theme of Jones's self-critique, a critique reinforced by writing on the page before the arrière pensée of the day after.

Jones's note is divided into two parts, giving two rules for 'capricious' or 'composed' ornaments. The first rule deals with their design, the second with their proper situation. The fundamental doctrine which underlies these rules is the analogy (originating with Vitruvius) of a building to the human body, which Jones had developed in his previous note at what came to be disproportionate length. The framework in which the rules are generated from this doctrine is derived – again, as in the previous note – from Alberti, whose texts were fundamental for Renaissance architectural and art theory. Jones is trying to work out basic principles.

The idea that 'capricious ornaments' in architecture must be designed by adding to an elementary form, 'the thing plain', follows Alberti's theory of ornament. This was most strikingly expressed, as we have seen, by comparing the application of ornament to a building with the dressing of a naked body:

> è bisogno haver finito cosi ignuda tutta la tua muraglia avanti che tu la vesti di ornamenti, & l'ultima cosa sarà lo addornala.[56]

> We should erect our Building naked, and let it be quite compleated before we dress it with Ornaments, which should always be our last Work...

Jones marked an instance of this in his Palladio, a drawing of the substructure of an Ionic capital before its ornament was added, described as 'il vivo senza la voluta del capitello' or as he translated in the margin 'ye naked of ye Capitell wthout the vollute'.[57] He has used Alberti's comparison already in his note of 19 January, and it underlies his first rule here. He adds the principle of decorum, that is, correspondence to the order being used. This is illustrated by the 'Cartouses' of Tarquinio Ligustri, a range of designs for consoles adaptable in their relative austerity or richness to the different orders.

Jones enunciates his second rule more speculatively, and develops the basic analogy into a more subtle parallel between a building and the human person. Again the matrix of the parallel comes from Alberti. He had made a distinction between public and private architecture, and then between the more public and more private aspects of the private house itself. It is imperative for public buildings to display 'gravità'; and private houses in the city will necessarily show 'molto piu del grave' than those in the country. As the eighteenth-century English translation puts it in charmingly Whiggish vein, 'you have much more Liberty in the Country'.[58] Within the private house some spaces are more public and some more hidden away. In general, says Alberti, the more private the place, the more can individual inclination and pleasure be consulted in its adornment. Jones picks up Alberti's contrast between public and private architecture, and using the same antithesis between gravity and freedom, develops it into his own contrast between the 'outward' and the 'inward', both in human and, as it were, architectural behaviour.

'Composed ornaments' are to be confined to interiors, just as the free range of imagination takes place 'inwardly'; and the confinement is reflected in the broad but careful manoeuvres of Jones's syntax, which this time he keeps under control. But within these limits he represents the creative workings of the mind in untowardly eloquent terms, even breaking the bounds of language and 'licentiously flying out' to invent the key word 'Immaginacy' – it appears in the manuscript extempore, over the word 'mynd', which is struck out. Like Lomazzo, Jones sees this faculty of creative fantasy as a force of nature, whose energies are so varied as to embrace opposite extremes, 'delight' and 'horror'. He is describing what Lomazzo called 'furia naturale' or 'natural bizarria', the special faculty needed by the artist in composing grotesques, which are the private language of universal nature. The last synonym he uses for 'capricious ornaments' or 'composed ornaments' – 'Cimeras' – is a version of the Latin *chimaera* (Italian *chimera*), often used in referring to grotesques as a more exact description. Jonson insisted on the term, '*Chimaera's*, by the vulgar unaptly called *Grottesque*'; Thomas Marshall recorded Jones's less pedantic reference to 'Juan of Udena [Giovanni da Udine] ... excellt in grotescs, wch the ancients called Chimaraes'.[59] It is quite logical for Jones to extend the discussion, which is made to move towards the decoration of interiors, from architectural ornament to grotesques; but the introduction of grotesques brings with it a turbulent tradition of debate, full of unresolved problems, which threatens to upset Jones's attempt to put 'composed ornaments' in their place, and legislate for ornament in general. There is a tension between this attempt to rationalise the role of 'capriccio' in architecture, and the powerfully anarchic model of mental activity which he invokes to illustrate its qualities.

In practice this tension could be very productive. The dichotomy between exterior and interior, expressed as a contrast of 'masculine' and feminine ('nature herself'), sometimes seemed to coincide with the varied demands of Jones's royal patrons, who fitted the stereotype roles of 'grave' kings – James I and Charles I, not to mention Prince Henry – and reputedly 'stravagant' queens, whose levity was taken to be compounded by their Catholicism. When Jones built the chapel at St James's for Prince Charles's intended Catholic bride, he designed an exterior of doctrinaire neo-antique *gravitas* to contain (and perhaps disguise) the baroque paraphernalia within. And at the Queen's House there was the antithesis between the Palladian exterior, and the fanciful complexity of the interior decoration, some of it ordained by Henrietta Maria in a French style, some by Jones in exactly the terms he sets out here – as in the surviving grotesque ceiling decoration of the Queen's Bedchamber.[60]

But there were other structures in which this tension between rationality and fantasy could be turned to creative account, and these were the masques. That Jones regarded them as a kind of architecture in their own right is shown by the title-page of the *Memorable Masque* two years previously, which is described as 'Invented, and fashioned, with the ground, and speciall structure of the whole worke, By our Kingdomes most Artfull and Ingenious *Architect* Innigo Jones.'[61] The possibilities of architecture are not exhausted by the dichotomy of exterior and interior. By invoking the principle of decorum in his first rule, he implies a spectrum or scale of different architectures, which can stretch from 'solid Architecture', through interior decoration to the temporary forms of masques; and in fact when he came to use the 'Cartouses' of Tarquinio Ligustri (plate 153), his illustrations of decorum, it was in a stage design. Obviously the masque is a more volatile medium than 'solid Architecture', but it is also more dynamic. In the contrasting comportment of the disorderly, anarchic antimasque and the stately main masque it dramatises the same kinds of social and psychic tensions out of which the 'wise man' creates his architecture. And in the social and psychic economy of the masque as an aristocratic entertainment, an occasion of courtly pleasure, its extreme visual supererogation, its necessary display of rich and varied ornament, raises a large question about the control of that 'licentiously flying out' fantasy which ornament for Jones represents. It was ornament which provoked Jones to think about 'Immaginacy'; and the masques are his most ornamented works.

The proscenium as a 'composed ornament'

In the surviving designs for the masques, ornament is everywhere; but in the published texts, description and discussion of ornament focusses on one element of the whole, the proscenium arch. Whereas in the earlier texts this was referred to as 'the arch' or 'arch triumphal', in the texts of the 1630s it is almost always called 'the ornament'. In *Chloridia* (1631) Jonson refers to the proscenium as 'The ornament, which went about the *Scene*', and this becomes a formula used with only slight variations by all the writers who came after him. So we have 'the border serving for ornament to the scene' (*Tempe Restored*, 1632), 'the ornament that enclosed the scene' (*Britannia Triumphans*, 1638), and so on.[62] The accompanying descriptions, which after Jonson's dismissal become fuller and fuller under Jones's influence, suggest not lazy writers repeating each other but an idée fixe of the designer.

The idea is a simple one, and can be explained in relation to Jones's notes in the Roman Sketchbook. It comes out in the opening description from Carew's *Coelum Britannicum* (1634):

> The first thing that presented itself to the sight was a rich *ornament* that enclosed the scene, in the upper part of which were great branches of foliage growing out of leaves and husks, with a cornice at the top; and in the midst was placed a large compartment *composed of grotesque work* wherein were harpies with wings and lions' claws, and their hinder parts converted into leaves and branches; over all was a broken frontispiece wrought with scrolls and mask-heads of children, and within this a table adorned with a lesser compartment with this

inscription: COELUM BRITANNICUM. The two sides of this *ornament* were thus ordered: first from the ground arose a square basement, and on the plinth stood a great vase of gold, richly enchased and beautified with sculptures of great relieve, with fruitages hanging from the upper part; at the foot of this sat two youths naked, *in their natural colours*; each of these with one arm supported the vase, on the cover of which stood two young women in draperies, arm in arm ... On the other side was *the like composition*, but the design of the figures varied ... All this *ornament* was heightened with gold, and for the invention and *various composition* was the newest and most gracious that hath been done in this place.[63]

There is a partial drawing of the design which (supplemented by the engraving from which it is copied) shows what it looked like; but, more revealingly, the text shows the terms in which Jones conceived it. Its virtue is said to be its 'various composition'. It is a 'composed ornament' on a grand scale.

The parts which it composes together are themselves 'composed ornaments', either in the strict sense, specially constructed or hybrid forms, like the 'large compartment ... of grotesque work wherein were harpies', or in the general sense of groupings of discrete forms, like the vases or plinths attended by 'youths naked, in their natural colours'. This mixture of naturalism with grotesques reproduces the ambivalence in all ornament of which grotesques themselves had become the paradigm, the unsettlingly divided allegiance to naturalism and 'unnatural' artifice. But by spelling out this ambivalence on a magnified scale Jones makes it much easier to handle, much more receptive of the meanings he uses it to mediate.

He makes sure that his proscenia follow his own rules for 'composed ornaments' worked out years before, especially the first rule: 'one must first design the Ground, or the thing plain, as it is for use, and on that vary it, adorn it'. One of his slightest drawings happens to demonstrate this perfectly. It is a very quick sketch for a landscape or pastoral setting, with the stage front and proscenium shown as the merest outline[64] (plate 129). But the outline reveals a basic form, precisely the 'frame' that Jones speaks of in the text of *Tempe Restored*. A few extra lines at the top hint at the notion of a frieze, reminding us that even in its most reduced form the basic frame is not an abstract scheme but intrinsically an architectural concept. A text which gives the same basic concept is Davenant's *The Triumphs of the Prince d'Amour* (1636). This was produced in the Middle Temple without the resources of the court, and designed not by Jones but probably by an assistant. Its impoverished version of the Jonesian proscenium shows at its most basic: 'a Front of *Architecture* with two Pillasters at each side, and in

Plate 129. Jones, ?Setting for a Pastoral, Chatsworth

the middle of the Cornich a Compartement with [the] inscription in an Ovall'.[65] Jones's own proscenia are much richer, but they all have this fundamental form. The point is quite clear in the designs; and sometimes receives emphasis in the texts:

> The border at the front and sides that enclosed all the scene had first a *ground* of arbour-work . . . (*The Triumph of Peace*)

> over these hung shield-like compartments . . . these had for finishing the capital of a great pilaster, which served as a *ground* to stick them of, and bore up a large frieze . . . (*The Temple of Love*)[66]

He always starts with 'the Ground, or the thing plain'.

He also obeys his own direction to 'Compose . . . with decorum according to the use, and the order . . . ' The texts contain general observations about the appropriateness of proscenia to the masques or plays they introduce:

> on [the stage] was raised an ornament of a new invention agreeable to the subject . . . (*The Temple of Love*)

> The ornament enclosing the scene was made of a pastoral invention
> proper to the subject ... (*Florimène*)[67]

The designs obviously go much further than this, and show in great detail how Jones used the classical orders, with decorum and also with ingenuity, on his proscenium arches.

At first sight the most finished designs seem to cover, within the repertory of the orders, a very narrow range, considering the variety of themes covered by the corresponding masques and plays. One unusual drawing, not yet attributed to a specific production, which uses Salomonic columns and the Composite order,[68] is the odd man out; nearly all the others use the Doric order, admittedly in varying versions. One reason is that they are all derived from Riccio's proscenium of 1560 (plate 31). This seems to have made a lasting impression on Jones, as if he regarded it as an archetypal design (which, in historical terms, it probably was) worthy of imitation and variation. It was also a very firm and clear design, ideal to copy and adapt. Its use of the orders is mixed. The basic order is Doric, but according to Serlio – the principal published authority up to that time – the frieze with modilions belongs to the Composite order. Serlio calls the Doric order 'robusto' and associates it with strength; whereas he points out that the modillions in the Composite frieze make the order look especially 'rich'. He licenses a mixture of the two, illustrating a Doric doorway with modillions in the frieze invented by his master Peruzzi, which he praises as decorous and pleasing to the eye.[69] Riccio has adapted Serlio's 'mescolanza' (as he calls it) probably to suggest a relationship between the main participants of the occasion. The gentlemen of the Accademia degli Intronati are represented by the strong, simple Doric, and Duke Cosimo, to whom they are presenting their play, by the exalted Composite frieze, which bears his arms at the centre. This symbolic mingling of the orders within a firm, basic framework is taken over from Riccio by Jones and used as a precedent for continued imitation.

One pair of designs demonstrates this mingling very well. These are drawings of proscenia for Queen Henrietta Maria's pastoral plays, *Artenice* (1626) and *The Shepherds' Paradise* (1633). The first, for *Artenice* (plate 33), is not a full arch, because of the space in which the play was performed.[70] It consists of an entablature with a (probably feigned) curtain gathered under it and hanging down at the sides. Both are taken from Riccio (plate 31). They are matched with a rusticated basement. Jones's problem with architectural decorum here is evident. He has to find an order to suit both the humble genre of pastoral and the high rank of the actors, the Queen and her ladies. To English eyes, a Queen acting in a play was a gross indecorum anyway, so that Jones has to make a virtue of necessity, and try at least to compose the awkward social 'mescolanza' on an aesthetic level. He enriches the entablature, giving the architrave two fascias and the frieze more modillions, while preserving some Doric austerity. Then he tries to relate it to the picturesque rustication which has more affinity with the neighbouring Tuscan order. But the physical setting of the production, which ruled out columns or pilasters linking the rustic base to the entablature, forces him to design his royal pastoral order on separate levels, and these remain literally and metaphorically too far apart to make a plausible composition.

The same problem is brilliantly solved seven years later, for *The Shepherds' Paradise* (plate 114). Jones's drawing leaves the basement neutral, although at a later stage it would have been fully realised and related to the order of the proscenium, which this time includes pilasters.[71] The order is recognisably Doric, but ingeniously enriched. The frieze contains consoles, more elaborate than the plain modillions copied from Serlio via Riccio for the frieze of *Artenice*, but paradoxically more correct. Jones found authority for them in an antique frieze fragment owned by Lord Arundel (plate 3), which he had already followed in designing the Doric order of the Queen's closet in Somerset House chapel.[72] The pilasters are covered with figurative ornament alluding to the neo-Platonic themes of the play. This is mostly copied from an engraving by Battista del Moro (plate 130),[73] where it is articulated over a rigid scheme of compartments. Jones abandons the compartmentalisation, and makes the sense of an orderly arrangement implicit, showing the pilasters as a clearly defined 'ground' for the figuration. The pilasters are slender, and the entablature unusually shallow. Vitruvius associates slenderness with the 'feminine' orders, the Ionic and Corinthian; since, as before, the play was performed by the Queen and her ladies, Jones's subtle adjustment of proportions follows decorum. By enriching and feminising the Doric order he shifts it towards the other, grander end of the spectrum, and gives it a Corinthian feel. With a careful eye on classical theory and precedent, Jones invents an order which combines the pastoral and the regal, signifying with the most exact decorum both the shepherdess and the Queen.

Jones's use of the proscenium as a 'ground' on which to make a rapprochement between different orders, or to 'compose' hybrid orders out of the familiar types, can be seen over a range of his designs. In each case decorum is a prime concern. For the masque *Albion's Triumph* (1632)[74] (plate 8), in which Charles I appears as an imperial triumphator, he uses again Riccio's Doric/Composite prototype (plate 31). Doric is appropriate to the military theme; and to suggest imperial splendour Jones enriches the prototype in his own way. He complicates the surface texture by introducing compartments into the pilasters and frieze, increases the ornament, and, instead of leaving the curtain just to hang, he loops it around the pilasters. This enhancement of the order is reinforced when the first scene appears (plate 4), a Roman atrium in the Composite order,[75] which seems to make visible the grandeur implicit in the Doric of the proscenium. A similar design is for *The Temple of Love* (1635)[76] (plate 144), set in a legendary East, with Henrietta Maria as Indamora, Queen of Narsinga. Here the basic Doric of Riccio's proscenium receives a wealth of new ornament, 'consisting of Indian trophies'. The key additions seem to be the maskheads and festoons inserted in the neck of the pilasters. By giving the Doric an exotic inflection Jones has improvised an 'Indian' order, appropriate to the Queen's persona.

The decorum of the orders on these proscenia of the 1630s shows Jones experimenting, in the relative freedom offered by stage design, with the classical vocabulary which he knew so well. One of his most refined experiments is the proscenium of *Florimène* (1635)[77] (plate 97). This was another of the Queen's pastorals, but performed for her by a visiting French company. Yet again Jones uses Riccio's design, but this time strips it down almost to its elementary outline. The spaces left are architecturally defined, but no architectural ornament remains, and he substitutes figuration instead, 'of a pastoral invention proper to the subject'.[78] Doric, the order of pastoral, becomes wholly implicit, paraphrased by the figures. A reticence or absence represents the appropriate plainness of the order; while the beautifully handled complexity of the figural relationships provides an aesthetic enrichment which rises to the demands of the royal occasion.

The Jonesian style

In response to the complex problems of decorum often raised in the court theatre, Jones learned to treat the orders not just as a series of separate types but as a continuous spectrum, in which primary effects could either be complicated and intensified or dissolved into gradations and nuances. This kind of shifting, as the *Florimène* proscenium illustrates so well, was related to the role of figurative and other detail in the total economy of the grand 'ornament' which the proscenium constituted. On the architectonic matrix or 'ground' there could be a variety of relationships between the identifying features of the order and other ornament of a more general kind. The *Florimène* design especially directs our attention to that more general repertory of ornament, its vocabulary and syntax.

The proscenium designs of the 1630s show that Jones had evolved a personal style of ornament, which he practised with as much assurance as his variations of the orders. Its special character can perhaps best be captured by considering its lineage. It derives from two main sources. One is the School of Fontainebleau. The other is Italian late mannerism, the style of ornament

Ornament

Plate 130. Battista del Moro, Fame

which prevailed in pre-baroque Rome between the pontificates of Sixtus V and Paul V. The locus classicus for the first is the Galerie François Ier, which Jones probably visited in 1609. The second would have been all over Rome when he was there in 1614, and is most succinctly illustrated in the two chapels added by Sixtus and Paul to Santa Maria Maggiore.

Jones's synthesis and revision of these two differing styles was worked out, like much of his scenic design, with the help of prints. Although there was a great variety of etchings and engravings by or after Fontainebleau artists, he relied on quite a narrow range of this work. His favourite standby was *Le Livre de la conqueste de la Toison d'or*, a book of engravings with explanatory verses by Jacques Gohory, published by Jean de Mauregard in 1563. It is dedicated to King Charles IX, and Mauregard offers it as a pattern book, either for tapestries or for painting 'to adorn one day the rooms of your splendid palaces . . . or enrich some gallery'.[79] Whether this is a rhetorical gesture or a practical hope, it puts the book in a tradition. Just as the famous gallery of François I was published in various prints, Mauregard is publishing its successor, an ideal gallery which as yet has no material existence. In fact the prints did come to be used as patterns by other artists before Jones,[80] although not for the King – even so they do have the aesthetic and historical value Mauregard claimed, and Jones's fascination with them suggests an awareness of their importance.

The engravings are by René Boyvin after the designs of Léonard Thiry. Both artists were close to Rosso Fiorentino, the creator of the Galerie François Ier. Thiry was one of Rosso's most able assistants during the painting of the Galerie, according to Vasari unusually skilled in the execution of the master's designs; and many motifs from these designs reappear in the *Livre de la Toison d'or*. Boyvin was one of the leading engravers of Rosso's work, as Vasari again testifies.[81] Vasari does exaggerate their relationship, but at least this points up Boyvin's reputation as a pre-eminent interpreter of Rosso. The complementary efforts of Thiry and Boyvin produced a brilliant pastiche of Rosso's Galerie. The existing reproductive prints of it were sparse and unsatisfactory; their work is much closer to the original ensemble. The *Livre de la Toison d'or* is a unique aesthetic document, since it offers the most suggestive recollection of the capital achievement of the School of Fontainebleau.

As such, it was peculiarly useful to Jones for the design of proscenium arches in relation to the perspective scenery behind them. In a telling aside, he had called the proscenium a 'frame' and the scenes 'pictures' – to us now a platitude, but to him a central metaphor of his work, which he wanted to see as a kind of monumental art. Rosso's great contribution to monumental art had been to problematise the relationship between picture and frame, and the ornamental style of the Galerie was not just a dazzling repertoire of idiosyncrasies but an intrinsic part of his subversive project. Thiry and Boyvin's pastiche epitomises this project, and reiterates Rosso's searching questions about frames and framing. These were questions which arose continuously for Jones as a scenographer, and even more acutely for Jones as an aspiring designer of 'pictures with light and motion'.

By placing his allegories within settings of challenging complexity, where extreme formal variety was intensified by the mixture of media (painting and stucco), Rosso unsettled the conventional relationship between the central *storia* and the peripheral ornament used to frame it. In the *Livre de la Toison d'or* Rosso's challenge is reproduced: Thiry easily matches his formal inventiveness, and Boyvin succeeds, solely through engraving, in suggesting different media and levels of relief. The *encadrements*, like Rosso's, are strikingly ambiguous. They seem to subserve the meaning of the scenes which they frame, but at the same time take on a life of their own, which distracts the spectator's attention from the centre to the periphery. When the figures echo or respond to the actions of the main tableaux they do so in a melodramatic or irreverent fashion; and they thrive in a much richer, more intricate spatial environment than the titular protagonists of the story, whose space they at times carelessly impinge on. Psychologically and physically they challenge the centrality of the main narratives.

Jones took up this stimulating problem, but made something very different of it. On the positive side, he saw his 'frame', the proscenium, not just as a neutral architectural kit but as an 'ornament', a form to be made as aesthetically active as possible, saturated with signification. On the other hand, his 'pictures' were animated tableaux of the most exalted persons in the state, whose central importance could not be challenged. While his frames were as visually animated as possible, there had to be distinction and subordination in the relationship between frame and picture.

We can see him working this out in the unfinished drawing for a Proscenium and Hunt Scene of 1621 (plate 128). Many of the proscenium motifs – the scrolls in the centre of the frieze, the figures stretching across the corners, the large scrolls on the left containing fruit, the plinths with goats' heads – are recognisable from Thiry's *encadrements*, as are the discrepancies of scale between figures and ornament, and the irrational continuities of the composition. The boldness of the handling and the strong indications of different levels of relief (on the left side of the frieze, for example) remind one in turn of Boyvin's technique. Jones's design is very close to the *Livre de la Toison d'or* (e.g. plate 134), and thereby a tribute to Rosso. But it also revises what it borrows, recomposing the motifs on a 'ground' of architecture, probably (it is hard to make out) Riccio's familiar Doric arch. Jones contrives to relate this to the landscape scene by a historical conceit. Scamozzi had written that pedestals under columns originated in primitive

Plate 131. Jones, Copy of detail of encadrement, *Livre de la conqueste de la toison d'or*, Chatsworth

building from fixing tree trunks on mounds of packed earth; and Jones's pilasters rise from mounds or hillocks.[82] This other, neo-classical Jones is busy trying to rationalise his Rossoesque *encadrement*. The adaptation of it to frame a stage picture means that the central space necessarily becomes more powerful. It has to be enlarged, and Jones in classicising vein makes it a perfect square. The perspective scenery makes it deeper and more complex, so that the marginal area, albeit strongly modelled, now looks superficial by comparison, and not vice versa. Jones diminishes the marginal space, although here he hesitates. In the *Toison d'or* designs the ratio of width of picture to width of frame is about 1 : 3; he scales this down to between 1 : 6 and 1 : 10. Since the drawing is squared up, we can measure his hesitations. The scenic opening is 30 units square. On the right, the proscenium varies in width from 3 to 4 units; on the left it is 5 units at least. This is because on the left motifs from the *Toison d'or* spread far beyond the edges of the pilaster; on the right the ornament is changed or redrawn on a more meagre scale so as to fit the outline of the pilaster more nearly. The question of whether to let ornament or architecture gain the upper hand is unresolved. Even so, the conflict takes place in a situation where classical norms have been reinstated. While reproducing the style of the *Toison d'or* designs as if he were slavishly

Plate 132. René Boyvin after Léonard Thiry, *Toison d'or*, plate 24, British Library

under their spell, Jones turns the spatial and formal relations of these designs inside out.

It is logical for this drawing to be unfinished, as it shows Jones welcoming and undoing Rosso's work at the same time. He could only complete the process by developing an ornamental style of his own, which would consort more easily with the architecture of his proscenia. This was achieved by the next decade. In a preliminary drawing for one section of the proscenium of *Luminalia* (1638), which seems at first glance to be copied literally from the *Livre de la Toison d' or* (plates 131–2), he has made subtle adjustments in the poses of the figures and the relations of the decorative forms so as to gather them into a more contained, harmonious composition; and even his drawing technique, which softens the contrasts and relaxes the tensions in Boyvin's engraving, enables this overall reordering.[83] The *Florimène* proscenium of 1635 (plate 97) uses motifs from the *Toison d'or*, but assimilates them decisively. They are the figures on the left side of the frieze (plate 133); the title cartouche with its scrolls, garlands and reclining putti; and the compartment on the front of the stage platform[84] (plate 134). One feature he retains is the way figures and forms extend outside their local frames, like the putti with upraised arms or the hanging garlands, and he has even produced the scrolls in the centre upwards, adding gratuitously to this effect. But the effect is contained by the rational subdivision of the space, not at all in the spirit of the original. The most indicative change is to the compartment

Plate 133. Boyvin after Thiry, *Toison d'or*, plate 13, British Library

at the bottom, which Thiry showed curved, in imitation of Rosso's stuccowork. Jones redraws it as a properly graphic form – and straightens it out, which epitomises his new attitude to the Fontainebleau ornament stemming from Rosso which he still found so fascinating. His new personal *maniera* was a powerful medium of assimilation, powerful enough to reverse the historical tendency of Rosso's work. Jones used it to make restitution for Rosso's brilliant derangement of High Renaissance classicism, to straighten Rosso out. In this perspective we could give a name to the style of ornament Jones had evolved, and call it classical mannerism.

This style first becomes visible, through the surviving designs and texts, in the masques of 1632, *Albion's Triumph* on Twelfth Night for the King, and *Tempe Restored* on Shrove Tuesday for the Queen. These were the first productions for which Jones, having ousted Jonson, assumed overall responsibility. D. J. Gordon has shown that the proscenium for *Albion's Triumph* (plate 8) announces the new order of things: with the figures of Theory and Practice Jones makes a programmatic statement of his intellectual and aesthetic principles.[85] As a stylistic statement the proscenium is just as decisive. The motifs come from both Fontainebleau and Italian sources. The cartouches on the pilasters are adapted from the *Toison d'or* (plate 135). The putti lying on garlands in the frieze are from a kindred print of Fontainebleau decoration, an etching by Fantuzzi after Primaticcio[86]

Plate 134. Boyvin after Thiry, *Toison d'or*, plate 22, British Library

(plate 136). The other cartouches are from a series originally designed by Federigo Zuccaro (plate 137), but Jones has copied them from two engravings by his Roman friend Francesco Villamena.[87] Looking at one of these, the portrait of Clement VIII (plate 138), we can see how its composition makes structure as explicit as possible, whereas the Fontainebleau designs make structure so implicit as to attenuate or dissolve it. Jones takes his cue from the explicit compartmentalisation of the Italian design, adapting it to his basic architectural matrix, the Riccio proscenium (plate 31). The enclosure of Primaticcio's sleeping putti in carefully defined compartments is typical: discipline is reimposed on the fantasy and licence of Fontainebleau ornament.

That ornament positively throngs the proscenium of *Tempe Restored*. Again Jones makes a visual statement of principle, now with figures in the frieze of Invention and Knowledge, who are shown under attack:

Near to these were children holding ugly masks before their faces, in action as if they would affright them; others riding on tame beasts ... in the corners sat other children hardening of darts in lamps. But Invention and Knowledge seemed not to be diverted from their study by these childish bugbears. In the midst of the two sides of this border in short niches sat two ugly figures, the one a woman ... with the

Plate 135. Boyvin after Thiry, *Toison d'or*, plate 2, British Library

under-part of a satyr; this hag held in her hand a smiling vizard ... and was figured for Envy, under the mask of Friendship. On the other side was as horrid a man satyr ... this represented Curious Ignorance. The rest of the border was filled up with several fancies ... [88]

All these motifs come from the *Toison d'or* (plates 132, 139); Jones has simply recharacterised them. Although no drawing of the proscenium survives, it is easy to see what he is doing. By pressing the Fontainebleau motifs into a new stylistic context, he generates a stylistic conflict which translates into a moral and philosophical drama, the drama of his own aims as an artist. Their stylistic character – comprising such qualities as irrationality, licence, irreverence, inconsequence – can be allegorised into a bizarre but ineffectual assertiveness: they become 'childish bugbears'. At the same time they retain their aesthetic vivacity, as the lively description suggests, but under the disarming control of Jones's ruling concepts, Invention and Knowledge.

The 'descriptions' in the text of *Tempe Restored* are specifically attributed to Jones. His account of the proscenium, read alongside the visual material that went into the design, suggests with how much self-consciousness he went about constructing his own ornamental style. It was an attempted synthesis of conflicting historical tendencies: the classicism of the High

Plate 136. Antonio Fantuzzi after Francesco Primaticcio, Jupiter sending the three Goddesses to the Judgment of Paris

Renaissance and the mannerism which had undone and superseded it. In an even broader perspective this synthesis rehearsed, and attempted to compose, a problem about all ornament which Vitruvius had bequeathed to later writers and artists in the debates waged around grotesques: the conflict between a rational naturalism and 'unnatural' fantasy. Jones's line on this was a compromise, in keeping with his synthesis of styles. In the proscenium descriptions he often stresses that motifs from the natural world, such as swags of fruit, or human figures, are 'in their natural colours'. But he also stresses the element of inventive fantasy in his ornaments, expressed by describing them as 'fancies'.[89] His qualified tolerance of what he called 'composed ornaments' places him in the tradition which tended to view grotesques, in their controversial complexity, as paradigmatic of all ornament, rather than among those Vitruvian purists who dismissed them as perverse and eccentric. In effect, his use of ornament in the proscenia of the 1630s echoes Lomazzo's rationalisation of grotesques – and by implication all ornament – as a secondary language, a gloss on the central discourse of *storia*. So, in the proscenium of *Tempe Restored*, he takes over the gratuitous aesthetic discourse of Rosso's ornamental vocabulary and makes it mean something more, and tells us what it means.

Plate 137. Federigo Zuccaro, Design for a cartouche

On other proscenia of this period, stylistic dialogues – between mannerism and classicism, fantasy and nature – contribute to the allegorical meaning of the compositions. For the proscenium of *The Triumph of Peace* (1634) (plate 140) Jones derived numerous motifs from the *Toison d'or*: the placards with grotesque heads in profile (plate 141), the festoons of fruit, the central compartment in the frieze with putti blowing trumpets, and the 'trophies proper to feasts and triumphs, composed of masquing vizards and torches'[90] (plate 142). The masque was presented to the King by the Inns of Court, and was meant to be a conspicuously pleasurable divertissement which would also deliver a message about the relation between law and royal prerogative. The enterprise of constraining the King's attention (especially from outside the court) was a very delicate one, and the dialogue of styles on the proscenium acknowledges this. The many decorative motifs are not so sternly recharacterised as they were for *Tempe Restored*, but allowed to repeat their own language of aesthetic pleasure. And although they are reworked into much more carefully built up compositions than those they came from, Jones retains the idea from Thiry's *encadrements* of an overall structure as implicit or unobtrusive as possible, so as to pleasurably minimise the sense of constraint or regimentation. On the proscenium of the

Plate 138. Francesco Villamena after Marco Arconio,
Clement VIII

King's masque of two years before, *Albion's Triumph*, the sense of discipline and control had been appropriately uppermost; here the stylistic economy has a different balance.

We can see from these examples that the Jonesian style of ornament, while having a recognisable identity, is adaptable in different directions. Its identity is affirmed by two interesting drawings of John Webb (plate 143), where he paraphrases the *Triumph of Peace* design in a style which moves towards the baroque;[91] the experiment helps to bring his master's style into sharper focus. But that style could assume different inflections, in keeping with the decorum of the occasion. It has a more informal character, shown in *Florimène* and *The Triumph of Peace*, where as well the architectural order tends to retire off-stage. It can also appear grand and powerful, as in *Albion's Triumph* (plate 8), where the order is also more salient and assertive.

Naturally it is in the royal masques, those presented by the King or Queen, that the Jonesian style appears at its most powerful. The one surviving design for a Queen's masque is the proscenium of *The Temple of Love* (1635)[92] (plate 144), just as grand as that for *Albion's Triumph*. It uses motifs from Italian sources, and emphasises their classicising panache. The figures of the elephant and camel are excerpted from a fresco by Giulio Romano in the Palazzo del Tè (plates 145–6); and the other motifs are scaled up to that monumental pitch. The putti holding up the curtain come from the Villamena print of Clement VIII (plate 138). The cartouches on the pilasters are taken from a series of etchings of grotesques by Tempesta[93] (plate 147). Some of his etched motifs are delineated with very thin, delicate lines, and Jones has reproduced this effect in his frieze: the result is to increase the depth and contrast of relief, and add to the richness of the composition.

This 'royal' style came to be used not only in the court theatre but for schemes of interior decoration in the King's and Queen's residences. The association is a logical one, given the idea of seeing the stage 'pictures' and their 'frames' as equivalent to large decorative projects. The connexion between the two fields is neatly expressed in a sheet on which Jones has sketched a mixture of figuration and ornament (plate 148). The principal figure, copied (via an etching) from Primaticcio's Galerie d'Ulysse at Fontainebleau (plate 149) is intended for the proscenium of an unidentified scenic project entitled 'The Tragic Scene'[94] (plate 51). This consists only of a frieze, with reclining figures of Truth and Hercules (presumably meant for Fortitude). On another sheet, Jones tried to adapt a further figure from the Ulysses series for Hercules (plates 150–1). In the end he derived the figure of Truth from another Fontainebleau print (of Diana) after Primaticcio[95] (plate 152). What is suggestive about the first sheet is that the figure for the proscenium frieze accompanies sketches of grotesque ornament which, given their format, can only be meant for interior decoration. And the proscenium itself uses those 'cartouses of Tarquinio Ligustri' (plate 153) which Jones cited when making notes on 'composed ornaments' in architectural interiors. Clearly he regarded his ornamental style as a versatile medium, adaptable to either architecture or the theatre, just as he regarded his theatre projects as an integral part of his work overall.

Other artists also saw the Jonesian style as versatile, and adaptable from stage design to interior decoration. The figure of Truth on the Tragic Scene proscenium, for example, reappears in different contexts. She is on the ceiling of the Single Cube Room at Wilton, decorated by Jones's assistant Matthew Gooderick.[96] And in a slightly altered pose she figures in the frieze ornaments designed by Edward Pearce, another Jones assistant, published in 1640 (plate 154). Pearce here also uses motifs from Jones's decoration of Henrietta Maria's palace at Oatlands,[97] which he seems to regard no

Plate 139. Boyvin after Thiry, *Toison d'or*, plate 3, British Library

differently from the scenic ornament. What makes the two types stylistically homogeneous is their association with royalty, and in particular – since the Tragic Scene was also designed for Henrietta Maria – with the Queen.

Most of Jones's designs for interior decoration after 1625, and especially in the 1630s, were done for the Queen. Her French taste is much in evidence throughout this work. In some cases he was required to redraw and execute proposals by a French designer. Some of his own work is in the same vein, leaning towards the *style Louis XIII*, with which the Queen had been brought up. The use of French sources for the masque proscenia, such as the *Livre de la Toison d'or* and the prints of the *Galerie d'Ulysse*, may have been at the Queen's prompting. But Jones had always been interested in French art, especially since his visit to France in 1609; and he came to terms with the Queen's preferences in his own fashion. We have seen that he used the Fontainebleau ornament of the *Livre de la Toison d'or* in generous abundance, but he rationalised and classicised it. The use of the *Galerie d'Ulysse* for the Tragic Scene proscenium is another case in point. Here, as with Thiry's designs, he is prepared to turn the work inside out. Primaticcio's figures are summarily displaced from the centre to the margin,

Plate 140. Jones, Proscenium, for *The Triumph of Peace*, RIBA

taken from the *storie* where they belong and redesigned as ornament. Evidently Jones found Primaticcio's figures, with their more classical quality compared to Rosso's, eminently suitable for his ornamental repertory, where the figure is accorded the fullest value. So here he translates them from the ambience of Fontainebleau into that of the neo-antique friezes of Polidoro da Caravaggio, which he was studying around this time;[98] that is, he takes them back in time, closer to Raphael. On a wider front, Jones shows a determination to analyse and rehearse the history of French ornament on his own terms, and redesign that history according to his own principles. So just as he classicises the mannerism of the *style bellifontain*, he adds an antique resonance to the *style Louis XIII*. In this perspective one could make a further characterisation of the Jonesian style, which in general

Ornament

Plate 141. Boyvin after Thiry, *Toison d'or*, plate 7, British Library

Plate 142. Boyvin after Thiry, *Toison d'or*, plate 26, British Library

Plate 143. Webb after Jones, Reworking of proscenium from *The Triumph of Peace*, Chatsworth

terms I have called classical mannerism. In that it was the style of the Stuart monarchy, with a notable penchant towards the French culture of the Queen, it might be described as the *style Charles Ier*.

Even in its most French guise, that is, in its most domestic setting in the Queen's houses, the style fulfils the same function as it does in its more public vein on the proscenia of the masques. The anonymous French designs which Jones had to copy were for chimney-pieces, as are many of his independent designs commissioned by the Queen. The essential structure of these was always a double frame: the mantel framing the fireplace, and the overmantel framing a picture. In two of the drawings, one for Oatlands and another for Greenwich,[99] the pictures are actually sketched in – presumably they are paintings from the royal collections. A different but related type of design is for the wall of the garden gallery at Oatlands: a series of ornamental frames to contain landscape murals.[100] These are on a larger scale than the overmantel frames; and from them it is only a short step to the even

Plate 144. Jones, Proscenium, *The Temple of Love*, RIBA

larger proscenium arches for the masques, which according to Jones are 'frames' for his stage pictures. Differences of scale tend to determine the particular inflection that the Jonesian style receives: in the chimney pieces it is at its most purely ornamental and abstract, in the proscenia at its most figurative and allegorical. The mural frames for Oatlands come between these two extremes; and there is an interesting overmantel design for Basing House (plate 155) which shows alternative modes, one more abstract, one more figurative.[101] But wherever the accent is placed, the function is always the same: to frame pictures.

The Basing overmantel was apparently designed for a space above a wide, old-fashioned Tudor hearth, so that it approaches (on a smaller scale) the rectangularity and amplitude of the proscenium format. Jones makes it a more ambitious composition than those he was used to providing for the Queen. It has full-length allegorical figures of virtues standing before pilasters on plinths, and an implicit order which moves between Doric and

Plates 145–6. Diana Ghisi after Giulio Romano, Fresco from Palazzo del Tè (details)

Ionic with many adventitious enrichments. And just as he gives it something of the grandeur of a proscenium, he was to give his proscenia an added grandeur in their final phase.

The masques of the late 1630s show a special urgency in justifying and celebrating Charles I's policies in the face of growing resistance. *Salmacida Spolia* (1640), which was to be the last ever presented, is the grandest of these efforts, especially as it was a joint masque of the King and Queen. The proscenium is a design of unprecedented complexity, as Jones makes clear in the description (which the printed text ascribes to his authorship). He uses

Plate 147. Tempesta, Grotesque panel, Victoria and Albert Museum

a new term, calling it 'the border that enclosed the scenes and made a frontispiece to all the work . . .'[102] The word 'frontispiece', taken from the vocabulary of architecture, gives the proscenium even more importance. Scamozzi's account of frontispieces had explained that they were adapted from antique temple fronts to modern buildings. They made the principal aspect of a building look especially majestic; and they were useful bearers of ornament, such as *storie*, trophies of arms, imprese, and so on.[103] Jones annotated this passage, which explains the precise point of seeing a proscenium as a 'frontispiece'. Scamozzi insists that they must be 'fatti con ragione', and Jones's careful description and explanation of the figures on his proscenium entirely fulfils this requirement. In fact Reason is the first of his figures to be mentioned, and the ensuing paragraphs detail a rationally planned programme.

Plate 148. Jones, Truth, for the proscenium of The Tragic Scene, Chatsworth

Ornament

Plate 149. Theodoor van Thulden after Primaticcio, *Les Travaux d'Ulysse*, plate 50

This programme is of a new order of magnitude. An idea of its scope can be gained from the concluding section: in the frieze there were

> children, with significant signs to express their several qualities: Forgetfulness of Injuries, extinguishing a flaming torch on an armour; Commerce, with ears of corn; Felicity with a basket of lilies; Affection to the Country, holding a grasshopper; Prosperous Success, with the rudder of a ship; Innocence with a branch of fern . . . [104]

Some of these figures had already appeared in Rubens's Banqueting House ceiling, installed five years before. The putto 'extinguishing a flaming torch on an armour' can be paralleled exactly. Elsewhere on Jones's proscenium were 'winged children, one riding on a furious lion, which he seems to tame with reins and a bit;' and Rubens has a very similar figure.[105] Whether or not Jones devised the programme of the ceiling, as Roy Strong believes, his allusions to it stress that his own composition has a shared figurative repertory and a similarly ambitious scope. Rubens is the measure, even

Plate 150. Hercules, for the proscenium of The Tragic Scene, Chatsworth

before the grand tableaux of the masque are revealed, simply of the proscenium alone.

Jones's ideological design is equally ambitious. He sums up his description of the 'children, with significant signs' as

> expressing the several goods, followers of peace and concord, and forerunners of human felicity; so as the work of this front, consisting of picture qualified with moral philosophy, tempered delight with profit.[106]

The final words echo one of the most well known counter-Reformation treatises on the proper function of the arts. This is Gregorio Comanini's *Il Figino, overo del fine della pittura* (1591). The book is a dialogue between the poet Guazzo, the theologian Martinengo, and the painter Figino, whose name supplies the title. Among other topics, they argue around Aristotle's point that imitation, because it produces knowledge, causes pleasure – the underlying doctrine of Jones's motto 'Altro diletto che imparar non trovo'. Martinengo is adamant however that pleasure cannot be the principal end of 'picture':

Plate 151. Van Thulden after Primaticcio, *Les Travaux d'Ulysse*, plate 9

Plate 152. Master L. D. after Primaticcio, Diana

Plate 153. Tarquinio Ligustri, Designs for consoles

Plate 154. Robert Peake after Edward Pearce, Frieze design, British Museum

That imitation has pleasure as an end, I must not and cannot deny to you. But that imitation, insofar as it is qualified and governed by moral philosophy (qualificata e governata dalla morale filosofia), has pleasure as its chief end, that I am quite free to confute... [107]

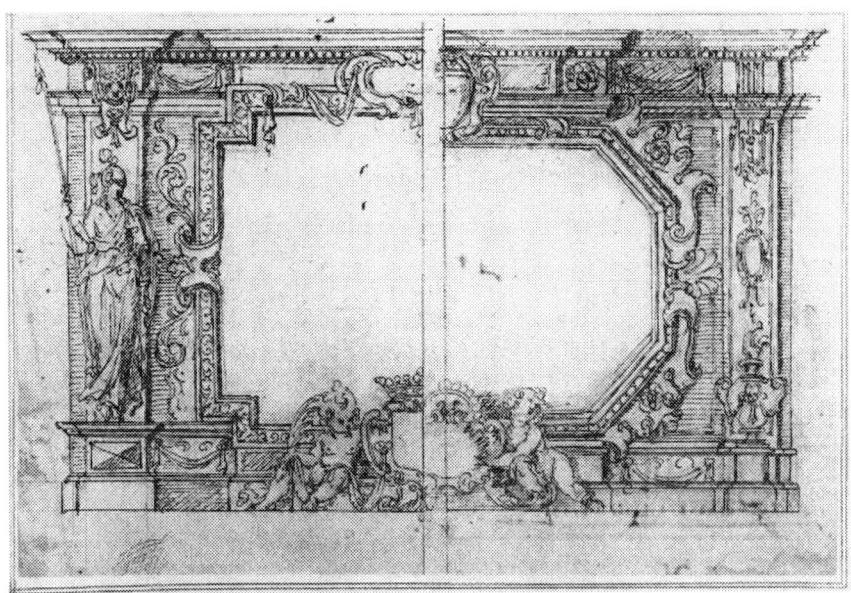

Plate 155. Jones, Two half elevations for an overmantel, possibly for Basing House, RIBA

Jones, in echoing the words, transposes them into a milder ideological key. 'Picture' is only 'qualified' by moral philosophy, and not 'governed'. This is in keeping with the idea of 'delight' being 'tempered... with profit', an idea which anticipates the central political theme of the masque. It turns out that the power which vanquishes the King's opponents is not force but his civilising gentleness. Similarly, Jones claims, the power of his art lies in the moderating balance of its effects.

The claim is at odds with the overpowering ambition of his pictorial programme, which stretches the concept of the proscenium as 'ornament' to its limits, and perhaps beyond. Lomazzo's idea of ornament as a coherent system of language, a code of 'significant signs' (to adapt Jones's expression), is taken so far that ornament turns into *storia* proper, 'picture qualified with moral philosophy'. Jones certainly describes enough figures to make up the staffage of a full-scale history painting. Whether in practice his design and the work as executed lived up to its programme we do not know, since no identifiable drawings have survived. Two drawings for parts of a frieze in the RIBA may relate to *Salmacida Spolia*, and if so, they show the problems involved.[108] There are various putti with attributes (plates 156–7), but these are difficult to distinguish; and even if they were plainer, it might be difficult to read their symbolism fluently. The problem of realising an ambitious programme of 'picture' within the restricted and marginal field of ornament, which is scarcely susceptible of being so scaled up, seems related to the

Plates 156–7. Jones, Panels of frieze, for *Salmacida Spolia*, RIBA

reverse problem of scaling down an insistent representation of political and aesthetic ideology to make it appear gentle and temperate.

Salmacida Spolia, by trying to assert both the King's authority and his clemency, was Charles I's most complex demonstration of royal power in symbolic form. Typically, Jones used the occasion to push his own art further than it had gone before. In the overwrought context of this extraordinary occasion he overreached himself, but in a characteristically searching experiment: the contradictory attempt to treat ornament as *storia*.

7

Antiquity

The spectacle of antiquity

Some of Jones's masque designs represent antiquity; many more (perhaps most) of them make use of it in one way or another. There are masquers figured *all'antica*, scenes with antique sculpture and architecture, and views of Roman ruins. As well, the art of the Renaissance tradition which he copied and adapted is by its very nature imbued with the forms and motifs of antique art. Edmund Bolton had envisaged Jones introducing 'all the elegant arts of the ancients' into England, assuming in a strict neo-classical spirit that to be the protagonist of the Renaissance was to be the reviver of antiquity. The whole range of Jones's masque work might be examined from this point of view; but in this chapter I want to focus on those designs which derive from antique or neo-antique sources, and see how antiquity is actually represented in the masques.

In sixteenth-century Italy, the proximate historical context of Jones's intellectual and aesthetic culture, the representation of antiquity could have different aims and effects. This can be seen in the various publications, from the mid-century onwards, recording the remains of ancient Rome. Some are sets of topographical views, executed carefully but in a self-consciously picturesque way by northerners like Cock and du Pérac. Occasionally, as in the series by Hendrick van Cleef, these can be almost outrageously inflected with the idiosyncrasies of northern landscape. Some are scholarly analyses and reconstructions of the remains by native architects such as Labacco and Palladio, which concentrate schematically on buildings to the utter exclusion of their settings. Some lie between these two extremes, like the eclectic compendium of Antonio Lafreri (properly Antoine Lafréry), the *Speculum Romanae Magnificentiae*, or Vincenzo Scamozzi's *Discorsi sopra l'antichità di Roma*.[1] Jones knew Scamozzi, and he used this volume, which is an admitted piece of book-making by the publisher Girolamo Porro. It deliberately, but rather awkwardly, combines picturesque topography with antiquarian and architectural scholarship. The plates, by Battista Pittoni, are copies of a set of views by Cock. Scamozzi's text is loosely modelled on the style of analysis and commentary used by Palladio in his book on antique temples, Book IV of the *Quattro Libri* (which Jones referred to as 'ye Booke of antiquities').[2] But Pittoni had copied Cock's views in reverse, producing an insecure relationship between pictures and text. The attempt to marry the two modes of representing antiquity points up their divergences.

Porro admits in his preface that he started with Pittoni's prints, and felt the need for a text to fill them out, commissioned eventually from Scamozzi. His serious purpose was to extend their usefulness. Till the present, 'they have chiefly been able to help those painters who delight to represent landscapes in their works'. But he wanted to give them a life of their own, 'to bestow a spirit on these designs with some accompanying remarks, so that they can be useful not only to painters, but to architects also . . . ' The idea that only words can give 'spirit', intellectual animation, to 'designs', is exactly the doctrine asserted by Jonson in his conflict with Jones; although unlike Jonson, Porro sees the architect as intellectually pre-eminent, at least over the painter. And he concludes that the text will now make the pictures worthy of the architect's attention: 'the work will now come before the public not only to give pleasure, but to be useful to scholars of the revered classical past (la veneranda antichità)'.[3]

This analysis of how Roman remains might be published is much more successful than the actual ill-fitting publication. Porro distinguishes two ways of representing antiquity: both are related, but one is superior in its effect to the other. The first, associated with the painter, produces pleasure; the second, associated with the architect, produces knowledge.

Scamozzi's *Discorsi* are peculiarly successful, says Porro, because he is professionally competent in both fields: he not only practises architecture, but also the art of perspective. This is illustrated by the title-page: allegorical figures of Architecture and Perspective point through a framing arch at a perspective of Roman ruins (plate 158). It consists of recognisable monuments – the Colonnacce, the temple of Minerva, Jano Quadrifronte – arranged along a street vista like a stage-set. The vista is closed by Trajan's Column; then, in the background, where we see the Colosseum and the Pyramid of Cestius on the slopes of a hill, it extends further into the realm of fantasy.[4] Ancient Rome is presented as a *spettacolo*. Scamozzi justifies this in his comments on the last of Pittoni's designs. It shows, he claims, no recognisable view, but is 'un bel capriccio' of the artist himself, whose skill in the exact transcription of the monuments is enhanced by his ability to

Plate 158. Title-page of V. Scamozzi, *Discorsi Sopra L'Antichità Di Roma*, 1582, British Library

devise 'una bella inventione'.[5] The painterly view of antiquity complements the strict architectural record.

Porro's discussion, supplemented by Scamozzi, articulates and clarifies the questions involved in publishing the *antichità di Roma*, a new, expanding field of representation. It also provides an informative context for Jones's work in this field. As both painter/scenographer and architect Jones represents antiquity in different ways. There is not just a simple split between the view on antiquity given in the masques and that given by implication and imitation in his built architecture. Within the masques themselves, with their overall 'painterly' mode, there is a shifting between romantic topography and scholarly archaeological reconstruction. And there is a corresponding relationship between the two effects identified by Porro, pleasure and knowledge. Jones's motto declared that, for him, the two were one and the same; and the spectators of the masques are drawn invitingly towards this goal. By representing antiquity as a *spettacolo*, he encourages them to take pleasure in its appearances, and acquire knowledge of its authentic forms.

This would produce a different kind of view of the ancient world from that which most of his audience held, or were predisposed to by their education. Its difference lay precisely in the fact that it was a view, a visual and aesthetic apprehension, something other than the discursive knowledge produced through the usual study of classical texts. This kind of knowledge, Jonson had insisted, was fundamental to a genre like the masque which used classical mythology and history for the purpose of allegory. In his preface to *Hymenaei* (1606), where he tried to dictate a theoretical agenda for the masque, he wrote that the 'high, and heartie *inuentions*' required 'to furnish the inward parts' (to constitute the 'soul' of the masque) should be 'grounded vpon *antiquitie*, and solide *learnings*'.[6] This is borne out in his text by marginal references to an imposing array of antique and later literary sources. They are often so bulky as to exceed the bounds of the margin and fill sections of the page under the poetic text, which appears literally to rest on a 'solide' foundation of '*antiquitie*'.[7] For the spectators to see a re-enactment of a Roman wedding ceremony in *Hymenaei* must have been a novel experience; but when they read Jonson's published version later, they would have been returned to familiar ground. He implies that textual evidence must be the authoritative basis for any representation of antiquity – which tends to reduce Jones's role to that of an illustrator of texts. Jones must have come to be deeply dissatisfied with this. The first masque after Jonson's dismissal, *Albion's Triumph* (1632), is a scholarly reconstruction of antiquity which, however, draws heavily on numismatic sources, architectural remains, and sculpture, as if Jones felt the need to show the validity of such evidence.

His own knowledge of classical culture was no less reliant than Jonson's on wide and careful reading. Without a training in the ancient languages, he could not emulate Jonson's grasp of classical literature and neo-Latin scholarship. But he studied many of the same authors, in modern Italian and French translations. Of the books surviving from Jones's library, the greater number are classical history, philosophy and science. He read modern works on many aspects of classical civilisation, often ranging beyond his particular interests in architecture, sculpture, numismatics, topography and archaeology. This reading was a necessary complement to his expert knowledge of the material remains of Roman civilisation. The tradition of Renaissance art into which he so deliberately inserted himself demanded of the artist, who was to combine theory with practice, a wide intellectual culture; and the root of this had to be a dedicated familiarity with the antique world.

Learning from ancient Rome

For Jones, this world was most accessible through ancient Roman architecture, which, according to Vitruvius, brought to a focus history, science, art, philosophy and religion. In 1614 came his best opportunity to study it systematically at first hand, consolidating earlier acquaintance with antique remains on previous visits to Italy (around 1600) and France (1609). His principal guide was Palladio, especially in the Fourth Book of the *Quattro Libri* on antique temples. He also used Palladio's little volume on the topography of ancient Rome, where the usual inaccuracies and longueurs of such publications were sifted out. This terse distillation of research so struck Jones that he translated many pages of it verbatim into the Roman Sketchbook, which at this initial stage contained mostly notes rather than sketches. But the programme of study in 1614 cannot be separated from the studies which preceded it, nor from the continuous rehearsal and rethinking of those Roman observations in the years following. Jones's annotations in his copy of the *Quattro Libri* contain a network of cross-references to other authors whom he read alongside it, probably over a long period of time. The main ones are Bernardo Gamucci on the antiquities of Rome; Antonio Labacco, who published reconstructions of various Roman buildings; and Serlio, whose Third Book pursued Roman architecture beyond Rome into the provinces of the empire. Palladio was simply the centre of a constellation of authors whom he constantly studied to deepen his knowledge of Roman architecture, which was for him the epitome of antique civilisation.

This never-ending perusal of the fabric of ancient Rome, kept up after 1614 via the publications – with their drawings, measurements and descriptions – of Palladio and the others,[8] is characteristic of Jones's entire attitude to antiquity. He wrote in Book IV of his Palladio, 'who follows the best of the ancients cannot much err'.[9] If, as his motto suggests, his whole life as an artist was a process of learning, then his principal teachers were 'the ancients'. Of course the whole Renaissance tradition stresses receptiveness to the lessons of antiquity, but for Jones, on the margins of this tradition, the acknowledgement has a fresh force. Among those who interpreted that teaching for him, Serlio best signals the didactic power of antiquity, as manifest in the remains of its architecture. On the title-page of his Book III, 'in which the antiquities of Rome are figured and described', he shows a view of monumental classical buildings, partly intact and partly decayed (plate 159). It is styled in *opera rustica*, at the most primitive, fundamental extremity of the classical orders, connoting strength and power. The nature of its power is signified in an inscription, strongly composed and delineated: 'ROMA QUANTA FUIT IPSA RUINA DOCET'.[10] It is the power to teach.

Serlio's pastiche of antique architecture, existing between integrity and ruin, is also placed between representation and symbolism. The inscription fills a compartmentalised space which can be read either as the fascia of the building or as the bottom line of the title above it. With similar ambivalence, its meaning hovers between past and present, and partly evokes medieval laments for vanished glory, sermons in stones. But Serlio's text is positive, and looks forward: what the ruins have to teach is not how to meditate on the vanity of earthly things, but how to reconstruct the grandeur of Roman architecture, both on paper and in practice.

As Serlio shows them, the ruins have two ways of teaching the architect. As imperfect but suggestive remnants of once great works, they allow him to deduce (or at least to conjecture) the original form of those works, and record them in drawings. And as fragmentary parts of compositions in a definitive architectural language, they help him to analyse those compositions and extend his grasp of that language. On Serlio's title-page, the imposing mass of the principal building, shown in perspective to reveal as much of its structure as possible, is surrounded by pieces of column shaft, a detached base, a capital, a section of an entablature, and similar fragments. There is a very immediate, material sense of that interrelation between the whole and the parts which is the essence of classical architecture. And this becomes the keynote for all the illustrations throughout Book III. Even though the graphic conventions used are more 'scientific' – a system of plans, elevations, sections and perspectives – the same essential relation is kept between the form of the whole and the parts.

It is by forcibly undoing this relation that 'ruina docet', ruin teaches the Renaissance architect how to remake it. The exposure is an exposition, from which much can be learnt. Serlio sees himself as interpreter, as mediator of the lessons. This role is perfectly exemplified in his discussion of the Frontispiece of Nero. One solitary corner of a large structure was left standing, a section of wall bounded by a giant Corinthian pilaster, topped by a section of entablature and pediment. Serlio has an elevation drawing of this, showing a section of wall with entablature and pediment, which is erased at the margin of the printed page[11] (plate 160). In showing parts or details of buildings he habitually marks a border by a jagged line of erasure. But here the conventional erasure line corresponds to the ruined edge of the actual building. The architect acknowledges the analytical aptness of ruin, and simply passes on the demonstration. To understand classical buildings, he has to ruin them in his own way, undo them through analysis. But this

Plate 159. Title-page of Serlio, *Architettura*, Book III (English version of 1611)

intellectual dismemberment has already been forestalled by the material ruination of antiquity, which expounds the knowledge necessary to recreate it.

Serlio's convention of erasure, which 'ruins' buildings in order to focus attention on parts or details, was an analytical device charged with a very powerful idea. It was taken up by later treatise writers, such as Palladio and Rusconi, who extended its use, to look into not just the formal but the material structure of antique buildings.[12] Jones used it in a design for *Love Freed from Ignorance and Folly* (1611), to show the Prison of Night, a

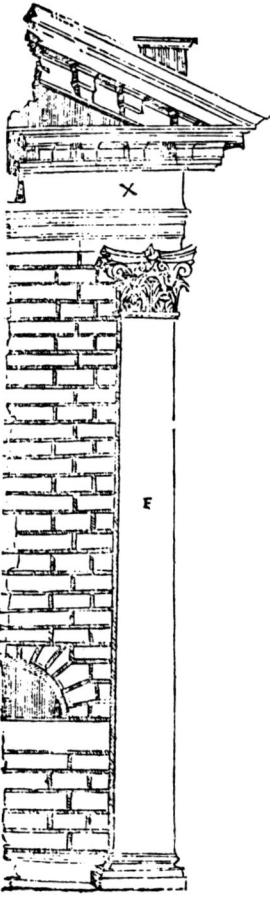

Plate 160. Frontispiece of Nero, from Serlio, *Architettura*, 1619

medieval fortress from which Queen Anne and her ladies, as the Daughters of the Morn, miraculously break free (plate 161). The building has a sweeping, jagged edge, exactly like the erasure line in one of Serlio's elevation drawings (of Bramante's exedra in the Belvedere) (plate 19) which Jones had already copied for another design.[13] Here he is adapting Serlio's convention from a didactic device into an expressive motif – perhaps only for the drawing rather than the final design – but in doing so he testifies to its power.

If what is absent or imperfect in the fabric of antiquity can be strikingly informative, then what survives into the present must be even more so. Time and again Serlio stresses what the modern architect can learn from the ancients. Sometimes he draws attention to the basic idea or the overall plan

Plate 161. Jones, The Release of the Daughters of the Morn, for *Love Freed from Ignorance and Folly*, Chatsworth

of a building (the 'inventione'); sometimes to specific details in the use of the classical orders. He refers so often to the architect in the role of learner that he resorts to formulaic phrases to describe this role: 'l'Architetto prudente' or 'l'ingegnoso Architetto'. The 'ingenious Architect' especially becomes a sort of stereotypical hero of Serlio's discussion. In antiquity this figure shows a bold resourcefulness, like the designer of the amphitheatre of Pola who adapted the seating to the slope of a hill. In modern times he is resourceful in adapting the bold works of the ancients, like the Baths of Caracalla and Diocletian, which Serlio recommends him to study. This role fits Jones. When Chapman describes him as 'our Kingdomes most . . . Ingenious *Architect*', he is giving him a character out of Serlio – the worthy, intelligent modern architect who learns from the ancients by imitating them.[14]

On the level of detail, the deployment of the vocabulary and syntax of the classical orders, Serlio tirelessly points out usages which can be recommended. This involves him in a comparative critique of ancient buildings. For example, he criticises the impost mouldings on the Arch of Constantine, for being over-elaborate, and including incompatible elements (116, 106v).[15] Instead, he recommends those on the Theatre of Marcellus, as 'the finest and best considered that I have ever seen, from which one can learn how similar things can be made' (45, 70v). Jones seems to take this kind of advice to heart. His own adaptation of the Arch of Constantine – the design for Temple Bar[16] (plate 12) – is not detailed enough to indicate the minutiae of the ornament, but it certainly seems to be a more sober revision of the original. Serlio's entire discussion of triumphal arches, in Rome and abroad, makes comparative evaluations as well as detailed analyses. Jones gave it the closest attention – it is the most heavily annotated section in the earlier of his two surviving editions of the treatise. Serlio awards the palm to the Arch of Trajan at Ancona, because all its parts are composed into a perfect whole. Its beauty, he says, is obvious to all observers; but architects will be particularly grateful 'to be able to learn ... from this fine and well considered structure' (118, 107v). Jones responds in exactly this way – his notes are much fuller here than on any of the other arches. He notes one feature of the design which he adapted into his own work, the small cornices between the pilasters, for holding bronze busts, 'as [I] made in ye scea[ne] of ye Theatiridium at Whight hall' (i.e. on the *frons scenae* of the Cockpit-in-Court).[17] But altogether what he learns from Serlio's analysis and critique of triumphal arches is a more general lesson: how to design one of his own, the 'fine and well considered' project for Temple Bar.

Serlio is anxious to explain how, in learning from the ancients, criticism does not contradict respect for their achievements, 'dalle quali tanto se impara'. The grounds of criticism are to be found in antiquity itself:

> my aim is to make known those things which are well designed, as distinct from those designed badly, and not just in my opinion, but on the authority of Vitruvius and of good antique buildings, which are those most conformable to the teaching (dottrina) of that author. (45, 70v)

Critical discriminations do not come from mere personal judgment; they must have an authoritative basis, the doctrine of Vitruvius. For Serlio, the authority of Vitruvius is supreme: 'to go against his precepts is to err' (43, 69v). This holds for the ancients as much as the moderns: no usage can be sanctioned, even in antiquity, merely because it is customary. So Serlio criticises the habit of using dentils and modillions in the same cornice, and denies that modern architects may do this because it was prevalent in antiquity. Where he finds it, in the Arch of Titus and the Arco di Castelvecchio in Verona, he condemns it out of hand. The point is that Vitruvius will not allow it, and argues against it 'with very effective reasons' (102, 99v; 128, 112v). Serlio sees no appeal from the prohibition, but wants it not to seem arbitrary. Vitruvius's authority derives from knowledge and reason, and that is why we should submit to it: 'when reason does not convince us otherwise, we have to hold to the teaching of Vitruvius as a guide and infallible rule . . . ' In fact, Serlio does not recognise any rational objections to Vitruvius; and his bias appears as his sentence slides from the concept of rationality to that of infallibility. He comes to characterise the supremacy of Vitruvius in religious terms, with metaphors borrowed from counter-Reformation debate. Should not his writings be 'sacrosanct and inviolable' he asks, to be regarded with 'complete and unquestionable faith', and those who resist them as 'heretics in architecture' (43, 69v)?

These metaphors are excessive and revealing. To attack custom in favour of 'faith' in a 'sacrosanct' text is one thing; to exalt the infallible primacy of a single doctrinal authority is another. Serlio presents Vitruvius as the Protestant Bible and the Catholic Pope in one. The insistent conflation shows up the split he is trying to heal, which is apparently comparable to the contemporary rupture in the fabric of Christianity. It is a split in the concept of antiquity. The division is between theory and practice, between the doctrine of Vitruvius and the sometime heterodoxy of antique architecture; and it is compounded by modern architects who take only the practice of the ancients as their guide. Serlio's commanding effort to close this division, by asserting the primacy of Vitruvian theory, reveals it for what it is.

The more he insists on the unity of antiquity, as a clear source of leadership to its modern followers, the more Serlio exposes its disunity. To explain the 'licentious' deviations of Roman architecture, he compares it with the 'marvellous works' of the Greeks, from whom the Romans learned the true principles of building. As the conquerors of the Greeks, the Romans may have found it difficult to submit to them culturally, receiving their teaching with a measure of captious resistance. Greek architecture is largely destroyed, says Serlio, but whoever manages to see it has to acknowledge that here it was the Greeks who overcame the Romans (43, 69v). Unfortunately, this neat historical hypothesis undermines his general argument. It produces a pristine corpus of antique architecture in which theory and practice are at one, only to allow that this has vanished, leaving behind a second body of work in which they are in conflict. And it makes a split in antiquity between Greece and Rome, of which the split between theory and practice is both a parallel and an effect. Serlio's Vitruvius is required to speak with a single voice for an antiquity which is in conflict with itself.

Serlio's attempt to construct a unitary concept of antiquity, which will form an authoritative model for modern architects, is undermined by his own sense of history and practicality. This also emerges when he tries to include High Renaissance buildings among the work of the ancients, to suggest that antiquity is an entity that can be manifestly revived. He canonises the work of Bramante; but at the same time records that some of it had to be modified by Peruzzi (his own master), or even rebuilt, like the loggia of the cortile del Belvedere, which was falling down (140, 118v). This ambivalence between an idealised Bramante, whom Serlio emphatically admires, and the historical Bramante, of whom he is critical and jealous, points up his problems with the ancients. He knows the ancient remains too well to convince us that their diversity can be rationalised by a doctrinaire resort to Vitruvius. Some Roman buildings, he observes, like the Septizonium, are made of recycled materials, so that questions of theoretical propriety could scarcely enter directly into their design (78, 87v). He suggests that most of the triumphal arches in Rome are like this, 'fatti di spoglie', because they were put up in a hurry after the emperors' victories; as a result they are 'licentiosi', neglectful of the rules (102, 99v). But if the material corpus of ancient architecture could be remade and transformed in this way, it becomes something more elusive than a homogeneous set of objects on which rules can operate.

Jones was well aware of Serlio's view of triumphal arches, as his copious notes on those pages of the treatise suggest. He took the point that antiquity was remade by the ancients themselves, that an antique building could be a pastiche. His own design for Temple Bar acknowledges this fact, being a pastiche based on the Arch of Constantine, which was itself – Vasari confirmed – a pastiche, 'fatto di spoglie'.[18] He was also aware of the wider problem illustrated, although not intentionally, by Serlio: that 'antiquity', an idea fundamental to the whole Renaissance, was nonetheless a highly unstable concept. The earliest masque collaborations with Jonson implicitly dramatise this instability, as the poet creates a version of antiquity based on texts, and the designer one based on visual records and reconstructions; they may complement each other, but they are still distinct. Even in his own world, 'the arts of design', Jones had many different versions of antiquity to resort to, which themselves ranged from the purely visual to the purely textual, and from original objects to various forms of reproduction. There were the collections of sculpture made by Charles I, Arundel, and others, which also included architectural fragments;[19] the antique works of art recorded in sixteenth-century prints; the graphic records and reconstructions of architecture in the treatises, especially by Serlio and Palladio;

the publications of antiquarian scholarship, from books on the topography of Rome to, nearer home, Franciscus Junius on *The Painting of the Ancients*. There were also imaginative reconstructions of antiquity, based on such primary evidence, by Renaissance artists, like Mantegna's *Triumph of Caesar* in the royal collection. 'Antiquity' was manifold.

Even when he encountered antiquity directly on its home ground, as in Rome in 1614, he recognised that it had to be intellectually constructed in some way to make it meaningful. The version of ancient Rome he opted for was Palladio's. So into his own notebook, which might be expected to include only personal, first-hand observations, he translated many pages of Palladio's *Antichità di Roma*, accepting entirely its model of the city's topography. He interpolates one point only, on the Forum of Nerva: 'The ruines of this wear Pulled doune whilst I was in roome, and on/ly to have ye marbell.'[20] This single sentence of his own explains why all the rest is copied: 'ancient Rome' is constantly in flux, and can only be fixed and inspected in a deliberate representation, such as Palladio's brusque text makes of it. As for the monuments, Jones viewed them through the medium of Palladio's *Quattro Libri*, especially Book IV, coming to use it (John Harris has suggested)[21] as a grammar of classical architecture — years later he was still reading and annotating it, refining his observations. So although Jones's Rome is in a sense Palladio's Rome, even this concept can change, starting from the difference between the city as a historical locality and the city as a thesaurus of architectural composition. And this shift from a historical to a more abstract, ideal view of antiquity is not only pertinent for Jones the architect: it is the key to his representation of antiquity in the masques.

Antiquity pictured and antiquity rebuilt

From the inception of the masques, antiquity was bound to figure largely in them. Jonson, a neo-classical poet, wanted to assimilate the genre to his classicising poetics, based on Aristotle and the Renaissance doctrine of imitation which descended from him; and its content too had to be derived from classical and neo-Latin literature, 'grounded vpon *antiquitie*, and solide *learnings*'. Jones was an aspiring neo-classical artist, who was to bring 'all the elegant arts of the ancients across the Alps into our England'. For their royal patrons, antiquity furnished powerful political metaphors. James I wanted to stress the union of the kingdoms, and to represent the enlarged domain of Great Britain as an empire; the archetypal imagery of imperial rule was obviously to be found in Roman history. Prince Henry wanted to go further than the King, and figure this imperial power in aggressive military terms, symbolising his desire to pursue political aims through warfare.

In *Hymenaei* (1606), the marriage of Lady Frances Howard and the Earl of Essex, instigated by the King to reconcile rival political groups, was symbolised by an antique Roman wedding ceremony, and the whole made into a metaphor of the 'marriage' of England and Scotland into one united realm.[22] Prince Henry preferred chivalric military festivals designed *all'antica*, such as the *Barriers* of 1610, in which he strove, against the King's disapproval and censorship, to show his willingness to use force on behalf of truth. Jones, as Henry's Surveyor, became especially involved in representing the Prince's politics in these shows, with imagery drawn from the antique.

The synthesis of neo-medieval chivalric exercises and the forms of classical antiquity had become a characteristic feature of Renaissance court culture. In the classicising intellectual milieux of Jonson and Jones the connexion was intrinsically established. Both Jonson and Prince Henry possessed copies of the *Pandectae Triumphales* of Franciscus Modius,[23] a vast, learned compilation which traced modern chivalric festivals back to the public celebrations of ancient Rome. Jones saw the same connexion made in Lafreri's *Speculum Romanae Magnificentiae*. It contains two engravings of the neo-antique theatre constructed for Pius IV by Pirro Ligorio inside Bramante's cortile del Belvedere, 'one of the most beautiful buildings put up since antiquity'. The prints record a joust to celebrate an aristocratic marriage in 1565: one is a perspective view of the buildings, the spectators and the jousters; the other is a ground-plan, which includes a diagram of the paths traced by the combatants in their encounters.[24] Lafreri represents the forms of neo-antique chivalry according to the same conventions as the forms of neo-antique architecture, as if they share a common objective matrix.

In designing the Prince's chivalric fêtes, Jones uses the kind of imagery to be found in Lafreri, while transposing its archaeological character into a looser, more pictorial style. A Cave and a Mount (plate 162) is a scenic unit for a tilt, evidently designed for Prince Henry. The mount is crowned by a beacon, which Camden records as a device of 'that most martiall Prince King *Henry* the fift',[25] an ancestor on whom Henry particularly modelled himself. Around the entrance to the cave are shields, painted with the devices of the other tilters, and over the top are three trophies of antique arms. The motif of a doorway surrounded by arms is found on the base of Trajan's Column, illustrated in Lafreri and elsewhere; and in other designs Henry is associated with Trajan, the 'worthiest prince'.[26] The overall image, of trophies mounted on a rocky, overgrown eminence, recalls the so-called Trofei di Mario, another of the famous monuments of Rome. Such trophies were the predecessors of triumphal arches, and these were reputed to commemorate Marius's victory over the Cimbri. Lafreri has an archaeological recon-

Plate 162. Jones, A Cave and Mount, Chatsworth

struction of them; but in the guide books to Rome the site is shown as a picturesque ruin (plate 163), and Jones's image is in this vein.[27] No doubt this has to do with the theme of the tournament, of which no record seems to survive. But it is characteristic of these early designs that they do use accidents of history and topography in figuring antiquity, rather than showing an ideal place abstracted from circumstance.

For costumes and accoutrements Jones often used Antonio Tempesta's prints of the *Twelve Caesars on Horseback*, published in 1596.[28] Tempesta had a huge and varied output, but one of his specialities was horses; and as a Florentine he was influenced by the Medicean festivals, which had refined jousting into spectacular equestrian ballets. So these neo-antique images are already transposed into a chivalric key. In using them, Jones draws them back a little closer to ancient Rome. He copies a horse caparison from

Tempesta's Domitian (plates 164–5), but adds a motif of vine branches with bunches of grapes seen in Lafreri's reconstruction of the Trofei di Mario.[29] He also adapts it for a pageant – of the type used in the parade before a tilt – representing an elephant (plate 166); but this extravagant conception too, which actually comes from Giulio Romano's tapestry designs for the History of Scipio,[30] is further Romanised. Painted panels ('storiette' Jones called them) showing battles are sketched in a style imitated from the Columns of Trajan and M. Aurelius, as shown by Lafreri. For Prince Henry's role in *Oberon* (which was originally intended to be an equestrian entertainment) Jones designed a costume derived from two of Tempesta's Caesars (plates 165, 167–8), but based the actual figure on two Roman bas-reliefs, engraved by Marcantonio (plates 69–70), one of which lies behind one of Tempesta's emperors.[31] Just as Jones brings Lafreri's ideal reconstructions closer to actual reality, he returns Tempesta's romantic fantasies towards their antique origins. Each type of imagery is referred to antiquity as it historically now exists.

This interest in the actual remains of antique civilisation is put to work on a large scale in the set designs for *Prince Henry's Barriers* (1610). The designs reflect Jones's recent experience of Roman buildings in southern France – two of them make an appearance, alongside buildings from Rome itself (studied from engraved sources) and 'Roman remains' of a generic sort. As we have seen, these formed the setting for a martial fête, presented through an Arthurian fiction. Henry is Meliadus – 'Miles a deo', 'God's knight'. Jonson and Jones translate the Arthurian past into classical antiquity. Jonson sees Henry and his fellow combatants as 'old *Graecian Heroes*', and his narrative makes allusions to Homer. Jones echoes this in his design for Merlin, which is copied from the figure of Homer in Raphael's *Parnaso*;[32] and for his sets turns to his own source of antique authority, ancient Rome.

Two scenes are required, since the plot moves from dejection to celebration. The first shows the House of Chivalry, which is 'decayd / Or rather ruin'd' because chivalry is no longer practised (plate 169). But Meliadus is going to 'restore / These ruin'd seates of vertue'; and as he appears the scene changes to St George's Portico (plate 170), the site of a revived British chivalry.[33] Scene 1 was painted on a shutter, moved aside to reveal Scene 2, a solidly constructed set. The two drawings which we have do not seem to represent Jones's final thoughts, as their relationship is not entirely logical. But his idea apparently was that the ruined structures of Scene 1 should appear restored in Scene 2, so that a revival of architecture mirrors the revival of chivalry.

To present the ruins of Rome as a scenic spectacle Jones scanned and selected from a diversity of sources. For the sake of analytical clarity, we could say that he treated his material in three stages. He picked out

Plate 163. Trofei di Mario, from A. Donato, *Roma Vetus ac Recens*

individual motifs; he assembled and composed them in a conventionalised 'picturesque' style; and he articulated these compositions according to a perspective scheme. In practice, these stages sometimes overlapped. He may start with a motif and work it into the stage-picture; or he may quote a motif from an existing picture, and place it in his own, using its existing perspective alignment. In the first category comes a building he had recently seen in France, the Piliers de Tutelle at Bordeaux. He copied a restored version of this into Scene 2 from a print by Jacques Androuet du Cerceau (plate 171), turning it at an angle to fit his perspective;[34] and worked out a ruined version for the corresponding place in Scene 1. In the second category is the Torre delle Milizie, excerpted from an etched view by Willem van Nieulandt[35] (plate 172), and redrafted into Scene 2, with a corresponding decayed version in Scene 1. This overlap of different procedures, in the attempt to compose together an almost unmanageable range of material, helps to explain why Jones's designs look rather crowded and hyperactive.

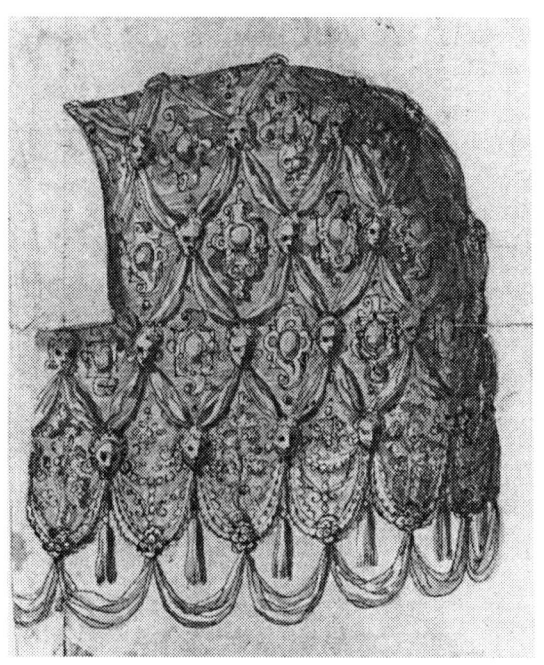 

Plate 164. Jones, A Horse Caparison, Chatsworth

Plate 165. Tempesta, Domitian, from *The Twelve Caesars*, Metropolitan Museum of Art

The three kinds of organisation – motivic, pictorial and perspectival – do not always blend happily. Some of the individual motifs come from a pictorial context, like the Torre delle Milizie, as we saw; the Torre de' Conti and the Pyramid of Cestius in Scene 1 are also from views by van Nieulandt[36] (plate 190). These contribute to the general picture of antiquity and ruin, while sometimes making individual symbolic points: for example, the Pyramid, as a tomb, may be associated with the demise of chivalry: in the background of the scene it echoes Merlin's tomb in the left foreground. This in turn is a quotation by Jones from his own work, reproducing (as we have seen) the neo-antique sarcophagus on Lady Cotton's funeral monument,[37] so that it fits in but also draws attention to itself. The same is true of the broken column in the right foreground (echoed by Trajan's Column in the background). It comes from a landscape by Paolo Farinati (plate 173), and has a general pictorial function in following Jonson's description of the ruined House of Chivalry, with its '*Obelisks* and *Columnes* broke, and downe'.[38] But it is also a personal device of Lord Arundel, who was one of the Prince's companions in the *Barriers*,[39] so that like the sarcophagus it stands out from the ensemble with a specific meaning, and a different way of producing that meaning – it works

Plate 166. Jones, Elephant Pageant, Chatsworth

emblematically, while the *veduta* of ruins works metaphorically. Jones's scenic pictures represent too much to form entirely harmonious compositions.

Their pictorial style is similarly overstressed, although its character is fairly precise. Jones sees the ruins of Rome through the eyes of those recent and contemporary northern European artists for whom they had a unique fascination. Not only do both scenes excerpt from van Nieulandt; Scene 1 in its overall feeling is reminiscent of his etchings of the Forum and other places after the drawings of Matthias Bril, with decayed monuments bordering on uneven and unkempt terrain.[40] Scene 2 suggests the early landscapes of Paul Bril with their strong vertical accents: half-ruined buildings on top of rocks and hills. The steps climbing up a rock on the right, and the tower on a cliff in the left background, are typical Paul Bril motifs.[41] The complementary talents of the Bril brothers – that of Matthias for description, and that of Paul for fantasy – were closely related not only by their subject matter but by the self-consciously romantic nostalgia with which it was viewed. Together they supply Jones with a particular vision of the vanished glories of Roman antiquity. It is a vision in which loss and regret become the medium of aesthetic pleasure.

Plate 167. Jones, Oberon, for *Oberon*, Chatsworth

Plate 168. Tempesta, Caligula, from *The Twelve Caesars*

But visual pleasure is not the final effect of Jones's scenes. The appeal of the Italianate ruin landscapes which he invokes lies in a feeling of resignation, of acquiescence in the depredations of time and history. But the plot of the *Barriers* celebrates action and restoration. The pleasure with which he attracts his spectators' attention to the sight of antiquity and its power to signify is a means to an end: the knowledge of how antiquity can be revived.

This knowledge is revealed in the change from Scene 1 to Scene 2. The technical mode of the change parallels the thematic movement. Just as a pair of painted flats give way to a solidly built set, the idea of picturing antiquity (with passive nostalgia) gives way to the idea of reconstructing it. The move from picture to architecture gives substance to the transformation of the ruined House of Chivalry into St George's Portico. Of course Jones's scenic architecture, while solid, is necessarily feigned; but he can make it look real by complementing his construction with the mental 'construction' (as the Italians called it) of linear perspective. Girolamo Porro, introducing his views of Roman remains, had seen Scamozzi activating them with a new

Antiquity

Plate 169. Jones, The Fallen House of Chivalry, for *Prince Henry's Barriers*, Chatsworth

Plate 170. Jones, St George's Portico, for *Prince Henry's Barriers*, Chatsworth

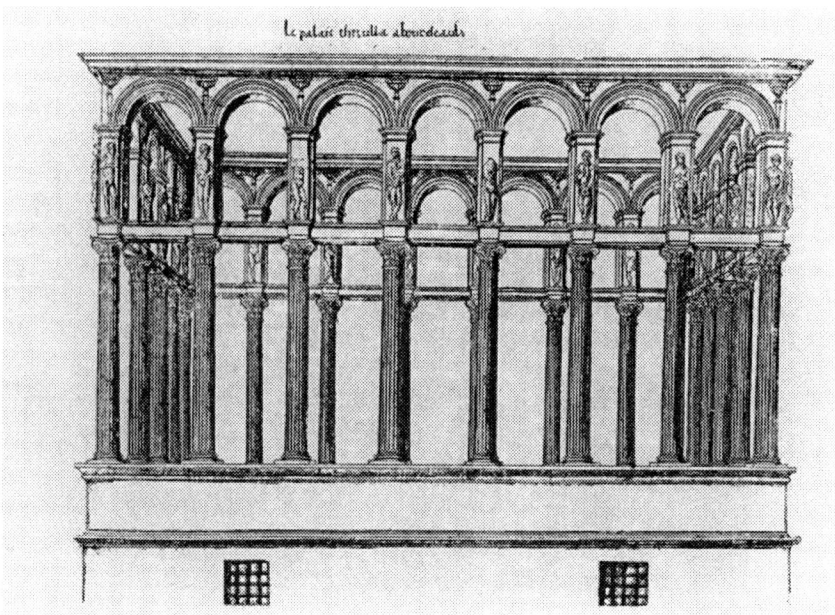

Plate 171. Du Cerceau, Les Tutelles, Bordeaux

Plate 172. Van Nieulandt, Torre delle Milizie

Plate 173. Paolo Farinati, Virgin and Child with St John

knowledge, appropriating them from the province of the painter to that of the architect; and part of his qualifications was the science of perspective, the capacity to 'make' architecture in the sense of representing it knowledgeably. It is this science which Jones here calls to his aid, in order to make real – to represent as powerfully as possible – his ideal of antiquity reconstructed.

The project of putting antiquity in perspective both literally and metaphorically, of making a visual and ideological construction of it from a determined point of view, is intrinsic to the Renaissance tradition. Perspective construction becomes crucial not only to Renaissance painting but also to architecture: we recall that, according to Vitruvius, *scaenographia* was one of the essential skills of architectural design. The scenographers who recomposed the fabric of antiquity on the stage were also the architects who undertook to revive it, and their scenic recompositions of ancient architecture are related to their programmes for building it over again. This tradition passes through Bramante, Raphael and Peruzzi to Serlio, who gives it publicity in his widely read treatise. Serlio's perspective view of the ruins of Rome on his title-page to Book III is complemented by his Tragic Scene in Book II (popularising his master Peruzzi's designs),[42] an idealised reworking of Roman architecture (plate 30), and by his own designs for neoclassical buildings. This relationship is most neatly expressed by his contemporary Antonio Labacco, a pupil of Antonio da Sangallo as Serlio was of Peruzzi, and so another scion of the Roman High Renaissance. His

Book on Architecture was also in Jones's library.[43] Its reconstructions of antique Roman buildings, with a supplement of modern classical designs, have as frontispiece a scenographic view of Roman ruins. The point is economically made: in order to recreate antiquity one must first take hold of it, take the commanding view of it that is offered by perspective.

This synthetic view of antiquity, most vividly realised in stage-design, necessarily complements the analytic view which is the staple of the architectural treatises. Jones obviously receives it from the scenic tradition direct, as well as from the programmatic frontispieces of Serlio and Labacco which use scenic conventions. In practice both sources of imagery become interrelated. Labacco's frontispiece reappears in elaborated guise in Scamozzi's *Discorsi*. Scamozzi's frontispiece, and motifs from his illustrations, are used by Giulio Parigi to compose a ruin scene entitled 'Palazzo della Fama' for an *intermedio* of 1608 (plate 20). Jones uses this for his House of Fame in *The Masque of Queens* in 1609 (plate 21), and again for the *Barriers* in 1610.[44] By doing so he does not merely resort to a tried expedient, but opens up further a context or perspective of ideas – ideas about how to see the antique in relation to the present.

His own idea of this relationship is a complex one, and unsettled, but at the same time insistently displayed. The perspective which, in Scene 1, is waveringly implicit, becomes schematically visible in Scene 2, with converging lines traced on the stage floor. These lines meet in the central structure, St George's Portico, the floor of which is patterned to coincide with them, so that they may appear to radiate from its interior. The Portico seems to be producing the perspective scheme, as well as being the product of it. This kind of ambivalence, as we saw in chapter 2, is built into it, since it is required to stand as a double metaphor, of the revival of chivalry by Henry and the union of the kingdoms by James. And doubleness is compounded by the second theme, of 'kingdomes mixt / And nations ioyn'd'[45] in Merlin's words. Jones expresses this by making the structure combine diverse building types, differing plans, and a range of architectural styles. The perspective network looks like an instrument to handle the result, to discipline and mediate the excess of meanings.

Part of this excess is a latent political conflict which cannot be resolved on the level of representation. Jones's antique model here of a structure combining different building types was Janus Quadrifrons (plate 174), which Serlio claimed had originally been called the Temple of Janus. Jonson's text has the figure of Chivalry apostrophise St George's Portico as if it were a temple of Janus: 'Breake, you rustie dores, / That haue so long beene shut'.[46] This identifies it with the militant political line of Prince Henry rather than King James's preference for conciliation. In having to be both a shrine of battle and a symbol of union it cannot help but mean too

Plate 174. Etienne du Pérac, Tempio di Jano Quadrifronte, from *Vestigi Dell'Antichità Di Roma*, 1575, British Library

much, and display the conflict of policies between Prince and King, with a Janus-like ambivalence between war and peace.

A latent religious conflict, on the contrary, can be turned to advantage. We have seen that the idea behind St George's Portico, the technique of architectural condensation, came from Domenico Fontana's catafalque for Sixtus V (plate 5); and that the setting of the Portico, which disposes restored Roman monuments into a perspective vista, is inspired by the Pope's renewal and replanning of the city of Rome to glorify Catholic Christianity. Jones takes the paradigm of the Sixtine *renovatio Romae* and adapts it to the praise of his Protestant Prince. He does so by shifting the meaning of his imagery: its Christian associations, instead of papal become imperial. The key to this translation is Trajan's Column, which appears in both scenes, and in the second very distinctly. Sixtus had replaced the figure of the emperor, with that of St Peter and his keys, symbolic of papal claims to supremacy. Jones we must presume puts Trajan back in his place; and in the adjacent buildings provides an appropriate milieu for him. The Torre delle Milizie was reputed to have been the barracks of Trajan's soldiers (hence its traditional name). The figure of Chivalry in front of it is based on the antique relief of Weeping Dacia (plate 175), commemorating the same conquest as the reliefs on the Column; and the trophies above Chivalry use motifs from the Column itself. In this context it looks as if the building in front of the

Plate 175. Weeping Dacia, from G. Franzini, *Le cose maravigliose dell'alma città di Roma*

Column, based on the Piliers de Tutelle, is meant as an external view of Trajan's Forum, resembling as it does the reconstruction by Palladio.[47]

These associations point towards Prince Henry. Jonson's text confirms this by calling him 'worthiest prince', a translation of the title *optimus princeps* conferred on Trajan by the Senate, and inscribed on his coinage.[48] The emperor who above all combined virtue and military success is reborn in Henry, heir to the Empire of Great Britain. Recent continental scholarship had annexed Trajan to the history of Christianity, seeing the 'worthiest prince' as the precursor of Constantine, who identified imperial power with true religion. And English Reformation polemics had written Constantine into the history of Protestantism, as the type of the 'godly prince', stressing his British origins.[49] This explains the connexion between Jones's Trajanic buildings and St George's Portico, with its Lateran motifs. The Lateran (plate 176), reputedly established by Constantine, was the 'archbasilica', the primal foundation of imperial Christianity.[50] In this context St George's Portico can be seen as the primitive church restored under the appropriate control of the state. Trajan and Constantine prefigure the virtuous modern ruler whose power governs and promotes true religion. These are the full dimensions of the imperial role which Jones's imagery offers Prince Henry.

Jones's costume design for Henry does not survive, but it was probably like that for *Oberon* a year later, which mixes features from Tempesta's *Caesars* with details from the Trajanic reliefs incorporated in the Arch of

Plate 176. S. Giovanni in Laterano, from G. F. Bordino, *De Rebus Praeclare Gestis a Sixto V*, 1588, British Library

Constantine.[51] Whatever its composition, it must have followed the eclecticism of his set designs. This eclecticism is by no means unreflective. The *Barriers* is organised round a clear theoretical programme, as the text shows. At the centre is the doctrine of imitation. The Prince is urged to imitate his virtuous predecessors; Jonson deliberately imitates classical poetry; Jones reconstructs ancient Rome.[52] However, in representing the 'truth of architecture' as a revival of antiquity, he acknowledges the historical complexity of the antique, and suggests the range of choices which such a revival involved. Over the next two decades, as his study of the classical past matured under the compelling influence of Palladio, his representations of it were to become more doctrinally resolved.

Antiquity and the arts of empire

The Roman and imperial vein of Jones's designs for the *Barriers* was continued in the two masques he staged for Prince Henry over the next year. *Tethys' Festival* (1610) was presented by Queen Anne to her son on his

Plate 177. Jones, Headdress for Tethys, *Tethys' Festival*, Chatsworth

creation as Prince of Wales. In fact the usual title was enlarged: he was created Prince of Great Britain and of Wales, to stress that he was heir to an enlarged imperial state. A design by Jones for the Queen as Tethys is suggestively based on an imaginary portrait by Aegidius Sadeler of the empress Livia, wife of Augustus[53] (plates 177–8). The proscenium carried a motto from the Augustan poet of empire, Virgil: *His artibus*. Daniel, the writer of the text on this occasion, indicates the allusion, Anchises prophesying to Aeneas the imperial mission of Rome:

> excudent aliis spirantia mollius aera,
> (credo equidem), et vivos ducent de marmore vultus,
> orabunt causas melius, coelique meatus
> describent radio, et surgentia sidera dicent.
> tu regere imperio populus Romane memento
> (hae tibi erunt artes) pacique imponere morem,
> parcere subiectis et debellare superbos.[54]

Others, I doubt not, shall beat out the breathing bronze with softer lines; shall from marble draw forth the features of life; shall plead their causes better; with the rod shall trace the paths of heaven and tell the

Plate 178. Aegidius Sadeler, Livia, Courtauld Institute

rising of the stars: remember thou, O Roman, to rule the nations with thy sway – these shall be thine arts – to crown Peace with Law, to spare the humble, and to tame in war the proud.

The last line, as everyone knew, was King James's motto. He had quoted the passage in *Basilicon Doron* and interpreted it for Henry's benefit: 'being content to let others excell in other things, let it be your cheefest earthlie glorie, to excell in your own craft . . . '55 But in the context of a masque this separation is unnecessary: the figurative, linguistic and mathematical arts can here contribute to a forceful representation of the arts of imperial rule, just as (contrariwise) the 'craft' of monarchy lends support to promoting 'the elegant arts of the ancients'.

Oberon the Fairy Prince (1611) returns to the mode of the *Barriers*, a mixture (as we have seen) of medieval and antique elements. Material from the romance *Huon of Bordeaux* is drafted into a modern adaptation of a Greek satyr play. Ben Jonson makes a radical reduction of the romance narrative: his hero is a fusion of its knight errant protagonist, Huon, with his opposite number and helper, the fairy king Oberon. Jonson and Jones take advantage of the cultural syncretism of romance, where pagan antiquity and medieval Christianity exist side by side. A key motif is Oberon's parentage, which brings both worlds together: he is the son of Julius Caesar and the Lady of the Secret Isle, a figure with Arthurian affiliations. Moreover he is a militant Christian, warring successfully against 'the Paynims' and killing all who refuse baptism.[56] This was the symbolic role Prince Henry, as 'Miles a deo', composed of invincibility and godliness, had already chosen to represent his accession to political maturity. Through the figure of Oberon, Roman conqueror and Christian paladin, he could express his idea of the proper relationship between political and religious power. Jones's costume design (plate 167) is taken from two of the prints in Tempesta's *Twelve Caesars* (plates 165, 168), with their suitable blend of chivalry and antiquity. To derive a standing figure from the mounted emperors he also refers to two Roman bas-reliefs engraved by Marcantonio (one showing Trajan)[57] (plates 69–70). A romanticising touch is given by shaping the tunic and bases of the Roman military uniform as if they were Jacobean trunk hose; but this did not prevent a reporter of the occasion from recognising the fashion in which 'the Roman emperors are represented'.[58]

Prince Henry's sudden death inevitably affected the character of the masques. They were no longer dominated by the figure of 'God's soldier', the would-be Christian emperor, the modern reincarnation of an antique hero. But the special impetus which Henry's personal mythology had given to Jones's design work was not spent; and it was to reappear twenty years later in the masques celebrating his brother Charles's decade of personal rule, when the myth of an imperial principate with a religious mission (its bias very different from Henry's) became an unforeseen reality.

Henry's place was momentarily supplied by one of the leading Protestant princes of the Holy Roman Empire, his intended brother-in-law, the Elector Palatine. In the two masques which Jones designed for the Elector's marriage to Princess Elizabeth, both poets with whom he collaborated, Campion and Chapman, credit him with the 'invention'; and we find him recapitulating motifs from Henry's masques, as if working through ideas which would have been further developed had the Prince still been living. In fact Chapman's *Memorable Masque* reads as if it were intended for Henry in the first place, to be presented either by him or in his presence. Here, the myth of Christian empire is extended to the New World, and the masquers are native Americans, Virginian princes, who are persuaded to turn from the pagan worship of the sun god and pay homage to 'our Briton Phoebus', King James, 'whose bright sky' is 'Enlightened with a Christian piety'.[59] These 'Virgin knights' cannot fail to recall Prince Henry in many ways – his martial ardour, his sexual restraint, his sympathy for the political style of the

Virgin Queen and for Elizabethan ventures in colonisation. They also recall his friend and political adviser Sir Walter Raleigh, the knight above all associated with Virginia, who was still begging to be released from the Tower and allowed to mine for gold in America, as a way of settling his political accounts with the King. Since the basic scene of the masque is a rocky mountain which opens, 'discovering a rich and refulgent mine of gold'[60] – exactly what Raleigh claimed to have discovered in Guiana – there was no difficulty in discerning him as the covert or repressed hero of the masque, as the Prince is its lost patron, and the Elector (a fellow anti-Habsburg Protestant imperialist) its present dedicatee.

The propagation of Christianity to justify the seizure of territory and wealth is the mainspring of early modern imperialism, and the masque handles the imperial theme by resorting to the 'appropriate' cultural forms, those of antiquity. Chapman states the 'argument' as a philosophical allegory, involving a rapprochement between the goddess Honour – who is attended by Eunomia (Law) and Phemis (Fame) – and Plutus, god of riches. The abstraction of myth, and the use of not just Latin but Greek names, confers the greatest possible authority on the allegorical narrative of empire. Jones's corresponding effort is the design of the Temple of Honour, which dominates one of the two peaks of the golden mountain. No drawing survives, but from the very precise description in the text the design can be clearly envisaged.[61] It is an enriched version of Bramante's Tempietto (plate 7), which both Serlio and Palladio had elevated into the canon of antique architecture. Jones had produced an earlier variant for the first, rejected series of *Oberon* designs, which took elegant liberties with its model; but this one is closer to the original, and preserves its neo-antique character. The text represents this by reproducing the Latin inscription on the front, 'HONORIS FANUM'; and by suggesting that here is a recreation of the ancient Roman Temple of Honos, which could only be approached through the Temple of Virtus,

> since to Honour none should dare access,
> But helped by Virtue's hand . . . [62]

In an elegy written around this time, John Webster made the Temple of Honour very much the dead Prince Henry's:

> And as *Marcellus* did two Temples reare
> To *Honour* and to *Vertue*, plac't so neare
> They kist; yet none to Honours got accesse
> But they that past through Vertues: So, to expresse
> His Worthinesse, none got his Countenance
> But those whom actuall merite did advance.[63]

The *Memorable Masque* can be seen as the final chapter of Jones's work for Prince Henry. This last attempt to design a symbolic monument which would represent the Prince's political aims in terms of the glory of antiquity revived is the most successful. St George's Portico and Oberon's Palace had tried to compose into some kind of totality a wealth, almost a surfeit, of visual sources. For the Temple of Honour, having to rely only on a literary tradition, Jones had made a simpler design, in the knowledge that the text could elaborate on the clear central motifs which he produced. To pursue this relative simplicity of design he needed the full cooperation of his chief collaborator, the poet. Chapman gave this cooperation more fully than Jonson had probably ever been prepared to.

Although the wedding masques were focussed retrospectively on Prince Henry, and owed a great deal to Jones's eight-year collaboration with Jonson, it was perhaps the absence of both which allowed him as a designer to refine his dealings with the antique. Both the patron and the colleague had been enabling but encroaching figures, and the tripartite relationship – involved as it was in an even wider network of connexions – must have brought both stimulus and difficulty. Without Henry's romantic obsessions and (for the moment) Jonson's sense of superiority as a classical scholar, but with the warm respect of the equally scholarly and self-esteeming Chapman, Jones was able to give his images of antiquity greater definition and distinction. Immediately afterwards he was released from the production line of court entertainments, to encounter the antique world on its own ground, Italy, and at its centre, Rome.

Roman notes: the Roman Sketchbook and the masques

The notebook Jones began in Rome shows him starting from scratch, looking at antiquity as if he had never looked before. The first page announces simply his arrival at the centre of the antique world, eager to learn; he is at the source of knowledge. His early notes are written in a practical, descriptive style. They are headed 'The Manner Of Drapery all antica', and seem to come from direct observation of antique sculpture. The longest is on Roman military dress, headed 'Emperors habbite in warr':

> A Shorte Roabe, Reaching aboufe [the] knee, and to the mid arme aboufe ye sleeues On this a cllose Curass, Musclied, that Comes a littell beneath the wast, y^t wast girtt with a Narroe belt, and a knott and ye ends tucked formally on ether syed onder yt, a dubbell bassis of labels: on reached Sumwhat beneath the [?] and the other Sumwhat aboufe the short roabe. Singel labels att the shoulders, that reach Somwhat abouf the sleeues of the short roabe ... [64]

This detailed note is illustrated by a figure drawing, taken from Trajan's Column (plates 179–80).

There is a clear contrast with the same type of dress as it had been represented in the masques. The costume of the lords in *Hymenaei* 'had part of it . . . taken from the *antique Greeke* statue; mixed with some *moderne* additions . . .' Jonson's description, with the details no doubt supplied by Jones, goes on:

> Their bodies were of *carnation* cloth of siluer, richly wrought, and cut to express the *naked*, in manner of the *Greeke Thorax*; girt vnder the brests with a broad *belt* of cloth of gold imbroidered, and fastened before with iewels: Their Labels were of *white* cloth of siluer, lac'd, and wrought curiously betweene, sutable to the vpper halfe of their sleeues; whose nether parts, with their bases, were of *watchet* cloth of siluer, chev'rond all ouer with lace.[65]

The notion of Greekness here involves a symbolic invocation of antiquity rather than a literal reference: this is a mannerist paraphrase of Roman military dress, as found in any court festival of the period. The basic structure is similar to that carefully detailed in the Roman notes. Jones used this so often, in numerous decorative variants, that he made its meaning perfectly familiar; even in the record of payments for a masque we find routine mention of 'antique Coate armor, with baces, Labelles, breeches and Mantle'.[66] Under the elaborate decorative overlays often copied from Tempesta's Caesars Jones's audience learned (more or less, since 'Coate armor' is an approximation) to recognise Roman military 'habbite', although it was never presented authentically.

But Jones himself meanwhile developed a much exacter conception of antique dress than the courtiers were ready for. The figure of Entheus (Poetic Fury) in *The Lords' Masque* is described as 'attired in a close cuirass of the antique fashion, bases with labels, a robe fastened to his shoulders and hanging down behind, on his head a wreath of laurel . . .' And this list of essentials is matched by Jones's drawing, which, while rapidly executed, gives an accurate summary of this particular 'antique fashion'.[67] It seems that in Rome he was able to open his eyes afresh, and start again from first principles, precisely because he had already been making and refining his own versions of the antique.

So even his notes on antique costume, made as if on a tabula rasa from direct inspection of the sources, reveal on closer scrutiny some implication in the world of the masque designs. The illustration of Trajan, for example, is copied not from the Column reliefs themselves but from the engraved copies published in book form. And the figure is not taken from a single engraving but compounded of at least two separate images from different

Plate 179. Jones, Emperor's habit in war, from
the *Roman Sketchbook*

scenes.[68] There are good reasons for both these expedients: it would have been difficult or impossible to draw directly from the Column; and no one scene shows the figure of the Emperor in the unencumbered pose required to display his uniform fully. But the procedures he uses here – copying from prints, and compounding different images into one – are exactly the same he was accustomed to use in the masque designs. The notes themselves contain references to the engravings of the Column reliefs, and to an analogous series of Raphael's Vatican Loggie. These are there for comparative purposes, to provide a context for the pure observations; but they bring back into those observations the sense of an intricate network of imagery which had been made manifest in the masque designs. Even the heading, 'The Manner of Drapery all antica', suggests with the phrase 'all antica' a self-consciously mediated view of the past.

The other set of notes which Jones made while in Rome itself is headed 'of the Antiquites of Roome'. Again there is a sense of preconceptions being left aside, together with a mediating context. But this is the material translated

Plate 180. Scene from Trajan's Column, from Chacón, *Historia Utriusque Belli Dacici*, 1576, British Library

from Palladio, and it is he who has stripped away the accretions of preconceived ideas; Jones is 'simply' reproducing his radically rethought topography.

If we were to categorise each set of notes in terms of Jones's chief interests, the Palladio translations would be classified under 'architecture', the observations on costume in antique sculpture under 'design' or 'picture' – and the latter were to contribute to Jones's characteristic mode of 'picture', the masques. We have only to compare the design of 1632 for Charles I as the emperor Albanactus[69] (plate 68) – in the light of the studies recorded in the Roman Sketchbook – with similar designs made before the Roman visit (plate 167). The later design is not an essay in archaeological purism, but while remaining inside the decorative and symbolic ambience of court festivals, it makes much surer reference to its antique models. Jones learnt many things from Rome: one was how to be a better masque designer.

This was not only demonstrated in the years following the Italian journey: it was publicly recognised. In 1616, the year following his return to England and his succession to the Surveyorship, Jones was again saluted by Chapman in the terms used to praise him earlier in the published text of the *Memorable Masque*. This time Chapman dedicated his translation of Musaeus 'To the Most generally ingenious, and our only Learned Architect, my exceeding good Friend, INYGO JONES'.[70] Again there is the suggestion, with the Serlian epithet 'ingenious' followed by the Vitruvian qualification 'learned', of the artist who has absorbed the lessons of the ancients. Musaeus was believed to be the first poet, and so for Jones to be the dedicatee of 'The Divine Poem Of Musaeus First of all Bookes' is a significant compliment. Chapman appeals to 'your most ingenuous Love to all Workes, in which the ancient Greeke Soules have appear'd to you',[71] referring to Jones's study of Greek philosophy. Thinking back to claims of 'Greek' elements in a masque like *Hymenaei* we may feel less sceptical, at least about Jones's intention to reach back to the pristine sources of antiquity. Chapman's compliments are confirmed by Ben Jonson, at the end of *The Masque of Augurs* (1622):

> For the expression of this, I must stand; The invention was divided betwixt Mr JONES, and mee. The SCENE, which your eye judges, was wholly his, and worthy his place of the King's *Surveyor*, and *Architect*, full of noble observation of Antiquitie, and high Presentment.[72]

This is only found in the second issue of the text, as if it were an afterthought; and its brevity contrasts with Chapman's fulsome dedication of six years earlier. But its reserve makes it even more striking, especially as it is couched in Jonson's most classically terse, 'Roman' vein. Jones's 'Presentment' of antiquity had received a hard won accolade.

The art of imperial government: Albion's Triumph

Jones's visit to Rome not only brought him to the centre of antiquity; it also brought antiquity back to England. As he was making his notes and drawings, his patron and fellow-traveller, Lord Arundel, was gathering the nucleus of his famous collection of antique sculpture. One of Jones's notes refers to 'yᵉ Messalina of my lo:',[73] a piece which turns up several years later in Daniel Mytens' painting of Arundel and his sculpture gallery. During the 1620s the collection was augmented with finds and purchases from the eastern Mediterranean, enlarging its scope to the ancient Greek world which neither Arundel nor Jones was ever to visit. Henry Peacham in 1634 stresses this connexion when writing in praise of Arundel,

> to whose liberal charges and magnificence this angle of the world oweth the first sight of Greek and Roman statues, with whose admired presence he began to honour the gardens and galleries of Arundel House about twenty years ago, and hath ever since continued to transplant old Greece into England.[74]

The Arundel Marbles put Jones in contact with 'old Greece'; and the wishful references in the masques to Greek art could be substantiated by the reality.

In practice, the more refined and knowledgeable versions of antiquity which Jones was able to show in the masques continued to have a Roman rather than a Greek inflection. In representing the ancient world at its most powerful rather than its pristine historical moment he was no different from any other Renaissance artist. Like many modern European states, Britain had been a province of the Roman empire; and the political aims of its modern rulers could be aptly displayed as a revival of Roman civilisation, of a culture promoted by invincible power. Prince Henry's masques had represented his political objectives in terms of a Romanised British past, although of a romantically fabulous kind. Jones was to recapitulate this project for Charles I, but in an idiom purified by the intervening years of work and study.

The 'British' masques of the 1630s, presenting Charles as Albanactus, Britanocles, and so on, essentially rework and extend the roles and settings designed for Henry (Meliadus, Oberon) twenty years earlier. Their effect is more striking and less diffuse because of the clearer position of both protagonist and designer. Unlike Henry, merely heir to the throne and not in accord with his father, Charles, having dispensed with parliament, is now very much a monarch. Jones, having cast off Jonson, and fortified by over twenty-five years' experience of designing the masques, is supreme in his own sphere. His view of the classical past has been decisively focussed by the choice of Palladio as a definitive guide for his architectural work. This commitment, and the sense of being in control, produce a greater resoluteness in his theatrical representations of antiquity, which now adopt a frankly idealist idiom, in contrast to the eclecticism and historicism of the masques for Prince Henry.

This combination of powers – the King's and the artist's – is most memorably seen in the first masque of the series, *Albion's Triumph* (1632). Politically, this is a celebration of Charles's personal rule, and looks forward to his coronation as King of Scotland.[75] The design impetus comes from his purchase of the Mantua collection, especially the recent arrival of the antique sculptures and Mantegna's monumental *Triumph of Julius Caesar* – as if Jones had decided to stage the great painter's vision of imperial Rome, with similarly close reference to original sources.[76] He specifically refers to the most famous sculptures in the Mantua collection, 'the rarest things which the Duke possessed', which were still to come: these were three sleeping Cupids, reputedly by Praxiteles, Michelangelo and Sansovino (plate 181). They figure allusively on the proscenium (plate 8), as a single motif repeated, reclining on either side of the royal arms in the centre,[77] which are supported by similar putti, but standing upright, raising trumpets and 'holding an imperial crown'. Jones deftly combines images of politics and art, presenting Charles as heroic ruler and heroic aesthete.

Plate 181. Sleeping Cupids, from the inventory of the Mantua Collection, Royal Library, Windsor Castle

The masque also pays tribute to another heroic aesthete (and to his political ambitions), the Earl of Arundel. The first scene

> represented a Roman atrium, with high columns of white marble, and ornaments of architecture of a composed manner of great projecture, enriched with carving, and between every return of these columns stood statues of gold on round pedestals, and beyond these were other pieces of architecture of a palace royal.[78]

This setting for the coming triumph of the King presents a highly idealised view of the Arundel Marbles. The statues in two rows facing each other reproduce the lay-out of Arundel's sculpture gallery. Jones's drawing shows square plinths, exactly as in the Mytens painting[79] (plate 182). The text

Antiquity

Plate 182. Daniel Mytens, Thomas Howard Earl of Arundel, Arundel Castle

mentions 'round pedestals', but Arundel also possessed a number of round Greek altars which, like other collectors of the period, he would have used as plinths for statues; and what this looked like can be seen in Jones's drawing for the proscenium of *The Triumph of Peace* (1634)[80] (plate 140). Not only the arrangement but the individual figures also recall the Arundel collection: it contained all the statue-types which are discernible in Jones's drawing. The first four figures are quite legible: a bearded togate figure ('consul' or perhaps 'philosopher' in the conventional typology), a Pudicitia, an Athena, a Hercules. Jones has copied his figures mostly from Italian engravings (plates 183–4), but this is merely a convenience: they all match statues which belonged to Arundel.[81]

Plate 183. Pudicitia, from G. B. Cavalieri,
*Antiquarum Statuarum Urbis Romae Primus et
Secundus Liber*, 1585

The 'carving' with which the 'architecture' is 'enriched' – that is, on the frieze of the Composite order – is also derived (as we have seen) from one of the Arundel marbles. This was a fragment of temple frieze from Asia Minor (plate 3). It had originally belonged to Buckingham, and appears in a painting he had commissioned from Van Dyck about ten years earlier, *The Continence of Scipio*.[82] Buckingham had made a large collection of antique sculpture, but his interests were not scholarly or historical: 'Neither am I so fond of antiquity', he wrote, 'to court it in a deformed or misshapen stone.'[83] He only wanted pieces which were handsome objects in their own right, and this is how the frieze fragment appears in Van Dyck's picture, rendered with

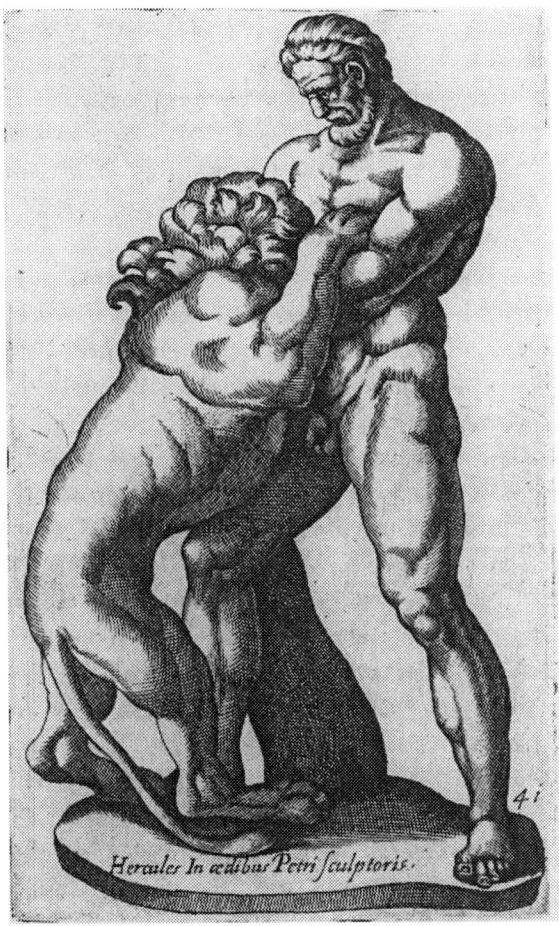

Plate 184. Hercules, from G. B. Cavalieri, *Antiquarum Statuarum Urbis Romae Primus et Secundus Liber*, 1585

considerable verve: it is a striking motif in the overall mise-en-scène. In Jones's stage-picture, the same piece, selected from the very different ambience of the Arundel collection, is assimilated much more intrinsically. Instead of being treated as a discrete sculptural object, its architectural implications are fully spelt out. Jones uses it as a touchstone to correct the grammar of the architecture which he has borrowed from Giulio Parigi. In his design of 1608 for a Temple of Peace (an idea obviously adaptable to the imagery of Charles's personal rule), Parigi had made Composite columns carry a Doric entablature (plate 37). Jones, by substituting the Arundel frieze with its heads and consoles, which can be seen as a richer equivalent of Doric metopes and triglyphs, makes the order Composite throughout.[84] Far from using the sculpture just to dress the set, he extrapolates a whole architectural ensemble from it.

Jones's design then, which provides a setting to glorify the King, pays a subsidiary compliment to the Arundel Marbles. It suggests the unique richness of that collection, from the resources of which antiquity can be reconstructed. And, as with the view of the King, part of this recreated antique world is a certain political stance.

Collections of antiquities made by rulers and aristocrats had political as well as cultural significance. The dynastic principle which was the guarantee of royalty and aristocracy could be tellingly represented by the possession of antique works of art, serving as symbolic credentials. They not only commanded respect as rare and valuable objects, but linked their owners to a concept of the past – the classical world – which was definitive. Antiquities gave the idea of ancient lineage a palpable form. In sixteenth-century Rome, leading collectors used antique inscriptions to claim descent from ancient Roman forbears, arranging their collections to draw attention to these claims. Cardinal Cesi displayed a series of 'ancient epitaphs, all recording members of the *gens Caesia*', who were said to be his ancestors. Asdrubale Mattei, Duke of Giove, placed one of his chief statues on a funerary altar of Quintus Mutius, implying the descent of the Mattei family from the Mutii.[85] Arundel would have seen such arrangements when he was in Rome in 1614, beginning to assemble his own classical sculptures. In his case, tracing descent from a Saxon of the tenth century, ancestry and the antique could only be brought together by association, but this he certainly did. In Mytens's twin portraits of Arundel and his wife, the Countess sits before a gallery of ancestral portraits and the Earl before his gallery of antique statues. Both compositions are symmetrically related, so that the pictures and the statues correspond exactly.[86] The parallel is inescapable: the antique sculptures are a metaphor for the antiquity of Arundel's family, and so for its right to social and political pre-eminence.

The statues represented in the first scene of *Albion's Triumph* imply the same kind of argument, especially the two figures closest in the foreground. The male figure, which breaks ranks, turning away from the set pattern of responsive poses and gazes to look out at the spectator in a meaningful way, seems to invite a search for further significance; and this can be found in his opposite number. She, even in the small scale sketch which we have, is clearly shown pointing, as if to warn or to show. The attitude is found in one type of Pudicitia statue, and this was the type in Arundel's collection.[87] But Jones exaggerates the gesture as if to emphasise that it should engage the spectator's attention, just as the man does by looking straight out at us.

Jones has placed his statues in significant relationships which are sometimes obvious, sometimes less so. To put Athena opposite Hercules is conventional, wisdom complementing fortitude. To put Pudicitia next to Hercules is to recall, more demandingly, Roman history and topography. Livy had recorded that the Temple of Pudicitia was set up next to that of Hercules; the information was repeated in all modern manuals about ancient Rome, such as those of Andrea Fulvio and Bernardo Gamucci, which were in Jones's library.[88] Livy also related that the goddess's full title was Pudicitia Patricia, since only women of the patrician order could sacrifice to her, plebeians being excluded. Strife broke out when the patrician Virginia, having married a man of consular rank who was however a plebeian, was expelled from the cult. She protested that all Roman matrons were entitled to revere *pudicitia*, just as their menfolk pursued the ideal of *virtus*; and she founded a shrine in her own house to Pudicitia Plebeia. Modern antiquarians rehearsed this drama of caste conflict with varying emphases. Gamucci stressed that the original temple had been founded with the intention of setting the patrician ladies apart from their social inferiors, 'so intent were the Romans on maintaining, through everything they did, an ancient, unadulterated nobility'.[89] The struggle for the cause of 'ancient, unadulterated nobility' was the mainspring of Arundel's career; and the figure of Pudicitia – the deity associated with the exclusivity of the ancient Roman patriciate – invokes this cause into the foreground of the first scene of the masque.

Jones had, we remember, done exactly the same kind of thing over twenty years before, in the first scene of *Prince Henry's Barriers*.[90] He had inserted in the foreground the image of a broken column (plate 169), an emblem of Arundel's family honour, solid but impaired. By the time of *Albion's Triumph* Arundel was much more secure in his social and political position. But he had never been restored to the full titles lost by supposedly treasonous forebears; and he had never seen his ideas about government put into practice. His basic idea was that the proper rulers of the state, under the monarch, were not professional politicians like Robert Cecil or royal favourites like Buckingham but men like himself, the members of the ancient nobility.[91] The only true title to political power was antiquity of lineage. Arundel symbolised this doctrine in his life by acquiring the products of antique culture; and Jones has projected it further in the magnified imagery of theatrical spectacle.

For Arundel to share the King's masque was both feasible and logical. Masques worked through complexity of discourse: they were intrinsically plural in their meanings. This particular masque was the first in which Jones had the upper hand. The action begins with the appearance of Mercury, who declares that it will deal not just in verbal descriptions but in demonstrations: 'We speak in acts, and scorn words' trifling scenes'.[92] In this context, 'acts' are visual demonstrations; and we can take what Mercury says as a programmatic point about the new importance of visual meaning. This enables Jones to extend meaning not just beyond, but outside of, the poetic text. So, while the masque moves towards its focus on the King, he can use the proscenium to make a visual statement about himself as an artist, and the first scene to make a similar statement about Arundel as a collector and politician. It is logical for Arundel, although only a spectator, to become a participating presence in the masque proper, since the doctrine which his imagery represents is a doctrine about privileged participation in the royal government. He also receives a share of the poetic text, in the third scene. This is a debate between two characters described as 'a patrician and a plebeian'. Both have seen the triumph of Albanactus. Publius, the plebeian, has witnessed it physically 'in the street'; Platonicus, the patrician, has stayed in his study and seen it 'with the eyes of understanding' – he explains that the real triumph of Albanactus is over vices and passions.[93] Only the aristocrat has the insight to enter into the emperor's real achievement. Townshend's dialogue is too lively to be always faithful to its programme, and the required idea of Platonicus has to be something of a put-up job. But the image which is constructed of a philosophical patrician exactly corresponds to the male figure posed in the foreground of the first scene, with his gravity of demeanour and piercing gaze. This can be seen as *virtus*, the male counterpart of *pudicitia*, but appropriately understood as *virtus patricius*, the moral force and intelligence beyond the reach of the common man.

At the centre of the masque is the King as the Romano-British emperor, Albanactus. This name taken from the legendary Trojan history of Britain is not mixed up with a romantic fiction, as it would have been in the time of Prince Henry, but treated purely allegorically. Townshend explains it through etymology, '*quasi in Albania natus*, born in Scotland',[94] anticipating Charles's coronation as King of Scots. As we have seen, Jones's design for Albanactus uses two Roman bas-reliefs, engraved by Marcantonio (plates 68–70). One of these has a coronation theme, with Trajan being crowned by Victory.[95] It appears on the Arch of Constantine with the inscription 'Fundatori Quietis'; and the motif of the emperor establishing peace and security provides the final scene of the masque, where 'Imperious Peace' descends and celebrates the blessings of Charles's pacific rule. The Trajanic relief was only one of a whole series of relief sculptures from previous reigns which Constantine incorporated into his triumphal arch. They record the deeds of three rulers of the Roman empire at its greatest – Trajan, Hadrian and Marcus Aurelius. In these scenes, the head of each emperor has been reworked into a portrait of Constantine,[96] so that he becomes literally identified with his virtuous and powerful predecessors, confirming his title to the empire. Jones in turn identifies Charles, as Albanactus, with the composite image of Trajan and Constantine, that is, with the imperial paragons of princely virtue and true religion. He had constructed the same role for Prince Henry in the *Barriers*, designing a setting which presented him as a modern Trajan and Constantine, while Jonson in the text identified him with worthy English kings of the past, such as Edward I and Henry V. Invoking the Roman and English past together had represented the rightful claim of the new Stuart dynasty to the 'empire of Great Britain'. *Albion's Triumph* does not need to repeat that claim, but revises it. Charles I takes the role of an antique emperor to show his right to adopt an antique style of government, an imperial principate, headed by a truly religious and virtuous autocrat.

This representation of the King chimed with Jones's new experience of 'personal rule' in his own domain. Having got rid of his formidable colleague, he now had overall control of the masques; and *Albion's Triumph* advertises this newly won power. Its triumphant visions of antiquity suggest how manifestly legitimate are the artist's – as well as the King's – claims to personal authority. As the balance of power comes down firmly on his side, Jones shifts emphasis away from Jonson's insistently literary view of the classical world towards material and visual evidence – architecture, sculpture and coins. On the use of coins there is an appropriate piece of special pleading by Jones's friend Henry Peacham:

> bookes and histories and the like are but copyes of Antiquity bee they never so truely descended unto us: but coynes are the very Antiquities themselves. But would you see a patterne of the *Rogus* or funerall pile burnt at the canonization of the Romane Emperors? would you see how the *Augurs* Hat, and *Lituus* were made? Would you see the true and undoubted modells of their Temples, Alters, Deities, Columnes, Gates, Arches, Aquaeducts, Bridges, Sacrifices, Vessels, *Sellae Curules*, Ensigns and Standards, Navall and murall Crownes, Amphytheaters, Circi, Bathes, Chariots, Trophies, Ancilia, and a thousand things more; Repare to the old coynes, and you shall find them, and all things else that they ever did, made, or used, there shall you see them excellently and lively represented.[97]

This was written for the chapter 'Of Antiquities' added to the 1634 edition of Peacham's *Compleat Gentleman*, dedicated to Arundel's younger son. But it might just as well have come from Jones. Study of the '*Rogus* or funeral pile . . . of the Roman Emperors' lay behind his catafalque for James I's funeral in 1625, and of the accoutrements of 'the *Augurs*' for *The Masque of Augurs* in 1622.[98] The passage makes an excellent gloss on his extensive use of numismatic material for *Albion's Triumph*.

We know that the royal collection included antique medals, together with a sizeable number of modern books about them, to which Jones had access.[99]

The stage designs of Inigo Jones

Plate 185. Jones, A Captive King, for
Albion's Triumph, Chatsworth

The King's headdress in *Albion's Triumph* of a laurel wreath and a radiant crown (Jones later added a helmet), very unusual in antique sources, is found on a medal of Alexander Severus.[100] Many of the costume designs for the triumph scenes are taken from a treatise on Roman circus games and triumphs by Onofrio Panvinio, which draws extensively on numismatic evidence. Panvinio publishes numerous medals, together with reconstructions of antique rituals and festivities which are worked up from them; Jones extends this method to design his own neo-antique triumph. So a design inscribed 'Armatus Saltator' is adapted from an etching in Panvinio (part of a large scene called 'Pompa Circensis') entitled 'Armata saltatio. Viri', which in turn derives from a medal reproduced earlier in the book, showing figures performing in a circus.[101] Altogether Panvinio provides practical guidance on how to work small-scale images from coins into large complex scenes.

His reconstructions of Roman festivals also use imagery from sculpture. From the engraving of a Roman triumph Jones derived a design inscribed

Plate 186. Reges Captivi, from O. Panvinio, *De Triumpho Romanorum Commentarius*, 1600, Bodleian Library

'Rex Captivus' (plate 185). The figures in Panvinio – there are two, identified as 'Reges Captivi' (plate 186) – are based on a familiar type of antique statue, the barbarian captives found in several Roman collections of the sixteenth century and, most notably, on the Arch of Constantine.[102] Jones follows this method in a design for a flute-player, inscribed 'Tibicen', which is copied from the reliefs on Trajan's Column.[103] Again, the basis of his imagery is 'the very Antiquities themselves'.

One drawing which sums up this approach is for the King's headdress. Jones has excerpted this from his full-length design for the figure of Albanactus, based on the Trajanic relief grafted onto the Arch of Constantine. Instead of realising the head only and leaving the other outlines vague, as he usually did, he has defined the contours of the drawing all round, and made the truncated shape cast a shadow (plate 187). The result is a pastiche of a classical portrait bust, a self-conscious act of fantasy or forgery, which gives the fictional figure of Albanactus a 'historical' reality. This was a presentation drawing shown to the King for his approval, and he would certainly have understood the subtlety of the representation and the implied compliment. The drawing gives a promise, in the context of a private consultation, of the artist's power to represent the monarch in a peculiarly authoritative mode, the visual language of the classical world – a power which the actual production of the masque would display on a greatly magnified scale.

But *Albion's Triumph* is not simply a spectacular collusion between an artist and a king both asserting their respective supremacies. The implicit presence of Arundel, and the celebration of his proprietorial grasp of the antique, gives the metaphor of antiquity a complex application, associating it not only with imperial rule but with aristocracy. Through that metaphor, the masques associated with Prince Henry had stressed the theme of empire, in an outward-looking spirit. King Charles's first masque to recapitulate the same theme looks inward, canvassing possible forms of domestic imperial government, notably the relationship between a principate and a patriciate. Jones's triumph is to deploy the imagery of the classical world so as to represent this large question: the idealising idiom in which that imagery is now couched can still be a vehicle for discussion and debate, albeit more coded and contained.

Ruin, revival and reform

Jones's extensive command of the imagery of antiquity, and his renewed exploitation of it as a symbolic language in the Caroline masques, is further shown in scenes representing the ruins of Rome. Here, the symbolism appears the same as it had been in *Prince Henry's Barriers*, the spectacle of ruin or decay giving way to the prospect of a new order, a revival or restoration; but the execution of the designs is more masterly than it had been in that earlier project. One Caroline design for a ruin scene shows an assemblage of Roman remains painted on a shutter,[104] like the first scene of the *Barriers*, but the composition has greater assurance (plate 188). The motifs are mostly adapted from prints by Willem van Nieulandt. The background, and the columns in the left foreground come from a landscape with the Flight into Egypt, which mixes imaginary ruins with a partial view of the Roman Forum and a romanticised paraphrase of the adjoining slope of the Palatine[105] (plate 189). Jones has excerpted a section of the composition and 'stretches' the space so as to insert an accurate view of the Palatine ruins (now seen from the other side, because transposed from right to left of the picture), after du Pérac. These are balanced by the Temple of Romulus (SS. Cosma e Damiano) with the Temple of Peace, from a topographical etching by van Nieulandt[106] (plate 190). Whereas the left side of the composition had been dilated, this right side is condensed, to fit a balancing mass in the available space. Jones moves the buildings of SS. Cosma e Damiano closer to the Temple of Peace, so that they partly mask the first bay. He has rehearsed this effect in a rapid drawing on the back of the sheet (plate 191), sketching after another print by van Nieulandt which shows the

Plate 187. Jones, Design for Albanactus's Headdress, *Albion's Triumph*, Chatsworth

two buildings in this relationship, seen as they are from a more oblique point of view[107] (plate 192). All these compositional manoeuvres are performed with a facility which had been lacking in the drawings for the *Barriers*. Even in the space of a single design Jones proves his mastery in the recreation of antiquity.

One major design of this type can be associated with a specific masque. This is an elaborate drawing for the first scene of *Coelum Britannicum* (1634).[108] There are four, or perhaps five, pairs of wings – certainly there are five distinct pairs of buildings (plate 193). The first three pairs are copied from Giulio Parigi's scene for the *Palazzo della Fama* (plate 20). The fourth and fifth on the left come from a set of ruin views by van Nieulandt, and

Plate 188. Jones, Classical Ruins, Chatsworth

show the Temple of Jupiter Stator (plate 194) and part of the Baths of Caracalla. The corresponding structures on the right are from Battista Pittoni's etchings after Cock, illustrating Scamozzi's *Discorsi sopra l'antichità di Roma*: the fourth from a (somewhat fantasticated) view of the Quirinal (plate 195), the fifth showing part of the Colosseum.[109]

Jones needed to add these extra buildings because the Parigi design is only in part a ruin scene, and the omitted background leaves a space which has to be filled. The method he uses to supplement Parigi's ruins is exactly the same method by which they are composed. Parigi had also copied from Pittoni's etchings, using those of the Forum of Nerva, the Temple of Jupiter Stator and the Baths of Diocletian.[110] Jones, with his experience of adapting the ruin *vedute* into scenic designs, must have recognised what Parigi had done. The finesse with which he dovetails his own borrowed motifs into Parigi's suggests a complete familiarity with this mode of composition. He appears able to reconstruct antiquity in whatever way he pleases with competence and authority.

Jones's command of his art here serves to represent the commanding authority which the masque claims for the King. This first scene is described by the text as

Plate 189. Van Nieulandt, Flight into Egypt

Plate 190. Van Nieulandt, Temples in the Forum, British Museum

Plate 191. Jones, Temple of Peace and SS. Cosma e Damiano, Chatsworth

Plate 192. Van Nieulandt, Temple of Peace and SS. Cosma e Damiano, British Museum

representing old arches, old palaces, decayed walls, parts of temples, theatres, basilicas and *thermae*, with confused heaps of broken columns, bases, cornices and statues, lying as underground, and altogether resembling the ruins of some great city of the ancient Romans or civilised Britons.[111]

The words 'representing' and 'resembling', which frame a résumé of the scene in the rhetorical mode of ekphrasis or verbal picturing, draw attention to the whole stage-picture as a representation. The text goes on to note that it was designed to be looked at on its own account: before the action started, 'This strange prospect detained the eyes of the spectators some time';[112] which is to say that the scene itself constituted the first phase of the action. Its illusionistic verisimilitude, and the fact that the initial dialogue makes no reference to it whatsoever, leaving it in a realm beyond the contingencies of mere realism, confirms its function as a self-contained picture discoursing its own language of visual symbolism. Its special impact is reinforced by its lack of economy. The distinction of means made in the *Barriers*, between painting and architecture – where the passive picturing of decayed antiquity in a mood of resigned nostalgia gave way to the active reconstruction of it –

Plate 193. Jones, A City in Ruins, for *Coelum Britannicum*, Chatsworth

Plate 194. Van Nieulandt, Temple of Jupiter Stator, British Museum

Plate 195. Battista Pittoni, Monte Quirinale, from V. Scamozzi, *Discorsi Sopra L'Antichità di Roma*, 1582, British Library

is not preserved here. This scene is a solid, practicable stage set which nevertheless works primarily as a pictorial spectacle. It uses extravagant resources simply to produce a 'strange prospect' which will 'detain the eyes of the spectators'. It is an overpowering sight; and it anticipates the overpowering sight of the royal authority which the masque will later reveal.

The precise historical meaning of the scene is left open, so as to enhance its symbolic meaning. The ruins are 'of some great city of the ancient Romans or civilised Britons', that is, the spectators are invited to supply them with significance of a general and idealising, rather than specific and localising, kind. As in *Albion's Triumph*, the British past is assimilated to Roman antiquity; and as in the *Barriers*, the premise of the action is the ruinous decay of antique virtue. But whereas the *Barriers* showed virtue being revived and 'restored', *Coelum Britannicum* is about 'reformation', a more ideologically pointed concept. Antique virtue, 'whatever elder times can boast / Noble or great',[113] is to be recovered by reforming, not just human institutions, but the cosmos.

This ambitious idea (borrowed from a typically daring text of Giordano Bruno)[114] can only be carried out by supreme power, that of the King. Once again antiquity provides a metaphor not only of pristine virtue but of what is needed to renew it, imperial might. The opening speech, delivered in front of the ruins, salutes the King and Queen as an 'imperial' couple, since they reign over a multiple state, comprising 'three warlike nations'. Before the ruined city appears we see on the proscenium the King's *impresa*, a lion wearing 'an imperial crown'.[115] When the ruin scene gives away to another, instead of an ensemble of restored antique architecture, which would be expected from the precedent of the *Barriers*, we see an equally overpowering image but of a different kind: a gigantic figure of Atlas holding up the celestial sphere (plate 1). This has a clear reference: it comes from the iconography of the Habsburg rulers, and symbolises the burden of imperial monarchy. The poet William Drummond had compared James I to Atlas.[116] Here he is an image of King Charles, who has taken the heroic resolve to shoulder the burden of governing his empire alone. Sole imperial power, through a policy of reformation, will bring back the pristine values of antiquity.

Although the basic structure of this sequence is recapitulated from the *Barriers* nearly a quarter of a century before, the striking change of political context and the equally striking development of Jones's art as a designer give the recapitulation an unusual force. The scenes of ruins in the *Barriers* had their ideological force weakened by uncertainties of design: they tend to read like assemblies of separate items (which is how the spoken text reads them). The corresponding initial scene of *Coelum Britannicum*, for all its diverse provenances, is composed so skilfully that it can register as a single image; and the spoken text aids this effect by not analysing or even describing it, leaving it to make its impact alone. So even though the city is an image of plurality, it shows many motifs as one, just as, in the next scene, the globe borne by Atlas includes all the celestial signs. By changing appropriately from one unitary monumental image into another, Jones implies that the city and the god are equivalent, and makes only too plausible the figuration of the King as a kind of imperial Leviathan, who subsumes all particularities and individual agencies into his omnipotent, divine person. The King's will to command the state, which at the time was by no means uncriticised or uncontested, is only too powerfully represented by the designer's incontestable command of his art. It may seem that as the 1630s unfolded, Jones's imagery of the antique world was used more and more to manifest the authority of Charles's personal rule.

This impression is initially borne out by his collaborator in *Coelum Britannicum*, the poet Thomas Carew. The printed text has this epigraph in the centre of the title-page:

> Non habeo ingenium; *Caesar* sed iussit: habebo.
> Cur me posse negem, posse quod ille putat?

I have no skill to write, but Caesar has commanded me; well, I will have it. Why should I deny that I can do what he thinks I can?[117]

This couplet is by Ausonius, from the dedication of his poems to the emperor Theodosius: they have been produced by the imperial command, which is the irresistible command of a god. So Carew attributes the masque to the King's power; and neither his name nor Jones's appears. This adulation of the imperial, divine ruler seems to anticipate Jones's figuration of Charles in the change from the first scene to the second. But in fact Carew's text turns out to be very ambivalent. The first of its two sections, which contains a number of danced antimasques, and could be described as an antimasque itself, is highly irreverent. Its most voluble speaker is Momus, god of censure and satire, who makes a disrespectful running commentary on the King's programme of reform. Eventually this gives way to the usual apotheosis of royalty when the masquers appear. But during the earlier phase of the action, which is unusually long, it can seem as if Carew is producing one kind of masque, and Jones quite another. Most notably, Carew's view of the King seems nuanced and critical, Jones's simple and idealising. The difference is accentuated by the relative independence of Carew's text. It is extra to requirements – more loquacious and brilliant than it needs to be, more an individual tour de force than a functional contribution to a collaborative work. And Jones's scenography – at least in the early phase we have been looking at – with its monumental assertiveness, seems a supplement not a complement to the text, as if composed in rivalry, in a forceful bid for preeminence.

If there is competition between designer and poet, and if at first Carew's King is not the same as Jones's, in the end he has to conform, since all masques end with the unanimous adulation of the King in propria persona. And the exaltation of the King also by implication exalts the designer who is responsible for that final, total effect. Jones was Carew's social inferior (Carew was a Gentleman of the Privy Chamber) and even more markedly the King's servant, but he had no occasion to express the diffidence which the poet, as a courtier and an amateur, gracefully prefaced to his text. As a visual artist he was exempt from the etiquette imposed on writers – his inarticulacy a kind of de facto privilege – and as a professional he exercised a special power. Jones's professionalism, acquired through an ambitious, laborious and unremitting programme of self-education, was of a type unprecedented in English history. It put him in command of the most powerful cultural tradition in early modern Europe, the classical tradition of the Italian Renaissance, in command of cultural territories and resources for which the analogy of an empire is not inapt.

In this perspective, Jones's exaltation of King Charles as an imperial hero becomes a means of representing his own authority as a professional artist in the classical tradition – decidedly more secure than the King's authority in the state. Whether the King was reviving the moral and political *virtù* of the Roman emperors or not, Jones had patently revived the aesthetic culture of their era, in the forms in which that was understood in modern Italy. So these first two scenes of *Coelum Britannicum* are acts of self-assertion, not only towards his over-splendid collaborator but other artists in the wider European arena. The main scene not only copies but tries to outdo Giulio Parigi, the many-sided court artist of the Medici, famous for a role which Jones had for long been trying to imitate and make his own. And the image of Atlas measures up to the modern Carraccesque style of figuration and to the artist from whose drawing (plate 2) it is copied, Francesco Albani, whom Charles I had tried to attract to his court. It is based on an antique statue, the Atlante Farnese; but it also competes with antiquity directly by confronting the classic problem posed by Philostratus (and reported by Franciscus Junius), who had offered Atlas as a uniquely testing subject for the painter.[118] The monumental symbol of royal power also posed a titanic challenge to the artist, and whether or not the symbol is valid, the challenge is capably sustained.

Classical antiquity had to be at the centre of all Jones's ambitions as an artist. As he gradually learnt the classical tradition, he also learnt to divulge it most effectively to the Stuart court by developing it into the visual language of court spectacle and the symbolic language of monarchic power. This process reached its apogee in the years of Charles I's personal rule, where two sets of interests converged: the King's desire to be represented as a supremely virtuous ruler, and Jones's desire to show the supreme virtues of Renaissance classicism as a representational medium. Charles may not have revived his preferred version of antiquity in England, but Jones did better. In the end, considering the eventual results of Charles's government and of Jones's cultural regime, it may have seemed that the King served the artist better than the artist served the King.

Conclusion

The King had dispensed with parliament in 1629; Jones's 'personal rule' over the masque productions began after the displacement of Ben Jonson in 1631. Thereafter he was able to use the masques not only to glorify the monarchy (which had always been their purpose) and discuss the virtues of the present royal government, but to represent themes from his own cultural programme, for which so far the masques had been only a tacit vehicle. Some of these themes are fairly overt, like the didactic and polemical representations of Theory and Practice on the proscenium of *Albion's Triumph*, with their meaning glossed in the printed text, or those of Invention and Knowledge on the corresponding proscenium of *Tempe Restored*, reinforced by the pronouncement in the text about 'pictures with light and motion'. Some are less obvious but even more forceful: when at the start of *Albion's Triumph* Mercury declaims 'We speak in acts, and scorn words' trifling scenes',[1] he makes a double allusion, stressing both the King's preference for firm government instead of divisive and delaying parliamentary debate, and the designer's for direct visual demonstration over the obliquity of verbal discourse.

These opportunities to figure implicitly as the King's double, to identify his cultural politics with the principles of Charles's rule, allowed Jones to fortify the effect of his designs without as it were breaking cover and surrendering the role of hidden persuader. Many of the priorities of the Personal Rule were also Jones's priorities in his own sphere (quite apart from his being in the King's service). The King, for example, was bent on reform, in both church and state; Jones was equally bent on reforming the Italianate visual culture which he was striving (in parallel to the King's aesthetic tastes) to establish in England. Both kinds of reformism are shown to coincide in the first scene of *Britannia Triumphans*, with its 'English houses of the old and newer forms' and 'afar off a prospect of the city of

London'.² The houses in the foreground recall the King's efforts to regulate building in London (in which Jones was involved as an administrator) and the architect's efforts to promote a more regular, classical style of urban housing. The centrepiece of the background, St Paul's Cathedral in the course of restoration, symbolises both Charles's reform of the Anglican Church and Jones's austere revision of Italian classical architecture. The published text generalises and glosses this scene by explaining that Britanocles (King Charles) has 'reduced the land, by his example, to a real knowledge of all good arts and sciences'.³ The claim of the Caroline régime (by fostering peace and prosperity) to be a bringer of true civilisation duplicates the cultural enterprise entrusted to Jones by Edmund Bolton decades earlier, and carried on through the masques.

In the Queen's masques and plays, as Erica Veevers has convincingly argued,⁴ the exaltation of royalty could be even more closely identified with the exposition of ideas central to Jones's work as an artist. Given the stereotypical contrast between the masculine ruler and his feminine consort, Henrietta Maria was represented as an object of admiring regard, a focus of contemplation, and the neo-Platonic tendency of her entertainments affirmed that it was through beauty that virtue and truth became manifest. In *Tempe Restored*, the first Queen's masque of his 'personal rule', Jones took almost complete control of the production. The poet Townshend was responsible only for writing 'the verses', while Jones was credited as inventor of 'the subject and allegory of the masque, with the descriptions and apparatus of the scenes . . .'⁵ Tempe, the most beautiful place on earth and once 'the happy retreat of the muses and their followers',⁶ having been seized from them is restored: again we have a fable about the return or revival of the arts. The Queen figures as Divine Beauty, a concept which underlies all her succeeding roles throughout the 1630s; and the masque repeatedly stresses the primacy of sight and visibility in the mind's effort to acquire knowledge and apprehend virtue. In the prose account of 'The Allegory' which Jones added to the text he reinforces these neo-Platonic notions, stating for example that 'desire cannot be moved without appearance of beauty', an axiom pertinent to the reception of his own work. He also describes 'a perfect habit of virtue made by the harmony of the irascible and concupiscible parts obedient to the rational and highest part of the soul';⁷ this is the Platonic doctrine of the soul from *Republic* Book IX, where the 'highest part' is 'the desire to learn',⁸ the concept helping to constitute Jones's personal motto, which clearly informs his exposition here.

Luminalia: The Queen's Festival of Light (1638) brings together all these central themes of Jones's masque work: the migration of the arts, cultural reform, and true knowledge gained through the medium of visual beauty.

Jones is credited with the 'making' of the 'subject', which is explained in a preamble:

> The muses being long since drawn out of Greece by the fierce Thracians, their groves withered and all their springs dried up, and out of Italy by the barbarous Goths and Vandals, they wandered here and there indecently without their ornaments and instruments, the arch-flamens and flamens, their prophetic priests, being constrained either to live in disguises or hide their heads in caves; and in some places, whensoever they began to appear, they were, together with peace, driven out by war; and in the more civilised parts, where they hoped to have taken some rest, Envy and Avarice by clipping the wings of Fame drave them into a perpetual storm, till by the divine minds of these incomparable pair, the muses and they were received into protection and established in this monarchy, by the encouragement and security of those well-born wits represented by the Prophetic Priests of the Britanides.[9]

This cultural parable ingeniously weaves together favoured motifs of the Caroline régime – peace, social order, hierarchical religion, 'civility' – with a revised version of Vasari's history of the arts:[10] flourishing in antiquity, expelled by the barbarians, and latterly transplanted to the reviving climate of (not Italy but) Great Britain. The story is substantiated by the climax of the masque, set in 'the beautiful garden of the Britanides' where Henrietta Maria appears:

> behind all was a bright sky, and in the midst, above the Queen's majesty's seat, was a glory with rays, expressing her to be the queen of brightness.[11]

This neo-Platonic tableau, which equates knowing with seeing and truth with vision or enlightenment, has the impact of a baroque religious painting (Erica Veevers has suggested) in which the Catholic Queen figures as her namesake, the Virgin Mary.[12] Such an attempt to present modern European art (while in covert paraphrase) in its most characteristic guise fits in with the Vasarian parable of migration and renaissance, to point us back towards the charge laid on Jones by his friend Bolton, with which this book began.

Notes

Introduction: the court masque

1. Enid Welsford, *The Court Masque*, Cambridge, 1927; Stephen Orgel, *The Jonsonian Masque*, Cambridge, Mass., 1965; O&S, vol. I, pp. 1–75.
2. John Peacock, 'Ben Jonson's Masques and Italian Culture', in J. R. Mulryne and Margaret Shewring, ed., *Theatre of the English and Italian Renaissance*, London, 1991, pp. 73–94.
3. H&S, vol. VII, p. 631, lines 49–50.
4. Welsford, *Masque*, p. 122.
5. Ibid., p. 130.
6. The term 'main masque' is used by Francis Beaumont in *The Masque of the Inner Temple and Gray's Inn* (1613); see *A Book of Masques in Honour of Allardyce Nicoll*, ed. T. J. B. Spencer and Stanley Wells, Cambridge, 1967, p. 140. For a more detailed discussion of the antimasque see ch. 4, pp. 130–51.
7. Alastair Fowler, *Kinds of Literature*, Oxford, 1982, pp. 60–1.
8. O&S, vol. II, pp. 604, 606, no. 292.
9. Ibid., p. 662, lines 1–5.
10. H&S, vol. VII, p. 735, lines 5–6.
11. O&S, vol. II, p. 667, lines 622–5.
12. H&S, vol. VII, p. 209, lines 18–19.
13. H&S, vol. X, pp. 566, 612.
14. The masques presented at Whitehall by the Inns of Court in 1613 and 1634 are not really exceptions, since the presenters were 'gentlemen'.
15. The fact that courtly amateurs sometimes displayed their talents in this area was not taken to invalidate the general principle.
16. H&S, vol. X, p. 576; O&S, vol. II, p. 599.

1 The theory and practice of imitation

1. Roy Strong, *Art and Power: Renaissance Festivals 1450–1650*, Woodbridge, 1984.

2 Arthur R. Blumenthal, *Giulio Parigi's Stage Designs*, New York and London, 1986, p. 152.
3 H&S, vol. VII, p. 209, lines 17–19.
4 Ibid., p. 282, lines 7–9.
5 H&S, vol. VIII, p. 609, line 1309. Cf. Davenant's comment on Jones's proscenium for *Salmacida Spolia*, that it 'tempered delight with profit' (O&S, vol. II, p. 730, line 68).
6 John Orrell, *The Theatres of Inigo Jones and John Webb*, Cambridge, 1985, p. 101; the motto is 'Prodesse & delectare'.
7 M. F. S. Hervey, *The Life, Correspondence and Collections of Thomas Howard, Earl of Arundel*, Cambridge, 1921, p. 176, note 2.
8 This is the translation of Bolton's Latin usually adopted, which in the next section I revise.
9 Giovanni Francesco Bordino, *De Rebus Praeclare Gestis A Sixto V. Pon. Max. ... Carminum Liber Primus*, Rome, 1588.
10 Latin text from J. A. Gotch, *Inigo Jones*, London, 1928, p. 251 (the Bordino volume with the inscription has unfortunately disappeared from the library of Worcester College, Oxford). I use the translation by Gotch, ibid., p. 44, with a number of alterations. For a more detailed version of the following argument, including a discussion of Gotch's substantive mistranslations, see John Peacock, 'Inigo Jones and Renaissance Art', *Renaissance Studies*, 4 (1990), 245–72.
11 Alexander Ross, *Mystagogus Poeticus*, London, 1648 (facsimile New York and London, 1976), p. 262.
12 Vincenzo Cartari, *Imagini Delli Dei De Gl'Antichi*, Venice, 1647 (facsimile Graz, 1963), p. 173: 'Statue di Mercurio, dette Hermi, per esser lui stato l'inventore di tutte le buone arte ... erano poste ... per ornamento nelle scuole, & nelle Academie ... '
13 E. M. Portal, 'The Academ Roial of James I', *Proceedings of the British Academy*, 7 (1915–16), 189–208.
14 For representations of Mercury as patron of the arts of design, see Jan Saenredam, *Gods of the Seven Planets*, Bartsch III.78.245, and Hendrick Goltzius, *Mercury as patron of painting* in the Mauritshuis (on loan to the Franz Hals Museum); see also note 28 below.
15 Jones seems to have known some Latin, but he read Latin texts in Italian (or occasionally French) translations.
16 Quoted in Erwin Panofsky, *Renaissance and Renascences in Western Art*, Stockholm, 1960, p. 16 and note 3: '[Nescio] cur illae artes quae proximae ad liberales accedunt, Pingendi, Scalpendi, Fingendi, Architectandi, aut tamdiu tantoque opere degeneraverint, ac pene cum litteris ipsi demortuae fuerint, aut hoc tempore excitentur, ac reviviscant ... '
17 Ibid., p. 17, note 1.
18 Ibid.
19 Edmund Bolton, *The Elements of Armories*, London, 1610, p. 60: 'to imitate is generally imprest in the nature of man ... '
20 Orrell, *Theatres*, pp. 35, 31.

21 More detailed argument on this point in John Peacock, 'The Stuart Court Masque and the Theatre of the Greeks', *JWCI*, 56 (1993), pp. 183–208.
22 O&S, vol. I, p. 115.
23 H&S, vol. VII, pp. 209ff., 169ff. *Oberon* (1611) was to be a version of a Greek satyr play; see Peacock, 'Stuart Court Masque'.
24 H&S, vol. VII, p. 229, lines 584–5.
25 Bastiano de' Rossi, *Descrizione Del Magnificentiss. Apparato E De' Maravigliosi Intermedi Fatti Per La Commedia Rappresentata In Firenze nelle felicissime Nozze degl'Illustrissimi ed Eccellentissimi Signori Il Signor Don Cesare D'Este E La Signora Donna Virginia Medici*, Florence, 1586, fol. IV; Michelangelo Buonarroti, *Descrizione Delle Felicissime Nozze Della Cristianissima Maestà di Madonna Maria Medici Regina di Francia e di Navarra*, Florence, 1600, p. 36.
26 Daniele Barbaro, *La Pratica Della Perspettiva*, Venice, 1569, p. 1. For a full discussion of the Vitruvian usage see John White, *The Birth and Rebirth of Pictorial Space*, 2nd edn., London, 1967, pp. 250ff. Cf. also the beginning of chapter 3 below.
27 Cicero uses the word to describe certain effects of oratory, which operate powerfully but unobserved, e.g. *Orator*, ed. and trans. H. M. Hubbell, London and Cambridge, Mass., 1952, xxxii.97: 'Haec modo perfringit, modo irrepit in sensus ...' ('Now it storms the senses, now it creeps in ...').
28 Christopher White, *The Dutch Pictures in the Collection of Her Majesty the Queen*, Cambridge, 1982, pp. 53–5, no. 74; Ellis Waterhouse, *Painting in Britain 1530 to 1790*, 4th edn., Harmondsworth, 1978, p. 86, plate 65.
29 Bordino, *De Rebus Praeclare Gestis*, p. 5: next to a marginal note, 'Hereticorum & infidelium reditus ad Ecclesiae gremiu[m]', there is the couplet: 'Serviet armipotens Anglus, gens dura Lemanni / Bosphoridae Thraces, indomitique Getae.'
30 At least one sixteenth-century commentator points out the ambivalence ('equivocatione') in Aristotle's use of the concept of mimesis: Alessandro Piccolomini, *Annotationi ... Nel Libro Della Poetica d'Aristotele; Con La Traduttione Del medesimo Libro, in lingua Volgare*, Venice, 1575, p. 66.
31 For detailed discussion of this concept see Günter Berghaus, 'Theatre Performances at Italian Renaissance Festivals: Multi-Media Spectacles or *Gesamtkunstwerke*?', in J. R. Mulryne and Margaret Shewring, ed., *Italian Renaissance Festivals and Their European Influence*, Lewiston, Queenston and Lampeter, 1992, pp. 3–50.
32 Carlo Ridolfi, *Le Maraviglie dell'Arte*, ed. Detlev von Hadeln, 2 vols., Berlin, 1924, vol. II, p. 95: 'essendo stato il passato secolo un Teatro a punto, ove si fece l'apparato delle più rare maraviglie dell'Arte ...'
33 John Newman, 'The Inigo Jones Centenary', *Burlington Magazine*, 115 (1973), 559.
34 *King's Arcadia*, p. 68.
35 O&S, vol. I, p. 41.

36 O&S, vol. II, pp. 566, 588, no. 280; James Byam Shaw, *Old Master Drawings from Chatsworth*, London, 1973, p. 18, no. 12 (plate 12); Donald Posner, *Annibale Carracci*, 2 vols., London, 1971, vol. I, p. 81, vol. II, pp. 39–40, no. 92 (plate 92c).

37 Konrad Oberhuber, 'Hieronymus Cock, Battista Pittoni und Paolo Veronese in Villa Maser', in *Munuscula disciplinorum. Festschrift Hans Kaufmann*, Berlin, 1968, pp. 207ff.

38 Bril's 'Maius. Junius' from his series of the months in six prints made by Aegidius Sadeler (Hollstein XXI.35.125, reprod. XXII.33) was copied by Jones for *The Shepherd's Paradise* (O&S, vol. II, pp. 514–15, no. 250) and by Pozzoserrato in a landscape now in the Ca' d'Oro (Gino Fogolari et al., *La R. Galleria Giorgio Franchetti alla Ca' d'Oro*, Venice, 1929, p. 124). Callot's 'Fair at Impruneta' (Lieure 478) was used by Jones for *The Triumph of Peace* (O&S, vol. II, pp. 560–1, no. 270) and copied by Teniers in a painting now in Munich (Peter Eikemeier et al., *Alte Pinakothek München. Erläuterungen zu den ausgestellten Gemälden*, Munich, 1983, p. 523, no. 817).

39 This is on the page headed 'parmigano il meglio'. The prints, in order, are Bartsch XVI.6.2, 8.5, 49.17, XVIII.300.46, reprod., *The Illustrated Bartsch*, vol. 32, ed. Henri Zerner, New York, 1979, pp. 9, 11, 53 and ibid., vol. 40, ed. Veronika Birke, New York, 1982, p. 197.

40 Jill Finsten, *Isaac Oliver: Art at the Courts of Elizabeth I and James I*, 2 vols., New York and London, 1981.

41 Ibid., vol. I, p. 31.

42 In his copy (in Worcester College library) of Giorgio Vasari, *Delle Vite De' Piu Eccellenti Pittori Scultori Et Archittetori . . . Primo Volume della Terza Parte*, Florence, 1568, sig. *****2 verso: 'La maniera venne poi la piu bella, dall'havere messo in uso il frequente ritrarre le cose piu belle . . . ' For the role of copying in Jones's draughtsmanship see Jeremy Wood, 'Inigo Jones, Italian art, and the practice of drawing', *Art Bulletin*, 74 (1992), 247–70.

43 Vasari, Milanesi, vol. VII, pp. 140, 141, 144.

44 Ibid., pp. 279–80: 'Domandato da un amico suo quel che gli paresse d'uno che aveva contraffatto di marmo figure antiche del più celebrate, vantandosi lo immitatore che di gran lunga aveva superato gli antichi, rispose: Chi va dietro a altri, mai non li passa innanzi; e chi non sa far bene da sè, non più servirsi bene delle cose d'altri.' In translations of Vasari I have used or adapted the English version of A. B. Hinds, published in Everyman's Library: Giorgio Vasari, *The Lives*, 4 vols., London, 1963.

45 Vasari, Milanesi, vol. IV, p. 376.

46 Barocchi, *Scritti*, vol. II, p. 1598.

47 G. B. Armenini, *De' Veri Precetti Della Pittura . . . Libri Tre*, Ravenna, 1587 (facsimile Hildesheim and New York, 1971); *On the True Precepts of the Art of Painting*, trans. Edward J. Olszewski, New York, 1977. This treatise was in Lord Arundel's library: see BM MS Sloane 862, 'Catalogus librorum bibliothecae Norfolcianae', fol. 20v, no. 204 (Armenini is listed between Vasari and Lomazzo).

48 Armenini, *True Precepts*, p. 149; *Veri Precetti*, p. 78: 'quelli che per loro meschinità non possiendo inventione alcuna...' Ibid., p. 136; p. 65.

49 Ibid, p. 136; p. 65: 'i quali disegni si vedevano essere con tal'arte ridotti alla sua dolce maniera, che si potea più tosto quelli esser da lui nati, e trovati, che retratti da altrui...'

50 Armenini, *True Precepts*, p. 149; *Veri Precetti*, p. 78: 'percioche essendo impossibile, sì come pare à molti, di poter formarsi hoggimai cosa, la qual prima non sia stata trovata, & fatta, ne seguita, che il servirsi delle altrui inventioni si possa, & sia necessario, pur che si habbia avertimento di ridurle con qualche mutatione, & tenere una certa facoltà, che paiano esser nate, & fabricate per suo proprio ingegno...'

51 Barbaro, p. 32: 'il piacere dello intelletto è di apprendere il vero, perche niuna cosa è piu conveniente allo intelletto, che la verità, onde si dice: Altro diletto ch'imparar non trovo.' Jones's annotations quoted above are found on pp. 29, 32.

52 Elizabeth Cropper, *The Ideal of Painting. Pietro Testa's Düsseldorf Notebook*, Princeton, 1984, pp. 65–7, who notes that the motto was also used by Alessandro Allori and Pietro Testa.

53 Ibid., p. 67; *Nicomachean Ethics*, x.vii.9.

54 *Poetics* iv.2–4 in S. H. Butcher, *Aristotle's Theory of Poetry and Fine Art*, New York, 1951, p. 15.

55 Antonio Minturno, *L'Arte Poetica*, Venice, 1564 (facsimile Munich, 1971), Libro Primo, p. 7. Minturno's quotation is more accurate than Barbaro's, since Petrarch uses the word 'provo' not 'trovo'.

56 Barbaro, p. 12.

57 Rensselaer W. Lee, *Ut Pictura Poesis. The Humanistic Theory of Painting*, New York, 1967, pp. 9–16.

58 Franciscus Junius, *The Painting of the Ancients*, in *The Literature of Classical Art*, ed. Keith Aldrich, Philipp Fehl and Raina Fehl, 2 vols., Berkeley, Los Angeles and London, 1991, vol. I, p. 9.

59 Vasari, Milanesi, vol. I, p. 222: 'io so che l'arte nostra è tutta imitazione della natura principalmente, e poi, perchè da sè non può salir tanto alto, delle cose che da quelli che miglior maestri di sè giudica sono condotte...'

60 Vasari, *Vite* (Worcester College Library), sig. *****2 verso (reprod. Wood, 'Jones and Drawing', p. 248, fig. 1): 'Design was the imitation of the most beautiful aspects of nature in all figures, whether sculpted or painted – a capacity which comes from having a hand and intellect able to reproduce everything that the eye sees on a level surface...'

61 D. J. Gordon, 'Poet and Architect: The Intellectual Setting of the Quarrel between Ben Jonson and Inigo Jones', in *The Renaissance Imagination*, Berkeley, Los Angeles and London, 1975, pp. 89–90, 94.

62 Richard S. Peterson, *Imitation and Praise in the Poems of Ben Jonson*, New Haven and London, 1981.

63 Palladio, *Quattro Libri*, Bk. I, p. 51.

64 *Ten Books on Architecture by Leone Battista Alberti Translated into Italian by*

Cosimo Bartoli And into English by James Leoni, ed. Joseph Rykwert, London, 1965, p. 195: 'The Ancients ... did in their Works propose to themselves the Imitation of Nature, as the greatest Artist at all Manner of Compositions: and for this Purpose they laboured ... to discover the laws upon which she herself acted in the Production of her Works, in order to transfer them to the business of Architecture.' *L'Architettura Di Leon Battista Alberti, Tradotta in lingua Fiorentina da Cosimo Bartoli*, Monreale, 1565 (Jones's copy in Worcester College library): 'conoscendo i nostri Antichi dalla natura delle cose ... non poteva in modo alcuno intervenir' loro di far' cosa alcuna che fusse lodata, o honorata giudicarono che e' bisognava che e' cercasino di immitare la Natura ottima artefice di tutte le forme, & per questo adorno raccogliendo per quanto possette la industria de gli huomini, le leggi, le quali ella haveva usate nel produrre le cose, & le trasportarono alle cose da edificarsi.' Cf. Barbaro: 'l' Architettura ... imitando la natura perl'occulta virtù del suo principio ...'

65 Vitruvius, III.i.1–5 (vol. I, pp. 158–61).
66 Vasari, Milanesi, vol. I, p. 146.
67 Haydocke, Lomazzo, Bk. I, p. 26.
68 Vitruvius, IV.i.6–7 (vol. I, pp. 206–7).
69 Vasari, Milanesi, vol. I, p. 130: '[ha] forma somigliante, come si dice, alla persona di Ercole ...'
70 Vitruvius, V.i.3 (vol. I, pp. 256–7): 'Non minus quod etiam nascentium oportet imitari naturam, ut in arboribus ...'; Palladio, Bk. I, p. 51; Sir Henry Wotton, *The Elements of Architecture*, London, 1624, p. 32.
71 Note on Bk. IV, p. 132; see Bruce Allsopp, ed., *Inigo Jones on Palladio*, 2 vols., Newcastle upon Tyne, 1970. All references to Jones's notes on Palladio will be made to this edition, with details of transcription occasionally corrected.
72 Joan Sumner Smith, 'The Italian Sources of Inigo Jones's Style', *Burlington Magazine*, 94 (1952), 204. The other occurrence is in the Roman Sketchbook.
73 Barbaro, p. 37: 'L'arte quanto puo imita la natura: Et questo adviene per che il principio dell'arte, che è lo intelletto humano, ha gran simiglianza col principio, che muove la natura, che è una intelligenza. Dalla simiglianza delle virtù & de i principii nasce la simiglianza dell'operare, che per ora chiameremo imitatione.' [No annotation]
74 H&S, vol. VII, p. 170, lines 26–30.
75 *La Republica Di Platone*, trans. Pamphilo Florimbene, Venice, 1554 (Worcester College library), p. 108.
76 Ibid., p. 416: 'dimmi di gratia qual città per il tuo mezzo fu mai ordinata, & disposta? come Sparta per il mezzo di Ligurgo, & molte città, & picciole, & grandi, per il mezzo di molti altri; di qual citta predicano gli huomini che tu specialmente sia ottimo datore di leggi?'
77 Ibid., pp. 421–2: 'io dicevo *che la pittura, et ogni facoltà dell'*imitare, esercita l'opera sua lontano della verità, et di nuovo si accosta con qualche parte di noi, la quale del tutto sia priva di prudentia, & con quella fa amicitia, ma non ha cosa veruna di vero, ne di sincero' (Jones's underlining).

78 John Newman, 'Inigo Jones's Architectural Education before 1614', *Architectural History*, 35 (1992), 18–50.
79 Notes on Bk. II, p. 70; Bk. IV, p. 63.
80 For a fuller discussion see Peacock, 'Inigo Jones and Renaissance Art', pp. 267–8.
81 Note on Bk. IV, p. 14.
82 Newman, 'Centenary', p. 559.
83 Note on Bk. IV, p. 98.
84 Vasari, Milanesi, Vol. I, p. 225: 'L'architettura ... si andò mantenendo, se non così perfetta, in miglior modo: nè di cio è da maravigliarsi, perchè, facendosi gli edifizi grandi quasi tutti di spoglie, era facile agli architetti nel fare i nuovi imitare in gran parte i vecchi, che sempre avevano dinanzi agli occhi ...'
85 Note on the Baptistery of Constantine, Bk. IV, p. 61: 'paladio thinkes this Templ not Antike but I do Beeleeve yt to bee made in Constantines time when Architecture was much falen and they yoused to build wth fragmentes of antike buildinges as in his Arch. se Serlio.' Serlio's account of the Arch of Constantine in Book III does not contain what Jones referred to: he may have written Serlio in mistake for Vasari.
86 The roundels are derived from Roman medals, such as Jones would have known in the royal collection: *King's Arcadia*, p. 143, 67; H&H, p. 251, no. 82. See Antonio Agostini, *Dialoghi Intorno alle Medaglie*, Rome, 1625, p. 76 (medals inscribed 'Hilari Tempor' and 'Hilaritas' cf. Jones's 'Laetitia Publica'), pp. 32, 41 ('Pietas' and 'Pax Augusti' cf. Jones's 'Hylaritas Publica').
87 Armenini, *True Precepts*, p. 130; *Veri Precetti*, p. 61; Junius, *Painting of the Ancients*, pp. 33, 35: 'a good Imitator standeth in need of learned and well exercised eyes; not onely, because hidden things cannot be seen unlesse they are first searched out; but also, because the things apparent are very often so cunningly contrived and joyned, that none but quick-sighted Artificers and teachers can perceive them.'
88 Reprod. Roy Strong, *Festival Designs by Inigo Jones*, International Exhibitions Foundation, 1967–8, no. 41.
89 John Peacock, 'Roman Sketchbook', in H&H, pp. 288–90.
90 See pp. 18–19 above.
91 Plato, *Republica*, pp. 384–7 (*Republic* 581B–583A): 'Si questa terza parte la chiameremo desiderio d'imparare & Philosopho, non gli sarà imposto il nome fuor di proposito.' Jones was to use the Platonic theory of the soul as thematic material in *Tempe Restored* (1632), the first masque where he had an entirely free hand in the 'invention': O&S, vol. II, p. 483, lines 350–5, 366–8.
92 Vitruvius, I.i.3 (I, 8–9); Barbaro, p. 18: 'La Filosofia adunque ci giova alla virtu de i costumi, similmente ci giova quanto alla parte posta nella cognitione del vero ...'
93 *La Seconda Parte De Gli Opusculi Morali Di Plutarco*, trans. Giovanni Trachagnota, Venice, 1567 (Worcester College library), fol. 49r (Jones's underlinings).
94 *The Speeches at Prince Henry's Barriers*, line 53, in H&S, vol. VII, p. 324.

95 Titles listed in *King's Arcadia*, pp. 217–18.
96 *Opusculi Morali Di Plutarco... Parte Seconda*, trans. Marc'Antonio Gandino, Venice, 1614 (Worcester College library), p. 177. Jones annotated the section 'del Genio di Socrate', pp. 606ff.
97 The mutation of Aristotle's idea of poetry as a means of delightful learning into Horace's idea of it as delightful teaching was reenacted synchronically in the sixteenth century, when theorists tended to read Horace and Aristotle into each other: Lee, *Ut Pictura Poesis*, pp. 32–4; Marvin T. Herrick, *The Fusion of Horatian and Aristotelian Literary Criticism, 1531–1555*, Urbana, 1946, esp. ch. IV, 'The Function of Poetry', pp. 39–47.
98 For an example of Jonson's use of the language of mimesis in the masque commentaries, see note 74 above. Cf. his notes on *The Masque of Blackness*, H&S, vol. VII, p. 172, note l: 'There wants not inough, in nature, to authorize this part of our fiction...'; and on *The Masque of Beauty*, ibid., p. 184, note f: 'To give authoritie to this part of our fiction...' For his attitude to *imitatio*, see Peterson, *Imitation and Praise*, passim.
99 Eugenio Battisti, 'Il concetto d'imitazione nel Cinquecento italiano' in *Rinascimento e Barocco*, Turin, 1960, pp. 175ff. Armenini, *True Precepts*, p. 130.
100 Palladio, *Quattro Libri*, Bk. I, p. 51: 'non si può se non biasimare quella maniera di fabricare, laquale partendosi da quello, che la Natura delle cose ci insegna, & da quella semplicità, che nelle cose da lei create si scorge, quasi un' altra natura facendosi; si parte dal vero, buono, e bel modo di fabricare.'
101 Sir Philip Sidney, *An Apology for Poetry*, ed. Geoffrey Shepherd, Manchester, 1973, p. 100.
102 Haydocke, Lomazzo, Bk. II, p. 3.
103 *King's Arcadia*, p. 66.
104 This idea was influentially developed (following Wittkower) in Gordon Toplis, 'The Sources of Jones's Mind and Imagination', *King's Arcadia*, pp. 61–3, and O&S, vol. I, pp. 49–75 (Introduction, Chapter IV, 'Platonic Politics'). But for a convincingly contrary view see now Gordon Higgott, '"Varying with Reason": Inigo Jones's Theory of Design', *Architectural History*, 35 (1992), 51–77.
105 *Poetics* xxv.6 in Butcher, *Aristotle*, pp. 101, 107; Lee, *Ut Pictura Poesis*, p. 9.
106 Finsten, *Oliver*, passim; Ridolfi, *Maraviglie*, vol. II, p. 14; Posner, *Carracci*, vol. I, pp. 90–2.
107 *The Elder Pliny's Chapters on the History of Art*, trans. K. Jex-Blake, ed. E. Sellers, Chicago, 1968, p. 109 (*Historia Naturalis*, XXXV.64) and note 11; L. B. Alberti, *On Painting and Sculpture*, ed. Cecil Grayson, London, 1972, p. 99; Battisti, *Rinascimento e Barocco*, pp. 193–7.
108 *L'Opere Morali di Xenophonte*, trans. Lodovico Domenichi, Venice, 1567 (Worcester College library), fol. 95r.
109 Vasari, *Vite* (Worcester College library), sig. *****2 verso: 'Style then reached its finest pitch from the practice of constantly portraying the most beautiful things, and joining together these superlative hands, heads, torsos and legs, so as to make a complete figure of all those fine features...' Wood, 'Jones and Drawing', p. 267.

110 *King's Arcadia*, p. 209. Jones's tomb carried reliefs of the Banqueting House and the west front of St Paul's.
111 John Peacock, 'Inigo Jones's Catafalque for James I', *Architectural History*, 25 (1982), 1–5.
112 Cf. Stephen Orgel's comments on Jones's view of Stonehenge, *King's Arcadia*, p. 62.
113 John Summerson, *Inigo Jones*, Harmondsworth, 1966, p. 43.
114 Battisti, *Rinascimento e Barocco*, p. 192.
115 Ibid., p. 197 and note 2; Barocchi, *Scritti*, vol. II, pp. 1570–1.

2 The masques as pictures

1 J. A. Gotch, *Inigo Jones*, London, 1928, p. 44.
2 M. F. S. Hervey, *The Life, Correspondence and Collections of Thomas Howard, Earl of Arundel*, Cambridge, 1921, p. 176, note 2.
3 For the effect of Protestant iconoclasm on English culture see Margaret Aston, *England's Iconoclasts. Volume I. Laws against Images*, Oxford, 1988; Patrick Collinson, *The Birthpangs of Protestant England*, New York, 1988; Frances Yates, 'Broken Images', in *Ideas and Ideals in the North European Renaissance. Collected Essays Volume III*, London, 1984, pp. 40–8.
4 Aston, *Iconoclasts*, p. 436.
5 Ibid., p. 461.
6 O&S, vol. I, p. 14.
7 Pliny, *Historia Naturalis*, XXXIV.15, in trans. K. Jex-Blake, ed. E. Sellers, *The Elder Pliny's Chapters on the History of Art*, Chicago, 1968, pp. 12–13; *The Historie Of The World. Commonly called The Naturall Historie Of C. Plinius Secundus*, trans. Philemon Holland, 2 vols., London, 1601, vol. II, p. 489: 'this art of founding and casting brass proceeded farther and passed on, untill it was commonly practised in making the idols and images of the gods.'
8 Haydocke, Lomazzo, Bk. IV, p. 152.
9 Henry Peacham, *The Arte of Drawing*, London, 1606, p. 8.
10 Henry Peacham, *The Gentlemans Exercise*, London, 1612, p. 11.
11 Peacham, *Drawing*, p. 1.
12 Edward Norgate, *Miniatura or The Art of Limning*, ed. Martin Hardie, Oxford, 1919, pp. 44, 88–9.
13 *Discoveries*, lines 1523–8, in H&S, vol. VIII, p. 610.
14 Ibid., pp. 609–10, lines 1509–16.
15 H&S, vol. VII, p. 172, lines 90–1.
16 *L'Opere Morali di Xenophonte*, trans. Lodovico Domenichi, Venice, 1567 (Worcester College library), fol. 95r.
17 H&S, vol. VIII, p. 611, lines 1575–6.
18 *Opuscoli Morali Di Plutarco ... Parte Seconda*, trans. Marc'Antonio Gandino, Venice, 1614 (Worcester College library), p. 177; *Opere Morali di Xenophonte*, fol. 95r.

19 *Opere Morali di Xenophonte*, fol. 95v.
20 Ibid., fol. 95r, where Jones had rendered 'quella soavissima ... imagine de l'animo' in the margin as 'the / bauti of the sowle'.
21 *Discoveries*, lines 1510–15, in H&S, vol. VIII, p. 609–10. For a contrary, Italian view see Irma A. Richter, *Paragone: A Comparison of the Arts by Leonardo da Vinci*, London, New York and Toronto, 1949, pp. 54–9.
22 Norgate, *Miniatura*, p. 55; cf. Lomazzo in Barocchi, *Scritti*, vol. I, p. 354: 'poeti, a' quali i pittori sono in molte parti simili ... non possa essere pittore che insieme anco non abbia qualche spirito di poesia ...'
23 *Discoveries*, lines 1580–4, in H&S, vol. VIII, p. 612.
24 Antonio Possevino, *Bibliotheca Selecta Qua agitur De Ratione Studiorum*, 2 vols., Cologne, 1607, vol. II, p. 472 (Jonson used the Rome, 1593, edition).
25 O&S, vol. I, p. 12.
26 Campion, on the contrary, in his text of *Lord Hay's Masque* (1607) included music for the songs and the costume design for the masquers (he had composed the music himself).
27 Barbaro, p. 12: 'Bisogna adunque leggere, & le cose lette, per la mente rivolgere ...'
28 Rudolf Wittkower, 'Inigo Jones, Architect and Man of Letters', in *Palladio and English Palladianism*, London, 1974, p. 60. John Bold, *John Webb: Architectural Theory and Practice in the Seventeenth Century*, Oxford, 1989, pp. 23ff.
29 *La Seconda Parte De Gli Opusculi Morali Di Plutarco*, trans. Giovanni Trachagnota, Venice, 1567 (Worcester College library), fol. 7v (Jones's underlining).
30 D. J. Gordon, 'Poet and Architect: The Intellectual Setting of the Quarrel between Ben Jonson and Inigo Jones', in *The Renaissance Imagination*, Berkeley, Los Angeles and London, 1975, pp. 87–90.
31 *Dialogo di pittura* (1548), in Barocchi, *Trattati*, vol. I, p. 117: 'Sono infinite le cose appertinenti al colorire et impossibil è isplicarle con parole ...'
32 O&S, vol. II, p. 454, line 99.
33 Ibid., lines 102ff.
34 H&S, vol. VIII, pp. 402–6. Again, there is something fundamentally Protestant about the refusal to leave imagery to its own devices, without an accompanying text. In the Elizabethan homily on idolatry, narrative religious art, explained by a text, is admitted as tolerable: 'And a process of a story, painted with the gestures and actions of many persons, and commonly the sum of the story written withal, hath another use in it, than one dumb idol or image standing by itself', *Certain Sermons and Homilies*, Oxford, 1844, p. 178 (quoted in Aston, *Iconoclasts*, p. 405).
35 Roy Strong, 'Some Early Portraits at Arundel Castle', *The Connoisseur*, 197 (1978), 202.
36 Haydocke, Lomazzo, p. 23: 'The skilfull Painter in drawing a King or Emperor, expresseth them grave and full of Maiestie, although peradventure they bee not so naturallie ... So that the precepts of Arts permit us to represent the Pope, the

Emperor ... or anie other person, with that Decorum which truely belongeth to them.'
37 Franciscus Junius, *The Painting of the Ancients*, in *The Literature of Classical Art*, ed. Keith Aldrich, Philipp Fehl and Raina Fehl, 2 vols., Berkeley, Los Angeles and Oxford, 1991, vol. I, p. 66.
38 Roy Strong, *The English Icon*, London, 1969, pp. 318–19, 330–1, nos. 330–2, 354–7.
39 Oliver Millar, *The Tudor, Stuart and Early Georgian Pictures in the Collection of Her Majesty the Queen*, 2 vols., London, 1963, vol. I, p. 81, no. 104 (pl. 45).
40 John Peacock, 'Inigo Jones and the Arundel Marbles', *Journal of Medieval and Renaissance Studies*, 16 (1986), 78.
41 Keith Andrews, *Adam Elsheimer*, London, 1977, pp. 10, 26, 36, 141, 151, 166.
42 See p. 24 above, note 86. Oliver Millar, ed., *Abraham van der Doort's Catalogue of the Collections of Charles I* (The Thirty-Seventh Volume of the Walpole Society, 1958–60), Glasgow, 1960, p. 155: 'Mijst sorffijer has bin taking and viewing de sam and nombring.'
43 A. P. Oppé, *English Drawings at Windsor Castle*, London, 1950, pp. 79–80.
44 O&S, vol. II, p. 480, lines 47–50. For a discussion parallel to what follows (which was conceived independently) but with a different emphasis see Erica Veevers, *Images of Love and Religion. Queen Henrietta Maria and court entertainments*, Cambridge, 1989, pp. 112–19.
45 H&S, vol. VII, p. 190, lines 272–6.
46 Barocchi, *Trattati*, vol. I, pp. 171ff.
47 H&S, vol. VII, p. 209, lines 1–19.
48 Benedetto Varchi, *Lezzione ... della maggioranza delle arti* (1556): 'i poeti imitano il di dentro principalmente ... et i pittori imitano principalmente il di fuori'; 'Pare che sia tanta differenza fra la poesia e la pittura, quanta è fra l'anima e'l corpo'; G. B. Armenini, *De' Veri Precetti della Pittura* (1587): 'si chiama la pittura poetica che tace, e la poetica pittura che parla, e questa l'anima dover essere, quella il corpo'; in Barocchi, *Scritti*, vol. I, pp. 264, 265, 373. See ch. 4 for a fuller discussion of this topic.
49 Vasari, Milanesi, vol. VI, p. 439: 'quella maniera di pitture' (translation from Giorgio Vasari, *The Lives*, trans. A. B. Hinds, 4 vols., London, 1927, vol. III, p. 295).
50 Giulio Mancini, *Considerazioni sulla pittura*, ed. Adriana Marucchi and Luigi Salerno, 2 vols., Rome, 1956–7, vol. I, p. 113.
51 *King's Arcadia*, 65–6, 217, where the list of Jones's books does not make clear that his edition of Alberti, *L'Architettura di Leon Battista Alberti*, trans. Cosimo Bartoli, Monreale, 1565, also contains Ludovico Domenichi's translation of the *De pictura*. The two most substantial passages Jones translated from Lomazzo are headed: 'Of colloring – lomatzo li. 6 fo 301' and 'lomatzo li: 6 fo. 290 Of the proportion of children &c'.
52 Vasari, Milanesi, vol. I, p. 173: 'l' invenzione ... fa mettere insieme in istoria le figure a quattro, a sei, a dieci, a venti, talmente che si viene a formare le battaglie e l' altre cose grandi dell' arte.'

53 See Erwin Panofsky, *Idea: A Concept in Art Theory*, New York, 1968, p. 98, on how mannerist artists 'often wished to express in their works an allegorical or symbolical content beyond the merely visual'; and how 'the Mannerist transformation of the compositional principles accepted by the Renaissance operated as a "spiritualization" of the representations themselves . . . ' Lomazzo regards the terms 'historia' and 'forma' as interchangeable: see the first chapter of Book VII of his *Trattato*, entitled 'Della virtù, & necessità dell' historia, ò forma che vogliam dire della pittura.' He explains that no painter can 'esprimere co'l pennello . . . inventione alcuna; se non sa la forma esteriore di ciò che hà ritrovato', but he goes on to gloss 'forma esteriore' by saying 'è meno apprezzato nella pittura da savi quello che si vede, che quello sotto si gli nasconde come splendore velato da belli colori . . . ' (Lomazzo, *Scritti*, vol. II, p. 459).
54 Haydocke, Lomazzo, Bk. II, pp. 2ff., 8.
55 Ibid., Bk. I, p. 13, for Lomazzo's definition of painting.
56 Vasari, Milanesi, vol. IV, pp. 9–12.
57 Ibid.
58 See ch. 5.
59 Panofsky, *Idea*, pp. 61–2, 82, 86.
60 Giorgio Vasari, *Delle Vite De' Piu Eccellenti Pittori Scultori Et Architettori . . . Primo Volume della Terza Parte*, Florence, 1568 (Worcester College library), p. 327.
61 Historical Manuscripts Commission, *Rutland*, IV (1905), p. 446: 'Item, 28 *Junii* [1603], to henygo Jones, a picture maker, xli.'
62 *King's Arcadia*, p. 17.
63 O&S, vol. I, no. 81; vol. II, no. 384. The apparent facility of these sketches must be the result of Jones's perpetual exercise in drawing.
64 Junius, *Painting of the Ancients*, p. 244: 'It is easie to hit the shadowes of them that lie downe . . . or stand upright: and it requireth small wisdome to do it accurately. But the shadowes of *Atlas* go beyond all art: for the shadows of him that stoopeth after this manner, though they fall one into another, yet do they not darken any of these things that should rise, but cause some light about the hollownesse of his belly.' Cf. Philostratus, *Imagines*, II.20.
65 John Peacock, 'Figurative Drawings' and 'Roman Sketchbook' in H&H, pp. 284–90; Jeremy Wood, 'Inigo Jones, Italian Art, and the Practice of Drawing', *Art Bulletin*, 74 (1992), 247–70.
66 Daniele Barbaro, *La Pratica Della Perspettiva*, Venice, 1569 (facsimile Bologna, 1980), p. 129: 'alle . . . pastori . . . per quello, che accade tra loro si da una mostra di paesi, d'alberi, d'acque, di case rusticali, & quella mostra, che in tale pittura si rappresenta, Scena Satirica nominarono . . . '
67 Barbaro, p. 319.
68 Barbaro, *Perspettiva*, p. 3.
69 Barbaro, p. 257. See ch. 3.
70 Barbaro, *Perspettiva*, pp. 3, 175; for his tendency to assimilate scene-painting to other types of picture see also pp. 130 (where he speaks impartially of 'la tavola,

ò la tela, ò il piano dove si dipinge'), 155 (on 'uno modo di accordare le fabriche delle scene con le pitture de i muri e pareti'). For the relevance of 'scenographia' to architecture, and to the representation of architecture on the stage, see ch. 3.
71 Ibid., p. 3.
72 Vitruvius only implies that scene-design is a paradigm for monumental mural painting. Barbaro goes further, and uses 'scenographia' to mean both scene-design and large-scale painted compositions which obey the same laws of perspective as presumably underlay 'scenographia' in antiquity. See David Rosand, 'Theatre and Structure in the Art of Paolo Veronese', in *Painting in Cinquecento Venice*, New Haven and London, 1982, pp. 178–81.
73 Jones's annotations on Barbaro, pp. 29–30, reveal eventual doubts about Barbaro's handling of the term 'scaenographia'.
74 Facsimile London, 1832, page headed 'Thursday ye 19 January 1614' [i.e. 1615]. For further comment on this important passage see chs. 4 and 6.
75 Andrew Martindale, *The Triumphs of Caesar by Andrea Mantegna in the Collection of Her Majesty the Queen at Hampton Court*, London, 1979, p. 32; Cecil Gould, 'Sebastiano Serlio and Venetian Painting', *JWCI*, 25 (1962), 61–2.
76 Roy Strong, *Britannia Triumphans. Inigo Jones, Rubens and Whitehall Palace*, London, 1980, pp. 15ff.
77 Oliver Millar, *Van Dyck in England*, London, 1982, pp. 86–7, no. 43.
78 John Peacock, 'New Sources for the Masque Designs of Inigo Jones', *Apollo*, 107 (1978), 104–10.

3 Architecture

1 John Summerson, *Inigo Jones*, Harmondsworth, 1966, pp. 31–3.
2 Vitruvius I.i.1.
3 Barbaro, pp. 8–9; see also the preface by Francesco de' Franceschi, sig. a4r, where the crucial relation of theory to practice is stressed.
4 Vitruvius VII.v.5–7; Barbaro, p. 320, with note by Jones: 'Apaturio All / abandeo Repro / ued of Liscinio / matematico for / not yousing Deco / rum:'
5 John Bold, *John Webb: Architectural Theory and Practice in the Seventeenth Century*, Oxford, 1989, pp. 181–2.
6 Vitruvius VII.Preface.11; Barbaro, p. 308, with notes by Jones: 'Agatharco writ of / ye sceane // Democrito & Anaxagō: / of ye sceane // Greeke authors / of Architecture'.
7 Serlio, Bk. II, fol. 18v; for Jones's early use of Serlio see John Orrell, *The Theatres of Inigo Jones and John Webb*, Cambridge, 1985, pp. 24–38, and John Newman, 'Inigo Jones's architectural education before 1614', *Architectural History*, 35 (1992), 18–52.
8 Vitruvius I.ii.2; Barbaro, pp. 29ff. (Jones's note, p. 29).
9 Vitruvius I.i.3–4; Barbaro, pp. 12, 14.

10 Vitruvius VI.ii.2 and textual note 2; Barbaro, pp. 278, 282 (Jones's note, p. 282): 'And here it becomes evident how necessary perspective is to the architect...' See also John Newman, 'Italian Treatises in Use: the Significance of Inigo Jones's Annotations' in Jean Guillaume ed., *Les traités d'architecture de la Renaissance*, Paris, 1988, p. 438.
11 O&S, vol. I, p. 194, lines 162–5.
12 Barbaro, pp. 6–7. For a similar etymological definition see Pirro Ligorio, *Trattato de alcune cose appartenente alla nobiltà dell' antiche arti*, in Barocchi, *Scritti*, vol. II, p. 1445.
13 Barbaro, p. 6, Jones's note: 'What an Architect / is according to / Plato nell Regnio fo 3:6.'; this refers to *Di Tutte L'Opere Di Platone tradotte In lingua volgare da Dardi Bembo*, Venice, 1601, Parte Seconda, *Il Regno*, fol. 3v. See J. B. Skemp, *Plato's Statesman. A Translation of the 'Politicus' of Plato*, London, 1952.
14 Bembo, *Platone*, fol. 3v: 'Conciosia, che ogni Architetto non sia egli operario; ma a gli operari signoreggi... Mentre dà la cognitione: ma non il ministero delle mani.' Skemp, *Plato's Statesman*, p. 126, 259e–260a.
15 Barbaro, p. 7, Jones's note: 'Se Zenofon Socr / ates and Eutide / mus Li 4. fo 104'; this refers to *L'Opere Morali Di Xenophonte Tradotte Per M. Lodovico Domenichi*, Venice, 1567, fol. 104r: 'Ma vuoi tu paraventura a diventare architetto? perche egli dee essere molti pieno di sentenze.' In his copy Jones has drawn in the margin a hand pointing to this sentence. For the context see Xenophon, *Memorabilia*, IV.ii.8–10.
16 Aristotle, *Nicomachean Ethics*, I.i.4; cf. Benedetto Varchi, *Lezzione... della maggioranza delle arti*, Florence, 1549, in Barocchi, *Scritti*, vol. I, pp. 140–1.
17 Leon Battista Alberti, *On the Art of Building in Ten Books*, trans. Joseph Rykwert, Neil Leach and Robert Tavernor, London and Cambridge, Mass., 1988, pp. 3 (Prologue), 315 (IX.x).
18 Vitruvius I.i.1 and textual note 1, Barbaro, p. 7: 'la dignità dell'Architettura esser alla sapienza vicina, & come virtù heroica nel mezo di tutte le arti dimorare;' I.i.11, Barbaro, p. 21.
19 Barbaro, p. 25. But when Barbaro, p. 101, commenting on Vitruvius III.i–ii (the proportions and planning of temples), declares that some of the mathematical implications are too complex to discuss, Jones is prepared to agree: 'this is to high / conceates for Archi / tecture.' His handwriting suggests that the more modest comment is earlier.
20 *Opusculi Morali Di Plutarco... Parte Seconda... Tradotti in volgare Dal Sig. Marc'Antonio Gandino*, Venice, 1614, p. 317; cf. *La Seconda Parte De Gli Opuscoli Morali Di Plutarco*, trans. Giovanni Trachagnota, Venice, 1567, *De Le Cose Civili Di Plutarcho a Traiano Imp.*, fol. 14v, where the statesman is compared to the architect as both need willing subordinates, and Jones notes: 'an Archi / tect shoud / chose good / and obedi / ent work[m]en'.
21 *The Order and Solemnitie of the Creation of the High and mightie Prince Henrie, Eldest Sonne to our sacred Sovereigne, Prince of Wales... Whereunto*

is annexed the Royall maske, presented by the Queene and her Ladies . . . , London, 1610.
22 Vitruvius v.Preface.2; Barbaro, p. 204.
23 Alberti, *Art of Building*, p. 154 (VI.i).
24 O&S, vol. I, p. 244, lines 182–7.
25 George Chapman, *The Memorable Maske of . . . the Middle Temple, and Lyncolns Inn*, London, 1613, title-page.
26 H&S, vol. VII, pp. 90–1, lines 251–3.
27 O&S, vol. I, p. 124, no. 13; cf. Roy Strong, *Art and Power: Renaissance Festivals 1450–1650*, Woodbridge, 1984, fig. 57.
28 O&S, vol. I, p. 168, no. 39; Serlio, Bk. II, fol. 31r. Further details from these Serlio illustrations: the style of rustication, Bk. III, fol. 86r; the small domes, Bk. V, fol. 18r; the round-headed section of the arch, Bk. VI, fol. 3r; the battlements, Bk. VII, p. 91.
29 Vitruvius IV.i.6; Serlio, Bk. IV, fol. 139r; cf. Jones's annotation of the same passage in *Libro primo [–quinto] d'architettura di Sebastiano Serlio*, Venice, 1559–62 (Queen's College library), Bk. IV, fol. 17r: 'The Ansients dedicated This Dorricke Order T[o] most Roboustious good[s] . . . Also to Sooldierly an[d] Robustious parsones of what Condittion Soeuer'.
30 H&H, 'Gateway and Entrance Designs', pp. 124–43.
31 Palladio, Bk. IV, p. 64; cf. Serlio, Bk. IV, fol. 139r.
32 Serlio, Bk. III, fols. 119v, 120r. Cf. Jones's note repeating the characterisation of Bramante in Serlio, *Libro primo*, Bk. IV, fol. 17r: 'Bramanti The Renuer of yᵉ good archi(tect)ure In Ittali'.
33 H&H, pp. 186–7, nos. 53–4; John Peacock, 'Inigo Jones's Catafalque for James I', *Architectural History*, 25, (1982), 1–5.
34 Arnaldo Bruschi, *Bramante*, London, 1977, pp. 104–6. Serlio reproduces Bramante's unexecuted plan for the loggia round the Tempietto (Serlio, Bk. III, fol. 67r), which implies that it may have been viewed through an older Gothic arch (part of the 'chiostro vecchio'), just as Jones's pastiche is.
35 O&S, vol. II, pp. 796–7, no. 452; Lorenzo Sirigatti, *La Pratica Di Prospettiva*, Venice, 1625, Libro Secondo, fol. 52.
36 Serlio, Bk. III, fol. 67r.
37 O&S, vol. I, pp. 128–9, no. 14 and fig. 6; Serlio, Bk. III, fols. 119v–120r.
38 John Peacock, 'Inigo Jones's Stage Architecture and Its Sources', *Art Bulletin*, 64, (1982), 197–8; André Chastel, 'Palladio et l' escalier à double mouvement inverse', *Bollettino del Centro Internazionale di Studi d'Architettura Andrea Palladio*, 2 (1960), 26–9.
39 Serlio, Bk. VI, fol. 5v, on a design for a 'porta rustica': 'La presente porta è tutta Dorica ma stravestita, & fatta maschera . . .'
40 Serlio, Bk. III, fol. 119v.
41 Ibid., fol. 120r.
42 O&S, vol. I, pp. 158, 163, no. 36 and fig. 14A; John Newman, 'An Early Drawing by Inigo Jones and a Monument in Shropshire', *Burlington Magazine*, 115 (1973), 360–7; Gordon Higgott, 'Inigo Jones in Provence', *Architectural*

History, 26 (1983), 30. H&H, pp. 42–4, no. 6. For a more detailed discussion of the *Barriers* see John Peacock, 'Jonson and Jones Collaborate on *Prince Henry's Barriers*', *Word and Image*, 3 (1987), 172–94.

43 Copied from one of Cort's engravings: see Walter L. Strauss and Tomoko Shimura, ed., *The Illustrated Bartsch*, vol. 52, New York, 1986, pp. 230–1.

44 O&S, vol. I, pp. 354, 356, no. 122.

45 H&S, vol. X, pp. 514, 515; Richard S. Peterson, *Imitation and Praise in the Poems of Ben Jonson*, New Haven and London, 1981, p. 63. Chapman calls Thetis 'the silver-footed': *Homer's Iliads*, XVIII, lines 124, 327, in *Chapman's Homer*, ed. Allardyce Nicoll, 2 vols., London, 1957, vol. I, pp. 376, 381.

46 H&S, vol. VII, p. 324, lines 53–4.

47 Barbaro, p. 115; Jones's note: 'An excelle[n]tt Compa / rason of Barbaro / betwene the Orra: / tor and the architec / te:'. From the early style of handwriting the comment looks roughly contemporaneous with the *Barriers*.

48 Peacock, 'Jonson and Jones', pp. 173, 178–80. For Jones on Stonehenge, see *King's Arcadia*, pp. 82–3, and Bold, *Webb*, pp. 48ff.

49 O&S, vol. I, pp. 163, 164.

50 Henri de Geymüller, *Les du Cerceau. Leur vie et leur œuvre*, Paris, 1887, p. 105, fig. 80.

51 Hollstein XIV.163.7 (wrongly identified on the plate as the Torre de' Conti).

52 H&S, vol. VII, p. 333, lines 339–40, 345–6.

53 Etienne du Pérac, *I Vestigi Dell'Antichità Di Roma*, Rome, 1575, plate 12, where it is described as a 'tempio ... à guisa d'un portico quadro ...'

54 A. E. Santaniello, ed., *The Book of Architecture by Sebastiano Serlio London, 1611*, New York, 1970, Bk. III, fol. 47v; Serlio, Bk. III, fols. 97v–98r.

55 Rudolf Wittkower, *Architectural Principles in the Age of Humanism*, 3rd edn., London, 1962, pp. 1–32; Palladio, Bk. IV, ch. 2.

56 James S. Ackermann, *Palladio*, Harmondsworth, 1966, pp. 128–9.

57 Wittkower, *Principles*, p. 39.

58 He resolved the planning problem by making the interior a double cube, which could be seen as the simplest compromise between centralised and longitudinal plans; and the façade problem by following a model which was Christian by tradition but classical in origin – the façade of the Senate House in the Forum Romanum, which had been converted into the church of S. Adriano (Du Pérac, *Vestigi*, plate 3).

59 The other projects listed in Domenico Fontana, *Della Trasportatione Dell'Obelisco Vaticano 1590*, ed. Adriano Carugo, intro. Paolo Portoghesi, Milan, 1978, pp. 3–4, and described pp. 37ff.

60 For the Lateran after Fontana's work see the etching in G. F. Bordino, *De Rebus Praeclare Gestis A Sixto V Pon. Max. ... Carminum Liber Primus*, Rome, 1588, p. 44 (see plate 176), which impressionistically stresses as the main features of the church façade the pointed towers and the new portico. The tabernacle was shown in an engraving of G. B. Panzera, reprod. Philippe Lauer, *Le palais de Latran*, Paris, 1911, p. 305, fig. 112.

61 *The Ancient, Honorable, Famous, and delightfull Historie of Huon of Bordeaux*, trans. John Bourchier, Lord Berners, London, 1601.
62 O&S, vol. I, p. 206.
63 Ibid., pp. 210–14, no. 61, pp. 216–17, no. 63.
64 Mary Sullivan, *Court Masques of James I*, New York and London, 1913, pp. 61–2; *Calendar of State Papers Venetian*, vol. XII, 1610–13, nos. 153, 159.
65 *Les Illustres Observations Antiques Du Seigneur Gabriel Symeon Florentin*, Lyons, 1558, p. 96. Engraving of gateway reprod. O&S, vol. I, p. 212, fig. 25, mistakenly attributed to du Cerceau; it is from Philibert de l'Orme, *Le Premier Tome de l'Architecture*, Paris, 1568, fol. 247r.
66 T. D. Kendrick, *British Antiquity*, London, 1950, plate 1; John Speed, *The Theatre Of The Empire Of Great Britaine*, London, 1611, p. 163.
67 *The Basilicon Doron of King James VI*, ed. James Craigie, Scottish Text Society, 3rd series, 16 (1942), 18 (1944) 2 vols., Edinburgh and London, 1944–50, vol. I, pp. 189–91.
68 Serlio, Bk. III, fol. 68r.
69 Vitruvius IV.viii.3.
70 De l'Orme, *Premier Tome*, fol. 246v; Anthony Blunt, *Philibert de l'Orme*, London, 1958, p. 34. It is possible that the figures in Jones's drawing were meant to be automata, designed in collaboration with de Caus.
71 For more details of provenance see Peacock, 'Stage Architecture', p. 203; for Jones's list of the parts of the palace see O&S, vol. I, pp. 218–20, no. 64.
72 Serlio, Bk. VII, pp. 78–9.
73 Terms used by John Summerson, 'Inigo Jones', *Proceedings of the British Academy*, 50 (1965), 188. For Jones's phrase see note 71 above.
74 H&S, vol. VII, p. 341, line 6, notes a,b; John Peacock, 'Inigo Jones and the Florentine Court Theatre', *John Donne Journal*, 5 (1986), 216–17.
75 Vitruvius IV.i.6; Serlio, Bk. IV, fol. 139r: 'che habbiamo havuto del virile, & del forte ad esporre la vita per la fede di Christo . . .' For Jones's annotation on this see note 29 above.
76 Mark Girouard, *Robert Smythson and the Elizabethan Country House*, New Haven and London, 1983.
77 *King's Arcadia*, pp. 28–34; *Il potere e lo spazio* (Firenze e la Toscana dei Medici nell'Europa del Cinquecento), Florence, 1980, pp. 164f.
78 H&S, vol. VII, p. 353, lines 346–7.
79 Ibid., p. 463, line 2; O&S, vol. I, pp. 273–5, no. 89.
80 Serlio, Bk. II, fols. 45v–46v; John Peacock, 'New Sources for the Masque Designs of Inigo Jones', *Apollo*, 107 (1978), 98–102.
81 *King's Arcadia*, p. 100; H&H, pp. 84–93.
82 O&S, vol. I, pp. 342–3, no. 117 verso.
83 H&H, pp. 88–91, figs. 24–5.
84 O&S, vol. I, pp. 328–9, no. 113. The design may be linked with the story of Cupid and Psyche, which Van Dyck was later to illustrate in one of his rare mythological paintings for Charles I.
85 Summerson, *Jones*, pp. 73–4; H&H, pp. 274–5, no. 94.

86 *Capitolii. Sciographia. Ex. Ipso. Exemplari. Michaelis. Angeli. Bonaroti. A. Stephano. Du Perac. Parisiensi. Accurate. Delineata. Et. In. Lucem. Aedita. Romae. Anno. Salutis. MDLXIX*, in Antonio Lafreri, *Speculum Romanae Magnificentiae*, Rome, n.d.
87 O&S, vol. I, pp. 376, 378, no. 129.
88 Ibid., pp. 385–7, no. 135; Serlio, Bk. II, fols. 45v–47v.
89 John Peacock, 'The French Element in Inigo Jones's Masque Designs' in David Lindley, ed., *The Court Masque*, Manchester, 1984, pp. 155–6.
90 See T. E. Lawrenson, *The French Stage in the XVIIth Century*, Manchester, 1957, figs. 40–53.
91 O&S, vol. II, pp. 646–8, no. 326; G. B. Guarini, *Il Pastor Fido*, Venice, 1602, sig. biv; Peacock, 'New Sources', p. 104, figs. 16–17, 19.
92 O&S, vol. II, pp. 644–5, no. 324.
93 See ch. 6.
94 O&S, vol. II, pp. 60–1, no. 191, pp. 483–5, no. 216.
95 Gordon Toplis, 'The Sources of Jones's Mind and Imagination' in *King's Arcadia*, p. 63; cf. Rudolf Wittkower, 'Inigo Jones, Architect and Man of Letters', *Palladio and English Palladianism*, London, 1974.
96 Gordon Higgott, '"Varying with Reason": Inigo Jones's Theory of Design', *Architectural History*, 35 (1992), 51–77.
97 O&S, vol. I, pp. 349, 354, 356–7, no. 122.
98 There is a similar view at the end of *Artenice* of Somerset House, where the performance was taking place, a proto-classical building which Jones had begun to transform: O&S, vol. I, p. 385; H&H, pp. 193ff.
99 O&S, vol. II, p. 662, lines 59–61.
100 John Newman, 'The Inigo Jones Centenary', *Burlington Magazine*, 115 (1973), 558, suggests that Jones's tall, gabled town-houses may represent a conscious choice of style, rather than being stylistically 'transitional'. Viewed in this context, the first scene of *Britannia Triumphans* could be alluding with approval to Jones's modernisation of London street-building. There would still be the element of self-conscious assessment of his own work.
101 O&S, vol. II, pp. 460–1, no. 191 and fig. 70.
102 Newman, 'Centenary', p. 559.
103 O&S, vol. II, pp. 462–3, no. 192 and figs. 71–2.
104 Ibid., p. 547, line 201.
105 Cf. Roman Sketchbook, notes 'of the Antiquities of Roome' (following Palladio) have a section 'Of Fori or Piazi'.
106 Full details and illustrations in Peacock, 'New Sources', 102.
107 O&S, vol. II, p. 794, no. 448; Jan Vredeman de Vries, *Perspective*, ed. Adolf K. Placzek, New York, 1968, Part I, plate 49, Part II, plate 9; Diane DeGrazia Bohlin, *Prints and Related Drawings by the Carracci Family*, Washington, 1979, p. 326, no. 203.
108 O&S, vol. II, pp. 650–1, no. 328; Vredeman de Vries, *Perspective*, Part II, plate 8; Vincenzo Scamozzi, *L'Idea Della Architettura Universale*, 2 vols., Venice, 1615, vol. II, p. 89, 'Aspetto del Colonnato Ionico'; Wittkower,

'Architect and Man of Letters', pp. 59–60. Palladio, Bk. I, p. 28, associates the Ionic order with Diana.

109 O&S, vol. II, p. 634, lines 311–12, pp. 658–9, no. 333; *Libro d'Antonio Labacco appartenente a l'architettura*, Rome, 1569, p. 20.

110 Scamozzi, *L'Idea*, vol. II, p. 89. The adjustment can be checked by counting the modilions in the cornice.

111 O&S, vol. II, p. 677, no. 339; Vredeman de Vries, *Perspective*, Part II, pl. 13.

112 Jean Jacquot, *Les fêtes de la Renaissance*, 3 vols., Paris, 1959–75, vol. II, plate II, fig. 4.

113 On decorum see Vitruvius I.ii.5, Barbaro, pp. 34–6 (the Vitruvian text is annotated by Jones with headings, in early handwriting); Summerson, *Jones*, p. 43; and the passage in the Roman Sketchbook linking architectural decorum and social behaviour.

114 O&S, vol. II, p. 585, fig. 94.

115 O&S, vol. I, pp. 130, 138, no. 15; A. M. Nagler, *Theatre Festivals of the Medici 1539–1637*, New Haven and London, 1964, p. 105.

116 O&S, vol. II, pp. 652–3, no. 329, fig. 105A.

117 See ch. 5.

118 O&S, vol. II, p. 480, lines 52–3.

119 *The Tempest*, ed. Frank Kermode, London, 1953, IV.i.152–3.

120 Describing the scene Peruzzi designed on the Campidoglio in 1515, 'percio che la varietà e bella maniera de' casamenti, le diverse loggie, la bizzarria delle porte e finestre, e l'altre cose che vi si videro d'architettura, furono tanto bene intese e di così straordinaria invenzione, che non si può dirne la millesima parte': Vasari, Milanesi, vol. IV, p. 596. Cf. Serlio, Bk. II, fol. 44r: 'Fra l'altre cose fatte per mano de gli huomini che so possono riguardare con gran contentezza d'occhio, & satisfattione d'animo, è (al parer mio) il discoprirsi lo apparato di una Scena, dove si vede in piccol spatio fatto dall'arte della Prospettiva, superbi palazzi, amplissimi Tempii, diversi casamenti, & da presso, & di lontano spatiose piazze ornate di varii edificii, diritissime & lunghe strade incrociate da altre vie, archi trionfali, altissime colonne, piramidi, obelischi, & mille altre cose belle...'

121 O&S, vol. I, pp. 397–9, no. 141 (the suggested date of 1629 is too early: see Peacock, 'French Element', p. 160 and n. 52); Daniele Barbaro, *La Pratica Della Perspettiva*, Venice, 1569, p. 1.

122 Peacock, 'Stage Architecture', pp. 209–12.

123 Martin Butler, 'Politics and the Masque: *Salmacida Spolia*' in Thomas Healy and Jonathan Sawday, eds., *Literature and the English Civil War*, Cambridge, 1990, 59–74; O&S, vol. II, p. 729.

124 O&S, vol. II, p. 734, lines 452–7.

125 Ibid., pp. 752–4, no. 409.

126 Bartsch XX.118.17; Callot, from *La Petite Passion*, Lieure 54.

127 Hollstein XIV.163.9a. The entire print reprod. Thomas Ashby, *Topographical Study in Rome in 1581*, London, 1916, plate 19 (fig. 31). A variant of the right

hand section of this scene (in reverse) reprod. in Didier Bodart, *Les peintres des Pays-Bas méridionaux et de la principauté de Liège à Rome au XVIIème siècle*, 2 vols., Brussels and Rome, 1970, vol. II, plate LXXVI, fig. 120.
128 E.g. *Diverse Vedute Designate In Fiorenza Per Jacopo Callot*, in H. Diane Russell, *Jacques Callot. Prints and Related Drawings*, Washington, 1975, p. 287, no. 233.
129 O&S, vol. II, p. 731, lines 109–10.
130 Ibid., pp. 754–6, nos. 410–11.
131 O&S, vol. II, p. 734, lines 459–60.
132 David Howarth, *Lord Arundel and His Circle*, New Haven and London, 1985, p. 185; Kevin Sharpe, *The Personal Rule of Charles I*, New Haven and London, 1992, pp. 404–5.
133 In so far as the new Whitehall might have been inspired by the Escorial it would have been a city in itself: see Roy Strong, *Britannia Triumphans: Inigo Jones, Rubens, and Whitehall Palace*, London, 1980.
134 H&H, pp. 251–3, nos. 82–3.
135 O&S, vol. II, p. 734, lines 471–4.

4 Figures

1 H&S, vol. VII, pp. 209–10, lines 1–28.
2 See ch. 2.
3 H&S, vol. VII, p. 172, lines 90–2.
4 Ibid., p. 190, lines 272–6.
5 Barocchi, *Trattati*, p. 172.
6 Lomazzo, *Scritti*, vol. II, p. 420.
7 Giorgio Vasari, *Delle Vite De' Piu Eccellenti Pittori Scultori Et Architetti... Primo Volume della Terza Parte*, Florence, 1568, (Worcester College library), p. 84.
8 Ibid., sig. *****2 verso; Vasari, Milanesi, vol. IV, pp. 7ff. For the Italian see ch. 1, pp. 20, 30.
9 Ibid., vol. I, p. 168.
10 Barocchi, *Scritti*, vol. I, p. 497.
11 Ibid., p. 535.
12 Vasari, Milanesi, vol. I, p. 173.
13 Pliny, *Historia Naturalis*, XXXV.64, in *The Elder Pliny's Chapters on the History of Art*, trans K. Jex-Blake, ed. H. Sellers, Chicago, 1968, p. 109.
14 *L'Opere Morali di Xenophonte*, trans. Lodovico Domenichi, Venice, 1567 (Worcester College library), fol. 95r.
15 Vitruvius III.i.1–3; Barbaro, p. 109. The male body is meant.
16 Vitruvius III.i.5–9; Barbaro, pp. 111–12.
17 Ibid., p. 110.
18 Haydocke, Lomazzo, Bk. I, p. 85. Vitruvius IV.i.6–8 had derived the columns of the orders from different body types, male and female; Barbaro, pp. 163–4 (almost continuous marginal annotation by Jones); and see ch. 1, p. 21. Cf.

Vitruvius I.i.5–6 on the origin of caryatids; Barbaro p. 15 traces the story to Athenaeus, to whom Jones supplies a marginal reference.

19 Haydocke, Lomazzo, Bk. I, pp. 108–10.
20 Lomazzo, *Scritti*, vol. II, p. 86.
21 Haydocke, Lomazzo, Bk. I, p. 107.
22 *Ten Books on Architecture by Leone Battista Alberti Translated into Italian by Cosimo Bartoli And into English by James Leoni*, ed. Joseph Rykwert, London, 1965, IX.v, p. 195; *L'Architettura di Leon Battista Alberti, Tradotta in lingua Fiorentina da Cosimo Bartoli*, Monreale, 1565, p. 256; L. B. Alberti, *On the Art of Building in Ten Books*, trans. Joseph Rykwert, Neil Leach and Robert Tavernor, London and Cambridge, Mass., 1988, p. 301. The reference to buildings being like animals is VI.iii, p. 158.
23 *Poetics* VII.4–5, in S. H. Butcher, *Aristotle's Theory of Poetry and Fine Art*, New York, 1951, p. 31.
24 Alberti, *Architecture*, IX.viii, p. 203; Bartoli, *L'Architettura*, p. 267.
25 Barbaro, p. 30 (Jones note: 'The great Benifite / of makyng ye Profile').
26 Vasari, Milanesi, vol. I, pp. 146–8; cf. Vincenzo Scamozzi, *L'Idea Della Architettura Universale*, 2 vols., Venice, 1615 (Worcester College library), vol. II, p. 312, summarised by Jones in the margin: 'Stairs compard to ye vaines in ye boddy'.
27 Palladio, *Quattro Libri*, Bk. II, p. 3; Livy II.xxxii.9–12.
28 Palladio, *Quattro Libri*, Bk. II, p. 3; Allsopp, vol. I, p. 43.
29 Leon Battista Alberti, *On Painting and On Sculpture*, ed. Cecil Grayson, London, 1972, p. 71 (*De pictura*, II.33); *La Pittura Di Leon Battista Alberti Tradotta Per M. Lodovico Domenichi*, Monreale, 1565 (Jones's copy, Worcester College, Oxford), p. 320, lines 8–11.
30 Vasari, Milanesi, vol. I, pp. 168ff.
31 This is the title of the second section of Fialetti's manual; the principal title is *Il vero modo et ordine. Per Dissegnar Tutte Le Parti Et Membra Del Corpo Humano*, Venice, 1608.
32 John Peacock, 'Figurative Drawings' and 'Roman Sketchbook' in H&H, pp. 284–90; Jeremy Wood, 'Inigo Jones, Italian Art, and the Practice of Drawing', *Art Bulletin*, 74 (1992), 247–70.
33 Vasari, Milanesi, vol. IV, pp. 11–13; and see ch. 2.
34 Roy Strong in O&S, vol. I, pp. 34–5, suggests Jones had instruction from Isaac Oliver.
35 Vincenzio Danti, *Trattato delle perfette proporzioni*, in Barocchi, *Scritti*, vol. II, pp. 1570ff.
36 Vasari, Milanesi, vol. V, p. 442.
37 Ibid., pp. 405–6.
38 O&S, vol. I, pp. 196–7, no. 53; Bartsch XIV.295.390.
39 O&S, vol. I, pp. 185, 187, no. 50; Bartsch XIV.13.12.
40 Vasari, Milanesi, vol. IV, p. 11.
41 O&S, vol. I, pp. 247, 250, no. 81; Bartsch XIV.186.23 and 248.329.
42 O&S, vol. I, pp. 262–3, no. 84; Bartsch XV.427.103 (engraving by

43 Vasari, Milanesi, vol. III, pp. 390, 396.
44 Bartsch XIV.343.461.
45 O&S, vol. II, pp. 452, 469, no. 204; Bartsch XIV.275.361 and 317.422; Phyllis Pray Bober and Ruth Rubinstein, *Renaissance Artists and Antique Sculpture*, London, 1986, pp. 191–2, no. 158, pp. 232–3, no. 199.
46 Bartsch XV.426.28; Massari, *Incisori*, pp. 53ff., no. 62 (illustrations for nos. 62 and 63 mistakenly transposed). The King appears to have owned a copy of this set of engravings; see Oliver Millar, ed., *Abraham van der Doort's Catalogue of the Collections of Charles I* (The Thirty-Seventh Volume of the Walpole Society 1958–60), London, 1960, p. 126, note 1: 'some Certeyne figurs of Sev[er]all postures of Michaell Angel Bonerotti in prints' (among the books kept in the Cabinet Room at Whitehall).
47 O&S, vol. II, pp. 536, 565, no. 274.
48 Fialetti, *Vero modo*, plates 3 (part 1), 7 (part 2); Bartsch XVII.296.202, 299.218.
49 Peacock, 'Roman Sketchbook', in H&H, pp. 288–90.
50 Vasari, *Vite*, sig.*****3, verso; Vasari, Milanesi, vol. IV, p. 12.
51 H&S, vol. VII, p. 282, lines 6–9.
52 Ibid., lines 10–22.
53 H&S, vol. V, p. 164 ('Another' Prologue to *Epicoene*), lines 2, 10; vol. VI, p. 16 (*Bartholomew Fair*. The Induction), lines 128–30; vol. V, p. 291 (*The Alchemist*. To the Reader), lines 5–8.
54 H&S, vol. VII, p. 633, lines 113–14.
55 Ibid., p. 638, lines 265–9.
56 William Rossky, 'Imagination in the English Renaissance: Psychology and Poetic', *Studies in the Renaissance*, 4 (1957), 49–73.
57 H&S, vol VII, pp. 465–7, lines 48, 57–116.
58 Ben Jonson, *The Complete Masques*, ed. Stephen Orgel, New Haven and London, 1969, p. 486.
59 Cesare Ripa, *Iconologia*, Rome, 1603 (facsimile Hildesheim and New York, 1970), p. 48.
60 O&S, vol. I, p. 256, line 65.
61 H&S, vol. VIII, p. 611, lines 1567–71. See ch. 6 for Barbaro's reading of Vitruvius along the same lines.
62 O&S, vol. II, p. 543, line 37.
63 Lomazzo, *Scritti*, vol. II, pp. 249–50.
64 O&S, vol. I, p. 292, no. 92 and fig. 38.
65 O&S, vol. I, pp. 276, 292–3, nos. 94–5.
66 O&S, vol. I, pp. 220–1, no. 65; Bartsch XIV.231.305.
67 Ibid., no. 66.
68 H&S, vol. VII, pp. 633, 104–6.
69 Erwin Panofsky, *Idea. A Concept in Art Theory*, New York, 1968, p. 215, note 51; see Franciscus Junius, *The Painting of the Ancients*, in *The Literature of Classical Art*, ed. Keith Aldrich, Philipp and Raina Fehl, 2 vols., Berkeley,

Los Angeles and London, 1991, vol. I, p. 23, note 4, on how this distinction comes from a misreading of Plato's text.
70 See above, ch. 6.
71 H&S, vol. VII, p. 633, lines 109–10.
72 O&S, vol. II, p. 707, lines 173–4, 177–8.
73 For the entire passage see ch. 6.
74 Junius, *Ancient Art*, vol. I, p. 23 and note 4; Junius does not interpret the Platonic distinction in exactly the same way as Comanini: see above p. 141, and note 69 above.
75 Ibid., p. 29.
76 Ibid., p. 40.
77 O&S, vol. II, pp. 619–21, nos. 304–7; John Peacock, 'The French Element in Inigo Jones's Masque Designs', in David Lindley, ed., *The Court Masque*, Manchester, 1984, pp. 158–9.
78 O&S, vol. II, pp. 618–19, nos. 302–3; Alonso Chacón, *Historia Utriusque Belli Dacici*, Rome, 1576, plate 34 (referred to as 'Col: Tra: fo 34' in the Roman Sketchbook notes on 'The Manner Of Drapery all antica').
79 Lomazzo, *Scritti*, vol. II, p. 255.
80 Cesare Vecellio, *Habiti Antichi Overo Raccolta Di Figure*, 3rd edn, Venice, 1664, sig. *5 verso, pp. 9, 40.
81 O&S, vol. I, pp. 169, 171–2, nos. 41–2, fig. 18.
82 O&S, vol. II, pp. 685, 687, no. 351; Vecellio, *Habiti*, p. 121.
83 Anne Lake Prescott, 'The Stuart Masque and Pantagruel's Dreams', *ELH*, 51 (1984), 407–30.
84 O&S, vol. II, pp. 688–90, nos. 357–8; cf. Callot, *Balli di Sfessania*, Lieure 379, 390. For other designs based on Callot see antimasque figures for *Love's Triumph through Callipolis* (1631), O&S, vol. I, pp. 409–15, and later masques.
85 O&S, vol. II, pp. 688, 690, no. 354; Bartsch VIII.189.184, 409.159.
86 O&S, vol. II, pp. 685–6, no. 349; I. Q. van Regteren Altena, *Jacques de Gheyn. Three Generations*, 3 vols., The Hague, Boston and London, 1983, vol. II, pp. 96–7, nos. 605–14: de Gheyn's plates are numbered 1–10, and Jones has used no. 3. For other designs based on de Gheyn see O&S, vol. II, p. 563, no. 272 (de Gheyn 2), pp. 764, 766, no. 417 (de Gheyn 8).

5 Landscape

1 H&S, vol. VII, pp. 170–1, lines 24–7, 58–9.
2 A. M. Nagler, *Theatre Festivals of the Medici*, New Haven and London, 1964, plates 1, 37.
3 Pembroke (then Philip Herbert) was married in London two days after the masque was produced, so presumably attended it: see *Calendar of State Papers Domestic*, 1603–10, 7 January 1605.
4 O&S, vol. I, p. 90.
5 John Nichols, *The Progresses of King James the First*, 4 vols., London, 1828, vol. I, p. 469: 18 December 1604, letter from Chamberlain to Winwood. In a letter

to Lord Cranborne of the same date, Archbishop Hutton of York criticised the excessive emphasis on hunting: *Calendar of State Papers Domestic, 1603–10*, p. 177.
6 Henry Peacham, *The Gentlemans Exercise*, London, 1612, pp. 40, 44.
7 Jonson's description implies that the curtain remained in view for some time: H&S, vol. VII, pp. 169–70, lines 24–6.
8 Ibid., line 24.
9 James Turner, '*Landscape* and the "Art Prospective" in England, 1584–1660', *JWCI*, 42 (1979), 290, note 12.
10 Edward Norgate, *Miniatura or The Art of Limning*, ed. Martin Hardie, Oxford, 1919, p. 42.
11 Henry Peacham, *The Arte of Drawing*, London, 1606, p. 25.
12 Norgate, *Miniatura*, p. 43.
13 Ibid.
14 Roy Strong, *The English Renaissance Miniature*, London, 1985, p. 156.
15 Christopher Brown, *Dutch Landscape. The Early Years*, London, 1986, p. 101.
16 Peacham, *Gentlemans Exercise*, p. 41. Jonson's mention of 'an obscure and cloudy night-piece' (H&S, vol. VII, p. 171, line 89) in the first scene of *Blackness* suggests the earlier habit of seeing landscape as an adjunct; a visual parallel would be Robert Peake's use of landscape in his portraits of Prince Henry.
17 H&S, vol. VII, pp. 170–2, lines 26–90.
18 Ibid., p. 195.
19 Cf. ibid., p. 189, *The Masque of Beauty*, line 264.
20 Ibid., pp. 171–2, lines 89–90.
21 Turner, '*Landscape*', p. 291.
22 Barocchi, *Trattati*, p. 100; Brown, *Dutch Landscape*, p. 37, stanzas 8–9. Van Mander's poem *Der Grondt der Edel Vry Schilder-const* contains a chapter 'Van het Landtschap', trans. Brown, ibid., pp. 35–43. Henry Peacham, *The Compleat Gentleman*, London, 1622, p. 137, refers to van Mander's work.
23 O&S, vol. I, p. 89; the phrase comes in a letter which is largely critical of the production.
24 H&S, vol. VII, p. 155, lines 26–7, 32–3.
25 John Peacock, 'Jonson and Jones collaborate on *Prince Henry's Barriers*', *Word and Image*, 3 (1987), 180.
26 O&S, vol. I, p. 243, lines 3–9.
27 T. E. Lawrenson, *The French Stage in the XVIIth Century*, Manchester, 1957, pp. 86ff., figs. 40–53.
28 O&S, vol. I, p. 116, lines 22–6.
29 Brown, *Dutch Landscape*, p. 39, stanzas 23–4.
30 Henry Wotton, *The Elements of Architecture*, London, 1624 (facsimile Farnborough, 1969), p. 4.
31 O&S, vol. I, p. 257, lines 133–5.
32 John Peacock, 'Inigo Jones's Stage Architecture and Its Sources', *Art Bulletin*, 64 (1982), 202ff.

33 O&S, vol. I, p. 257, lines 109f.; H&S, vol. VII, p. 250, lines 23ff.
34 Jean Dorat, *Magnificentissimi spectaculi... descriptio*, Paris, 1573, sig. Fii verso.
35 Brown, *Dutch Landscape*, p. 58, fig. 1a; p. 67, fig. 5.
36 O&S, vol. I, p. 243, lines 6–8.
37 O&S, vol. II, p. 481, lines 182–5, pp. 483, 486, no. 217.
38 A more 'primitive' version of this sequence can be seen not in an earlier masque but in a painting such as the Ditchley Portrait of Queen Elizabeth.
39 Barbaro, Vitruvius, p. 256: 'le Scene Satiriche sono ornate di alberi, & di spilonche, & di monti, & d'altre cose rusticali, & agresti in forma di giardini.'
40 Ibid.
41 Ibid., p. 319.
42 Ibid., p. 256: 'Satirici portavano cose silvestre, & boscarecci convenienti a pastori e ninfe & simile cose...'
43 Ben Jonson's English pastoral *The Sad Shepherd* follows Italian practice here: 'THE SCENE is *Sher-Wood*. Consisting of a Landt-Shape of Forest, Hills, Vallies, Cottages, A Castle, A River, Pastures, Heards, Flocks, all full of Countrey simplicity' (H&S, vol. VII, p. 7).
44 Quoted E. H. Gombrich, 'The Renaissance Theory of Art and the Rise of Landscape' in *Norm and Form*, London, 1966, p. 111; see *L'Architettura Di Leon Battista Alberti, Tradotta in lingua Fiorentina da Cosimo Bartoli*, Monreale, 1565, p. 254, lines 35–41.
45 Serlio, Bk. II, fol. 47r: 'arbori, sassi, colli, montagne, herbe, fiori, & fontane'; he uses the phrase 'Vitruvio vuole' as if certain that he is interpreting Vitruvius's requirements correctly.
46 Ibid., fol. 47v.
47 'In Flanders they paint... the green grass of the fields, the shadow of trees, and rivers and bridges, which they call landscapes, with many figures on this side and many on that. And all this, though it pleases some persons, is done without reason or art, without symmetry or proportion, without skilful choice or boldness and finally without substance or vigour... For good painting is nothing but a copy of the perfections of God and a recollection of His painting...' Francisco de Hollanda, *Four Dialogues on Painting*, trans. Aubrey F. G. Bell, London, 1928, p. 16.
48 Barocchi, *Trattati*, vol. I, pp. 133–4: 'gli oltramontani... fingono i paesi abitati da loro, i quali per quella lor selvatichezza si rendono gratissimi. Ma noi Italiani siamo nel giardin del mondo, cosa più dilettevole da vedere che da fingere...'
49 Donald Posner, *Annibale Carracci*, 2 vols., London, 1971, vol. I, p. 119.
50 Ibid.
51 Giovanni Baglione, *Le Vite De' Pittori Scultori Et Architetti*, Rome, 1642, p. 297: 'egli rimodernò la sua prima maniera Fiamenga, essendosi egli grandemente avanzato dopo aver veduto i belli paesi d'Annibale Carracci e copiato li paesi di Titiano, rarissimo dipintore; ond'egli dal buon giuditio portato mutò foggia, e diede più nel buono accostosi al naturale, & alla buona maniera Italiana...'
52 Giulio Mancini, *Considerazioni sulla pittura*, ed. Adriana Marucchi and Luigi

Salerno, 2 vols., Rome, 1956-7, vol. I, p. 260: 'con la longhezza del star in Italia, vedendo le cose dei Carracci ... ha ... nel paesaggio lasciato quello stento fiammengo, accostandosi più al vero, ne facendo l' horizonte cosi alto com'usan i fiamminghi, che cosi il loro paesaggio son più tosto una maestà scenica che prospetto di paese.'

53 Filippo Baldinucci, *Notizie dei professori del disegno*, Volume Terzo, Florence, 1846, pp. 24-5: 'il colorito ... fosse di bello, ma però di lor proprio invenzione; e per conseguenza fino ad un certo segno, e non più, simile al vero; onde poteassi lodare in loro piuttosto la bella maniera di far paesi, che una perfetta imitazione de' veri paesi.'

54 See ch. 1.

55 Oliver Millar, *The Age of Charles I*, London, 1972, p. 60.

56 Norgate, *Miniatura*, pp. 42-3, gives a list of the 'best' landscape painters – Brueghel, de Momper, Coninxloo, Bril, Elsheimer and Rubens – which may be taken to represent enlightened English taste during Jones's lifetime.

57 Maurizio Fagiolo, *La scenografia*, Florence, 1973, p. 87, plate 15. Daniele Barbaro calls the features of the Satyric Scene 'indeterminate': *La Pratica Della Perspettiva*, Venice, 1569 (facsimile Bologna, 1980), p. 158.

58 Vitruvius v.vi.9.

59 One of the earliest Renaissance treatises on perspective, Viator's *De Artificiali Perspectiva* (1509), suggests that 'l'espace champestre' can be rationally represented on the basis of a 'pavement' construction; see William M. Ivins Jr, *On the Rationalisation of Sight*, New York, 1975, *De Artificiali Perspectiva. Viator: Secundo*, sig. Avi recto.

60 O&S, vol. I, pp. 385-7, no. 135.

61 John Peacock, 'The French Element in Inigo Jones's Masque Designs', in David Lindley, ed., *The Court Masque*, Manchester, 1984, p. 155.

62 O&S, vol. I, p. 388, no. 136; this drawing reassigned to *The Shepherds' Paradise* in John Orrell, *The Theatres of Inigo Jones and John Webb*, Cambridge, 1985, p. 204, note 19.

63 John Peacock, 'New Sources for the Masque Designs of Inigo Jones', *Apollo*, 107 (1978), p. 104.

64 Battista Guarini, *Il Pastor Fido*, Venice, 1602.

65 O&S, vol. II, pp. 655-7, nos. 331-2; Bartsch XVII.179.1339 (Tempesta); Hollstein XXI.35.127 (Aegidius Sadeler after Bril).

66 Roseline Bacou, *Il paesaggio nel disegno del Cinquecento europeo* (Mostra all'Accademia di Francia, Villa Medici), Rome, 1972, p. 194, no. 137; Anton Mayer, *Das Leben und die Werke der Brüder Matthäus und Paul Brill*, Leipzig, 1910, plate 25.

67 O&S, vol. I, pp. 320-7, nos. 109-12; pp. 330-1, no. 114.

68 H&S, vol. VII, p. 535, line 180.

69 Ibid., pp. 672-3, lines 514-17, 533-6. On the honour and nobility of hunting cf. *The Basilicon Doron of King James VI*, ed. James Craigie, Scottish Text Society, 3rd series, 16 (1942), 18 (1944), 2 vols., Edinburgh and London, 1944-50, vol. I, pp. 189-91.

70 *The Triumph of Peace*, lines 445–6, in O&S, vol. II, p. 550.
71 Marco Chiarini, *Mostra di disegni italiani di paesaggio del seicento e del settecento*, Florence, 1973, pp. 15–16.
72 O&S, vol. I, p. 326, no. 112; Bartsch XVII.153.816.
73 O&S, vol. I, pp. 330–1, no. 114.
74 Bartsch XVII.169.1159, 154.822.
75 O&S, vol. II, p. 802, no. 457.
76 Bartsch XVII.153.813, 169.1161.
77 E.g. O&S, vol. II, pp. 725–7, no. 397.
78 Arthur R. Blumenthal, *Giulio Parigi's Stage Designs. Florence and the Early Baroque Spectacle*, New York and London, 1986, pp. 19–20.
79 Quoted Chiarini, *Disegni italiani*, p. 29.
80 See e.g. O&S, vol. II, p. 425, fig. 61.
81 Nagler, *Theatre Festivals*, plate 54.
82 Ibid., frontispiece and plate 69.
83 O&S, vol. II, pp. 422–5, no. 163 and fig. 61; H&S, vol. VII, p. 750, line 23.
84 O&S, vol. II, pp. 426–7, no. 164.
85 Nagler, *Theatre Festivals*, plates 52, 54.
86 O&S, vol. II, pp. 605, 608–9, no. 293.
87 Ibid., p. 609, fig. 97.
88 Bartsch XVII.173.1174.
89 O&S, vol. II, pp. 506, 510, no. 245.
90 Ibid., pp. 507–9, no. 246.
91 Hollstein XXI.51.250 (Aegidius Sadeler after Stievens; reprod. XXII, p. 63).
92 O&S, vol. II, pp. 518–19, no. 252 and fig. 90.
93 Hollstein XXI.35.125 (Aegidius Sadeler after Bril).
94 O&S, vol. II, pp. 516–17, no. 251.
95 Ibid., pp. 514–15, no. 250.
96 Bacou, *Il paesaggio*, p. 195, pl. 138; Mayer, *Brill*, plate 24.
97 O&S, vol. II, pp. 518–19, no. 252.
98 Malcolm R. Waddington, *Adam Elsheimer*, London, 1966, pp. 6, 8.
99 Relative dimensions given in O&S, vol. II, pp. 506–7, nos. 245–6.
100 O&S, vol. I, pp. 354, 356–7, no. 122; p. 385.
101 O&S, vol. II, pp. 805–6, nos. 459–60; Hollstein III.219.2 (View of the Coast of Campania). *The Illustrated Bartsch*, vol. 52, ed. Walter L. Strauss and Tomoko Shimura, p. 140, 119-1 (129) (St Onuphrius Penitent in the Wilderness).
102 Quoted in Gombrich, *Norm and Form*, p. 152, note 57.
103 O&S, vol. II, p. 706, lines 2ff.
104 H&S, vol. VII, p. 209, lines 14–15.
105 O&S, vol. II, p. 709, lines 409–11.
106 Ibid., p. 706, line 13.
107 Ibid., p. 708, line 357.
108 Ibid., lines 252–6.
109 Ibid., pp. 710–12, nos. 383–4 and fig. 114.
110 Ibid., p. 706, lines 57–62.

111 Keith Andrews, *Adam Elsheimer*, London, 1977, p. 155 and plate 136.
112 Anthony Griffiths and Gabriela Kesnerová, *Wenceslaus Hollar. Prints and Drawings*, London, 1983, p. 84, nos. 96a–f.
113 O&S, vol. II, p. 706, lines 64–5.
114 Roberto Longhi, *Caravaggio*, ed. Giovanni Previtali, Rome, 1982, pp. 70–2.
115 O&S, vol. II, p. 708, line 275.
116 Ibid., p. 707, line 171.
117 Ibid., pp. 714–15, no. 386.
118 Hollstein III.219.1–2 (Views of the Coast of Campania).

6 Ornament

1 O&S, vol. II, p. 666, lines 506–8, p. 677, no. 339; John Peacock, 'Inigo Jones's Stage Architecture and Its Sources', *Art Bulletin*, 64 (1982), 208.
2 John Harris and A. A. Tait, *Catalogue of the Drawings by Inigo Jones, John Webb and Isaac de Caus at Worcester College Oxford*, Oxford, 1979, p. 17, no. 15, p. 92, no. 249; John Orrell, *The Theatres of Inigo Jones and John Webb*, Cambridge, 1985, pp. 160–7, fig. 28.
3 Quoted Licisco Magagnato, *Teatri italiani del Cinquecento*, Venice, 1954, p. 43: 'A guardia della prospettiva erano posti in pittura di statura gigantesca dalla banda dextra Sansone e dalla sinistra Hercole, le quali due figure venivano appunto sopra due alie . . . ' See *La Magnifica et triumphale entrata del Christianissimo Re di Francia Henrico secondo*, Lyon, 1549, in Georges Guige, ed., *La Magnificence de la superbe et triumphante entrée . . .* , Lyon, 1927.
4 Sara Mamone, *Il teatro nella Firenze medicea*, Milan, 1981, p. 98; A. M. Nagler, *Theatre Festivals of the Medici*, New Haven and London, 1964, pp. 15–16; *La scena del principe* (Firenze e la Toscana dei Medici nell'Europa del Cinquecento), Florence, 1980, pp. 313, 325, no. 2.4
5 Bartsch XII.156.29-1; John Peacock, 'New Sources for the Masque Designs of Inigo Jones', *Apollo*, 107 (1978), 98 and note 3; Enzo Carli et al., *L'arte a Siena sotto i Medici 1555–1609*, Rome, 1980, pp. 27ff., 233ff.
6 Carli et al., *L'arte a Siena*, p. 233; Mary F. S. Hervey, *The Life, Correspondence and Collections of Thomas Howard, Earl of Arundel*, Cambridge, 1921, pp. 81–3.
7 Magagnato, *Teatri*, pp. 48–9 (quoting Bastiano de' Rossi); Nagler, *Theatre Festivals*, pp. 60–1.
8 John Peacock, 'Inigo Jones and the Arundel Marbles', *Journal of Medieval and Renaissance Studies*, 16 (1986), 221 (quoting Michelangelo Buonarroti the younger); Nagler, *Theatre Festivals*, p. 96.
9 H&S, vol. VII, p. 250, lines 23–41.
10 Ibid., p. 314, lines 694–5.
11 *The Works of Thomas Campion*, ed. Walter R. Davis, London, 1969, p. 268; H&S, vol. VII, p. 453, lines 1–2.
12 O&S, vol. I, pp. 130, 138, no. 15; Bartsch XVII.73.66; Peacock, 'Stage Architecture', p. 199, fig. 10.

13 O&S, vol. I, p. 194, lines 163–5, p. 193, lines 26–40.
14 J. G. van Gelder, 'Notes on the Royal Collection – IV: The "Dutch Gift" of 1610 to Henry Prince of "Whalis" and Some Other Presents', *Burlington Magazine*, 105 (1963), 541–4.
15 H&S, vol. VII, p. 231, lines 643–6.
16 Ibid., p. 681, lines 1–3; O&S, vol. I, pp. 376, 378, no. 129; Roy Strong, *Splendour at Court*, London, 1973, p. 80, fig. 66.
17 O&S, vol. I, pp. 322–3, no. 110; H&H, pp. 272–3, no. 93.
18 O&S, vol. I, pp. 354, 358–9, no. 123.
19 Ibid., p. 193, lines 125–6; H&S, vol. VII, p. 750, lines 14ff.
20 O&S, vol. II, p. 480, line 28.
21 Ibid., p. 662, lines 35–6, 48; p. 666, lines 506–8.
22 Ibid., p. 480, lines 48–9, p. 730, line 67.
23 See ch. 3.
24 Vitruvius VII.v.1–4; Barbaro, pp. 319–20: Jones's only note on the passage of denunciation is the impartial heading 'against grotesk'.
25 Vasari, Milanesi, vol. VI, pp. 550–4: 'restarono l'uno e l'altro stupefatti della freschezza, bellezza e bontà di quell'opere'; 'la più bella, la più rara e più eccellente pittura che mai sia stata veduta da occhio mortale'.
26 Ibid., p. 550: 'riusciva contraffare benissimo, per dirlo in una parola, tutte le cose naturali d'animali, di drappi, d'instrumenti, vasi, paesi, casamenti e verdure...'
27 Giorgio Vasari, *Delle Vite De' Piu Eccellenti Pittori Scultori Et Architetti... Primo Volume della Terza Parte*, Florence, 1568 (Worcester College library), p. 225.
28 Vasari, Milanesi, vol. V, p. 203: 'là onde egli ritornò a lavorare alle sue grottesche'.
29 *Il potere e lo spazio* (Firenze e la Toscana dei Medici nell'Europa del Cinquecento), Florence, 1980, p. 146: 'il primo, che portasse d'Italia in questi paesi l'arte del contrafare le grottesche al naturale'; Vasari, Milanesi, vol. VII, p. 589.
30 Vasari, Milanesi, vol. VI, p. 561, vol. II, p. 397.
31 Vasari, Milanesi, vol. V, pp. 206–10; Vasari, *Vite*, p. 225, Jones note: 'Andrea del Cosmo / exelent in grotteskes'.
32 Vasari, Milanesi, vol. I, p. 193: 'Furono poi regolate e per fregi e spartimenti fatto bellissimi andari...'
33 Serlio, Bk. IV, fol. 125r.
34 Ibid., fols. 191v, 192r.
35 Ibid., fol. 191v: 'fingerà il vero, servando il decoro'; 'degna di lode appresso di tutti quelli, che conoscono il vero dal falso'.
36 Ibid., fol. 192v.
37 Ibid., fol. 192r.
38 Barbaro, p. 321.
39 Ibid.
40 Lomazzo, *Scritti*, vol. II, p. 363.

41 Ibid., p. 364: 'In somma in questo fregio non entrava alcuna figura d'animale che fosse intiero, ma tutti erano diversamente composti . . .'
42 Ibid., p. 365.
43 Vitruvius VII.v.1; Barbaro, pp. 319, 321.
44 Lomazzo, *Scritti*, vol. II, pp. 367, 369.
45 Nicole Dacos, *La découverte de la Domus Aurea et la formation des grotesques à la Renaissance*, London and Leiden, 1969, pp. 130–1.
46 Lomazzo, *Scritti*, vol. II, pp. 365, 369–70.
47 Ibid., p. 370.
48 *Rime Di Gio. Paolo Lomazzi Milanese Pittore, divise In sette Libri . . . ad imitatione de i Grotteschi usati da' pittori . . .* , Milan, 1587.
49 Lomazzo, *Scritti*, vol. II, p. 369: 'nell'invenzione delle grottesche, più che in ogn'altra, vi corre un certo furore et una natural bizarria . . . in ciò l'una e l'altra hanno da concorrere insieme giuntamente furia naturale ed arte'.
50 Ibid., p. 369.
51 O&S, vol. I, p. 256, lines 62–7.
52 Ibid., p. 258, lines 260–2.
53 Palladio, Bk. I, p. 11; Allsopp, vol. I, p. 3.
54 In his counter-Reformation critique of grotesques, Cardinal Paleotti said that artists who used them 'sinned against the decrees' of Vitruvius: Barocchi, *Scritti*, vol. III, p. 2657.
55 Vincenzo Scamozzi, *L'Idea Della Architettura Universale*, 2 vols, Venice, 1615 (Worcester College library), vol. II, pp. 157 (headings noted in the margin by Jones), 160.
56 *L' Architettura di Leon Battista Alberti, Tradotti in lingua Fiorentina da Cosimo Bartoli*, Monreale, 1565, p. 267; *Ten Books on Architecture by Leone Battista Alberti Translated into Italian by Cosimo Bartoli And into English by James Leoni*, ed. Joseph Rykwert, London, 1965, IX.8, p. 203. See ch. 4.
57 Palladio, Bk. IV, p. 50; Allsopp, vol. I, p. 52.
58 Alberti IX.1–2, Bartoli, *L'Architettura*, pp. 250–2, Alberti, *Architecture*, p. 188; John Onians, *Bearers of Meaning*, Cambridge, 1988, p. 151.
59 H&S, vol. VIII, p. 611, *Discoveries*, lines 1568–9; Jeremy Wood, 'Inigo Jones, Italian Art, and the Practice of Drawing', *Art Bulletin*, 74 (1992), 269; A. F. Doni, *Disegno*, Venice, 1549 (facsimile Milan, 1970), p. 22; Vincenzio Danti in Barocchi, *Scritti*, vol. I, pp. 235–6.
60 G. H. Chettle, *The Queen's House, Greenwich*, London, 1937, frontispiece and plates 77–82.
61 George Chapman, *The Memorable Maske of . . . the Middle Temple, and Lyncolns Inn*, London, 1613, title-page.
62 H&S, vol. VII, p. 750, line 14; O&S, vol. II, p. 480, line 28, p. 662, lines 35–6.
63 O&S, vol. II, p. 570, lines 2–31 (my italics).
64 Ibid., p. 801, no. 456.
65 Murray Lefkowitz, *Trois Masques à la cour de Charles Ier d'Angleterre*. Paris, 1970, p. 126.
66 O&S, vol. II, p. 547, lines 163–4, p. 600, lines 50–4 (my italics).

67 Ibid., p. 600, lines 43–4, p. 632, lines 2–3.
68 John Harris, *Catalogue of the Drawings Collection of the Royal Institute of British Architects. Inigo Jones and John Webb*, Farnborough, 1972, p. 19, no. 95 (fig. 90).
69 Serlio, Bk. IV, fols. 139r, 183r, 145v (and cf. 153r).
70 O&S, vol. I, pp. 385–7, no. 135; Orrell, *Theatres*, p. 82.
71 O&S, vol. II, pp. 507, 510, no. 246.
72 John Harris, 'The Link between a Roman Second-Century Sculptor, Van Dyck, Inigo Jones and Henrietta Maria', *Burlington Magazine*, 115 (1973), 526–30.
73 Bartsch XVI.196.33.
74 O&S, vol. II, pp. 458–60, no. 190.
75 Ibid., pp. 460–1, no. 191.
76 Ibid., pp. 604, 606–7, no. 292.
77 Ibid., pp. 646–8, no. 326.
78 Ibid., p. 632, lines 2–3.
79 *Livre de la Conqueste de la Toison d'or, par le Prince Iason de Tessalie: faict par figures avec exposition d' icelles*, Paris, 1563. sig. A2r; the engravings reprod. Jacques Levron, *René Boyvin graveur angevin du XVIe siècle*, Angers, 1941.
80 E.g. the interior decoration of the château of Ancy-le-Franc: see S. Béguin, *L'Ecole de Fontainebleau*, Paris, 1960, p. 48.
81 Vasari, Milanesi, vol. V, pp. 155, 433–4.
82 Vincenzo Scamozzi, *L'Idea Della Architettura Universale*, 2 vols., Venice, 1615, vol. II, p. 11; cf. the proscenium of *Neptune's Triumph*, which paraphrases this motif to frame a submarine grotto, O&S, vol. I, pp. 376, 378–9, no. 129.
83 *Toison d'or*, plate 24; Jones drawings, Chatsworth, vol. 10, p. 19, no. 117. This drawing, hitherto unrecognised, can be identified from the description of the proscenium, O&S, vol. II, p. 706, lines 43–7: 'a second order, wherein were terms of women feigned of silver, and children in their natural colours standing on arches, some wantonising about those terms, and others holding great vizards before their faces. On the heads of the terms were cushions which served for capitals ... '
84 *Toison d'or*, plates 13, 22.
85 D. J. Gordon, 'Poet and Architect: The Intellectual Setting of the Quarrel between Ben Jonson and Inigo Jones' in *The Renaissance Imagination*, Berkeley, Los Angeles and London, 1975, pp. 86ff.
86 *Toison d'or*, plate 2; Henri Zerner, *The School of Fontainebleau*, London, 1969, Antonio Fantuzzi 55; John Newman, 'The Inigo Jones Centenary', *Burlington Magazine*, 115 (1973), 561.
87 Dorothee Kühn-Hattenhauer, *Das grafische Oeuvre des Francesco Villamena*, Berlin, 1979, pp. 102, 255. A copy of the second (the arms of Joanna Casimira Sobieska, Queen of Poland) is in the *Smaller Talman Album* (which originally belonged to Jones), Ashmolean Museum, fol. 48.
88 O&S, vol. II, p. 480, lines 34–47; Cf. *Toison d'or*, plates 24 (children with masks), 10 (children holding darts in lamps), 3 (female and male satyrs).
89 O&S, vol. II, p. 454, line 28, p. 547, lines 165–6; p. 480, line 47, p. 662, line 52.

90 O&S, vol. II, pp. 554–5, no. 267, p. 547, lines 187–9; *Toison d'or*, pls. 7, 26.
91 O&S, vol. II, pp. 554, 556–9, nos. 269–9; Orrell, *Theatres*, pp. 179ff.
92 O&S, vol. II, pp. 604, 606–7, no. 292.
93 Engraving after Giulio Romano by Diana Ghisi, Bartsch XV.499.40 (Jones made extensive notes on the decoration of Palazzo del Tè when reading Vasari's life of Giulio Romano); cartouches from Tempesta, *Esemplare Del Disegno*, IIII, Bartsch XVII.181.1381; and the tiger in the proscenium frieze from the same series, I, Bartsch XVII.181.1378.
94 O&S, vol. I, pp. 396, 401, no. 145; *Les travaux d'Ulisse dediez a Monseigneur de Liancourt par Theodor van Thulden*, Paris, 1633, plate 50 (Minerva appears to Penelope); O&S, vol. I, pp. 397–9, no. 141.
95 O&S, vol. I, pp. 400–1, no. 143; *Travaux d'Ulisse*, plate 9 (Polyphemus); Zerner, *Fontainebleau*, Master L. D. 13.
96 Edward Croft-Murray, *Decorative Painting in England 1537–1837: Volume I: Early Tudor to Sir James Thornhill*, London, 1962, p. 204.
97 Simon Jervis, 'A Seventeenth-Century Book of Engraved Ornament', *Burlington Magazine*, 134 (1992), 893–903, figs. 53, 60; H&H, pp. 224–5, no. 71.
98 H&H, p. 28.
99 Ibid., pp. 220–1, no. 69, pp. 234–5, no. 76.
100 Ibid., pp. 224–5, no. 71.
101 Ibid., pp. 217–19, no. 68.
102 O&S, vol. II, p. 730, lines 22–3.
103 Scamozzi, *L'Idea*, vol. II, p. 10; annotations by Jones: 'why frontispices wear maade / Praise of fro[n]tispices'.
104 O&S, vol. II, pp. 730, lines 58–64.
105 Ibid., p. 730, lines 31–2; Roy Strong, *Britannia Triumphans: Inigo Jones, Rubens and Whitehall Palace*, London, 1980, pp. 49–50, plate 46.
106 O&S, vol. II, p. 730, lines 64–8.
107 Barocchi, *Scritti*, vol. I, p. 410: 'Che l'imitazione ... abbia per fine il diletto, né debbo né posso negarlovi. Ma che l'imitazione, in quanta qualificata e governata dalla morale filosofia, abbia per fin principale il diletto, questo è quello che io liberamente vi niego ...'
108 Harris, *Catalogue*, p. 19, nos. 96–7.

7 Antiquity

1 Hieronymus Cock, *Praecipua Aliquot Romanae Antiquitatis Ruinarum Monimenta*, Antwerp, 1551; Etienne du Pérac, *I Vestigi Dell' Antichità Di Roma*, Rome, 1575; Hendrick van Cleef, *Ruinarum Vari Prospectus Ruriumq. Aliquot Delineationes*, Antwerp, 1587; Giovanni Antonio Dosio, *Cosmo Medici Duci Florentinor. Et Senes. Urbis Romae Aedificorum Illustrium Quae Supersunt Reliquiae*, Rome, 1569; Aegidius Sadeler, *Vestigi Delle Antichita Di Roma Tivoli Pozzuolo Et Altri Luochi*, Prague, 1606; *Il Terzo Libro Di Sebastiano Serlio Bolognese, Nelqual Si Figurano, E Descrivono Le Antiquita Di Roma, E Le Altre Che Sono In Italia, E Fuori D' Italia*, Venice, 1562; *Libro*

d'Antonio Labacco appartenente a l' architettura, Rome, 1569; *I Due Primi Libri Dell'Antichità Di M. Andrea Palladio*, Venice, 1570; Antonio Lafreri, *Speculum Romanae Magnificentiae*, Rome, n.d.; Vincenzo Scamozzi, *Discorsi Sopra L'Antichità Di Roma*, Venice, 1582. For a recent discussion of topographical ruin books see Anna Grelle, ed., *Vestigi delle antichità di Roma . . . et altri luochi. Momenti dell'elaborazione di un'immagine*, Rome, 1987.

2 Note on Bk. I, p. 13; Allsopp, p. 4.
3 Scamozzi, *Discorsi*, sig. [dagger] 2r (dedication to Giacomo Contarini).
4 John Peacock, 'Jonson and Jones collaborate on *Prince Henry's Barriers*', *Word and Image*, 3 (1987), 179, fig. 3.
5 Scamozzi, *Discorsi*, plate 40.
6 H&S, vol. VII, p. 209, lines 14–16.
7 See e.g. the facsimile of the first page of *Oberon* from the 1616 Folio, H&S, vol. VII, p. 339.
8 Jones also owned drawings by Palladio, and perhaps Pirro Ligorio: John Newman, 'Inigo Jones's Architectural Education before 1614', *Architectural History*, 35 (1992), 43, 49.
9 Allsopp, p. 62, IV.98; Gordon Higgott, '"Varying with Reason": Inigo Jones's Theory of Design', *Architectural History*, 35 (1992), 53, transcribes the entire note.
10 Serlio, Bk. III, sig. A1r. For other instances of the motto see Margaret R. Scherer, *Marvels of Ancient Rome*, New York and London, 1956, pl. 77.
11 Serlio, Bk. III, fol. 87r. Cf. du Pérac's view of the same building in Scherer, *Marvels*, pl. 175.
12 G. A. Rusconi, *Della Architettura*, Venice, 1590, pp. 36, 75.
13 O&S, vol. I, pp. 234–5, no. 74; Serlio, Bk. III, fol. 120r reprod. O&S, vol. I, p. 129, fig. 6.
14 Serlio, Bk. III, fols. 71v, 91v, 94r; George Chapman, *The Memorable Maske of the two Honorable Houses or Inns of Court; the Middle Temple, and Lyncolns Inn*, London, 1613, title-page (quoted O&S, vol. I, p. 253). Cf. Chapman's dedication to his translation of Musaeus in *George Chapman's Minor Translations*, ed. Richard Corballis, Salzburg, 1984, p. 1, 'To the Most generally ingenious, and our only Learned Architect . . . INYGO IONES'.
15 In this discussion of Book III, references in the text are to both editions of Serlio which Jones possessed and annotated: 1559–62, from which the quotations come, and 1601 (here represented by the 1619 reprint); see John Newman, 'Inigo Jones's architectural education before 1614', *Architectural History*, 35 (1992), 21.
16 H&H, pp. 168, 251–3, no. 82.
17 Note on *Libro primo [-quinto] d'architettura di Sebastiano Serlio Bolognese*, Venice, 1559–62 (Queen's College library), Bk. III, p. 121; John Orrell, *The Theatres of Inigo Jones and John Webb*, Cambridge, 1985, p. 102; H&H, pp. 268–9, fig. 87.
18 See ch. 1.
19 A note on Serlio, *Libro d'architettura*, Bk. IV, fol. 60v (Queen's College library)

refers to 'thes [s]camilli wch cam from delos and are in the magazin of his ma^ts [s]tattues'; see also John Harris, 'The Link between a Roman Second-Century Sculptor, Van Dyck, Inigo Jones and Henrietta Maria', *Burlington Magazine*, 115 (1973), 526–30.
20 Roman Sketchbook, 'of the Antiquities of Roome . . . of Fori or Piazi'.
21 H&H, p. 62.
22 D. J. Gordon, '*Hymenaei*: Ben Jonson's Masque of Union' in *The Renaissance Imagination*, Berkeley, Los Angeles and London, 1975, pp. 157–84.
23 For Jonson's copy see H&S, vol. XI, pp. 594–6 and David McPherson, 'Ben Jonson's Library and Marginalia. An Annotated Catalogue', *Studies in Philology*, 71 (1974), no. 5 (Texts and Studies, 1974), 71–2; Henry's copy is in the British Library, shelf number c.75.c.9.
24 Lafreri, *Speculum*, *Mostra della giostra fatto nel Teatro del Palazzo ridotto in questa forma dalla S.tà di N. S. Pio 40 come si vede nella stampa della pianta, con le sue misure* and *Fu della fe[lice] me[moria] di Giulio 2º fatto un Corridore . . .*
25 O&S, vol. I, pp. 178, 181, no. 46; William Camden, *Remains Concerning Britain*, ed. R. D. Dunn, Toronto, Buffalo and London, 1984, p. 181.
26 See p. 292.
27 Andrea Fulvio, *Delle antichità della Città di Roma*, Venice, 1543 (Jones's copy Worcester College library), fols. 136v, 141r; Bernardo Gamucci, *Libri Quattro Dell'Antichità Della Citta Di Roma*, Venice, 1565, fols. 99v–100v. The sculptured trophies were moved to the Campidoglio by Sixtus V in 1590.
28 Bartsch XVII.146.598–60, reprod. in *The Illustrated Bartsch*, vol. 35, ed. Sebastian Buffa, New York, 1984, pp. 325–7.
29 O&S, vol. I, pp. 182, 184, no. 47; *Twelve Caesars*, XII Domitianus Aug., Bartsch XVII.146.609; Lafreri, *Speculum*, *Trophea Marii De Bello Cymbr.Putat. Ad Aed. D. Euseb. Romae* (second of two plates).
30 O&S, vol. I, pp. 176–7, no. 45 and fig. 21; *Jules Romain. L'histoire de Scipion. Tapisseries et dessins. Grand Palais, 1978*, Paris, 1978, pp. 5, 95–7.
31 See p. 296, and note 57 below.
32 Richard S. Peterson, *Imitation and Praise in the Poetry of Ben Jonson*, New Haven and London, 1981, pp. 62–3; Peacock, 'Jonson and Jones', p. 175; O&S, vol. I, pp. 166–7, no. 38 and fig. 17.
33 H&S, vol. VII, p. 324, lines 33–4, p. 325, lines 84–5; O&S, vol. I, pp. 158, 163–5, nos. 36, 37.
34 Henri de Geymüller, *Les du Cerceau. Leur vie et leur œuvre*, Paris, 1887, p. 105, fig. 80.
35 Hollstein XIV.163.7 (wrongly identified on the plate as the Torre de' Conti).
36 Hollstein XIV.163.3 (*Tempio di Venere* . . .); 164.15 (*Monumenta Haec* . . . 5).
37 H&H, pp. 42–4, no. 6; John Newman, 'An Early Drawing by Inigo Jones and a Monument in Shropshire', *Burlington Magazine*, 115 (1973), 360–7.
38 Bartsch XVI.170.4; H&S, vol. VII, p. 324, line 37.
39 Peacock, 'Jonson and Jones', p. 190.
40 Frits Lugt, *Musée du Louvre. Inventaire général des dessins. Les écoles du nord.*

Ecole flamande, 2 vols., Paris, 1949, vol. I, pp. 16–19, nos. 356–62. A copy of no. 363 is among Jones's drawings at Chatsworth, O&S, vol. II, p. 796, no. 451.

41 See e.g. *Jonah Cast into the Sea*, c.1600, engraved after Paul Bril by Justus Sadeler, reprod. Arthur R. Blumenthal, *Giulio Parigi's Stage Designs. Florence and the Early Baroque Spectacle*, New York and London, 1986, fig. 63.

42 Serlio, Bk. II, fol. 46v; cf. Franco Mancini, *Scenografia italiana dal Rinascimento all'età romantica*, Milan, 1966, p. 11, plate 1.

43 Note in Jones's Palladio, *Quattro Libri*, Bk. IV, p. 129, Allsopp, p. 66: 'Anto: l'abaco dessignes this temple otherwise as I haue noted in his booke.'

44 See ch. 3.

45 H&S, vol. VII, p. 333, lines 339–40.

46 Ibid., p. 335, lines 397–8.

47 On the Tutelles see ch. 3; Palladio, Bk. IV, pp. 23–7.

48 Fulvio, *Antichità*, fol. 163v: 'Questo solo tra gli altri Principi per decreto del Senato meritò d' essere cognominato l'ottimo come apparisce nelle sue Medaglie.'

49 Peacock, 'Jonson and Jones', pp. 183–4 and notes 76–7.

50 Ibid., p. 182 and note 67.

51 See p. 229, and note 53 below.

52 Peacock, 'Jonson and Jones', p. 100.

53 O&S, vol. I, p. 198, no. 55; Hollstein XXI.78.360.

54 *Aeneid* VI.847–53, in *Virgil*, ed. and trans. H. Rushton Fairclough, revised edn, London and Cambridge, Mass., 1935; O&S, vol. I, p. 193, lines 28–30.

55 *The Basilicon Doron of King James VI*, ed. James Craigie, Scottish Text Society, 3rd series, 16 (1942), 18 (1944), 2 vols., Edinburgh and London, 1944–50, vol. I, p. 207.

56 *The Ancient, Honorable, Famous, and delightfull Historie of Huon of Bordeaux*, trans. John Bourchier, Lord Berners, London, 1601, sigs. Q4v, G1v ff.

57 O&S, vol. I, pp. 204, 220, no. 70; Bartsch XVII.146.600 (C. Caes. Ti. F.), 609 (Domitianus. Aug.); Phyllis Pray Bober and Ruth Rubenstein, *Renaissance Artists and Antique Sculpture*, London, 1985, pp. 191–2, no. 158 (Bartsch XIV.275.361), pp. 232–3, no. 199 (Bartsch XIV.317.422.).

58 O&S, vol. I, p. 206.

59 Ibid., p. 261, lines 599–600.

60 Ibid., p. 257, line 151.

61 Ibid., lines 116–22: 'a silver temple of an octangle figure, whose pillars were of a composed order, and bore up an architrave, frieze, and cornice, over which stood a continuous plinth ... above this was placed a bastard order of architecture ... Above all was a *Coupolo* or tipe ... '

62 Ibid., p. 260, lines 465–6. The printed text is dedicated 'To The Most Noble, and constant Combiner of Honor, and Vertue, Sir Edward Philips, Knight, Master of the Rolls': Chapman, *Memorable Maske*, sig. [reverse D] 2r. For the Temples of Honos and Virtus see Livy XXVII.xxv.7–10, Barbaro p. 120.

63 *The Complete Works of John Webster*, ed. F. L. Lucas, 4 vols., 2nd edn, London, 1966, vol. III, p. 277, lines 102–7.

64 Roman Sketchbook, 'The Manner Of Drapery all antica:'
65 H&S, vol. VII, pp. 229–30, lines 584, 592–600.
66 O&S, vol. I, p. 242.
67 Ibid., p. 243, lines 71–3, pp. 247–8, no. 78.
68 Alonso Chacón, *Historia Utriusque Belli Dacici A Traiano Caesare Gesti*, Rome, 1576, pls. 10, 44.
69 O&S, vol. II, pp. 469, 471, no. 205.
70 *Chapman's Translations*, ed. Corballis, p. 1.
71 Ibid.
72 H&S, vol. VII, p. 625.
73 Roman Sketchbook, 'The Manner Of Drapery all antica:'
74 *Peacham's Compleat Gentleman 1634*, ed. G. S. Gordon, Oxford, 1906, p. 107.
75 John Peacock, 'Inigo Jones and the Arundel Marbles', *Journal of Medieval and Renaissance Studies*, 16 (1986), 77, note 13, and passim for a more detailed discussion of the following points.
76 W. Noel Sainsbury, *Original Unpublished Papers Illustrative of the Life of Sir Peter Paul Rubens*, London, 1859, pp. 327–39.
77 O&S, vol. II, pp. 458–60, no. 190; John Newman, 'The Inigo Jones Centenary', *Burlington Magazine*, 115 (1973), 561; Peacock, 'Arundel Marbles', p. 86 and notes 53, 54.
78 O&S, vol. II, p. 454, lines 41–6.
79 Oliver Millar, *The Age of Charles I*, London, 1972, 13, no. 1.
80 Peacock, 'Arundel Marbles', p. 81; O&S, vol. II, pp. 554–5, no. 267.
81 Peacock, 'Arundel Marbles', pp. 81–3.
82 Harris, 'Link'; for the most recent and searching discussion of the painting see Jeremy Wood, 'Van Dyck's Pictures for the Duke of Buckingham', *Apollo*, 136 (1992), 37–47.
83 David Howarth, *Lord Arundel and His Circle*, New Haven and London, 1985, p. 198.
84 Newman, 'Centenary', p. 561.
85 Claudio Franzoni, '"Rimembranze d'infinite cose". Le collezioni rinascimentali di antichità', in *Memoria dell'antico nell'arte italiana. Tomo primo. L'uso dei classici*, ed. Salvatore Settis, Turin, 1984, pp. 330–1; the altar of Quintus Mutius is part of the early seventeenth-century lay-out of the principal cortile of Palazzo Mattei, which can still be seen.
86 Millar, *Charles I*, pp. 12–13, nos. 1–2.
87 Peacock, 'Arundel Marbles', pp. 82–3.
88 Livy x.xxiii.1–10; B. de Vigenère, *Les Decades Qui Se Trouvent De Tite-Live en Francois Avec Des annotations et figures pour l'intelligence de l'antiquite Romaine*, 2 vols., Paris, 1617, vol. I, pp. 435–6, 721, vol. II, p. 1743; Fulvio, *Antichità*, fols. 131v–132r; Gamucci, *Antichità*, fols. 76v–77r; Bartolomeo Marliano, *L'Antichità Di Roma*, Rome, 1548, fol. 50r.
89 Gamucci, *Le Antichità*, fol. 76v: 'tanto facevano conto di osservare i Romani in tutte le loro attioni, un antica incorrotta nobilità'.
90 See p. 284.

91 Kevin Sharpe, *The Personal Rule of Charles I*, New Haven and London, 1992, p. 237 and note 164.
92 O&S, vol. II, p. 454, line 99.
93 Ibid., p. 455, lines 133–4, 215, 203–4.
94 Ibid., p. 454, lines 8–9.
95 Ibid., pp. 452, 469–71, nos. 203–5; Bartsch XIV.275.361 and 317.422; Bober & Rubenstein, *Renaissance Artists*, pp. 191–2, no. 158, pp. 232–3, no. 199.
96 Ibid., p. 215.
97 *Compleat Gentleman*, ed. Gordon, pp. 123–4.
98 John Peacock, 'Inigo Jones's Catafalque for James I', *Architectural History*, 25 (1982), 3–4 ; O&S, vol. I, pp. 340–1, 343, no. 117 and figs. 43–43A.
99 Oliver Millar, ed., *Abraham van der Doort's Catalogue of the Collections of Charles I* (The Thirty-Seventh Volume of the Walpole Society, 1958–1960), London, 1960, pp. 124–5, 135, 218ff. Detailing his problems in keeping track of Prince Henry's medals, van der Doort, p. 155, writes [spelling modernised]: 'Master Surveyor has been taking and viewing the same and numbering ...'
100 O&S, vol. II, p. 472, no. 207; Octavius de Strada, *De Vitis Imperatorum Et Caesarum Romanorum*, Frankfurt, 1615, pp. 99–100, plate 143.
101 O&S, vol. II, p. 465, no. 194 and fig. 73; *Onuphrii Panvinii Veronensis, De Ludis Circensibus, Libri II. De Triumphis, Liber Unus*, Venice, 1600, X Pag.89, S Pag.62.IIII.
102 O&S, vol. II, pp. 476–7, no. 215; Onofrio Panvinio, *De Triumpho Romanorum Commentarius*, Venice, 1600, plate D, 'Reges captivi cum familia, filiis, filiabusque suis'; G. B. Cavalieri, *Antiquarum Statuarum Urbis Romae Primus et Secundus Liber*, Rome, 1585, plates 21, 30; Bober & Rubenstein, *Renaissance Artists*, pp. 197–8, no. 165 A–B.
103 O&S, vol. II, p. 468, no. 201; Chacón, *Historia*, plates 8–9.
104 O&S, vol. II, pp. 808–9, no. 463.
105 Hollstein XIV.162.2.
106 Du Pérac, *Vestigi*, plate 7 'Parte del Monte Palatino Verso Il foro Romano ...'; Hollstein XIV.163.3.
107 O&S, vol. II, pp. 808–9, no. 463 verso; Hollstein XIV.165.10.
108 O&S, vol. II, pp. 584–5, no. 279.
109 Hollstein XIV.165.17, 164.2; Scamozzi, *Discorsi*, plates 36, 12.
110 Ibid., plates 32, 2 (Parigi's first and second structures on the left), 7 (second right).
111 O&S, vol. II, p. 571, lines 33–7.
112 Ibid., lines 37–8.
113 Ibid., p. 577, lines 865–6.
114 Rhodes Dunlap, ed., *The Poems of Thomas Carew*, Oxford, 1964, pp. 275–6.
115 O&S, vol. II, pp. 570–1, lines 22, 47–8.
116 O&S, vol. II, pp. 566, 588, no. 280. Cf. Roy Strong, *Art and Power. Renaissance Festivals 1450–1650*, Woodbridge, 1984, fig. 63; Millar, *Van der Doort*, p. 141 (on one of Charles's medals): 'king Phillip the ... second at the other side Carrying a Gloabe on his shoulder'; *The Poetical Works of William Drummond*

of Hawthornden, ed. L. E. Kastner, 2 vols., Manchester, 1913, p. 146, lines 163–4: 'To know the Weight, and *Atlas* of a Crowne, / To spare the Humble, Prowdlings pester downe' (*Forth Feasting. A Panegyricke To The Kings Most Excellent Majestie*, 1617).

117 *Ausonius*, trans. Hugh G. Evelyn White, 2 vols., London and New York, 1919–21, vol. I, pp. 8–9 (I.iv.11–12).

118 Philostratus, *Imagines* II.xx.2, III.iii.6, the first passage quoted in Franciscus Junius, *The Painting of the Ancients* in *The Literature of Classical Art*, ed. Keith Aldrich, Phillip Fehl and Raina Fehl, 2 vols., Berkeley, Los Angeles and London, 1991, vol. I, p. 244: 'It is easie to hit the shadowes of them that lie downe . . . or stand upright: and it requireth small wisdome to do it accurately. But the shadowes of *Atlas* go beyond all art: for the shadowes of him that stoopeth after this manner, though they fall one into another, yet do they not darken any of these things that should rise, but cause some light about the hollownesse of his belly.' See ch. 2, p. 52.

Conclusion

1 O&S, vol. II, p. 454, line 99.
2 Ibid., p. 662, lines 59–61.
3 Ibid., pp. 22–3.
4 Erica Veevers, *Images of Love and Religion. Queen Henrietta Maria and Court Entertainments*, Cambridge, 1989, pp. 112ff.
5 O&S, vol. II, p. 483, lines 366–7.
6 Ibid., line 341.
7 Ibid., lines 327, 349–52.
8 See ch. 1.
9 O&S, vol. II, p. 706, lines 16–29.
10 Vasari, Milanesi, vol. I, pp. 215ff.
11 O&S, vol. II, p. 709, lines 355–7.
12 Veevers, *Images*, pp. 145–6.

Bibliography

Primary works

Agostini, Antonio, *Dialoghi Intorno alle Medaglie*, Rome, 1625

Alberti, Leon Battista, *L'Architettura di Leon Battista Alberti*, trans. Cosimo Bartoli, with *La Pittura Di Leonbattista Alberti*, trans. Lodovico Domenichi, Monreale, 1565

  Ten Books on Architecture by Leone Battista Alberti Translated into Italian by Cosimo Bartoli And into English By James Leoni, ed. Joseph Rykwert, London, 1965

  On the Art of Building in Ten Books, trans. Joseph Rykwert, Neil Leach and Robert Tavernor, London and Cambridge, Mass., 1988

  On Painting and On Sculpture, ed. Cecil Grayson, London, 1972

Allsopp, Bruce, ed., *Inigo Jones on Palladio*, 2 vols., Newcastle upon Tyne, 1970

Aristotle, *Poetics*, in *Aristotle's Theory of Poetry and Fine Art*, ed. and trans. S. H. Butcher, New York, 1951

  L'Ethica D'Aristotile, trans. Bernardo Segni, Venice, 1551

Armenini, Giovanni Battista, *On the True Precepts of the Art of Painting*, trans. Edward. J. Olszewski, New York, 1977

  De' Veri Precetti Della Pittura ... Libri Tre, Ravenna, 1587 (facsimile Hildesheim and New York, 1971)

Ausonius, *Ausonius*, trans. Hugh G. Evelyn White, 2 vols., London and New York, 1919–21

Baglione, Giovanni, *Le Vite De' Pittori Scultori Et Architetti*, Rome, 1642

Baldinucci, Filippo, *Notizie dei professori del disegno*, 5 vols., Florence, 1845–7

Barbaro, Daniele, *La Pratica Della Perspettiva*, Venice, 1569 (facsimile Bologna, 1980)

Barocchi, Paola, ed., *Trattati d'arte del Cinquecento*, 3 vols., Bari, 1960

  Scritti d'arte del Cinquecento, 3 vols., Milan and Naples, 1971–7

Berners, John Bourchier, Lord, trans., *The Ancient, Honorable, Famous, and delightfull Historie of Huon of Bordeaux*, London, 1601

British Library MS Sloane 862, *Catalogus librorum bibliothecae Norfolcianae*
Bolton, Edmund, *The Elements of Armories*, London, 1610
Bordino, Giovanni Francesco, *De Rebus Praeclare Gestis A Sixto V. Pon. Max. . . . Carminum Liber Primus*, Rome, 1588
Buonarroti, Michelangelo, *Descrizione Delle Felicissime Nozze Della Cristianissima Maestà de Madonna Maria Medici Regina di Francia e di Navarra*, Florence, 1600
Camden, William, *Remains Concerning Britain*, ed. R. D. Dunn, Toronto, Buffalo and London, 1984
Campion, Thomas, *The Works of Thomas Campion*, ed. Walter R. Davis, London, 1969
Carew, Thomas, *The Poems of Thomas Carew with his Masque Coelum Britannicum*, ed. Rhodes Dunlap, Oxford, 1964
Cartari, Vincenzo, *Imagini Delli Dei De Gl'Antichi*, Venice, 1647 (facsimile Graz, 1963)
Cataneo, Pietro, *L'Architettura*, Venice, 1567
Catani, Baldo, *La Pompa Funerale . . . di Papa Sisto il Quinto*, Rome, 1591
Cavalieri, G. B. [Cavalleriis, J. B. de], *Antiquarum Statuarum Urbis Romae Primus et Secundus Liber*, Rome, 1585
Chacón, Alonso, *Historia Utriusque Belli Dacici A Traiano Caesare Gesti*, Rome, 1576
Chapman, George, *Chapman's Homer*, ed. Allardyce Nicoll, 2 vols., London, 1957
  The Memorable Maske of the two Honorable Houses or Inns of Court; the Middle Temple, and Lyncolns Inn, London, 1613
Cicero, *Orator*, trans. H. M. Hubbell, London and Cambridge, Mass., 1952
Cleef, Hendrick van, *Ruinarum Vari Prospectus Ruriumq. Aliquot Delineationes*, Antwerp, 1587
Cock, Hieronymus, *Praecipua Aliquot Romanae Antiquitas Ruinarum Monimenta*, Antwerp, 1551
Daniel, Samuel, *The Order and Solemnitie of the Creation of the High and mightie Prince Henrie, Eldest Sonne to our sacred Sovereigne, Prince of Wales . . . Whereunto is annexed the Royall maske, presented by the Queene and her Ladies . . .* , London, 1610
Doni, Anton Francesco, *Disegno*, Venice, 1549 (facsimile Milan, 1970)
Dorat, Jean, *Magnificentissimi Spectaculi . . . descriptio*, Paris, 1573
Dosio, Giovanni Antonio, *Cosmo Medici Duci Florentinor. Et Senes. Urbis Romae Aedificorum Illustrium Quae Supersunt Reliquiae*, Rome, 1569
Drummond, William, *The Poetical Works of William Drummond of Hawthornden*, ed. L. E. Kastner, 2 vols., Manchester, 1913
Du Cerceau, Jacques Androuet, *Le Premier Volume des plus excellents Bastiments de France*, Paris, 1576; *Le Second Volume des plus excellents Bastiments de France*, Paris, 1607 (joint facsimile, Farnborough, 1972)
  Livre Des Edifices antiques Romains, Paris, 1584
Du Pérac, Etienne, *I Vestigi Dell'Antichità Di Roma*, Rome, 1575

Fialetti, Odoardo, *Il vero modo et ordine. Per Dissegnar Tutte Le Parti Et Membra Del Corpo Humano*, Venice, 1608

Fontana, Domenico, *Della Trasportatione Dell'Obelisco Vaticano 1590*, ed. Adriano Carugo, intro. Paolo Portoghesi, Milan, 1978

Fulvio, Andrea, *Opera Di Andrea Fulvio Delle antichità della Città di Roma*, Venice, 1543

Gamucci, Bernardo, *Le Antichità Della Città Di Roma*, 2nd edn, ed. Tommaso Porcacchi, Venice, 1580

Gohory, Jacques, *Livre de la Conqueste de la Toison d'or, par le Prince Iason de Tessalie: faict par figures avec exposition d'icelles*, Paris, 1563

Guarini, Battista, *Il Pastor Fido*, Venice, 1602

Hollanda, Francisco de, *Four Dialogues on Painting*, trans. Aubrey F. G. Bell, London, 1928

James VI and I, *The Basilicon Doron of King James VI*, ed. James Craigie, Scottish Text Society, 3rd series, 16 (1942), 18 (1944), 2 vols., Edinburgh and London, 1944–50

Jones, Inigo, Roman Sketchbook, facsimile prepared for the Duke of Devonshire, London, 1832

Jonson, Ben, *Ben Jonson*, ed. C. H. Herford and Percy and Evelyn Simpson, 11 vols., Oxford, 1926–52

The Complete Masques, ed. Stephen Orgel, New Haven and London, 1969

Junius, Franciscus, *The Painting of the Ancients*, in *The Literature of Classical Art*, ed. Keith Aldrich, Phillip Fehl and Raina Fehl, 2 vols., Berkeley, Los Angeles and London, 1991

Labacco, Antonio, *Libro d'Antonio Labacco appartenente a l'architettura*, Rome, 1569

Lafreri, Antonio, *Speculum Romanae Magnificentiae*, Rome, n.d.

Livy, *Les Decades Qui Se Trouvent De Tite-Live En Francois Avec Des annotations et figures pour l'intelligence de l'antiquite Romaine . . . Par.B[laise]. De Vigenere*, 2 vols., Paris, 1617

Lomazzo, Giovanni Paolo, *Trattato Dell'Arte Della Pittura, Scoltura, Ed Architettura*, Milan, 1585

Rime Di Gio. Paolo Lomazzi Milanese Pittore, divise In sette Libri . . . ad imitatione de i Grotteschi usati da' pittori . . ., Milan, 1587

A Tracte Containing The Artes of curious Paintinge Carvinge Buildinge, trans. Richard Haydocke, Oxford, 1598 (facsimile Amsterdam and New York), 1969

Scritti sulle arti, ed. Roberto Paolo Ciardi, 2 vols., Florence, 1973–4

l'Orme, Philibert de, *Le Premier Tome de l'Architecture*, Paris, 1568

Mancini, Giulio, *Considerazioni sulla pittura*, ed. Adriana Marucchi and Luigi Salerno, 2 vols., Rome, 1956–7

Marliano, Bartolomeo, *L'Antichità Di Roma*, Rome, 1548

Markham, Gervase, *Honour In His Perfection*, London, 1624

Mauro, Lucio, and Ulisse Aldrovandi, *Le Antichità Della Città Di Roma . . . Appresso, tutte le statue antiche, che in Roma . . . si veggono . . . Per M. Ulisse Aldroandi*, Venice, 1562

Millar, Oliver, ed., *Abraham van der Doort's Catalogue of the Collections of Charles I* (The Thirty-Seventh Volume of the Walpole Society 1958–60), London, 1960
Minturno, Antonio, *L'Arte Poetica*, Venice, 1564 (facsimile Munich, 1971)
Nichols, John, *The Progresses of King James the First*, 4 vols., London, 1828
Norgate, Edward, *Miniatura or The Art of Limning*, ed. Martin Hardie, Oxford, 1919
Orgel, Stephen, and Strong, Roy, *Inigo Jones: The Theatre of the Stuart Court*, 2 vols., Berkeley, Los Angeles and London, 1973
Palladio, Andrea, *I Quattro Libri Dell'Architettura*, Venice, 1570 (facsimile Milan, 1969)
  I Due Primi Libri Dell'Antichità Di M. Andrea Palladio, Venice, 1570
  L'Antichità di Roma di M. Andrea Palladio, Venice, 1588
Panvinio, Onofrio, *Onuphrii Panvinii Veronensis, De Ludis Circensibus, Libri II. De Triumphis, Liber Unus*, Venice, 1600
Peacham, Henry, *The Arte of Drawing*, London, 1606
  The Gentlemans Exercise (also issued as *Graphice Or The Most Auncient And Excellent Art Of Drawing and Limming*), London, 1612
  The Compleat Gentleman, London, 1622
  Peacham's Compleat Gentleman 1634, ed. G. S. Gordon, Oxford, 1906
Piccolomini, Alessandro, *Annotationi... Nel Libro Della Poetica d'Aristotele; Con La Traduttione Del medesimo Libro, in Lingua Volgare*, Venice, 1575
Plato, *Di Tutte L'Opere Di Platone*, trans. Dardi Bembo, 5 vols., Venice, 1601
  Plato's Statesman. A Translation of the 'Politicus' of Plato, ed. J. B. Skemp, London, 1952
  La Republica Di Platone, trans. Pamphilo Florimbene, Venice, 1554
Pliny the Elder, *The Historie Of The World. Commonly called The Natural Historie of C. Plinius Secundus. Translated into English by Philemon Holland*, London, 1601
  The Elder Pliny's Chapters on the History of Art, trans. K. Jex-Blake, ed. H. Sellers, Chicago, 1968
Plutarch, *La Seconda Parte De Gli Opuscoli Morali Di Plutarco*, trans. Giovanni Trachagnota, Venice, 1567
  Opuscoli Morali Di Plutarco... Parte Seconda, trans. Marcantonio Gandino, Venice, 1614
Possevino, Antonio, *Bibliotheca Selecta Qua agitur De Ratione Studiorum*, 2 vols., Cologne, 1607
Richter, Irma A., ed., *Paragone. A Comparison of the Arts by Leonardo da Vinci*, London, New York and Toronto, 1949
Ridolfi, Carlo, *Le Maraviglie dell'Arte*, ed. Detlev von Hadeln, 2 vols., Berlin, 1924
Ripa, Cesare, *Iconologia*, Rome, 1603 (facsimile Hildesheim and New York, 1970)
Ross, Alexander, *Mystagogus Poeticus*, London, 1648 (facsimile New York and London, 1976)
Rossi, Bastiano de', *Descrizione Del Magnificentiss. Apparato E De' Maravigliosi Intermedi Fatti Per La Commedia Rappresentata In Firenze nelle Felicissime*

Nozze degl'Illustrissimi ed Eccellentissimi Signori Il Signor Don Cesare D'Este E La Signora Donna Virginia Medici, Florence, 1586.
Rusconi, Giovanni Antonio, *Della Architettura*, Venice, 1590
Sadeler, Aegidius, *Vestigi Delle Antichita Di Roma Tivoli Pozzuolo Et Altri Luochi*, Prague, 1606
Sainsbury, W. Noel, *Original Unpublished Papers Illustrative of the Life of Sir Peter Paul Rubens*, London, 1859
Scamozzi, Vincenzo, *Discorsi Sopra L'Antichità Di Roma*, Venice, 1582
  L' Idea Della Architettura Universale, 2 vols., Venice, 1615
Serlio, Sebastiano, *Libro primo [-quinto] d'architettura di Sebastiano Serlio Bolognese*, Venice, 1559–62
  Tutte L'Opere D'Architettura, Et Prospetiva, Venice, 1619 (facsimile Ridgewood, N.J., 1964)
  The Book of Architecture by Sebastiano Serlio London, 1611, ed. A. E. Santaniello, New York, 1970
Sidney, Philip, *An Apology for Poetry*, ed. Geoffrey Shepherd, Manchester, 1973
Simeoni, Gabriele, *Les Illustres Observations Antiques Du Seigneur Gabriel Symeon Florentin*, Lyons, 1558
Sirigatti, Lorenzo, *La Pratica Di Prospettiva*, Venice, 1625
Speed, John, *The Theatre Of The Empire Of Great Britaine*, London, 1611
Spencer T. J. B., and Wells, Stanley, eds., *A Book of Masques in Honour of Allardyce Nicoll*, Cambridge, 1967
Strada, Octavius de, *De Vitis Imperatorum Et Caesarum Romanorum*, Frankfurt, 1615
Thulden, Theodoor van, *Les travaux d'Ulisse dediez a Monseigneur de Liancourt par Theodor van Thulden*, Paris, 1633
Vasari, Giorgio, *Delle Vite De' Piu Eccellenti Pittori Scultori Et Architetti ... Primo Volume della Terza Parte*, Florence, 1568
  Le opere di Giorgio Vasari, ed. Gaetano Milanesi, 9 vols., Florence, 1878–85
Vecellio, Cesare, *Habiti Antichi Overo Raccolta Di Figure*, 3rd edn., Venice, 1664
Vitruvius, *On Architecture*, ed. and trans. Frank Granger, 2 vols., London and Cambridge, Mass., 1931–4
  I Dieci Libri Dell'Architettura Di M. Vitruvio, Tradotti & commentati da Mons. Daniele Barbaro, Venice, 1567 (facsimile Milan, 1987)
Vredeman de Vries, Jan, *Perspective*, ed. Adolf K. Placzek, New York, 1968
Webster, John, *The Complete Works of John Webster*, 2nd edn, 4 vols., London, 1966
Wotton, Henry, *The Elements of Architecture*, London, 1624 (facsimile Farnborough, 1969)
Xenophon, *L'Opere Morali di Xenophonte*, trans. Lodovico Domenichi, Venice, 1567

Secondary works

Ackermann, James S., *Palladio*, Harmondsworth, 1966
Andrews, Keith, *Adam Elsheimer*, London, 1977

Ashby, Thomas, *Topographical Study in Rome in 1581*, London, 1916

Aston, Margaret, *England's Iconoclasts. Volume I. Laws against Images*, Oxford, 1988

Bacou, Roseline, *Il paesaggio nel disegno del Cinquecento europeo*, Rome, 1972

Bartsch, Adam von, *The Illustrated Bartsch*, New York, 1978– , vol. 32, ed. Henri Zerner, 1979; vol. 35, ed. Sebastian Buffa, 1984; vol. 40, ed. Veronika Birke, 1982; vol. 52, ed. Walter L. Strauss and Tomoko Shimura, 1986

Battisti, Eugenio, 'Il concetto d'imitazione nel Cinquecento italiano', in *Rinascimento e Barocco*, Turin, 1960

Béguin, Sylvie, *L'Ecole de Fontainebleau*, Paris, 1960

Berghaus, Günter, 'Theatre Performances at Italian Renaissance Festivals: Multi-Media Spectacles or *Gesamtkunstwerke?*' in J. R. Mulryne and Margaret Shewring, eds., *Italian Renaissance Festivals and Their European Influence*, Lewiston, Queenston and Lampeter, 1992, pp. 3–50

Blumenthal, Arthur R., *Giulio Parigi's Stage Designs. Florence and the Early Baroque Spectacle*, New York and London, 1986

Blunt, Anthony, *Philibert de l'Orme*, London, 1958

Bober, Phyllis Pray, and Rubenstein, Ruth, *Renaissance Artists and Antique Sculpture*, London, 1986

Bodart, Didier, *Les peintres des Pays-Bas méridionaux et de la principauté de Liège à Rome au XVIIème siècle*, 2 vols., Brussels and Rome, 1970

Bold, John, *John Webb: Architectural Theory and Practice in the Seventeenth Century*, Oxford, 1989

Brown, Christopher, *Dutch Landscape: The Early Years*, London, 1986

Bruschi, Arnaldo, *Bramante*, London, 1977

Butler, Martin, 'Politics and the Masque: *Salmacida Spolia*', in Thomas Healy and Jonathan Sawday, eds., *Literature and the English Civil War*, Cambridge, 1990, pp. 59–74

Byam Shaw, James, *Old Master Drawings from Chatsworth*, London, 1973

Carli, Enzo, *L'arte a Siena sotto i Medici 1555–1609*, Rome, 1980

Chastel, André, 'Palladio et l'escalier à double mouvement inverse', *Bolletino del Centro Internazionale di Studi d'Architettura Andrea Palladio*, 2 (1960), 26–9

Chettle, G. H., *The Queen's House, Greenwich*, London, 1937

Chiarini, Marco, *Mostra di disegni italiani di paesaggio del seicento e del settecento*, Florence, 1973

Collinson, Patrick, *The Birthpangs of Protestant England*, New York, 1988

Croft-Murray, Edward, *Decorative Painting in England 1537–1837: Volume I: Early Tudor to Sir James Thornhill*, London, 1962

Cropper, Elizabeth, *The Ideal of Painting. Pietro Testa's Düsseldorf Notebook*, Princeton, 1984

Dacos, Nicole, *La découverte de la Domus Aurea at la formation des grotesques à la Renaissance*, London and Leiden, 1969

DeGrazia Bohlin, Diane, *Prints and Related Drawings by the Carracci Family*, Washington, 1979

Fagiolo, Maurizio, *La scenografia*, Florence, 1973

Finsten, Jill, *Isaac Oliver: Art at the Courts of Elizabeth I and James I*, 2 vols., New York and London, 1981

Fowler, Alastair, *Kinds of Literature*, Oxford, 1982

Franzoni, Claudio, '"Rimembrenze d'infinite cose": Le collezioni rinascimentali di antichità', in Salvatore Settis, ed., *Memoria dell'antico nell'arte italiana: Tomo primo: L'uso dei classici*, Turin, 1984

Frutaz, Amato Pietro, *Le piante di Roma*, 3 vols., Rome, 1962

Gelder, J. G. van, 'Notes on the Royal Collection – IV. The "Dutch Gift" of 1610 to Henry Prince of "Whallis" and Some Other Presents', *Burlington Magazine*, 105 (1963), 541–4

Geymüller, Henri de, *Les du Cerceau: Leur vie et leur œuvre*, Paris, 1887

Girouard, Mark, *Robert Smythson and the Elizabethan Country House*, New Haven and London, 1983

Gombrich, E. H., 'The Renaissance Theory of Art and the Rise of Landscape', in *Norm and Form*, London, 1966, pp. 107–21

Gordon, D. J., 'Poet and Architect: The Intellectual Setting of the Quarrel between Ben Jonson and Inigo Jones' and '*Hymenaei*: Ben Jonson's Masque of Union', in *The Renaissance Imagination*, Berkeley, Los Angeles and London, 1975

Gotch, J. A., *Inigo Jones*, London, 1928

Grelle, Anna, *Vestigi delle antichità di Roma . . . et altri luochi. Momenti dell'elaborazione di un'immagine*, Rome, 1987

Griffiths, Antony, and Kesnerová, Gabriela, *Wenceslaus Hollar: Prints and Drawings*, London, 1983

Harris, John, *Catalogue of the Drawings Collection of the Royal Institute of British Architects: Inigo Jones and John Webb*, Farnborough, 1972

'The Link between a Roman Second-Century Sculptor, Van Dyck, Inigo Jones and Henrietta Maria', *Burlington Magazine*, 115 (1973), 526–30

Harris, John, Orgel, Stephen, and Strong, Roy, *The King's Arcadia: Inigo Jones and the Stuart Court*, London, 1973

Harris, John, and Tait, A. A., *Catalogue of the Drawings by Inigo Jones, John Webb and Isaac de Caus at Worcester College Oxford*, Oxford, 1979

Herrick, Marvin T., *The Fusion of Horatian and Aristotelian Literary Criticism, 1531–1555*, Urbana, 1946

Hervey, Mary F. S., *The Life, Correspondence and Collections of Thomas Howard, Earl of Arundel*, Cambridge, 1921

Higgott, Gordon, 'Inigo Jones in Provence', *Architectural History*, 26 (1983), 24–34

'"Varying with Reason": Inigo Jones's Theory of Design', *Architectural History*, 35 (1992), 51–77

Howarth, David, *Lord Arundel and His Circle*, New Haven and London, 1985

Il potere e lo spazio (Firenze e la Toscana dei Medici nell'Europa del Cinquecento), Florence, 1980

Ivins Jr, William M., *On the Rationalisation of Sight*, New York, 1975

Jacquot, Jean, ed., *Les fêtes de la Renaissance*, 3 vols., Paris, 1959–75

Jervis, Simon, 'A Seventeenth-Century Book of Engraved Ornament', *Burlington Magazine*, 134 (1992), 893–903

Johnson, A. W., 'Angles, Squares, or Roundes': Studies in Jonson's Vitruvianism, unpublished D.Phil. thesis, University of Oxford, 1987

Jules Romain: L'histoire de Scipion: Tapisseries et dessins. Grand Palais, 1978, Paris, 1978

Kendrick, T. D., British Antiquity, London, 1950

Kühn-Hattenhauer, Dorothee, Das grafische Oeuvre des Francesco Villamena, Berlin, 1979

La scena del principe (Firenze e la Toscana dei Medici nell'Europa del Cinquecento), Florence, 1980

Lauer, Philippe, Le palais de Latran, Paris, 1911

Lawrenson, T. E., The French Stage in the XVIIth Century, Manchester, 1957

Lee, Rensselaer W., Ut Pictura Poesis. The Humanistic Theory of Painting, New York, 1967

Levron, Jacques, René Boyvin graveur angevin du XVIe siècle, Angers, 1941

Lugt, Frits, Musée du Louvre. Inventaire général des dessins: Les écoles du nord: Ecole flamande, 2 vols., Paris, 1949

Magagnato, Licisco, Teatri italiani del Cinquecento, Venice, 1954

Mamone, Sara, Il teatro nella Firenze medicea, Milan, 1981

Mancini, Franco, Scenografia italiana dal Rinascimento all'età romantica, Milan, 1966

Martindale, Andrew, The Triumphs of Caesar by Andrea Mantegna in the Collection of Her Majesty the Queen at Hampton Court, London, 1979

Massari, Stefania, Incisori mantovani del '500, Rome, 1980

Mayer, Anton, Das Leben und die Werke der Brüder Matthäus und Paul Brill, Leipzig, 1910

McPherson, David, 'Ben Jonson's Library and Marginalia. An Annotated Catalogue', Studies in Philology, 71 (1974), no. 5 (Texts and Studies, 1974).

Millar, Oliver, The Tudor, Stuart and Early Georgian Pictures in the Collection of Her Majesty the Queen, 2 vols., London, 1963

The Age of Charles I, London, 1972

Van Dyck in England, London, 1982

Nagler, A. M., Theatre Festivals of the Medici 1539–1637, New Haven and London, 1964

Newman, John, 'An Early Drawing by Inigo Jones and a Monument in Shropshire', Burlington Magazine, 115 (1973), 360–7

'The Inigo Jones Centenary', Burlington Magazine, 115 (1973), 557–61

'Italian Treatises in Use: the Significance of Inigo Jones's Annotations', in Jean Guillaume, ed., Les traités d'architecture de la Renaissance, Paris, 1988

'Inigo Jones's Architectural Education before 1614', Architectural History, 35 (1992), 18–50

Oberhuber, Konrad, 'Hieronymus Cock, Battista Pittoni und Paolo Veronese in Villa Maser' in Munuscula disciplinorum: Festschrift Hans Kaufmann, Berlin, 1968

Oppé, A. P., English Drawings at Windsor Castle, London, 1950

Orgel, Stephen, *The Jonsonian Masque*, Cambridge, Mass., 1965
Orrell, John, *The Theatres of Inigo Jones and John Webb*, Cambridge, 1985
Panofsky, Erwin, *Idea: A Concept in Art Theory*, New York, 1968
  Renaissance and Renascences in Western Art, Stockholm, 1960
Peacock, John, 'New Sources for the Masque Designs of Inigo Jones', *Apollo*, 107 (1978), 98–111
  'Inigo Jones's Stage Architecture and Its Sources', *Art Bulletin*, 64 (1982), 195–216
  'Inigo Jones's Catafalque for James I', *Architectural History*, 25 (1982), 1–5
  'The French element in Inigo Jones's Masque Designs', in David Lindley, ed., *The Court Masque*, Manchester, 1984
  'Inigo Jones and the Arundel Marbles', *Journal of Medieval and Renaissance Studies*, 16 (1986), 75–90
  'Inigo Jones and the Florentine Court Theatre', *John Donne Journal*, 5 (1986), 201–34
  'Jonson and Jones collaborate on *Prince Henry's Barriers*', *Word and Image*, 3 (1987), 172–94
  'Inigo Jones and Renaissance Art', *Renaissance Studies*, 4 (1990), 245–72
  'Inigo Jones as a Figurative Artist', in Lucy Gent and Nigel Llewellyn, eds., *Renaissance Bodies. The Human Figure in English Culture c. 1540–1660*, London, 1990, pp. 154–79
  'Ben Jonson's Masques and Italian Culture', in J. R. Mulryne and Margaret Shewring, eds., *Theatre of the English and Italian Renaissance*, London, 1991, pp. 73–94
  'The Stuart Court Masque and the Theatre of Antiquity', *Journal of the Warburg and Courtauld Institutes*, 56 (1993), 183–208
Peterson, Richard S., *Imitation and Praise in the Poems of Ben Jonson*, New Haven and London, 1981
Portal, E. M., 'The Academ Roial of James I', *Proceedings of the British Academy*, 7 (1915–16), 189–208
Posner, Donald, *Annibale Carracci*, 2 vols., London, 1971
Prescott, Anne Lake, 'The Stuart Masque and Pantagruel's Dreams', *English Literary History*, 51 (1984), 407–30
Regteren Altena, I. Q. van, *Jacques de Gheyn: Three Generations*, 3 vols., The Hague, Boston and London, 1983
Rosand, David, 'Theatre and Structure in the Art of Paolo Veronese', in *Painting in Cinquecento Venice*, New Haven and London, 1982, pp. 145–81
Rossky, William, 'Imagination in the English Renaissance: Psychology and Poetic', *Studies in the Renaissance*, 4 (1957), 49–73
Russell, H. Diane, *Jacques Callot: Prints and Related Drawings*, Washington, 1975
Scherer, Margaret R., *Marvels of Ancient Rome*, New York and London, 1956
Sharpe, Kevin, *The Personal Rule of Charles I*, New Haven and London, 1992
Spencer, T. J. B., and Wells, Stanley, eds., *A Book of Masques in Honour of Allardyce Nicoll*, Cambridge, 1967
Strong, Roy, *Festival Designs by Inigo Jones*, International Exhibitions Foundation, 1967–8

Splendour at Court, London, 1973
'Some Early Portraits at Arundel Castle', *The Connoisseur*, 197 (1978), 194–202
Britannia Triumphans: Inigo Jones, Rubens and Whitehall Palace, London, 1980
Art and Power: Renaissance Festivals 1450–1650, Woodbridge, 1984
The English Renaissance Miniature, London, 1985
Sullivan, Mary, *Court Masques of James I*, New York and London, 1913
Summerson, John, 'Inigo Jones', *Proceedings of the British Academy*, 50 (1965), 169–92
Inigo Jones, Harmondsworth, 1966
Sumner Smith, Joan, 'The Italian Sources of Inigo Jones's Style', *Burlington Magazine*, 94 (1952), 200–7
Turner, James, '*Landscape* and the "Art Prospective" in England, 1584–1660', *Journal of the Warburg and Courtauld Institutes*, 42 (1979), 290–3
Veevers, Erica, *Images of Love and Religion. Queen Henrietta Maria and Court Entertainments*, Cambridge, 1989
Waddington, Malcolm R., *Adam Elsheimer*, London, 1966
Welsford, Enid, *The Court Masque*, Cambridge, 1927
White, John, *The Birth and Rebirth of Pictorial Space*, 2nd edn., London, 1967
Wittkower, Rudolf, *Architectural Principles in the Age of Humanism*, 3rd edn, London, 1962
'Inigo Jones, Architect and Man of Letters', in *Palladio and English Palladianism*, London, 1974
Wood, Jeremy, 'Inigo Jones, Italian Art, and the Practice of Drawing', *Art Bulletin*, 74 (1992), 247–70
Yates, Frances, 'Broken Images', in *Ideas and Ideals in the Northern European Renaissance: Collected Essays Volume III*, London, 1984
Zerner, Henri, *The School of Fontainebleau*, London, 1979

Index

The masques for which Jones provided the designs are listed by title (with the name of the writer in brackets), and Jones's drawings and sketches for them are given as subheadings under the titles. References to plate numbers are in italics.

A. V.
   Apollo Belvedere, 125–6; *65*
academy, project for, 8
Agatharcus, 56
Albani, Francesco, 176
   Hercules, 14, 47, 176, 324; *2*
Alberti, Leon Battista, 20, 50, 61, 63, 71
   and body analogy, 120–1, 232–3
   and 'compositio', 230
   De pictura, 29, 116
   De re aedificatoria, 60
   Dell'architettura, 172
   and *historia*, 53, 122–3
   and landscape, 173
   and variety, 140
Albion's Triumph (Aurelian Townshend), 130, 183
   Albanactus: Preliminary Sketch, 128–9, 301, 310; *68*
   An Amphitheatre, 92; *38*
   and antiquity, 270, 303–14, 321
   Design for Albanactus's Headdress, 312–14; *187*
   Proscenium, 42, 216, 240, 246–7, 251, 303–9, 325; *8*
   A Roman Atrium, 23, 88, 92, 98; *4*
   and royal collections, 45–7, 303–4
Aldegrever, Albrecht
   Dancing Couple, 149; *89*

Aleotti, G. B.
   Scena Tragica, 102; *52*
Anaxagoras, 57
Andreani, Andrea
   Engraving of Neroni's Design for *L'Ortensio*, 210–11; *31*
Anne of Denmark, Queen, 4, 59, 132, 140
   interest of, in arts, 15, 159, 161
   as masquer, 3, 274
   as patron, 165, 293–4
antimasque
   concept of, 2, 131–43, 150–1
   costume design for, 130–1, 140–51
antiquities
   as evidence, 311–14
   possession of, 308–9
antiquity
   and Christianity, 291–8
   disunity within, 277–9
   and political power, 303–14, 316–24
   representation of, 267–324
   revival of, 11, 286–93
   as spectacle, 268–70, 280–93, 314–24
arches, designs for, 62–4
architect, concept of the, 58–62, 67, 275–6
architecture
   English, reform of, 79–81
   and figuration, 118–22
   as focus of antiquity, 271–9, 286–93, 301

and imitation, 20–7, 30–2
landscape as, 178–81, 190
and ornament, 230, 243–51
proscenia as, 213–16, 218
and representation of antiquity, 268–9, 306–7
and stage design, 55–112
aristocracy, and antiquity, 308–10, 314
Aristotle, 60, 69, 279
Ethics, 19
Metaphysics, 18–19
and mimesis, 26, 27, 28–9
Poetics, 10, 12, 19–20, 22, 26, 29, 121
see also imitation; mimesis
Armenini, G. B., 25, 26, 33
De' veri precetti della pittura, 17–18
Artenice (Honorat de Beuil, Sieur de Racan), 198
Proscenium and Standing Scene, 87–8, 178–9, 238; *33*
arts, combination of, 3, 10–11
Arundel, Earl of (Thomas Howard), 142, 284, 302, 304–5, 308–10, 314; *182*
and Elsheimer, 203
as patron, 7, 35, 81
Arundel Marbles, 92, 239, 278, 302, 304–8, 314; *3, 183–4*
Ausonius, 323

Bacon, Francis, 6
Baglione, Giovanni, 174, 175
Baldinucci, Filippo, 175, 176, 190
Ballet des provinces de la France, 167; *93*
Barbaro, Daniele
on architecture, 41, 55–6, 60, 69, 92, 102
on bodily proportion, 119, 120, 121
on imitation, 18, 19, 20, 21
on landscape, 170, 172
on ornament, 223–4, 225
on philosophy, 27
on *scaenographia*, 11, 52–3, 57–9, 90, 340 n72
Barocci, Federico, 94
Beham, Hans Sebald
Dancing Couple, 149; *88*
Bellarmine, Cardinal, 37
body, 113–30
as model for architecture, 118–22, 232–3

Bolton, Edmund, 7–13, 30, 32, 35, 74, 326
mentioned, 36, 42, 74, 267, 327
Bordino, Gianfrancesco
De Rebus Praeclare Gestis a Sixto V, 7, 12, 74
Bosch, Hieronymus, 138
Boyvin, René
Toison d'or (after Thiry), 242–6, 248, 250, 253; *132–5, 141–2*
Bramante, Donato, 57, 64–7
and antiquity, 278, 280, 289
Exedra of the Belvedere, 65–6, 274; *19*
Tempietto, 30, 64–5, 77, 94, 297; *7, 17*
Breenbergh, Bartolomeus, 176
Bril, Matthias, 183, 285
Bril, Paul
landscapes, 167, 185, 196, 198, 202, 205–6; *120, 127*
and landscape painting, 160, 165, 174–7, 353 n56
Maius. Junius, 194–6; *116*
September. October, 180, 181; *100*
as source, 15, 103, 192, 285
Britannia Triumphans (William Davenant), 2–3, 216–17, 235
Antimasque Characters, 148–9; *86*
A Crier of Mouse Traps, 149; *87*
English Houses with London and the Thames afar off, 91–2, 103–4, 325–6; *36*
A Man with Gridiron and Shoehorn, 149; *90*
The Palace of Fame, 95–6, 97–8, 208; *49*
A Porter Laden, 147; *83*
Brueghel, Jan, 176, 353 n56
Brueghel, Pieter, the Elder, 161
Brueghel, Pieter, the Younger, 160
Bruno, Giordano, 321
Bruschi, Arnaldo, 65
Buckingham, Duke of, 3, 12, 306, 309
Buonarroti, Michelangelo, 16–17, 141, 173, 220
Buontalenti, Bernardo, 11, 178, 188–91
Apollo Slays the Python, 191
proscenium design of, 211–12

Caccini, Giulio
Il rapimento di Cefalo, 11

Callot, Jacques, 15, 88, 105–7, 145, 147–9, 180, 191
  Capitano Spagnuolo, 92, 103–4; *41*
  Capricci, 147
  Christ Presented to the People, 92–3, 106; *55*
  Diverse Vedute, 106
  The Fair at Impruneta, 93
  Fantaisies, 147
  Grand Parterre de Nancy, 194
  Pantalone, 92
  The Punishments, 93
  The Two Pantaloons, 148; *85*
Calvin, Jean, 36
Camden, William, 280
Campion, Thomas, 168, 213, 296
Cantagallina, Remigio
  for *Il giudizio di Paride* (after Parigi), 190, 191; *20, 37, 109*
capriccio, as principle, 228–34
Caravaggio, Michelangelo Merisi da, 203
Carew, Thomas
  Coelum Britannicum, 322–3
Carleton, Dudley, 164
Carracci, Agostino, 29, 123, 191
Carracci, Annibale, 14, 29, 123, 174–5, 176, 177, 191, 205
Cartari, Vincenzo, 8
Catholicism, 12, 35
Caus, Salomon de, 55
  Grotto design, *Les Raisons des forces mouvantes*, 76; *26*
Cecil, Robert, 55, 309
Cesi, Cardinal, 308
Chapman, George, 142, 275, 296, 301–2
Charles I, King of England
  and Arundel, 303–8, 309–11
  as Jones's double, 109–11, 323–6
  as masquer, 3, 131, 239
  and nature, 170
  as patron, 176, 234, 250, 258
  and Reformation, 36
  representation of, 2–3, 12, 107, 128–9, 266, 296, 301, 313–14, 316–26
  and royal collection, 47, 53, 278
Charles II, King of England, 56
chivalry, and antique sources, 280–91
  passim, 296

Chloridia (Ben Jonson), 216, 235
  Scene 1: A Landscape, 191; *110*
Christianity
  and imperial power, 291–8
  and Renaissance Virtuvianism, 119–20
  renewal of, 71–4
  see also Catholicism; Protestantism
church design, 71–3
classicism
  Jones's use of, 64–7, 69–74, 80, 82–3, 89–96
  and Jonson, 68–9, 279–80, 293
  in landscape painting, 174–7, 184–8, 197
  in ornament, 252–6
  in proscenia, 242–9
  and variety, 99–112
  see also Renaissance visual culture
Cleef, Hendrick van, 267
Cock, Hieronymus, 15, 267, 268, 316
Coelum Britannicum (Thomas Carew), 235–6
  Atlas, 14, 47, 52, 322–4; *1*
  A City in Ruins, 315–24; *193*
coins, as source, 311–12
Comanini, Gregorio
  Il Figino, 141, 262
comedy, as principle of antimasque, 136–9
'composing', practice of, 24–6
compositio, 119, 122, 230
Coninxloo, Gilles van, 161, 353 n56
Constantine, Emperor, 292, 310–11
Coppola, Giovanni Carlo
  Le nozze degli dei, 105
copying
  and figuration, 124–5
  and transmission of Renaissance culture, 12, 13–34
  see also imitation
Correggio, Antonio, 51
Cosimo I, Duke of Tuscany, 238
costume design
  and antiquity, 298–300
  and figuration, 113, 123–31, 140–51

dancing, role of, 2, 4, 149–51
Daniel, Samuel, 59, 61, 139
Danti, Vincenzio, 32, 124
Davenant, William, 2, 105, 109

decorum, principle of, 3–4, 96–104
   and antimasque, 132–6
   and architecture, 234–5
   and the orders, 237–40
della Bella, Stefano, 96
Democritus, 57
design, and mimesis, 20
didacticism, 6–7, 27–8
disegno, concept of, 114–19, 122–4, 211–12
'disguising', 1–2
Dolce, Lodovico, 52, 115
   Dialogo della pittura, 48, 114
Domenichi, Ludovico, 39
Donatello, 221
drawing, 51–2
Drummond, William, 322
Du Cerceau, Jacques Androuet, 70, 92, 283
   Les plus excellents Bastiments de France, 77; 24, 27
   Les Tutelles, 283; *171*
Du Pérac, Étienne, 267, 314
   Tempio di Jano Quadrifonte, 290; *174*
Dürer, Albrecht, 125

Eikon Basilike, 36
Elector Palatine, 4, 228, 296–7
Elizabeth, Princess, 4, 228, 296
Elsheimer, Adam, 47, 160, 174, 176, 205, 353 n56
   Flight into Egypt, 202–3
Erasmus, Desiderius, 9, 10
Essex, Earl of, 280

Fantuzzi, Antonio
   Jupiter (after Primaticcio), 247; *136*
Farinati, Paolo
   Virgin and Child, 284; *173*
Feltre, Morto da, 220, 221
Feltrini, Andrea di Cosimo, 221
Ferrari, Gaudenzio, 50
Fialetti, Odoardo
   Il vero modo et ordine, 123, 129; *74*
figuration
   and architecture, 119–22, 214–15
   and costume design, 123–31, 140–51
   theory of, 115–23
figure drawing, 115–16, 124–31, 140–51
Finsten, Jill, 15

Florimène (Anon.), 251
   The Fourth Intermedium: Autumn, 180–1; *99*
   Proscenium and Standing Scene, 88, 98, 179–80, 240–2, 245–6; *97*
   The Temple of Diana, 94–5; *45*
   The Second Temple of Diana, 95; *47*
Floris, Cornelis, 220
Fontainebleau, School of, 240–51
Fontana, Domenico, 30, 64, 72–3
   Catafalque for Sixtus V, 291; *5*
For the Honour of Wales (Ben Jonson), 136
foreground and background, 193–6
The Fortunate Isles and Their Union (Ben Jonson), 87
frame and picture, relation of, 243–9, 256–7
Francia, Francesco
   David with the Head of Goliath, 125; *62*
frontispieces, 259, 290
Fulvio, Andrea, 309

Gamucci, Bernardo, 271, 309
Genga, Girolamo, 57, 173
Gesualdo, G. A., 18
Gheyn, Jacques de, II
   Masquerade figures, 147, 149; *91*
Giorgione, 220, 223
Giovanni da Udine, 219–21, 222
Gohory, Jacques, 242
Goltzius, Hendrik, 167
Gooderick, Matthew, 252
Gordon, D. J., 42, 246
Gotch, J. A., 35
Goudt, Hendrik, 202, 203
Greek art, 302
Gregory the Great, 36
grotesques, controversy over, 139, 219–34, 236, 249
Guarini, Battista
   Il Pastor Fido, 88, 179; *98*
Guicciardini, Francesco, 220
The Gypsies Metamorphosed (Ben Jonson), 3

The Haddington Masque (Ben Jonson), 4, 164, 167, 212–13, 215
Harris, John, 85, 279

Harrison, Stephen
   Arches of Triumph, 62
Hay, Lord, 3
Haydocke, Richard, 37, 120
Henrietta Maria, Queen
   and decorum, 238–9
   as masquer, 2, 3, 178
   and nature, 170
   representation of, 12, 203, 326–7
   as patron, 4–5, 87–8, 144, 201–2, 234, 238–9, 252–3
Henry, Prince of Wales
   and architecture, 55
   and continental art, 15
   investiture of, 4, 59, 214, 293–4
   as masquer, 3, 130–1, 141, 282
   as patron, 68, 161, 165, 234, 279–80
   representation of, 79, 290–2, 295–8, 303
Hercules, 305, 308–9; *184*
Higgott, Gordon, 85, 90
Hilliard, Nicholas
   Young Man Among Roses, 44; *9*
Holbein, Hans, 7
Holland, Philemon, 36
Hollar, Wenceslaus, 203
Homer, 68–9, 282
Honthorst, Gerrit van
   Mercury Presenting the Arts to Apollo and Diana, 12
Horace, 6, 132–4
   Ars poetica, 19
Howard, Lady Frances, 280
humanism, Quattrocento, 7–9
Huon of Bordeaux (Anon.), 74, 295
Hutton, Matthew, Archbishop of York, 351 n5
Hymenaei (Ben Jonson), 10–11, 113–14, 48, 202, 270, 280, 299, 302
   and architecture, 215

iconoclasm, 36–8
ideal city, concept of, 81–6, 105–9
imagination, and architecture, 82–3
   see also phantasia
imitation
   and the grotesque, 219–26
   and nature, 76, 219–20
   and phantasy, 141, 142–3

   in Renaissance culture, 18–34, 219
   and revival of antiquity, 293
   see also antiquity; copying; mimesis
imperial power, and representation of antiquity, 291–8, 310–14, 316–23
interior decoration, 252–7
intermedio, 4, 6, 11, 190–1
   see also scenography

James I, King of England
   Basilicon Doron, 75, 295
   as patron, 234, 279
   representation of, 68, 70, 74, 182–3, 290–1, 296–7
   as spectator, 3, 75
Jones, Inigo
   and architecture, 64–112
   as 'architector', 55–62, 67, 112
   conception of masque, 48–54
   conflict with Jonson, *see under* Jonson
   and copying, 13–34
   grotesque, use of, 227–34
   ornament, conception of, 235–66
   and painting, 51–3
   professional authority of, 323–7
   and Renaissance visual culture, 6–54, 323–4
   study of antiquity, 271–324
   trip to Rome, 298–302
Jones, Inigo – designs, sketches and buildings
   Archway, *13*
   Back Shutter, 184; *101*
   Back Shutter for a Landscape, 184; *103*
   Banqueting House, 54, 58
      quotation of, 69, 90–1, 198; *35*
   Basing overmantel, 257–8; *155*
   A Captive King, 312–13; *185*
   Catafalque for James I, 30–1, 64, 311; *6*
   A Cave and a Mount, 280–1; *162*
   Classical Ruins, 314–15; *188*
   Copy of detail from *Toison d'or*, 245; *131*
   Cotton, Lady, funeral monument for, 68, 284
   Covent Garden piazza, 82
   Cupid's Pallas, 85–6; *32*
   Elephant Pageant, 282; *166*
   Emperor's habit in war, 298–9; *179*

Forest Scene, 186; *106*
A Horse Caparison, 281–2; *164*
A Mountainous Valley, 167; *94*
Page Bearing a Helmet, 125; *61*
A Palace, 42
The Palace of Fame, 95–6; *49*
Prince's Lodging at Newmarket, 85
Proscenium and Hunt Scene, 215; *128*
Queen's Chapel, 71
Queen's house, 85, 234
?Setting for a Pastoral, 236–7; *129*
Sketches of heads, 129; *73*
Somerset House, 198, 239, 345 n98
Temple of Apollo, 65; *16*
Temple Bar, 47–8, 276, 278; *12*
Temple of Peace, 314–15; *191*
A Throne, 65–6; *18*
The Tragic Scene, 100–3, 252–3; *51*, *148*, *150*
Tree Wings, 198–9; *119*, *121*
Jonson, Ben
  on antimasque, 130, 131–9, 140–50 *passim*
  and antiquity, 270, 279–80, 282, 292, 293, 295–6, 298, 299
  on arches, 62–3
  on architecture, 60
  collaboration with Jones, 1, 7, 278, 302
  conflict with Jones, 19, 38–43, 61–2, 128, 139, 140–1, 268, 303, 325
  on imitation, 27–8, 137–41
  on landscape, 158, 159, 162, 164, 166, 182, 191
  on masque, 1, 2, 3, 6, 202, 311
  on poetry and picture, 19, 38–40, 48–9, 61–2, 113–15
  on proscenia, 212–14, 216, 235
Jonson, Ben – works (masques are listed under title)
  Discoveries, 38–9
  Expostulation (with Jones), 20, 43
Julius II, Pope, 10, 72
Junius, Franciscus, 26, 44, 52
  The Painting of the Ancients, 20, 142–3, 279

Labacco, Antonio, 267, 271
  Book on Architecture, 289–90
  Temple of Jupiter Stator, 95; *48*

Lafreri, Antonio
  Speculum Romanae Magnificentiae, 267, 280–1, 282
landscape
  as architecture, 178–81
  concept of, 158–63
  pictorialisation of, 163–206
Lanier, Nicholas, 213
Laud, William, Archbishop of Canterbury, 36
Lee, Rensselaer, 19
Leonardo da Vinci, 50, 51, 115, 220
light, and pictorial unity, 203
Ligorio, Pirro, 225, 280, 360 n8
Ligustri, Tarquinio
  designs for consoles, 235, 252; *153*
literariness, of English culture, 38–43
Le Livre de la conqueste de la Toison d'or (Anon.), 242–52 *passim*
Livy, 121, 309
Lomazzo, Giovanni Paolo
  on architecture, 21
  and bodily proportion, 119–20
  and figuration, 140, 145
  Le Grottesche, 226
  Idea del tempio della pittura, 17
  on Leonardo, 115
  on ornament, 218, 224–7, 231, 233–4, 249, 265
  on painting, 37, 50, 51
  Trattato della pittura, 28–9, 224–7
London, architectural reform of, 108–9
Longhi, Roberto, 203
Lord Hay's Masque (Thomas Campion), 11, 165
The Lords' Masque (Thomas Campion), 61, 139, 165, 299, 337 n26
  A Fiery Spirit, 125; *63*
l'Orme, Philibert de, 24
Love Freed from Ignorance and Folly (Ben Jonson)
  The Release of the Daughters of the Morn, 273–4; *161*
Love Restored (Ben Jonson), 3, 136, 138
Lovers Made Men (Ben Jonson), 3, 213
Luminalia (William Davenant), 47, 245, 326–7
  Back Shutter for Scene 1, 201–6; *124*
  The City of Sleep, 201–2, 205–6; *126*
  Scene 1: Night, 201–5; *123*

Index

Mancini, Giulio, 50, 175, 176, 177, 181, 200, 205, 206
Mander, Karel van, 163, 166
maniera (style), 116–18, 123, 125–30
mannerism, critique of, 32, 176–7, 184–8, 242–9
   see also classicism
Mantegna, Andrea
   Allegory of Servitude, 127; *67*
   Triumph of Caesar, 47, 53, 279, 303, *11*
Mantua Collection, Sleeping Cupids, 303; *181*
Marcantonio, *see* Raimondi, Marcantonio
Marshall, Thomas, 234
Martin, Jean, 63
Masaccio, 16
'maske', Italian, 1-2
The Masque of Augurs (Ben Jonson), 1, 83, 137–8, 302, 311
The Masque of Beauty (Ben Jonson), 11, 48, 114, 164
The Masque of Blackness (Ben Jonson), 10–11, 21, 114, 158, 159, 161-2, 164, 182, 183
The Masque of Queens (Ben Jonson), 4, 6, 132, 213
   The House of Fame, 72, 97–8, 290; *21*
   proscenium, 214
masques
   and architecture, 112, 234–5
   as mimesis, *see* mimesis
   origins and definition of, 1–5
   and ornament, 234–66
   as pictures, 40–3, 48–54, 164
   and Renaissance visual culture, 6–7, 13–14, 44–54
   see also stage designs
Mattei, Asdrubale, 308
Mauregard, Jean de, 242
Medici, Francesco de', 158, 210
Medici, Maria de', 212
The Memorable Masque (George Chapman), 61, 126, 139, 166, 167, 228, 296–8, 301
   An Indian, 126–7; *66*
Michelangelo Buonarroti, *see under* Buonarroti
   Cupid, 303; *181*
   Ignudo from the Sistine Ceiling, 129; *71*
   Last Judgement, 130
   Medici Chapel tombs, 68
   Piazza del Campidoglio, 86
Milton, John
   Comus, 167, 169, 170
   Eikonoklastes, 36
mimesis, art of, 10–13, 19–20, 21–2, 28–9, 32–4
   in antimasque, 137–9
   see also Aristotle; imitation
Minturno, Antonio, 19
mixture of styles, 70–81, 91–2
Modius, Franciscus
   Pandectae Triumphales, 280
Momper, Joos de, 353 n56
monarchy
   and politics of masque, 2–3, 109–11, 293–8, 303–8, 309–14, 316–27
   and proscenia, 210, 211
   see also political power
Moro, Battista del
   Fame, 239; *130*
Muziano, Girolamo, 174, 191
   St Onuphrius in a Landscape, 198; *122*
Mytens, Daniel, Earl of Arundel, 302, 304, 308; *182*

Nannoccio, 209, 210, 211
nature
   definition of, 166–70, 173, 176
   and the grotesque, 225–6
   imitation of, 28–9, 137–9, 220
Neptune's Triumph for the Return of Albion (Ben Jonson), 86, 215
Neroni, Bartolomeo (called Riccio)
   Design for *L'Ortensio*, 82, 88, 102, 210–11, 238, 239; *31*
   and proscenia, 210–11, 214, 238, 239, 240, 243
Newman, John, 14
Nieulandt, Willem van, 103, 165, 284, 285, 314, 315–16
   Flight into Egypt, 314; *189*
   Ponte Quattro Capi, 106; *57, 58*
   Temple of Jupiter Stator, 315–16; *194*
   Temple of Peace, 314–15; *192*
   Temples in the Forum, 284, 314; *190*
   Torre delle Milizie, 70, 283; *172*

Norgate, Edward, 39, 40, 159, 160, 176
   Miniatura, 37–8

Oberon the Fairy Prince (Ben Jonson), 61, 68, 74–81, 292, 297
   mixture of medieval and antique, 295–6
   and nature, 166, 167, 170
   Oberon, 282, 296, 301; *167*
   Oberon's Palace, 75–81; *23*
   Palace within a Cavern, 64–5, 75–7; *22*
   Satyrs, 140–1; *75*
   Scene of Rocks, 167; *92*
Oliver, Isaac, 15, 29, 44, 161
Oliver, Peter, 47
orders of architecture, 78–9, 208, 238–40, 276
Orgel, Stephen, 14, 138, 184
ornament
   'capricious' and 'composed', 232–66
   definition of, 208, 216–18
   as 'picture', 262–6
   theory of, 218–34

pageants and pageant machines, 1, 164–5
painting
   Barbaro on, 223
   stage designs as, 50–4
Paleotti, Cardinal, 357 n54
Palladio, Andrea
   Antichità di Roma, 279
   and antiquity, 267, 268, 271, 273, 278–9, 292, 293, 301, 303
   and body analogy, 121
   on Bramante, 64, 66, 297
   and church design, 71
   and classicism, 107
   and imitation, 20–8 passim
   proscenium, 211
   Quattro Libri, 268, 271, 279
   and Vitruvian theatre, 209, 214–15
Pan's Anniversary (Ben Jonson), 170, 182
Panvinio, Onofrio, 312
   Amphitheatre, *39*
   Reges Captivi, 313; *186*
Parigi, Alfonso
   designs for *Le nozze degli dei*, 105
   Sbarco di Venere, 192–3; *112*
Parigi, Giulio, 6, 96, 102, 178, 188–9, 192, 198, 324
   La liberazione di Tirreno, 191

   for *Il giudizio di Paride*
      Palazzo della Fama, 72, 97–8, 290, 315, 316, *20*
      Scene of Mount Ida, 191; *109*
      Il tempio della Pace, 92, 307; *37*
pastoral drama, 87–8, 98–9, 172–3, 178–81
Peacham, Henry, 302
   The Art of Drawing, 37, 161
   The Compleat Gentleman, 311
   The Gentleman's Exercise, 37, 159, 160, 161
Peake, Robert, 351 n16; *154*
Pearce, Edward, 252–3; *154*
Pembroke, Earl of (Philip Herbert), 158–9
Perino del Vaga, 17–18, 174
perspective
   and architecture, 57–8, 74
   and proscenium, 211, 212
   and public's sense of vision, 44–5, 162–6
   and representation of antiquity, 268–9, 286–91
   and scene design, 53, 57
   urban, 82–97, 105–9
   use of, in landscape, 162–6, 203
   and variety, 102–9
Peruzzi, Baldassare, 50, 57, 100, 222, 238, 278, 289
Petrarch, *Trionfo dell'Amore*, 18
phantasia
   in antimasque, 138–43
   and the grotesque, 226, 233–5, 249
   in painting, 223
philosophy, imitation as, 26–7
Piccolomini, Alessandro
   L'Ortensio, 210
pictorial space, *see* perspective
pictorial spectacle, stage-design as, 40–3, 48–54, 164, 318–23
Pino, Paolo, 42, 163, 173
Pittoni, Battista, 15, 268
   Monte Quirinale, 316; *195*
Plato, 26, 38, 59, 60–1
   and imitation, 28–9, 141, 142–3
   Politicus, 59
   Republic, 21–2, 26, 326
   Sophist, 141
Pleasure Reconciled to Virtue (Ben Jonson), 4, 136, 140
Pliny, 10, 29, 36, 173

Plutarch, 27, 41, 60
  Moralia, 27
Poelenburgh, Cornelis van, 176
poetry and picture, 38–41, 113–15
Poitiers, Diane de, 75
Polidoro da Caravaggio, 174, 254
political power
  metaphysic of, in masque, 2–3, 290–3
  and representation of antiquity, 279–80, 303–14, 316–27
  see also Charles I; monarchy
Porro, Girolamo, 268–70, 286–9
Posner, Donald, 174, 177
Possevino, Antonio
  Bibliotheca Selecta, 40
Pozzoserrato, Lodovico, 15
Praxiteles
  Cupid, 303; *181*
Primaticcio, Francesco
  Diana, 252; *152*
  Jupiter, 246; *136*
  Les Travaux d'Ulysse, 252, 253–4; *149, 151*
Prince Henry's Barriers (Ben Jonson), 58–9, 280, 295, 311
  The Fallen House of Chivalry, 68–74, 282–93, 309; *169*
  St George's Portico, 68–74, 82, 165, 282–93; *170*
  ruins in, 314, 315, 318, 321, 322
proportion, use of, 75–6, 119–21
proscenium arches, 208–18, 235–52, 258–66
A Prospect of Trees and Houses, 194
'prospects', 163
Protestantism, 30–1, 69
  and visual arts, 35–8, 120
  see also Christianity
Pudicitia, 305, 308, 309; *183*
Pythius, 60

Quintilian, 16

Rabel, Daniel
  Entrée des Sorcières et des Monstres, 144; *78*
  Entrée des Gelés, 144; *80*
Raimondi, Marcantonio, 140
  David with the Head of Goliath, 125; *62*
  Lion Hunt, 129, 282, 296, 310; *70*
  Satyrs abducting a Nymph, 141; *76*
  Temperance, 125; *60*
  Trajan, 129, 282, 296, 310; *69*
  Two Fauns, 125; *64*
Raleigh, Sir Walter, 297
Raphael, 17, 53, 57, 127, 130, 174, 219, 222
  and antiquity, 289, 300
  Parnaso, 282
  Temperance, 125; *60*
Raphael, School of, 219, 222, 224
realism, and ornament, 218–20
Renaissance visual culture
  concept of imitation in, 14–34
  and English architecture, 79–81
  Jones's revision of, 89–104
  and landscape, 158–66, 174–7, 199–200
  and perspective construction, 289–90
  transmission of, to England, 7–14, 44–54, 323–4
  and urban perspective, 82–96
Reni, Guido, 15
Reynolds, 54
Riccio, see Neroni, Bartolomeo
Ridolfi, Carlo, 14
Romano, Giulio, 52, 57, 222, 282
  Fresco from Palazzo del Tè, 252; *145–6*
Ross, Alexander, 8
Rosso Fiorentino, 214, 242–6, 249, 254
Rubens, Peter Paul, 7, 14, 35, 54, 174, 176, 202, 353 n56
  Banqueting House ceiling, 261
ruins
  as spectacle, 282–6, 314–22
  as teaching, 272–4
Rusconi, Giovanni Antonio, 273
Rutland, Earl of, 15

Sadeler, Aegidius
  Livia, 294; *178*
  Prints after Bril, 181, 194, 294; *100, 116*
Salmacida Spolia (William Davenant), 54, 104–11, 258–66
  Design for Bridge, 106; *56*
  Panels of frieze, 265–6; *156–7*
  The Suburbs of a Great City, 105–9; *53*
S. Giovanni in Laterano, 292; *176*
Sangallo, Antonio da, 289
Sangallo, Bastiano da, 50, 177

Sansovino, Jacopo
  Cupid, 303; *181*
Sarto, Andrea del, 209
Satyric Scene, 170–3, 177–82, 191
Scamozzi, Vincenzo, 94–5, 231, 243, 258
  Discorsi sopra l'antichità di Roma, 267–9, 316
  Title-page of *Discorsi*, 268–9, 290; *158*
scenography (*scaenographia*), 11, 52–3, 57–9, 90, 340 n72
  and architecture, 289–90
  Florentine, 188–91
Schiavone, Andrea, 15
Schongauer, Martin, 16
Scultori, Adamo
  Allegory of Servitude, 127; *67*
  Ignudo, 129; *71*
Serlio, Sebastiano
  on antiquity, 71, 271–8, 290
  on Bramante, 64, 297, 342 n34
  Bramante's Exedra of the Belvedere, 65–6, 274; *19*
  Bramante's Tempietto, 30, 64, 77; *7*
  City gate, 64; *15*
  Comic and Tragic Scenes, 87, 88, 100–2, 289; *29, 30*
  Delle Antichità, 64
  Frontispiece of Nero, 272–3; *160*
  and landscape, 172, 173, 177–8, 179, 180, 190
  Libro Straordinario, 66
  on orders, 78, 79, 238, 239
  on ornament, 218, 221–3, 224, 225, 231
  Perspective construction, 63–4; *14*
  Satyric Scene, 50, 87, 88, 170–80 *passim*, 190; *95*
  and scenography, 54, 57, 289, 290
  Title-page, *Architettura*, 271–2; *159*
  and urban perspective, 82
  and variety, 100
Servi, Costantino de', 55, 213
Sesto, Cesare da, 29
Shakespeare, William, 100
The Shepherds' Paradise (Walter Montagu), 89, 98, 99
  Love's Cabinet, 194–6; *117*
  A Palace in Trees, 194–8; *115*
  Proscenium and Standing Scene, 193–8, 239; *114*
  A Prospect of Trees and Houses, 194–6; *118*
  Sketch for Scene 1, 179; *96*
Sidney, Sir Philip
  Apology for Poetry, 28
Simeoni, Gabriele
  Fontaine d'Anet, 75; *25*
Sirigatti, Lorenzo
  Bramante's Tempietto, 65; *17*
Sixtus V, Pope, 9–10, 12, 30, 3;5, 72–4, 291
Smythson, John, 85
Socrates, 26, 27, 38–9, 59–60
Somer, Paul van
  James I, 44; *10*
The Somerset Masque (Thomas Campion), 213
Les songes drolatiques de Pantagruel (Anon.), 147
Spenser, Edmund, 36, 121
  The Faerie Queene, 69
stage designs
  as architecture, 55–61, 67–112
  and copying, 13–14, 22–8
  as paintings, 50–2
  and synthetic view of antiquity, 290–3
  see also masques
Stievens, Pieter, 194
storia (also *historia, istoria*)
  ornament as, 265–6
  primacy of, 50, 53–4, 122–4
Stradano, Giovanni, 161, 183
Strong, Roy, 184, 261
style and theory, 63–7, 74
Summerson, John, 31–2, 55, 85
symmetry, as master-idea, 190, 191, 192–7

Tempe Restored (Aurelian Townshend), 48, 98, 168, 326
  Proscenium, 48, 216, 235, 236, 246, 247–9, 325
  The Vale of Tempe, 88–9; *34*
Tempesta, Antonio, 99, 158, 161, 182, 183–8
  Death of Adonis, 184
  Diana and Callisto, 185; *105*
  Gazelle Hunt, 185; *104*
  Giugno, 180–1

Tempesta, Antonio (*cont.*)
  Grotesque panel, 252; *147*
  Narcissus, 186; *107*
  Palace Garden, 192–3; *113*
  Stag Hunt, 186; *108*
  Twelve Caesars on Horseback, 281–2, 292, 296, 299
    Caligula, 282, 296; *168*
    Domitian, 281–2, 296; *165*
The Temple of Love (William Davenant), 2, 4, 252
  An Airy Spirit, 144–5; *81*
  An Earthy Spirit, 144; *79*
  Proscenium, 240; *144*
  Scene 1: A Grove, 192–3; *111*
  A Watery Spirit, 144; *77*
tenebrism, *see* light
Teniers, David, 15
Tethys' Festival (Samuel Daniel), 4, 59, 61, 293–5
  Headdress for Tethys, 294; *177*
  Naiad, 125; *59*
  proscenium of, 214, 215, 216
theatricality, 4
Thiry, Léonard
  Toison d'or, 242–6, 248, 250, 253; *132–5, 141–2*
Time Vindicated (Ben Jonson), 182, 215
  Banqueting House, 68, 90–9, 198; *35*
Tintoretto, 29
  The Washing of the Feet, 53–4
Titian, 166, 175, 223
Townshend, Aurelian, 42, 310, 326
Trajan's Column, 145, 291–2; *82*
  Scene from, 299; *180*
The Triumph of Peace (James Shirley), 139, 251
  The Forum of Peace, 92–3; *40*
  Proscenium, 250–1, 305; *140*
  Reworking of the proscenium, 251; *143*
  The Sons of Peace, 129; *72*
The Triumphs of the Prince d'Amour (William Davenant), 236
Trofei di Mario, 280–1; *163*

unitary perspective set, 82, 86–9
urban environment, reform of, 81–96, 105–9

Valla, Lorenzo, 10
  Elegantiae linguae latinae, 8–9
Van Dyck, Anthony, 12, 54, 206, 344 n84
  The Continence of Scipio, 306–7
Vanni, G. B.
  The Marriage at Cana, 106; *54*
Varchi, Benedetto, 117
variety
  in antimasque, 134–6, 140
  architectural, 99–109
Vasari, Giorgio, 52, 209, 242, 327
  on antiquity, 278
  and figuration, 116–18, 121, 122–30 *passim*, 140, 151
  on imitation, 16–17, 20, 25, 30, 33
  and Michelangelo, 16–17
  on ornament, 218, 219–21, 222, 223
  Preface to the Lives, 24, 50, 51, 116, 118, 221
  on proportion, 21
  proscenium by, 210, 212
  on *rinascità*, 8
  on variety, 100
Vecellio, Cesare
  Habiti Antichi e Moderni di Tutto il Mondo, 145–7
  Facchino, 147; *84*
Veevers, Erica, 326, 327
Veronese, Paolo, 15
  The Marriage at Cana, 54, 105–6; *54*
Viator, *De Artificiali Perspectiva*, 353 n59
Villamena, Francesco
  Clement VIII (after Arconio), 247, 252; *138*
Vinckboons, David, 161
Virgil, 69
  Eclogues, 79
The Vision of Delight (Ben Jonson), 96, 138
  A Street in Perspective, 82–3, 87, 91, 96; *28*
visual culture
  and antiquity, 311–14
  English, and Renaissance art, 6–14, 44–54
  primacy of, 326–7
  Protestant attitudes towards, 35–43
visual pleasure, 285–6

Vitruvius
    on architecture and the architect, 10, 27, 41, 55–61 *passim*, 79, 232, 239, 271, 289
    as authority in antiquity, 276–8
    and decorum, 96, 102
    and doctrine of imitation, 18, 19, 26
    on grotesques, 139, 218–26 *passim*, 231, 249
    on proportion and harmony, 20–1, 119–22
    and Roman theatre, 209
    scenic types of, 170–3, 177–8, 190
    and stage design, 52, 53
    on urban perspective, 82
Vredeman de Vries, Jan
    Perspective, 93–6
        Courtyard, 95–6; *50*
        Ionic portico, 94; *46*
        Perspective construction, 94, 102–3; *43*

Walker, Robert
    Self-Portrait, 12
wall-painting, 222
Webb, John, 41, 51, 56, 112, 209
    The City of Sleep (after Jones), 206; *126*
    Reworking of the proscenium of *The Triumph of Peace* (after Jones), 251; *143*
    The Suburbs of a Great City (after Jones), 105; *53*
Webster, John, 297
Weeping Dacia, 291; *175*
Wotton, Sir Henry, 21
    The Elements of Architecture, 166

Xenophon, 27, 29, 38–9, 59, 60
    Memorabilia, 27

Zuccaro, Federigo, 158
    Design for a cartouche, 247; *137*